T0257547

Information Security: Principles and New Concepts

Volume IV

Information Security: Principles and New Concepts Volume IV

Edited by **Fiona Hobbs**

LANRYE
INTERNATIONAL

New Jersey

Published by Clanrye International,
55 Van Reypen Street,
Jersey City, NJ 07306, USA
www.clanryeinternational.com

Information Security: Principles and New Concepts
Volume IV
Edited by Fiona Hobbs

© 2015 Clanrye International

International Standard Book Number: 978-1-63240-309-4 (Hardback)

This book contains information obtained from authentic and highly regarded sources. Copyright for all individual chapters remain with the respective authors as indicated. A wide variety of references are listed. Permission and sources are indicated; for detailed attributions, please refer to the permissions page. Reasonable efforts have been made to publish reliable data and information, but the authors, editors and publisher cannot assume any responsibility for the validity of all materials or the consequences of their use.

The publisher's policy is to use permanent paper from mills that operate a sustainable forestry policy. Furthermore, the publisher ensures that the text paper and cover boards used have met acceptable environmental accreditation standards.

Trademark Notice: Registered trademark of products or corporate names are used only for explanation and identification without intent to infringe.

Printed in the United States of America.

Contents

Preface

In contemporary times, there is no dearth of information. In fact, since the advent of technology and the World Wide Web, there has been an overload of information. All data needs to be recorded, saved and stored. However, some information is more crucial as compared to others. And this is where the concept of Information Security comes in. The origins of Information Security can be traced to the times of Julius Caesar in 50 B.C, when he invented the Caesar cipher. This mechanism was used to protect the confidentiality of correspondence and provided a means of detecting tampering, in case any. Regardless of the form that the data may take, electronic or physical, Information Security is a must in present times.

Information Security has grown and evolved significantly in recent years. Numerous occurrences of international terrorism, through disruption of data fuelled the need for better methods of Information Security. Today, it is an indispensable part of all the business operations across different domains. Protecting information has also become an ethical and legal requirement in many cases. Essentially, the practice of defending information from unauthorized access, use, disclosure and destruction is referred to as Information Security. The CIA triad of confidentiality, integrity and availability is one of the core principles of information security.

There are two important aspects to Information Security. These are Information Technology Security, which is concerned with technology security and Information Assurance, whose aim is to ensure that data is not lost during critical times.

I would like to thank all the contributors who have shared their knowledge in this book. I would also like to thank my family for their constant trust and support.

Editor

Effectiveness of Built-in Security Protection of Microsoft's Windows Server 2003 against TCP SYN Based DDoS Attacks

Hari Krishna Vellalacheruvu, Sanjeev Kumar

*Networking Security Research Lab, Department of Electrical and Computer Engineering,
The University of Texas-Pan American, Edinburg, USA*

Abstract

Recent DDoS attacks against several web sites operated by SONY Playstation caused wide spread outage for several days, and loss of user account information. DDoS attacks by WikiLeaks supporters against VISA, MasterCard, and Paypal servers made headline news globally. These DDoS attack floods are known to crash, or reduce the performance of web based applications, and reduce the number of legitimate client connections/sec. TCP SYN flood is one of the most common DDoS attack, and latest operating systems have some form of protection against this attack to prevent the attack in reducing the performance of web applications, and user connections. In this paper, we evaluated the performance of the TCP-SYN attack protection provided in Microsoft's windows server 2003. It is found that the SYN attack protection provided by the server is effective in preventing attacks only at lower loads of SYN attack traffic, however this built-in protection is found to be not effective against high intensity of SYN attack traffic. Measurement results in this paper can help network operators understand the effectiveness of built-in protection mechanism that exists in millions of Windows server 2003 against one of the most popular DDoS attacks, namely the TCP SYN attack, and help enhance security of their network by additional means.

Keywords: Network Security, TCP SYN Based DDoS Attack, Prevention of Attacks

1. Introduction

When TCP/IP protocol suite was initially developed as a part of network research development by the United States Advanced Research Projects Agency (DARPA or ARPA) in 1970s [1], they were unaware of the security attacks. At that time the protocol suite designs were basically concerned with appropriate communication and the scalability of the network. There was no proper framework to defend against security attacks in the initial design of protocol suite. As time progressed TCP/IP gained more popularity than any other architecture. There has always been some hacker community who have been trying to exploit security breaches of popular TCP/IP architecture.

Whenever the hackers exploited the security breaches, the TCP/IP developer community tried to fix it by making some changes to the TCP/IP protocol suite. TCP/IP stack is still evolving to defend against security attacks. For example, recently Microsoft released a critical patch to TCP/IP on 8th September 2009 [2]. This patch corresponds to the zero window size of the TCP packet after the three-way handshake is complete and also time stamp code execution.

TCP implementation may permit the LISTEN state to be entered with either all, some, or none of the pair of IP addresses and port numbers specified by the applications. A link can become established with any user whose details are unidentified to the server ahead of time. This type of unbounded LISTEN is the target of SYN flooding attacks due to the way it is typically implemented by operating systems [3].

2. Three-Way Handshake

TCP uses three-way handshake (**Figure 1**) to establish a connection between any two nodes. The client sends a SYN request with its sequence number to the server. When a SYN is received by server for a local TCP port

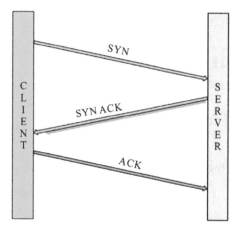

Figure 1. TCP three-way handshake.

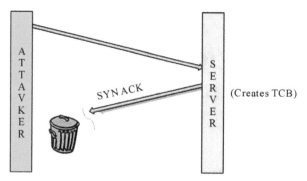

Figure 2. TCP SYN flood attack.

where the connection is in the LISTEN state, then the state transitions to SYN-RECEIVED. The Transmission control block (TCB, a data structure to store all the state information for an individual connection) is initialized with information from the header fields of the received SYN segment. In second step the server responds with an ACK to received SYN and it will also sends its own sequence number (SYN) to the client. In the last step, the client responds with final ACK packet. After the last ACK is received by the server, connection state changes from SYN_RECEIVED to ESTABLISH state. The real data transfer between the client and the server is initiated after the three-way handshake is complete.

3. TCP SYN Flood Attack

Over Internet today, it is common for users to access data by using application services of a remote machine. Most of these applications like HTTP, FTP and e-mail run on top of TCP layer. The accessibility and performance of application services depend on how well the underlying Transport protocol works. By some means, if the TCP layer is made unresponsive, the person who is trying to access these services from a remote machine may think that the services are busy/unavailable. In recent years increase in online shopping and online financial transactions make unavailability of the web services, simply intolerable.

In this attack, the attacker makes the server's TCP layer unresponsive by sending a large number of open connection requests or TCP SYN packets (**Figure 2**). This is known as SYN flooding or SYN Bombing, named after specific bit in TCP header specifications. The TCP SYN flooding weakness was discovered as early as 1994 by Bill Cheswick and Steven Bellovin [3]. The SYN flooding attack was first publicized in 1996, with the release of a description and exploit tool in Phrack Magazine. By September of 1996, SYN flooding

attacks has been observed more frequently on the internet around the world. SYN flooding was particularly serious in comparison to other known denial of service attacks at that time and even now. The community quickly developed different techniques for preventing or limiting the impact of SYN flooding attacks. Some of these techniques like SYN Cache protection and SYN Cookies protection have become important pieces of the TCP implementations in certain operating systems, although some significantly diverge from the TCP specification and none of these techniques have yet been standardized or sanctioned by the IETF process. SYN Chache is one of the most commonly used SYN flooding prevention methods, and variants of this method is implemented in many popular computer operating systems.

Suppose that an attacker directs a large number of SYN requests rapidly to the server with spoofed source IP addresses. In a traditional TCP 3-way hand shake, the server has to create a new TCB for each new connection request it received and save the incomplete state of the connection and the TCP options like window size, Maximum segment size etc. Since the TCB's are limited for each port of the server, the TCB's get filled up. In traditional TCP, the server will send several retransmissions for incomplete connections before the timeout period and eventually get deleted. Even though TCB's are going to be unallocated after certain timeout period, if the attacker manages to keep flooding the server so that no TCB's are free at any given point of time, the TCP layer becomes unresponsive to the legitimate clients.

One typical data structure used for communication is the Transmission Control Block (TCB) which is created and maintained during the lifetime of a given connection. The TCB contains the following information according to RFC 675 [4] (field sizes are notional only and may vary from one implementation to another):

  16 bits: Local connection name
  48 bits: Local socket
  48 bits: Foreign socket
  16 bits: Receive window size in octets
  32 bits: Receive left window edge (next sequence num-

ber expected)

16 bits: Receive packet buffer size of TCB (may be less than window)

16 bits: Send window size in octets

32 bits: Send left window edge (earliest unacknowledged octet)

32 bits: Next packet sequence number

16 bits: Send packet buffer size of TCB (may be less than window)

8 bits: Connection state

The typical TCB size is sum of all fields which is 280 bits. For each connection standard transport layer allocates one TCB. So the total number of connections that can be supported by the server depends on the number of TCB's available in the server. A TCP synchronize (SYN) attack is a denial-of-service attack that exploits the retransmission and time-out behavior of the Synchronize-Acknowledgement (SYN-ACK) segment during the TCP three-way handshake to create a large number of half-open TCP connections. Depending on the TCP/IP protocol implementation, a large number of half-open TCP connections could do any of the following [5]:

- Use all available memory.
- Use all possible entries in the TCP Transmission Control Block (TCB), an internal table used to track TCP connections. Once the half-open connections use all the entries, further connection attempts are responded with a TCP connection reset.
- Use all available half-open connections. Once all the half-open connections are used, further connection attempts are responded with a TCP connection reset.

4. SYN Attack Protection Performance

We measured the performance of SYN attack protection in the real time traffic circumstances by sending the legitimate client connections and SYN flood attack to the web server at the same time. The legitimate/authentic clients complete the there-way handshake with the server and then send HTTP request for a web page to the server (**Figure 3**). After receiving the web page the clients close the connection with server in traditional TCP way of terminating the connection by exchanging FIN packets. On the other hand the attacker's side is made to send a flood of TCP connection requests with spoofed source IP addresses to the web server with no intention to complete the three-way hand shake with the server. The attackers IP source address are fully randomized to overcome any sort of filtering done on the server side.

We measured the number of legitimate client connections that can be established per second with the server under increasing attack loads. The attack load is incremented from low to high intensity in nonlinear fashion

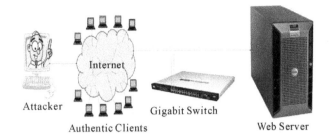

Figure 3. Experimental setup.

from 0 Mbps to 100 Mbps in all of the following experimental results to find the connection rate behavior at lower and higher intensity of attack traffic. The duration of each attack load is kept for 10 minutes (600 seconds) and the statistical readings are collected for each second. *i.e.* 600 reading for each attack load.

The server CPU utilization and Memory status of the server under different loads of SYN attack are shown in **Figures 4** and **5**. The powerful quad core CPU utilization of the server is increasing linearly as the attack load increases (nonlinear) when there is no protection. The maximum CPU utilization 41% is reached at 100 Mbps of SYN attack load. The memory consumption is just 387MB at 100Mbps attack load which is well below the 8 GB RAM installed in the server. From the graphs (**Figures 4** and **5**) it is observed that the server CPU and Memory are not consumed completely because of the SYN Attack.

The total number of TCP connections in SYN_RECEIVED state when the server is under SYN attack is shown in the **Figure 6**. Connections in SYN_RECEIVED state is also referred as half-open TCP connections means incomplete TCP connections The maximum number of half open connections supported by the server at any given instant depends on the backlog size. TCP half-open connections are increasing linearly at lower loads of SYN attack until 7 Mbps. After this point the number half open connections are falling at higher attack load. The average half open connections at each attack load shown in fig 6 is an average of 200 reading. These reading are manually logged with the help of NETSTAT command.

Netstat -n -p tcp|find/c "SYN_RECEIVED"

It is observed in **Figure 6** that the total number of half-open connections in server is unstable after 7 Mbps of SYN attack load.

Figures 7 and **8** show the average successful legitimate connections established with the web server when it is under attack, and no protection is enabled at the server. The legitimate client connections are found to decrease rapidly with increase in TCP-SYN attack load. Without any attack (as shown with 0 Mbps in the graphs), the legitimate clients connections are measured to be around

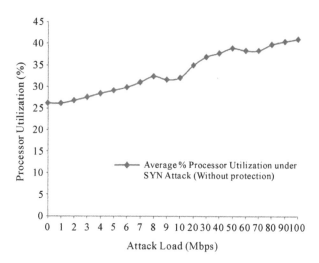

Figure 4. Server CPU utilization (without SYN attack protection) under SYN attack.

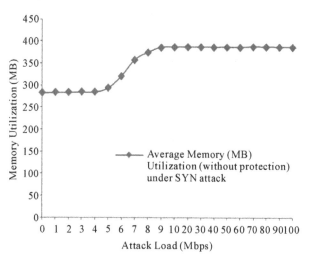

Figure 5. Memory consumption (without SYN attack protection) under SYN attack.

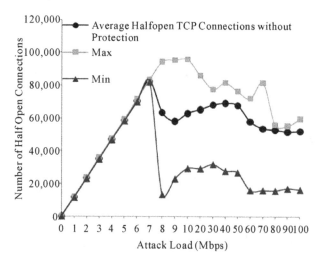

Figure 6. Server TCP connections in SYN_RECEIVED State (without SYN attack protection) under SYN Attack.

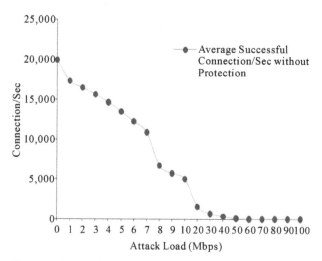

Figure 7. Successful legitimate client connections/sec vs. the attack load without SYN attack protection.

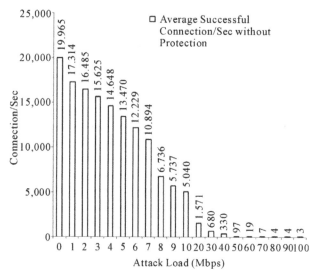

Figure 8. Successful legitimate client connections/sec without SYN Attack Protection.

20,000 connections per second (baseline value). After 60 Mbps of SYN attack load legitimate client connections/sec with the server are almost depleted well below 100 connections/sec. It is observed that around 5000 Connections per second are successful when the SYN attack load intensity is 10 Mbps.

Research community proposed different techniques to detect [6-12], Trace back [13,14] and Defend [15-21] against the TCP SYN flooding attacks. Most of the detection mechanisms proposed depend on the abnormal traffic flow statistics in the network/Internet and the prevention mechanisms depend on filtering, traffic policing and rate limiting. These mechanisms can be implemented in Internet core, firewalls, routers or end systems. When a SYN attack is detected, TCP/IP in Windows Server 2003 and Windows XP lowers the number of retransmissions of the SYN-ACK segment and does not allocate memory or table entry resources for the connection until the TCP three-way handshake has been completed. Microsoft provided a feature called SYN Attack Protect in the server operating system. This feature is available in all versions of windows server 2003 but enabled by default only in some versions of windows server 2003 operating systems. The Microsoft provided definition for this protection as follows [22].

"SYN attack protection involves reducing the amount of retransmissions for the SYN-ACK's, which will reduce the time for which resources have to remain allocated. The allocation of route cache entry resources is delayed until a connection is made and the connection indication to application is delayed until the three-way hand shake is completed."

The action taken by the SYN attack protection mechanism only occurs if TcpMaxHalfOpen and TcpMaxHalfOpenRetried settings are exceeded. The three configurable threshold parameters to trigger TCP's SYN attack flooding protection feature are explained below [23].

1) TcpMaxHalfOpen specifies how many connections the server can maintain in the half-open state before TCP/IP initiates SYN flooding attack protection, by default it is 500 in windows server 2003.

2) TcpMaxHalfOpenRetried specifies how many connections the server can maintain even after a connection request has been retransmitted before TCP/IP initiates SYN flooding attack protection by default it is 400 in windows server 2003.

3) TcpMaxPortsExhausted specifies how many connection requests the server can refuse before TCP/IP initiates SYN flooding attack protection by default it is 100 in windows server 2003.

All the three entries mentioned are used only when SYN flooding protection is enabled on the server, that is, when the value of the SynAttackProtect entry is 1 and the value of the TcpMaxConnectResponseRetransmissions entry is at least 2.

The behavior of TCP/IP protocol stack in the windows server 2003 operating system heavily depends on the registry parameters. We recognized the research efforts made by Microsoft in deciding these registry key parameters for the stable response of server and its services. So we kept most of these parameters in the default state or in the state recommended by the Microsoft as mentioned above for the stable response of the server.

The next step is to enable the SYN attack protection feature in windows server 2003 and observe the server behavior under SYN attack. In the remaining part of this chapter we will observe the server ability to provide services to legitimate clients when SYN attack protection is enable and compare it with the results we had when the

SYN attack protection is not active. The SYN attack protection thresholds mentioned earlier are in the default state/value for all the experiments we conducted in this paper.

The network topology created for this testing is same as shown in **Figure 3**. The CPU and Memory usage of the server under SYN attack when protection enabled is shown in the **Figures 9** and **10** respectively. The CPU utilization is nearly the same with and without protection. The memory consumed by server under SYN attack is significantly reduced when the SYN attack protection is active. Compared to the memory resources available in the server and the cost of memory today, it is not significant.

The successful legitimate client connections rate vs. attack load when the server SYN attack protection enabled is shown in the **Figures 11** and **12**. It is observed that even with protection enabled the successful connection rate is decreased as the attack load increases. The legitimate connections are unable to establish and the connection rate is less than 100 connections/sec after 80 Mbps attack load. This is an improvement over the previous scenario where the connections/sec fell below 100 at 60 Mbps without SYN protection. It is observed from **Figure 12** that the successful connection rate at 10 Mbps of attack load is around 16,000 connections/sec, which is more than two times the successful connection rate we achieved without the SYN flood attack protection. The successful connection rate is improved significantly for a given attack load but at higher attack loads after 60 Mbps, the legitimate connections are unable to be established.

Comparison of the results of these two experiments with and without TCP-SYN protection is shown in the **Figure 13**. When the TCP-SYN attack protection is used, the new client connection rate supported by the web server was improved by 226% under TCP SYN attack load of 10 Mbps.

From the results presented in this paper, it is evident that the legitimate client connection rate is improved by the use of SYN attack protection. However SYN attack protection is not effective at higher loads of SYN attack. But if we increase the number of half open connection limit on the server the successful connection rate of clients may improve [24]. A high bound for the half open connection limit can be computed from the bandwidth of the server's network and the timeout used by the servers to discard pending requests. This is kind of brute force solution that waste lots of kernel memory and slow down the server response time, but it can be effective in public servers serving large communities of clients, since such servers have extensive hardware resources. Even if you increase the half open connection limit, it is possible that at some higher load attack traffic the hash table fills up,

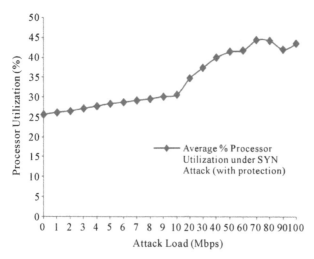

Figure 9. Server CPU utilization (with SYN attack protection) under SYN attack.

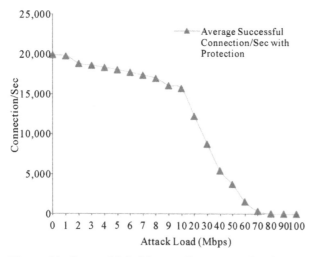

Figure 10. Memory consumption (without SYN attack protection) under SYN attack.

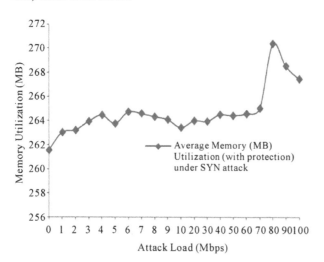

Figure 11. Successful legitimate client connections/sec vs. attack load with SYN attack protection.

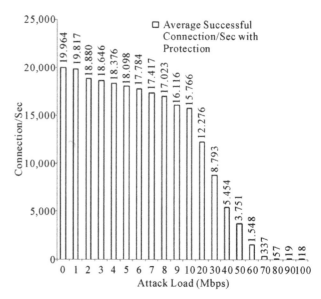

Figure 12. Successful legitimate client connections/sec with SYN attack protect (bar view).

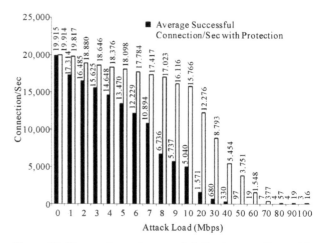

Figure 13. Comparison of successful client connections with and without TCP-SYN attack protection of the windows server.

and it could Overflow with forged connection requests.

5. Conclusions

In this paper, we evaluated the host based protection feature provided by Microsoft against TCP-SYN based DDoS attacks for its widely deployed Windows 2003 servers. It is observed that the built-in, host-based protection feature of Windows server 2003 has limited effectiveness in protecting against TCP-SYN based DDoS attacks. In the absence of any attack, Windows 2003 server was found to support around 20,000 client connections/sec, whereas when the TCP-SYN based DDoS attack traffic was increased to 50Mbps, only around 1700 client connections/sec could be established, which is a reduction of over 90% of legitimate client connection rate. The experimental measurements show that the built-in protection provided by Microsoft for its Windows server 2003 is effective only for low intensity of the TCP-SYN based DDoS attacks, but not effective against high intensity of the DDoS attacks (exceeding 50 Mbps), and many users are not aware of this fact. This paper conveys an important message for the network managers that they must not rely only on the host-based protection mechanism that exists in the Microsoft's server 2003, and they should deploy additional security devices to effectively defend against DDoS attacks.

6. Acknowledgements

This work was supported in part by the funding from US National Science Foundation, Grant No: 0521585.

7. References

[1] Information Science Institute, "Transmission Control Protocol" RFC 793, University of Southern California, Los Angeles, September 1981.
http://tools.ietf.org/html/rfc793

[2] Microsoft Corporation, "Vulnerabilities in Windows TCP/IP Could Allow Remote Code Execution (967723)," *Microsoft Security Bulletin MS09-048-Critical*, 8 September 2009.
http://www.microsoft.com/technet/security/Bulletin/MS09-048.mspx

[3] W. M. Eddy, "TCP SYN Flooding Attacks and Common Mitigations," RFC 4987, August 2007.
http://tools.ietf.org/html/rfc4987

[4] V. Cerf, Y. Dalal and C. Sunshine, "Specification of Internet Transmission Control Program," RFC 675, 1974.
http://tools.ietf.org/html/rfc675#section-4.2.2

[5] Microsoft Corporation, "Transmission Control Protocol/Internet Protocol (TCP/IP)," Windows Server TechNet Library, 2003.
http://technet.microsoft.com/en-us/library/cc759700(WS.10).aspx

[6] S. Shin, K. Kim and J. Jang, "D-SAT: Detecting SYN Flooding Attack by Two-Stage Statistical Approach," *The 2005 Symposium on Applications and the Internet*, Trento, 31 January-4 February 2005, pp. 430-436.

[7] B. Lim and M. S. Uddin, "Statistical-Based SYN-Flooding Detection Using Programmable Network Processor," *3rd International Conference on Information Technology and Applications*, ICITA 2005, Vol. 2, 4-7 July 2005, pp. 465-470.

[8] R. R. Kompella, S. Singh and G. Varghese, "On Scalable Attack Detection in the Network," *Integrated Marketing Communications*, IMC'04, University of California, San diego, 25-27 October 2004.

[9] Y. Ohsita, S. Ata and M. Murata, "Detecting Distributed Denial-of-Service Attacks by Analyzing TCP SYN Packets Statistically," *Global Telecommunications Conference*, 2004, *GLOBECOM'04*, Vol. 4, 29 November-3 December, 2004, pp. 2043-2049.

[10] D. M. Divakaran, H. A. Murthy and T. A. Gonsalves, "Detection of SYN Flooding Attacks Using Linear Prediction Analysis," 14*th IEEE International Conference on Networks*, ICON'06, Vol. 1, September 2006, pp. 1-6.

[11] B. Xiao, W. Chen, Y. He and E. H.-M. Sha, "An Active Detecting Method against SYN Flooding Attack," 11*th International Conference on Parallel and Distributed Systems*, Vol. 1, 20-22 July 2005, pp. 709-715.

[12] S. Kumar and E. Petana, "Mitigation of TCP-SYN Attack with Microsoft's Windows XP Service Pack3 (SP2) Software," *Proceedings of the* 7*th International Conference on Networking*, Cancun, 13-18 April 2008, pp. 238-242.

[13] H. N. Wang, D. L. Zhang and K. G. Shin, "SYN-Dog: Sniffing SYN Flooding Sources," *Proceedings of the* 22*nd International Conference on Distributed Computing Systems*, Vienna, 2-5 July 2002.

[14] M. Sung and J. Xu, "IP Traceback-Based Intelligent Packet Filtering: A Novel Technique for Defending against Internet DDoS Attacks," *Proceedings of the* 10*th IEEE International Conference on Network Protocols*, Paris, 12-15 November 2002, pp. 302-311.

[15] W. Chen and D. Yeung, "Defending against TCP SYN Flooding Attacks under Different Types of IP Spoofing," *Networking, International Conference on Systems and International Conference on Mobile Communications and Learning Technologies*, ICN/ICONS/MCL 2006, Morne, 23-29 April 2006, pp. 38-38.

[16] U. K. Tupakula, V. Varadharajan and A. K. Gajam, "Counteracting TCP SYN DDoS Attacks Using Automated Model," *Global Telecommunications Conference*, 2004, *GLOBECOM'04*, Vol. 4, 29 November-3 December 2004, pp. 2240-2244.

[17] B. AI-Dwmiri and G. Manimaran, "Intentional Dropping: A Novel Scheme for SYN Flooding Mitigation," 25*th IEEE International Conference on Computer Communications*, Barcelona, 23-29 April 2006, pp. 1-5.

[18] Q. Xiaofeng, H. Jihong and C. Ming, "A Mechanism to Defend SYN Flooding Attack Based on Network Measurement System," 2*nd International Conference on Information Technology*: *Research and Education*, ITRE 2004, London, 28 June-1 July 2004, pp. 208-212.

[19] H. Safa, M. Chouman, H. Artail and M. Karam, "A Collaborative Defense Mechanism against SYN Flooding Attacks in IP Networks," *Journal of Network and Computer Applications*, Vol. 31, No. 4, 2008, pp. 509-534.

[20] Y. P. Swami and H. Tschofenig, "Protecting Mobile Devices from TCP Flooding Attacks," *Proceedings of* 1*st ACM/IEEE International Workshop on Mobility in the Evolving Internet Architecture*, San Francisco, 1 Decem-

ber 2006.

[21] F. Kargl, J. Maier and M. Weber, "Protecting Web Servers from Distributed Denial of Service Attacks," ACM, May 2001.

[22] L. Jonathan, "Resisting SYN Flood Attacks with SYN Cache," *Proceedings of the BSDCon Conference on File and Storage Technologies*, February 2002.

http://people.freebsd.org/~jlemon/papers/syncache.pdf

[23] Microsoft Corporation, "Microsoft Windows Server 2003 TCP/IP Implementation Details," March 2006.

[24] A. Zuquete, "Improving the Functionality of SYN Cookies," *6th IFIP Communications and Multimedia Security Conference*, Portoroz, 26-27 September 2002.

2

Tanimoto Based Similarity Measure for Intrusion Detection System

Alok Sharma, Sunil Pranit Lal[*]

Faculty of Science, Technology and Environment, University of the South Pacific, Suva, Fiji

Abstract

In this paper we introduced Tanimoto based similarity measure for host-based intrusions using binary feature set for training and classification. The k-nearest neighbor (*k*NN) classifier has been utilized to classify a given process as either normal or attack. The experimentation is conducted on DARPA-1998 database for intrusion detection and compared with other existing techniques. The introduced similarity measure shows promising results by achieving less false positive rate at 100% detection rate.

Keywords: Intrusion Detection, *k*NN Classifier, Similarity Measure, Anomaly Detection, Tanimoto Similarity Measure

1. Introduction

Intrusion detection is an important area in the field of computers and security, and in the recent years it has generated considerable interest in the research community. The intrusion detection system (IDS) can be subdivided into two main categories namely, signature-based detection and behavior-based detection. In this paper we focus on behavior-based detection which is also known as anomaly detection. An important feature of anomaly detection is that it can detect unknown attacks. Behavior modeling can be done by either modeling the user-behavior or process. The system call data is one of the most common types of data used for modeling process behavior. Host-based anomaly detection systems mostly focus on system call sequences with the assumption that a malicious activity results in an abnormal trace. Such data can be collected by logging the system calls using operating system utilities e.g. Linux strace or Solaris Basic Security Module (BSM). In this framework, it is assumed that the normal behavior can be profiled by a set of patterns of sequence of system calls. Any deviation from the normal pattern is termed as intrusion in this framework. An intrusion detection system needs to learn the normal behavior patterns from the previously collected data and this is normally accomplished by data mining or machine learning techniques. The problem of intrusion detection thus boils down to a supervised classification problem to identify anomalous sequences, which are measurably different from the normal behavior. The system call sequences of normal instances are used as the training set. Though anomaly-based IDS can detect unknown attacks, it suffers from having unacceptable false-positive rate [1]. This is because of the fact that it is hard to perfectly model a normal behavior. Unlike the traditional pattern recognition approach for classification, the aim in the present context is not only to achieve high accuracy rate but also to minimize the false positive rate. In recent years, a lot of research activities in anomaly detection focus on learning process behaviors and building the profiles with system call sequences as data sources.

Various machine learning techniques such as Support Vector Machines [2] and Neural Network [3] have been proposed for designing intelligent intrusion detection systems. Interested readers are directed to Tsai *et al.* [4] for a comprehensive overview on this subject. In this paper we use the *k*NN classification scheme [5-7] as an efficient means for intrusion detection. In carrying out the classification, it is a common practice to use features represented as frequency of system calls observed. While this approach has produced outstanding results [7], we are more interested in reducing the computational cost associated with classification task. Instead of representing features as frequency, which involves repetitive counting, we only consider absence or presence of a system call and represent it as a single bit of data. Needless to say binary representation consumes less storage space compared to integer representation. To this end, we propose a Tanimoto binary similarity measure, and empirically evaluate and compare its performance. To the best of authors' knowledge the result is better than other binary similarity schemes for intrusion detection reported in literature.

2. A Brief Description of the Preceding Work

In this section we briefly describe the research work on behavior-based intrusion detection procedures. Denning [8] did a pioneering work on behavior-based intrusion detection. In this approach profiles of subjects are learnt and statistical methods are used to compute deviations from the normal behavior. Lane and Brodly [9] propose another approach for capturing a user's behavior. A database of sequences of UNIX commands that normally a user issues, is maintained for each user. Any new command sequence is compared with this database using a similarity measure. Forrest et al. [10,11] introduce a simple anomaly detection method based on monitoring the system calls invoked by active and privileged processes. The profile of normal behavior is built by enumerating all fixed length of unique and contiguous system calls that occur in the training data, and unmatched sequences in actual detection are considered abnormal. A similar approach is followed by Lee et al. [12], but they make use of a rule learner RIPPER, to form the rules for classification. Lee and Stolfo [13] use data mining approach to study a sample of system call data to characterize the sequences contained in normal data by a small set of rules. In monitoring and detection, the sequences violating those rules are treated as anomalies [14]. Warrender et al. [15] propose Hidden Markov Model (HMM) method for modeling and evaluating invisible events based on system calls. It is believed that the entire sequence of system calls in a process need not exhibit intrusive behavior, but few subsequences of very small lengths may possess the intrusive characteristics. Rawat et al. [16] showed using rough set technique that the intrusive behavior in a process is very localized. Sharma et al. [7] introduce kernel based similarity measure for host-based intrusions. They have used kNN classifier to classify a process as either normal or abnormal.

Most of the IDSs that model the behavior of processes in terms of subsequences, take fixed-length, contiguous subsequences of system calls. One potential drawback of this approach is that the size of the database that contains fixed-length contiguous subsequences increases exponentially with the length of the subsequences. Wespi et al. [17] propose a variable length subsequence approach. Asaka et al. [18] develop another approach based on the discriminant method in which an optimal classification surface is first learned from samples of the properly labeled normal and abnormal system call sequences. Wang et al. [19] develop another Principle Component Analysis based method for anomaly intrusion detection with less computation efforts. Tandon and Chan [20] propose to consider system calls arguments and other parameters, along with the sequences of system calls. They make use of the variant of a rule learner LERAD (Learning Rules for Anomaly Detection).

In order to detect the deviation of anomalous system call sequences from the normal set of sequences, Liao and Vemuri [5] used a similarity measure based on the frequencies of system calls used by a program (process), rather than the temporal ordering. Their approach draws an analogy between text categorization and intrusion detection, such that each system call is treated as a word and a set of system calls generated by a process as a document. They used a "bag of system calls" representation. Liao and Vemuri [5,21] adopted this representation to profile the behavior according to the trace of each process independently and a kNN method is used for classification. In this method, each system call is treated as a word and a collection of system calls during the execution of a process is treated as a document. The system call trace of a process is converted into a vector and cosine similarity measure is used to calculate the similarity among processes. In another study [22] by the same group, the Robust Support Vector Machine (RSVM) is applied to anomaly-based IDS. Recently, the emphasis of this RSVM study is on exhibiting the effectiveness of the method in the presence of noisy data. Rawat et al. [6] propose anomaly-based IDS. A new similarity measure called binary weighted cosine (BWC) is proposed and it is shown that by kNN classifier with the new measure, one can reduce the false positive rate substantially without sacrificing the detection rate. The authors have shown that by defining appropriate similarity measures, the detection by simple kNN can be as efficient as the sophisticated classification techniques like SVMs. Sharma et al. [7] propose a very efficient anomaly based IDS. They have introduced kernel based similarity measure and showed that it can capture similarity at very accurate level. They have used kNN as their classification scheme. The success of any such classification is hinged on two important aspects the similarity measure and the classification scheme.

3. Notations and Descriptions

In the remaining discussion $S = \{s_1, s_2, s_3, \cdots, s_m\}$ denotes a set of unique system calls where $m = |S|$ is the number of system calls. The training set X is defined as a set of labeled sequences $\{<Z_i, c_i>|Z_i \in S^*; c_i \in \{0, 1\}\}$ where Z_i is an input sequence of system calls or a process, c_i is a corresponding class label denoting 0 for "normal" label and 1 for "intrusion" label and S^* is the set of all finite strings of symbol of S. In this representation, the ordering information of adjacent system calls in the input sequence is not considered to be significant and only the frequency of each system call is preserved. Given the data set X, the goal of the learning algorithm is to find a classifier $h: S^* \rightarrow \{0, 1\}$ that maximizes detection rate and minimizes false positive rate.

The vector-space model of Information Retrieval (IR) is also often used to represent the set of processes. A process is depicted as a binary vector to represent the occurrences of system call. The value 1 represents the occurrences of a system call in a process and its absence is represented by 0. Thus we define Zb_i the binary representation of Z_i, where the entries of Zb_i is 1, if the corresponding system call is present, and 0, otherwise.

4. Tanimoto Similarity Measure

The concept of Tanimoto coefficient [23], is presented here for binary similarity. It is an extension of Jacquard coefficient, which is a binary similarity measure. Given two vectors of binary features, Zb_i and, Zb_j the binary Tanimoto coefficient is represented as

$$BT(Z_i, Z_j) = T(Zb_i, Zb_j) = \frac{Zb_i \cdot Zb_j}{\|Zb_i\|^2 + \|Zb_j\|^2 - Zb_i \cdot Zb_j} \quad (1)$$

where $\|\bullet\|$ is the Euclidean norm.

The Jacquard and Tanimoto coefficients have been extensively applied in several fields ranging from studying the diversity of species in ecosystem [24], to measuring similarity between chemical compounds [25]. In this paper we experiment using Tanimoto coefficient to measure the similarity between processes represented as binary features.

5. Binary Tanimoto Weighted Cosine (BTWC) Similarity Measure

In order to define BTWC similarity measure, we first define cosine similarity measure [5]. The cosine similarity measure $\lambda(Z_i, Z_j)$ between any two processes Z_i and Z_j is defined as follows.

$$CosSim(Z_i, Z_j) = \lambda(Z_i, Z_j) = \frac{Z_i.Z_j}{\|Z_i\| . \|Z_j\|} \quad (2)$$

The motive behind multiplying binary Tanimoto and $CosSim$ is that $CosSim(Z_i, Z_j)$ measures the similarity

based on the frequency and binary Tanimoto is the weight associated with Z_i and Z_j. In other words, binary Tanimoto tunes the similarity score $CosSim(Z_i, Z_j)$ according to the number of similar and dissimilar system calls between the two processes. The BTWC similarity measure can be given as

$$BTWC(Z_i, Z_j) = T(Zb_i, Zb_j) \times CosSim(Z_i, Z_j) \quad (3)$$

Therefore, the similarity measure BTWC takes frequency and the number of common system calls into consideration while calculating similarity between two processes.

6. *k*-Nearest Neighbors with the Similarity Measures

The *k*NN classifier is a generalized form of NN classifier. In this approach the behavior of a new process is classified by collecting the majority of k closest training processes. The average of these majority k measures is computed which is compared with the threshold value to determine if the process is normal or attack. The pseudo code of *k*NN procedure with similarity measure is as follows.

Let the training set X has n processes such that $Z_j \in X$. Let P be any new process.

```
for j = 1 to n
    sm_j = similarity_measure(P, Z_j)¹;
end
sm_k = find_top_k(sm_j);
avg = average(sm_k);
if avg > threshold
    P = 'normal'
else
    P = 'attack'
end
```

7. An Illustration

In this section, we analyze the proposed scheme with the help of an example. To illustrate, consider two training processes Z_1 and Z_2 associated with 10 unique system call S. Let also consider a test process Z to measure the similarity with the training processes. The processes and the unique system call set S are defined as follows:

$S = \{$auditon, chdir, close, creat, kill, login,
mkdir, stat, su, sysinfo$\}$

$Z_1 = \{$login, stat, stat, stat, stat, auditon,
auditon, auditon, auditon$\}$

---

[1] In place of *similarity_measure*, Equation (1) or (3) will be used.

$Z_2 = \{$login, close, su, sysinfo, stat, chdir,

chdir, mkdir, creat, kill$\}$

$Z = \{$login, auditon, auditon, stat, mkdir,

close, close, creat, kill$\}$

To find the similarity between a test and train processes, we observe that there are only three common system calls between Z and Z_1. However, there are six common system calls between Z and Z_2. This inferred that there is more similarity between Z and Z_2. Therefore, hypothetically $Sim(Z, Z_2) > Sim(Z, Z_1)$, where Sim is any similarity measure function. Computing the similarity score between these processes using $CosSim$, binary Tanimoto and BTWC similarity measures, we get,

$$CosSim(Z, Z_1) = 0.6276 \quad CosSim(Z, Z_2) = 0.5604$$
$$BT(Z, Z_1) = 0.4286 \quad BT(Z, Z_2) = 0.6000$$
$$BTWC(Z, Z_1) = 0.2690 \quad BTWC(Z, Z_2) = 0.3363$$

According to $CosSim$ similarity measure, Z is more similar to Z_1 than to Z_2, since $CosSim(Z, Z_1) > CosSim(Z, Z_2)$. However, this contradicts with the hypothesis. On the other hand, using binary Tanimoto and BTWC similarity measures, Z appeared to be more similar to Z_2 than to Z_1, since $BT(Z, Z_2) > BT(Z, Z_1)$ and $BTWC(Z, Z_2) > BTWC(Z, Z_1)$. The similarity scores measured by binary Tanimoto and BTWC validate the hypothesis. Therefore, it is more likely that by using these two techniques, better results for intrusion detection problem can be achieved.

In order to see the application of kNN classifier with binary Tanimoto and BTWC similarity measures, let us assume a third training process Z_3, such that $BT(Z, Z_3) = 0.5$ and $BTWC(Z, Z_2) = 0.3$. Suppose the threshold for binary Tanimoto is $\theta_{BT} = 0.58$ and for BTWC is $\theta_{BTWC} = 0.32$. If the classification procedure to label a process Z into either as attack or normal is conducted by comparing the highest similarity score then by binary Tanimoto the process will be classified as normal since, $BT(Z, Z_2) = 0.6 > \theta_{BT}$ and by BTWC it will also be classified as normal since, $BTWC(Z, Z_2) = 0.3363 > \theta_{BTWC}$. This could give statistically unstable results as the classification is dominated by a single training process (with the highest similarity score). A better classification scheme would be to evaluate the average of top k scores to arrive to the labeling of processes. If $k = 2$ then for binary Tanimoto using kNN classifier the average of top 2 similarity scores would be $avg < \theta_{BT}$. This means that the process Z is now classified as an attack since, $avg < \theta_{BT}$. In a similar way, process Z will be classified as an attack for BTWC using kNN classifier since, $avg = 0.3181 < \theta_{BTWC}$. Therefore binary Tanimoto and BTWC similarity measures with kNN classifier are expected to give statistically stable results by comparing the average similarity measure of top k processes.

8. Experimentation

In order to perform experimentation we use BSM audit logs from the 1998 DARPA data [26] for training and testing of our algorithm. This is the same data set used in previous research efforts [5-7] and thus it enables us compare the results. There are 50 unique system calls in the training data. All the 50 system calls are shown in **Table 1**.

In this dataset about 2000 normal sessions reported in the four days of data and the training data set consists of 606 unique processes. There are 412 normal sessions on the fifth day and we extract 5285 normal processes from these sessions. We use these 5285 normal processes as testing data. In order to test the detection capability of our method, we considered 54 intrusive sessions as test data. **Table 2** lists these attacks. A number in the beginning of the name denotes the week and day followed by the name of the session (attack).

Table 1. List of 50 unique system calls.

access, audit, auditon, chdir, chmod, chown, close, creat, execve, exit, fchdir, fchown, fcntl, fork, fork1, getaudit, getmsg, ioctl, kill, link, login, logout, lstat, memcntl, mkdir, mmap, munmap, oldnice, oldsetgid, oldsetuid, oldutime, open, pathdonf, pipe, putmsg, readlink, rename, rmdir, setaudit, setegid, seteuid, setgroups, setpgrp, setrlimit, stat, statvfs, su, sysinfo, unlink, vfork

Table 2. List of 54 attacks used in test data.

1.1_it_ffb clear,	1.1_it_format_clear,	2.2_it_ipsweep,
2.5_it_ftpwrite,	2.5_it_ftpwrite_test,	3.1_it_ffb_clear,
3.3_it_ftpwrite,	3.3_it_ftpwrite_test,	3.4_it_warez,
3.5_it_warezmaster,		4.1_it_080520warezclient,
4.2_it_080511warezclient,		4.2_it_153736spy,
4.2_it_153736spy_test,		4.2_it_153812spy,
4.4_it_080514warezclient,	4.4_it_080514warezclient_test,	
4.4_it_175320warezclient,	4.4_it_180326warezclient,	
4.4_it_180955warezclient,	4.4_it_181945warezclient,	
4.5_it_092212ffb,		4.5_it_141011loadmodule,
4.5_it_162228loadmodule,		4.5_it_174726loadmodule,
4.5_it_format,	5.1_it_141020ffb,	5.1_it_174729ffb_exec,
5.1_it_format,		5.2_it_144308eject_clear,
5.2_it_163909eject_clear,	5.3_it_eject_steal,	5.5_it_eject,
5.5_it_fdformat,	5.5_it_fdformat_chmod,	6.4_it_090647ffb,
6.4_it_093203eject,	6.4_it_095046eject,	6.4_it_100014eject,
6.4_it_122156eject,	6.4_it_144331ffb,	test.1.2_format,
test.1.2_format2,	test.1.3_eject,	test.1.3_httptunnel,
test.1.4_eject,	test.2.1_111516ffb,	test.2.1_format,
test.2.2_xsnoop,	test.2.3_ps, test.2.3_ps_b,	test.2.5_ftpwrite,
test.2.4_eject_a,	test.2.2_format1	

An intrusive session is said to be detected if any of the processes associated with this session is classified as abnormal. Thus detection rate is defined as the number of intrusive sessions detected, divided by the total number of intrusive sessions. We perform the experiments with $k = 5$.

In **Tables 3-6** we show Liao-Vemuri scheme [5], BWC scheme [6], BTWC scheme and binary Tanimoto scheme respectively for $k = 5$. In the tables, the first column represents the threshold values used in the experiments. The second column depicts the false positives rates and the third column depicts the detection rate.

It can be seen from **Table 3** that for Liao-Vemuri scheme the false positive rate is very high (25.8%) at a detection rate of 100%. It can be observed from **Table 4** that BWC is a better technique than Liao-Vemuri as it provides lesser false positive rate (4.65%) at a detection rate of 100%. However, this false positive rate (4.65%) still may not be acceptable. The BTWC scheme (**Table 5**) gives better performance by getting false positive rate of 4.1% at 100% detection. Next, the binary Tanimoto scheme performs the best by giving 3.7% false positive rate at a detection rate of 100%. **Table 7** summarizes the results obtained in **Tables 3-6**. It can be seen the binary

Table 3. Liao-vemuri scheme.

Threshold	False Positive Rate	Detection Rate
0.52	0.0000	0.3519
0.89	0.0009	0.7593
0.99	0.0096	0.9630
0.995	0.2575	1.0000

Table 4. Binary weighted cosine scheme.

Threshold	False Positive Rate	Detection Rate
0.52	0.0000	0.3704
0.86	0.0095	0.9444
0.90	0.0238	0.9815
0.90099	0.0465	1.0000

Table 5. BTWC scheme.

Threshold	False Positive Rate	Detection Rate
0.52	0.0000	0.3704
0.86	0.0348	0.9630
0.88	0.0401	0.9630
0.889	0.0411	1.0000

Table 6. Binary tanimoto scheme.

Threshold	False Positive Rate	Detection Rate
0.52	0.0000	0.3519
0.86	0.0312	0.9630
0.92	0.0369	0.9630
0.9219	0.0369	1.0000

Table 7. Summary: false positive rate at 100% detection rate for all the schemes.

Method	False Positive Rate	Detection Rate
Liao-Vemuri	25.75%	100.0%
BWC	4.7%	100.0%
BTWC	4.1%	100.0%
Binary Tanimoto	3.7%	100.0%

Tanimoto scheme is better than other schemes. The advantage of this scheme is that it utilizes only binary data which has lesser computing and managing requirements.

The receiver operating characteristic (ROC) curve is also depicted in **Figure 1**. It provides a comparison between the techniques. The ROC curve is a graph between the attack detection rate and false positive rate. It can be seen in the figure that binary Tanimoto converges to 100% detection rate faster than other three schemes. The curve of BTWC scheme is better than binary Tanimoto for smaller values of false positive rate. However, it converges slower to 100% detection rate than binary Tanimoto scheme. Nonetheless, the benchmark is to obtain lowest false positive rate at 100% detection rate and the proposed schemes are outperforming other similarity measures.

9. Conclusions

The Tanimoto based similarity measure schemes have been introduced in this work. It was observed that these schemes produced better results than other techniques. The best result obtained by Tanimoto scheme was 3.7% at the detection rate of 100%. To the best of the authors' knowledge the performance of the proposed technique is better than any previously documented result using binary similarity measure in the area of intrusion detection.

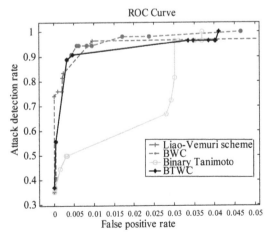

Figure 1. ROC curve for Liao-vemuri, BWC, binary tanimoto and BTWC schemes.

It is worth highlighting that a binary representation of features captures less detailed information about a process compared with features represented as frequency. Even with this limitation, we obtained good results, which gives validity to our proposed approach.

10. Acknowledgements

The authors would like to thank the reviewers and the Editor for providing constructive comments about the paper.

11. References

[1]   T. Lane and C. E. Brodley, "Temporal Sequence Learning and Data Reduction for Anomaly Detection," *In Proceedings of 5th ACM Conference on Computer & Communication Security*, San Francisco, 3-5 November 1998, pp. 150-158.

[2]   Y. Yi, J. Wu and W. Xu, "Incremental SVM Based on Reserved Set for Network Intrusion Detection," *Expert Systems with Applications*, Vol. 38, No. 6, 2011, pp. 7698-7707.

[3]   G. Wang, J. Hao, J. Ma and L. Huang, "A New Approach to Intrusion Detection Using Artificial Neural Networks and Fuzzy Clustering," *Expert Systems with Applications*, Vol. 37, No. 9, 2010, pp. 6225-6232.

[4]   C. F. Tsai, Y. F. Hsu, C. Y. Lin and W. Y. Lin, "Intrusion Detection by Machine Learning: A Review," *Expert Systems with Applications*, Vol. 36, No. 10, 2009, pp. 11994-12000.

[5]   Y. Liao and V. R. Vemuri, "Use of K-Nearest Neighbor Classifier for Intrusion Detection," *Computers & Security*, Vol. 21, No. 5, 2002, pp. 439-448.

[6]   S. Rawat, V. P. Gulati, A. K. Pujari and V. R. Vemuri, "Intrusion Detection Using Text Processing Techniques with a Binary-Weighted Cosine Metric," *Journal of Information Assurance and Security*, Vol. 1, 2006, pp. 43-50.

[7]   A. Sharma, A. K. Pujari and K. K. Paliwal, "Intrusion Detection Using Text Processing Techniques with a Kernel Based Similarity Measure," *Computers & Security*, Vol. 26, No. 7-8, 2007, pp. 488-495.

[8]   D. E. Denning, "An Intrusion-Detection Model," *IEEE Transactions on Software Engineering*, Vol. 13, No. 2, 1990, pp. 222-232.

[9]   T. Lane and C. E. Brodly. "An Application of Machine Learning to Anomaly Detection," *Proceeding of the 20th National Information System Security Conference*, Baltimore, 1997, pp. 366-377.

[10]   S. Forrest, S. A. Hofmeyr, A. Somayaji and T. A. Longstaff, "A Sense of Self for Unix Processes," *Proceedings of the 1996 IEEE Symposium on Research in Security and Privacy*, Los Alamos, 1996, pp.120-128.

[11]   S. Forrest, S. A. Hofmeyr and A. Somayaji, "Computer Immunology," *Communications of the ACM*, Vol. 40, No. 10, 1997, pp. 88-96.

[12]   W. Lee, S. Stolfo and P. Chan, "Learning Patterns from Unix Process Execution Traces for Intrusion Detection," *In Proceedings of the AAAI97 Workshop on AI Methods in Fraud and Risk Management*, AAAI Press, Menlo Park, 1997, pp. 50-56.

[13]   W. Lee and S. Stolfo, "Data Mining Approaches for Intrusion Detection," *Proceedings of the 7th USENIX Security Symposium*, Usenix Association, 1998, pp.79-94.

[14]   E. Eskin, A. Arnold, M. Prerau, L. Portnoy and S. Stolfo, "A Geometric Framework for Unsupervised Anomaly Detection: Detecting Intrusions in Unlabeled Data," Applications of Data Mining in Computer Security, Kluwer Academics Publishers, Berlin, 2002, pp. 77-102.

[15]   C. Warrender, S. Forrest and B. Pearlmutter, "Detecting Intrusions Using System Calls: Alternative Data Models," *Proceedings of 1999 IEEE Symposium on Security and Privacy*, Oakland, 1999, pp. 133-145.

[16]   S. Rawat, V. P. Gulati and A. K. Pujari, "A Fast Host-Based Intrusion Detection System Using Rough Set Theory," *Computer Science*, Vol. 3700, No. 2005, 2005, pp. 144-161.

[17]   A. Wespi, M. Dacier and H. Debar, "Intrusion Detection Using Variable-Length Audit Trail Patterns," *Proceedings of the Third International Workshop on the Recent Advances in Intrusion Detection (RAID'2000)*, Toulouse, 2000.

[18]   M. Asaka, T. Onabuta, T. Inove, S. Okazawa and S. Goto, "A New Intrusion Detection Method on Discriminant Analysis," *IEICE Transaction on Information and Systems E84D*, Vol. 5, 2001, pp. 570-577.

[19]   W. Wang, X. Guan and X. Zhang, "A Novel Intrusion Detection Method Based on Principle Component Analysis in Computer Security," *Proceedings of the International IEEE Symposium on Neural Networks*, Dalian, *Lecture Notes in Computer Science*, Vol. 3174, No. 2004, 2004, pp. 657-662.

[20]   G. Tandon and P. K. Chan, "Learning Useful System Call Attributes for Anomaly Detection," *Proceedings of the 18th International Florida Artificial Intelligence Research Society (FLAIRS) Conference*, Clearwater Beach, 2005, pp. 405-410.

[21]   Y. Liao and V. R. Vemuri, "Using Text Categorization Techniques for Intrusion Detection," *Proceedings USE NIX Security 2002*, San Francisco, 2002, pp. 51-59.

[22]   H. Wenjie, Y. Liao and V. R. Vemuri, "Robust Support Vector Machines for Anomaly Detection in Computer Security," *In International Conference on Machine Learning*, Los Angeles, 2003, pp. 1-7.

[23]   T. T. Tanimoto, "IBM Internal Report 17th," November 1957. http://en.wikipedia.org/wiki/Jaccard_index for details.

[24] J. A. Wallwork, "The Distribution and Diversity of Soil Fauna," Academic Press, London, 1976.

[25] P. Willett, "Chemical Similarity Searching," *Journal of Chemical Information and Computer Sciences*, Vol. 38,

1998, pp. 983-996.

[26] DARPA 1998 Data, "MIT Lincoln Laboratory," 2007. http://www.ll.mit.edu/IST/ideval/data/data index.html

3

Vulnerabilities of LDAP as an Authentication Service

Charlie Obimbo*, **Benjamin Ferriman**
School of Computer Science, University of Guelph, Guelph, Canada

Abstract

Lightweight Directory Access Protocol (LDAP) servers are widely used to authenticate users in enterprise level networks. Organizations such as universities and small to medium-sized businesses use LDAP for a variety of applications including E-mail clients, SSH, and workstation authentication. Since many organizations build dependencies on the LDAP service, a Denial-of-Service (DoS) attack to the service can cause a greater number of services disrupted. This paper examines the danger in the use of LDAP for user authentication by executing a DoS attack exploiting the TCP three-way handshake required when initializing a connection to an LDAP server.

Keywords: LDAP, SYN Flooding, Denial-of-Service, Authentication Service

1. Introduction

In computing today organizations including universities and small to medium-sized businesses need to provide a wide range of services to a vast number of users. Many of these services require a form of authentication and/or authorization to securely verify the identity of their respective subscribers. Services that may require such authentication include email clients like Zimbra and remote terminal clients such as SSH. A denial-of-service attack on a Lightweight Directory Access Protocol Server (LDAP server) left vulnerable could effectively disrupt productivity and/or economic gains of an organization.

Since LDAP servers are critical [1] in business environments, they are typically hidden behind firewalls and IDS software (see **Figure 1**). One major flaw that usually causes security policies to be degraded, is the fact that LDAP is also an active directory meaning that IT departments will usually make these servers open to the Internet. Despite the efforts of firewalls, well-crafted TCP SYN packets can often cause SYN flooding symptoms.

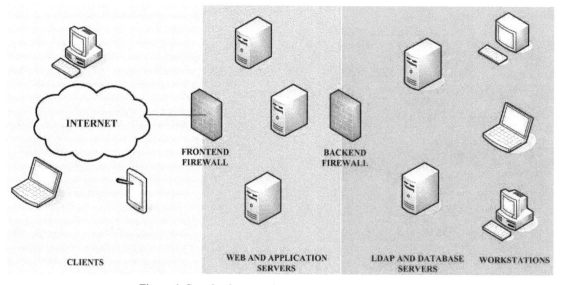

Figure 1. Standard enterprise network configuration [2].

This paper intends to assert the argument that active directory systems like LDAP in their current states are poor choices as authentication services through the design and implementation of a SYN flooding denial-of-service attack. The attack is intended as a simple denial-of-service scenario to bring forth issues that may arise when a LDAP server is used as an authentication service.

1.1. LDAP Overview

LDAP directories are hierarchical databases [1] that hold information about people and entities [3] (such as workstation PAM or SAM files). Inside each directory, data is stored in a tree structure with every level of the tree being a different domain. This structure resembles that of DNS servers; the top-level domain (TLD) is .com or .ca and the fully qualified domain name (FQDN) is ldap.example.com. All sub-directories also follow this structure (see **Figure 2**).

LDAP is designed for providing directory services with other open systems [3]. This means that by design LDAP is an open system for accepting and returning queries. The difference between directories and regular databases is that a directory typically has its data organized to allow quick search results for rapid querying [4].

1.2. Security in LDAP

Originally passwords were sent over networks in plaintext. Since LDAP was designed to facilitate communication among directories for organizations, LDAP's design assumed it would be implemented inside existing (secure) network infrastructures. To combat this shortcoming, LDAP had to incorporate the use of SSL to provide encryption of traffic containing plain-text passwords. The result was that a listener had to be opened on port 636 to support SSL. The solution provided the intended confidentiality but still was an ad-hoc solution. A better solution proposed in LDAP v3 was the incorporation of a Transport Layer Security (TLS) session [6] when initializing a connection with a LDAP server. Though LDAPs protocol security has been implemented there still exists many LDAP servers that allow less secure binding methods. This is usually due to lack of server configuration and/or interaction with legacy systems.

1.3. LDAP Authentication Model

LDAP as an authentication service follows the client/server model. The LDAP model has two main steps when a user requests non-TLS bind authentication. These are (in order):

1) TCP three-way handshake (SYN, SYN/ACK, ACK)
2) LDAP bind() function (performed synchronous or asynchronous)

All TCP traffic to a LDAP server is typically sent to port 389 [7], although v2 of the protocol allows communication with port 636 over the Secure Socket Layer (SSL). Since v3, the protocol has introduced the Simple Authentication and Security Layer (SASL) [8,9] using port 389, port 636 has become obsolete but still remains in use due to legacy directories still using v2 and client applications seeking confidentiality through SSL.

1.4. LDAP Authentication Protocol

As seen in the section above LDAP has two actions when initializing an authentication request. The three-

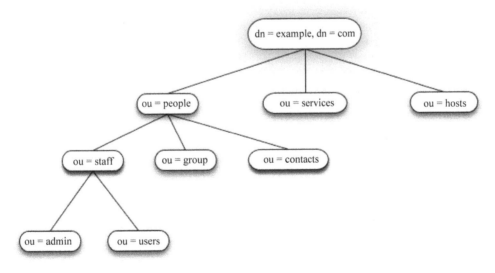

Figure 2. Basic LDAP heirachy [5].

way handshake required of a TCP connection forms the first step of authenticating. The second step requires the use of the LDAP protocol. The LDAP protocol is encapsulated in the TCP layer of a packet band has three standard fields. They are the messageID, protocolOp, and controls. Since authentication with LDAP only adds data in with the messageID and the protocolOp, the controls field will not be addressed.

The messageID field holds a unique value to the session from 0 to 231-1. Message IDs cannot be reassigned until a client has received a response corresponding to that message.

The protocol Op field holds three choices that are important functions of authenticating with LDAP. They include:

- bindRequest
- bindResponse
- unbindRequest

A bindRequest follows the following syntax: version, name, and authentication. Version is used to specify v2 or v3. The name field follows the LDAP standard for querying the directory (see **Figure 3**), while the authentication field specifies the encryption used.

In **Figure 3** the term simple refers to a password that has no encryption (*i.e.* plain-text). This practice is still common among many organizations.

1.5. Related Work

A lot of research has been done on LDAP injections [1,4] while far less is known about proper protection and implementation of LDAP servers. Denial-of-service of LDAP usually targets one of two OSI network layers. Attacks discovered on the **application layer** [10] of LDAP communication include *null byte injection*, where a carefully crafted *POST request* with a null byte inside can cause *unauthenticated authentication* to a system [11]. On the transport layer [12] denial-of-service attacks including *SYN flooding* have also been used to disrupt services. In another paper, security policy was adjusted from semantic threat graphs [13] that were generated by conducting *SYN flooding* on vulnerable high usage systems including LDAP. Though threat analysis is not the intention of this paper, the findings did show how network systems such as routers and servers reacted to heavy attacks. Also illustrated are many default configu-

rations to prevent such an attack.

2. Proposed Attack

An attack was chosen to demonstrate the vulnerability of a denial-of-service attack and reinforce the idea that LDAP directory servers are not good candidates for authentication services. The proposed attack is a **SYN flood** attack on the three-way handshake of TCP protocol. Since we are attacking the way which TCP initializes a connection, the attack is to the transport layer. *SYN* **flood** was chosen as the best-suited attack for its simplicity and to emphasize that the problem is the usage of LDAP as an authentication system. In the TCP three-way handshake, a client and server send three packets between each other to initiate a synchronous connection. The three packets consist of:

1) a **SYN** (synchronize) client request

2) a **SYN/ACK** (synchronize/acknowledgement) server reply

3) a **ACK** (acknowledgement) client reply

An example of the handshake can be seen in **Figure 4**.

Since every TCP connection commences with a **SYN request**, attacks can be constructed with raw sockets [15] to spoof sender IP addresses causing server side SYN/

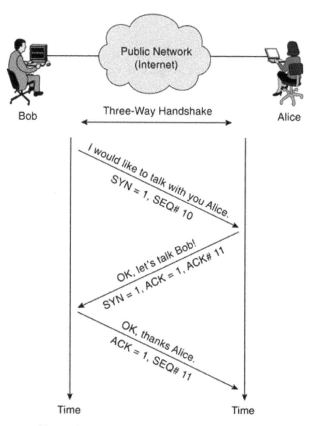

Figure 4. Basic TCP three-way handshake [14].

```
version: 3
name: uid = username, ou = people, o = uoguelph.ca
authentication: simple
simple: 55555555
```

Figure 3. Common format of bind request.

ACK packets to be redirected to the spoofed address. SYN flooding can potentially cause denial-of-service to two victims. One victim is the destination address if the service cannot properly handle many half-open connections. The other victim can be the spoofed address if it's service cannot handle random traffic well. An example of SYN flooding can be seen in **Figure 5**.

2.1. Packet Design

The packets were carefully constructed to impersonate the genuine *SYN* requests to a LDAP server running on port 38.

A standard IP header was created with the *spoofed* source IP address and the LDAP server IP as the destination address. The IP header takes up 20 bytes of the packet size.

The TCP header consisted of a *spoofed* source port and the LDAP destination port (389) as well as having the *SYN flag* bit flipped on. The TCP header also initializes its offset value to 6 (for six 32 bit words; 5 for the TCP header and 1 for TCP options) and sets the window size to 5840. The TCP header size is also 20 bytes. As an option the maximum segment size (MSS) is set to 1460. The option adds an additional 4 bytes to the TCP header size. In total the packet size is 44 bytes (IP and TCP headers). The TCP header used can be seen in **Figure 6**.

2.2. Attack Implementation

The TCP SYN packets were generated using raw sockets in C. The software sends any number (n) of SYN packets from a source address to a destination address and port (see **Figure 7**).

The attack was tailored for a LDAP server (tested against OpenLDAP [17]) but also has a testing suite

made up of a client and server that constantly send and reply to messages. A live LDAP server was also used up until the implementation of the attack but was not able to be tested against since many systems were reliant of it. An implementation of OpenLDAP was used on a closed network.

To test whether the LDAP server was still reachable, a Python program was used to attempt authentication with the LDAP server. Every time a bind request with the correct credentials returned a connection error an alert (chime) would sound. To communicate with the LDAP server the program utilized the Python LDAP library.

3. Analysis of Attack

The number one adversary of this attack is the use of firewalls. That said the use of static firewall policies are highly ineffective to planned attacks and dynamic policy changes are needed. Even with dynamically written poli-

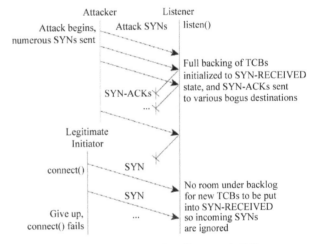

Figure 5. Basic SYN flooding attack [16].

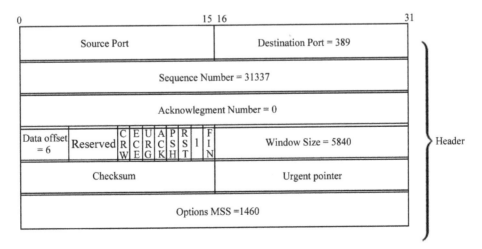

Figure 6. TCP Header—modified for connections with LDAP servers.

```
SYN flooding procedure:

begin
iphdr: = set_iphdr(src_ip, dst_ip);
tcphdr: = set_tcphdr(dst_port);
packet: = iphdr + tcphdr + payload;
for i: = 1 to n step 1 do
sendto(dst_ip, packet); od
where
proc set_iphdr(srcaddr, dstaddr) ≡

*ip: = header;
ip- > ip_src: = srcaddr;
ip- > ip_dst: = dstaddr;
return(header);
        .
proc set_tcphdr(dstport) ≡

*tcp: = header;
tcp- > th_sport: = rand();
tcp- > th_dport: = dstport;
tcp- > th_seq: = 31337;
tcp- > th_off: = 6;
tcp- > th_flags: = TH_SY N;
tcp- > th_win: = 5840;
comment: TCP Options (MSS = 1460);

*tcpOp: = header + sizeof(tcp);
tcpOp[0]: = 2;
tcpOp[1]: = 4;
tcpOp[2]: = 5;
tcpOp[3]: = 180;
return(header);
        .
end
```

Figure 7. SYN flooding and basic header construction and execution algorithms; used in flood.c.

cies a lot of administrative effort is diverted to victimized firewall.

3.1. Packet Generation

In order to create obfuscation of the source of the attack, every packet sent changes its IP address from the previously sent address. This method makes it harder to implement an ad-hoc firewall policy that might disrupt an

attack to regain control. It is for this same reason that the port number of the sender is randomized. The actual execution of the flood program (written in C) is done inside a shell script (see **Figure 8**) that changes the senders IP as well as adding the ability to set a *delay* between each packet sent.

3.2. Effectiveness of Attack

In the test environment the attack *successfully* denied service to all applications relying on LDAP for authentication. It must be noted that the LDAP server in the test environment handled many less queries than real-life implementations. Since the attack was devastatingly successful in the test environment, it is predicted to have the same effect in a real-life exercise. Just the increased amount of SYN requests is enough to require rapid modification and/or constant monitoring of firewall policies.

One major factor in the *effectiveness* of an attack is if the LDAP server has an IP that is resolvable to the Internet. This practice is still common since first and foremost LDAP is *a directory access protocol*. The random appearance of the source IP and port also prolonged the attacks effectiveness at defeating firewall policies. In terms of effectiveness, since LDAP is a critical authentication system and can effectively be denial-of-service, the attack (SYN flooding) is seen as highly effective when orchestrated properly.

4. Effectiveness as an Authentication Service

As of 2011 (when this paper was written) there are many choices of authentication services. One such example developed by the Massachusetts Institute of Technology is Kerberos [18]. Though Kerberos is also vulnerable to DoS attacks due to the fact that it a *centralized authentication server*, it addresses two extremely important flaws

```
#!/bin/bash
# 131.104.0.0 is part of the uoguelph.ca namespace
# -n 1 -w 2 -x 4 -y 5 -z 180: one packet sent, with MSS=1460 in TCP options

while true; do
  for j in `seq 254`
  do
    for i in `seq 256`
    do
      ./flood -s "131.104.$j.$i" -d 131.104.93.16 -p 389 -n 1 -w 2 -x 4 -y 5 -z 180
      sleep 0
    done
  done
done
```

Figure 8. Synflood.sh—script to control TCP SYN packets sent.

of LDAP. The two flaws presented are not design flaws of the protocol, rather implementation flaws due to increases in functionality.

4.1. Issues

The first problem with LDAP is the fact that it is an *active directory*. This means that it (the LDAP server) is constantly being inundated with new queries. An authentication service should never have **more traffic than necessary**. Since LDAP services provide more than just authentication, LDAP is a poor candidate as an authenticator. There are three measures that can be taken to better protect an organizations LDAP server(s).

1) Only bind to connections for authentication that are inside an organization's **IP range** and on **a known hosts list**

2) Bind all **blind authentication** connections to a **second physical LDAP server** that is a **clone** of the directory tree for the scope of a blind authentication

3) If allowing connections from the Internet, only allow **blind authentication**

The *first* measure ensures that only known clients inside the network have access to the directory for authentication and *privileged querying*. The *second* measure ensures that all non-critical traffic hitting the LDAP server is directed at a clone server instead ensuring **data integrity**. The *final* measure is ensured by the second measure that all Internet traffic is by policy sent to the clone server. With proper security policies set up **internal attacks** can also be traced easier and shut down faster since the abuse can be logged through internal networks.

The second flaw of LDAP is that since it was designed first for **directory access**, security was appended to the design, and not initially supported. As a result passwords can be sent over networks in *plain-text*. Any authentication service that allows *transmission* plain-text passwords of or *stores* plain-text passwords is not suited for use given computing in the 21st Century. Although v3 of the protocol allows TLS sessions [6], the use of such security has not fully carried over due to historic security policies using the obsolete SSL-session method, which can be easily compromised by *SSL certificate spoofing* [19]. There are also three precautions that can be taken for the second flaw in LDAP.

1) Not allowing **plain-text** passwords to be used for authentication; hash them with at least SHA-256

2) Using the **TLS service** LDAP supports

3) Having all authentication connections connect to server through a **virtual private network (VPN)**

Of course one could try and implement all of the above safe-gaurds but it would be much easier to use

software designed for authentication. Due to the required extra policies needed to combat denial-of-service attacks, LDAP does not make a good authentication provider.

4.2. Alternative Authentication Services

As discussed previously in section 4.1, LDAP is a poor choice for authenticating users and entities. One service already described above is **Kerberos**. It is worth mentioning due to the fact that it is present in several systems including the BSD operating system and the X Window System [20]. Many other operating systems use a variant of Kerberos.

Kerberos incorporates the use of strong cryptography in order to ensure the **confidentiality** of authentication credentials. Kerberos is often used in conjunction with a LDAP server that only allows access from connections where an authentication ticket has been granted. Tickets are authentication tokens that verify a users identity to the requested service and tells the user where to create a connection with the service requested.

5. Conclusions

We have shown that the use of LDAP software in its current state is not suitable as an authentication service. In Section 3 the attack proposed was successful at causing denial-of-service due to SYN flooding and was thus able to render the LDAP service disrupted. In Section 3.2 it was argued that due to the fact authentication is a critical service a successful DoS attack is highly effective.

Section 4.1 brought forth two fundamental flaws of LDAP. They included protecting LDAP servers from DoS attacks and protecting user passwords from being discovered over a network. Finally section 4.2 suggested the use of Kerberos as an alternative authentication service to LDAP.

Attack Definition
The characteristics of the attack prompt the use of a better-suited definition: *denial-of-dependent-services* or DoDS.

Denial-of-dependent-services is a planned denial-of-service attack on a service with the intension to disrupt dependent services. This type of attack attempts to optimize the services denied while minimizing its (the attackers) targets. An example of an infrastructure that would be susceptible to this attack is *central authentication services*.

6. References

[1]   J. M. Alonso, R. Bordon, M. Beltran and A. Guzman,

"LDAP Injection Techniques," 11*th IEEE Singapore International Conference on Communication Systems*, Guangzhou, 19-21 November 2008, pp. 980-986.

[2]   J. M. Alonso, R. Bordon, M. Beltran and A. Guzman, "LDAP Injection & Blind LDAP Injection," Figure 1 in URJC, 2008, ICCS 2008, p. 4.

[3]   "RFC 4512: Light Directory Access Protocol (LDAP): Directory Information Models," 2006. http://tools.ietf. org/html/rfc4512

[4]   J. M. Alonso, R. Bordon, M. Beltran and A. Guzman, "LDAP Injection & Blind LDAP Injection," URJC, 2008, ICCS 2008.

[5]   "OpenLDAP—Secure Computing Wiki," 2010. http://www.secure-computing.net/wiki/index.php/OpenLDAP

[6]   "RFC: 2830: Lightweight Directory Access Protocol (v3): Extension for Transport Layer Security," 2000, http://www.rfceditor.org/rfc/rfc2830.txt

[7]   "RFC 1487: X.500 Lightweight Directory Access Protocol," 1993. http://www.faqs.org/rfcs/rfc1487.html

[8]   "RFC 2251: Lightweight Directory Access Protocol (v3)," 1997. http://www.faqs.org/rfcs/rfc2251.html

[9]   "RFC 4422: Simple Authentication and Security Layer (SASL)," 2006. http://tools.ietf.org/html/rfc4422

[10] "Application Layer-Wikipedia, the Free Encyclopedia," 2011. http://en.wikipedia.org/wiki/Application_Layer.

[11] A. Everett, "Unauthenticated Authentication: Null Bytes and the Affect on Web-Based Applications which Use LDAP," IT Information Security Office, Oklahoma State University, Stillwater, December 2006.

[12] "Transport Layer-Wikipedia, the Free Encyclopedia," 2011. http://en.wikipedia.org/wiki/Trans-port_Layer

[13] S. Foley and W. Fitzgerald, "An Approach to Security Policy Configuration Using Semantic Threat ᵼGraphs," Data and Applications Security XXIII, 2009. University College Cork Cork Constraint Computation Centre, Computer Science Department Ireland, Vol. 5645, pp. 33-48, 2009

[14] "TCP 3 WAY HANDSHAKE: Educational Resources, Tips, Tricks, and More," 2010. http:// www.3wayhandshake.com/

[15] "Raw Socket-Wikipedia, the Free Encyclopedia," 2011. http://en.wikipedia.org/wiki/Raw_so-cket

[16] W. Eddy, "Cisco—Defenses against TCP SYN Flooding Attacks," 2006. http://www.cisco.com/web/about/ac123/ac147/images/ipj /ipj_9-4/94_syn_fig2_lg.jpg

[17] "OpenLDAP, Download," 2011. http:// www.openldap.org/software/download/

[18] "MIT Kerberos Distribution Page," 2010. http://web.mit.edu/kerberos/dist/index.html

[19] "SSLSTRIP," 2009. http://tools.ietf. org/html/rfc4422

[20] "Kerberos: The Network Authentication Protocol," 2010. http://web.mit.edu/kerberos/what_is.

4

Secure Spread-Spectrum Watermarking for Telemedicine Applications

Basant Kumar[1], Harsh Vikram Singh[2], Surya Pal Singh[3], Anand Mohan[3]
[1]*Motilal Nehru National Institute of Technology, Allahabad, India*
[2]*Kamla Nehru Institute of Technology, Sultanpur, India*
[3]*Institute of Technology, Banaras Hindu University, Varanasi, India*

Abstract

This paper presents a secure spread-spectrum watermarking algorithm for digital images in discrete wavelet transform (DWT) domain. The algorithm is applied for embedding watermarks like patient identification/ source identification or doctors signature in binary image format into host digital radiological image for potential telemedicine applications. Performance of the algorithm is analysed by varying the gain factor, subband decomposition levels, size of watermark, wavelet filters and medical image modalities. Simulation results show that the proposed method achieves higher security and robustness against various attacks.

Keywords: Watermarking, Spread-Spectrum, Discrete Wavelet Transform, Telemedicine

1. Introduction

In recent years image watermarking has become an important research area in data security, confidentiality and image integrity. Despite the broad literature on various application fields, little work has been done towards the exploitation of health-oriented perspectives of watermarking [1-7]. While the recent advances in information and communication technologies provide new means to access, handle and move medical information, they also compromise their security against illegal access and manipulation. Sensitive nature of patient's personal medical data necessitates measures for medical confidentiality protection against unauthorized access. Source authenticcation and data integrity are also important matters relating to health data management and distribution. Data hiding and watermarking techniques can play important role in the field of telemedicine by addressing a range issues relevant to health data management systems, such as medical confidentiality protection, patient and examination related information hiding, access and data integrity control, and information retrieval. Medical image watermarking requires extreme care when embedding additional data within the medical images because the additional information must not affect the image quality. Security requirements of medical information, derived from strict ethics and legal obligations imposed three mandatory characteristics: confidentiality, reliability and availability [8]. *Confidentiality* means that only authorized users have access to the information. *Reliability* has two aspects; 1) *Integrity*: the information has not been modified by non-authorized people, and 2) *Authentication*: a proof that the information belongs indeed to the correct source. *Availability* is the ability of an information system to be used by entitled users in the normal scheduled conditions of access and exercise. Authentication, integration and confidentiality are the most important issues concerned with EPR (Electronic Patient Record) data exchange through open channels [1,5]. All these requirements can be fulfilled using suitable watermarks. General watermarking method needs to keep the three factors (capacity, imperceptibility and robustness) reasonably very high [9]. Robustness is the ability to recover the data in spite of the attacks in the marked image, imperceptibility is the invisibility of the watermark and capacity is the amount of data that can be embedded. These requirements are hindering each other. There must be some trade off among these requirements according to the applications. Two common approaches of information hiding using image covers are spatial domain hiding and transform (frequency) domain hiding. Spatial domain techniques perform data embedding by directly manipulating the pixel values, code values or bit stream of the host image signal and they are computationally simple and straightforward. *LSB substitution*, *patchwork*, and *spread spectrum image steganography* are some of the important spatial domain techniques [10,11]. In transform domain hiding, data are embedded by modulating coefficients in transform domain, such as DFT (Discrete Fourier Transform), DCT (Discrete Cosine Transform) and DWT (Discrete Wavelet Transform). Transform techniques can offer a higher degree of robustness to common image processing operations, compared to spatial domain techniques. Wavelet domain watermarking has recently received considerable attention due to its ability to provide both spatial and frequency resolution [12-14]. Many wavelet based watermarking schemes were proposed for medical images [15-18]. Watermarking technique can be further classified into two categories, reversible and irreversible [19,20]. The main idea behind reversible watermarking is to avoid irreversible distortion in original image (the host image), by developing techniques that can extract the original image exactly. Medical image watermarking is one of the most important fields that need such techniques where distortion may cause wrong diagnosis. The strict specifications regarding the quality of medical images could be met by reversible watermarking, which allows the recovery of the original image without any loss of information. Medical identity theft has been a serious security concern in telemedicine [21]. This demands development of secure watermarking schemes. Digital watermarking studies have always been driven by the improvement of robustness. On the contrary, security has received little attention in the watermarking community. The first difficulty is that security and robustness are neighboring concepts, which are hardly perceived as different. Security deals with intentional attacks whereas robustness is observed as degradation in data fidelity due to common signal processing operations. Digital watermarking may not be secure despite its robustness [22,23]. Therefore, security of the watermark becomes a critical issue in many applications. The problem of watermark security can be solved using spread-spectrum scheme [24-27]. Spread-spectrum is a military communication scheme invented during World War II [28]. It was designed to be good at combating interference due to jamming, hiding a signal by transmitting it at low power, and achieving secrecy. These properties make spread-spectrum very popular in present-day digital watermarking.

This paper proposes a new secure spread-spectrum based watermarking algorithm for embedding sensitive medical information like physician's signature/identification code or patient identity code into radiological image for identity authentication purposes. This medical information in binary image form is taken as watermarks. The proposed algorithm relies on n distinct pseudo-random (PN) matrices pairs with low correlation, where n is the number of bits that are to be hidden. The rest of the paper is organized as follows. Section 2 provides a brief overview of spread-spectrum image watermarking schemes in wavelet domain. Working of the proposed spread-spectrum algorithm is explained in Section 3. Performance of the new algorithm has been analyzed in Section 4 and Section 5 provides conclusion of overall work.

2. Spread Spectrum Watermarking in Wavelet Transform Domain

Wavelet-based watermarking has recently gained great attention due to its ability to provide excellent multi-resolution analysis, space-frequency localization and superior HVS modeling [12]. DWT (Discrete Wavelet Transform) separates an image into a lower resolution approximation image (LL) as well as horizontal (HL), vertical (LH) and diagonal (HH) detail components. The process can then be repeated to computes multiple "scale" wavelet decomposition. The dyadic frequency decomposition of wavelet transform resembles the signal processing of the HVS and thus allows adapting the distortion introduced by either quantization or watermark embedding to the masking properties of human eye [29]. The watermarks are inserted in different decomposition levels and subbands depending on their type, and in locations specified by a random key; thus, they can be independently embedded and retrieved, without any interference among them. It is evident that the energy of an image is concentrated in the high decomposition levels corresponding to the perceptually significant low frequency coefficients; the low decomposition levels accumulate a minor energy proportion, thus being vulnerable to image alterations. Therefore, watermarks containing crucial medical information like *doctor's signature, patient identification code or patient identification codes* requireing great robustness are embedded in higher subbands. In general, horizontal and vertical subbands have more or less the same characteristics and behavior, in contrast to diagonal ones. Thereupon, watermark embedding in the horizontal and vertical subbands guarantees increased robustness, since their energy compaction makes them less vulnerable to attacks.

The proposed image watermarking scheme uses spread-spectrum technique in which, different watermark messages are hidden in the same transform coefficients of the cover image using uncorrelated codes, *i.e.* low cross correlation value (orthogonal/near orthogonal) among codes. A brief overview of spread-spectrum watermarking technique is presented below:

2.1. Spread-Spectrum Watermarking Principle

The watermark should not be placed in insignificant regions of the image or its spectrum, since many common signal and geometric processes affect these components.

The problem then becomes how to insert a watermark into the most perceptually significant regions of the spectrum while preserving fidelity. Clearly, any spectral coefficient may be altered, provided such modification is small. However, very small changes are very susceptible to noise. This problem can be addressed by applying spread-spectrum watermarking which can be easily understood with spread-spectrum communications analogy in which frequency domain of the image is viewed as a *communication channel*, and correspondingly, the watermark is viewed as a *signal* that is transmitted through it [24]. Attacks and unintentional signal distortions are treated as *noise* that the immersed signal must be immune to. In spread-spectrum communications, one transmits a narrowband signal over a much larger bandwidth, such that the signal energy present in any single frequency is undetectable. Similarly, the watermark is spread over many frequency bins so that the energy in any one bin is very small and certainly undetectable. Nevertheless, because the watermark verification process knows the location and content of the watermark, it is possible to concentrate these many weak signals into single output with high signal-to-noise ratio (SNR). However, to destroy such a watermark would require noise of high amplitude to be added to all frequency bins. Spreading the watermark throughout the spectrum of an image ensures a large measure of security against unintentional or intentional attack: First, the location of the watermark is not obvious. Furthermore, frequency regions should be selected in a fashion that ensures sufficiently small energy in any single coefficient. A watermark that is well placed in the frequency domain of an image will be practically impossible to see.

2.2. Spread Spectrum Watermark Design

There are two parts to building a strong watermark: the *watermark structure* and the *insertion strategy*. In order for a watermark to be robust and secure, these two components must be designed correctly. This can be achieved by placing the watermark explicitly in the perceptually most significant components of the data, and that the watermark is composed of random numbers drawn from a Gaussian ($N(0,1)$) distribution (where $N(\mu, \sigma^2)$) denotes a normal distribution with mean μ and variance σ^2). Once the significant components are located, Gaussian noise is injected therein. The choice of this distribution gives resilient performance against collusion attacks. The Gaussian watermark also gives strong performance in the face of quantization [30].

- *Watermark Structure:* In its most basic implementation, a watermark consists of a sequence of real numbers $X = x_1, x_2, \cdots, x_n$. In practice, we create a watermark

where each value x_i is chosen independently according to $N(0,1)$.

- *Watermarking Procedure*: We extract from host digital document *D*, a sequence of values $V = v_1, v_2, \cdots, v_n$, into which we insert a watermark $X = x_1, x_2, \cdots, x_n$ to obtain an adjusted sequence of values $W = w_1, w_2, \cdots, w_n$ and then insert it back into the host in place of V to obtain a watermarked document *D**.

- *Inserting and Extracting the Watermark*: When we insert X into V to obtain W, a scaling parameter k is specified, which determines the extent to which X alters V. Formula for computing W is

$$w_i = v_i + kx_i$$

We can view k as a relative measure of embedding strength which is also known as gain factor. A large value of k will cause perceptual degradation in the watermarked document.

- *Choosing the Length n, of the Watermark*: The choice of length *n*, dictates the degree to which the watermark is spread out among the relevant components of the host digital document. In general, as the numbers of altered components are increased the extent to which they must be altered decreases.

- *Evaluating the Similarity of Watermarks*: It is highly unlikely that the extracted mark X^* will be identical to the original watermark X. Even the act of requantizing the watermarked document for delivery will cause X^* to deviate from X. We measure the similarity of X and X^* by

$$sim(X, X^*) = \frac{X^* . X}{\sqrt{X^* . X}} \qquad (1)$$

Many other measures are possible, including the standard correlation coefficient. To decide whether X and X^* match, one determines whether $sim(X, X^*) > T$, where T is some threshold. Setting the detection threshold is a classical decision estimation problem [31].

3. Proposed Algorithm

This paper proposes a new DWT based spread-spectrum watermarking algorithm using medical image cover. Dyadic subband decomposition is performed on the radiological image using Haar wavelet transform. The watermark used in the algorithm is in binary image form. Different watermark messages are hidden in the same transform coefficients of the cover image using uncorrelated codes, *i.e.* low cross correlation value (orthogonal/ near orthogonal) among codes. For each message bit, two different Pseudo Noise (PN) matrices namely of size identical to the size of the wavelet coefficient matrices, are generated. Since the security level of the watermarking algorithm depends on the strength of its secret key, a grey scale image of size 1×35 is used as a strong key for generating pseudorandom sequences. Based on the value of the bit for the message vector, the respective two PN sequence matrices are then added to the corresponding second level HL and LH coefficients matrices respectively according to the data embedding rule as follows:

$$W = V + kX \quad \text{if} \quad b = 0$$

Where V is wavelet coefficient of the cover image, W is the wavelet coefficient after watermark embedding, k is the gain factor, X is the PN matrix and b is the bit of watermark that has to be embedded. Generation of a pair of PN matrices for embedding each bit enhances the security of the watermarking algorithm. Following steps are applied in data embedding process.

3.1. Data Embedding

Read the host image $I(M,N)$ of size $M \times N$
1) Read the message to be hidden and convert it into binary sequences D_d ($D_d = 1$ to n)
2) Transform the host image using "Haar" Wavelet transform and get second level subband coefficients ccA, ccH, ccV, ccD
3) Generate n different PN-sequence pairs (PN_h and PN_v) each of size $\frac{M}{4} \times \frac{N}{4}$ using a secret key to reset the random number generator
4) For $D_d = 1$ to n, add PN sequences to ccH and ccV components when message = 0

$$\text{ccH} = \text{ccH} + k^*\text{PN\_h};$$
$$\text{ccV} = \text{ccV} + k^*\text{PN\_v};$$

where k is the gain factor used to specify the strength of the embedded data.

Apply inverse "Haar" Wavelet transform to get the final stego (watermarked) image $I_w(M,N)$.

3.2. Extraction of Hidden Data

To detect the watermark we generate the same pseudorandom matrices used during insertion of watermark by using same state key and determine its average correlation with the two detail subbands DWT coefficients. Average of n correlation coefficients corresponding to each PN matrices is obtained for both LH and HL subbands. Mean of the average correlation values are taken as threshold T for message extraction. During detection, if the average correlation exceeds T for a particular sequence a "0" is recovered; otherwise a "1". The recovery process then iterates through the entire PN sequence until all the bits of the watermark have been recovered. For extracting the watermark, following steps are applied to the watermarked image:

1) Read the stego image $I_w(M,N)$
2) Transform the stego image using "Haar" Wavelet transform and get ccA1,ccH1,ccV1,ccD1 coefficients
3) Generate one's sequences (msg) equal to message vector (from 1 to n)
4) Generate n different PN-sequence pairs (PN_h1 and PN_v1) each of size $\frac{M}{4} \times \frac{N}{4}$ using same secret key used in embedding to reset the random number generator
5) For $i = 1$ to n
   Calculate the correlations store these values in corr_H (i) and corr_V (i).

   $corr\_H(i) =$ correlation between
   $$\text{PN\_h1}(i) \text{ and ccH1}(i)$$

   $corr\_V(i) =$ correlation between
   $$\text{PN\_v1}(i) \text{ and ccV1}(i)$$

6) Calculate average correlation
   $$avg\_corr(i) = (corr\_H(i) + corr\_V(i))/2$$

7) Calculate the
   $corr(n) =$ mean of all the values
   $$\text{stored in } avg\_corr(i)$$

8) Extract the hidden bit 0, using the relationship given below
   For $j = 1$ to n

   if $avg\_corr(j) > corr(n)$, $msg(j) = 0$

9) Rearrange these extracted message

4. Performance Analysis

Performance of the proposed spread-spectrum watermarking algorithm was tested for telemedicine applications. Experiments were carried-out using 8-bit grey scale CT scan image of size 512×512 available in reference [32]. Medical information such as telemedicine origin centre (watermark 1) and doctor's signature (watermark 2) were embedded into host CT scan image as watermarks. These watermarks are in binary image formats which add robustness by allowing recovery of the watermarks even at low correlation between original and extracted watermarks. Strength of watermarking is varied by varying the gain factor in the watermarking algorithm. Perceptual quality of the watermarked radiological image is measured by calculating PSNR between host and watermarked image. At the receiver side, watermark is extracted from the watermarked image. Extracted watermark is evaluated by measuring its correlation with the original watermark. **Figure 1** shows the host CT scan image and watermarked images obtained by applying watermarking algorithm in second level LH and HL subband DWT coefficients at different gain factors. Extracted watermarks along with the original watermarks are shown in **Figures 2** and **3**. It is observed from **Table 1** that with the increase in the gain factor, PSNR of the watermarked image decreases and the degree of similarity between original and extracted watermark increases. To show the effect of the decomposition levels, proposed algorithm with gain factor 2.0 was applied for embedding watermark in the horizontal and vertical subband coefficients of level 1, 2 and 3. It is observed from **Table 2** that the PSNR value of the watermarked image increases and correlation between original and extracted watermark decreases with the increase in subband level for watermarking. **Figure 4** shows the watermarks ex-

Table 1. Effect of gain factor.

Gain Factor	Watermark 1 (Origin centre)		Watermark 2 (Doctor's Signature)	
	PSNR	Correlation	PSNR	Correlation
0.5	37.518	0.376	39.680	0.295
1.0	31.497	0.535	33.659	0.289
1.5	27.976	0.597	30.138	0.461
2.0	25.477	0.635	27.639	0.485
3.0	21.955	0.657	24.117	0.527
4	19.456	0.659	21.614	0.562

Table 2. Effect of subband levels (gain factor 2.0).

Levels	Watermark 1 (Origin centre)		Watermark 2 (Doctor's Signature)	
	PSNR	Correlation	PSNR	Correlation
1	19.421	0.677	21.659	0.638
2	25.477	0.635	27.639	0.485
3	31.541	0.413	33.706	0.229

Figure 4. Extracted watermarks from (a) level 1 (b) level 2 and (c) level 3.

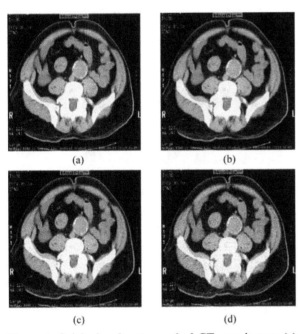

Figure 1. Original and watermarked CT scan images (a) original image and watermarked images with gain factor; (b) 0.5; (c) 1.5 and (d) 3.0.

Figure 2. Telemedicine centre watermarks (a) original and extracted watermarks with gain factor; (b) 0.5; (c) 1.5; (d) 3.0 and (e) 4.0.

Figure 3. Doctor's signature watermarks (a) original and extracted watermarks with gain factor; (b) 0.5; (c) 1.5; (d) 3.0 and (e) 4.0.

tracted from different levels of subband DWT coefficients. Performance of the watermarking algorithm also depends on the size of watermark. **Table 3** shows the effect of watermark size on the performance of the proposed watermarking algorithm. It is obvious that the PSNR performance of the watermarked image decreases with the increase in the size of the watermark, but subsequently we observe an improvement in the correlation between original and extracted watermarks. It can be also observed from **Figure 5** that larger size watermarks are more clearly identified during extraction. To observe the effect of host image, proposed algorithm was tested for other medical images like MRI and ultrasound images where watermarking is done in second level subband coefficients considering a gain factor of 1.5 and watermark size of 32 × 64. Host and watermarked MRI and ultrasound images are shown in **Figure 6**. It is observed from **Table 4** that the PSNR performance of all watermarked medical images are same where as there is a little variation in the similarity performance of original and

Table 3. Effect of watermark size.

Watermark size	Watermark 1 (Origin centre)		Watermark 2 (Doctor's Signature)	
	PSNR	Correlation	PSNR	Correlation
16 × 32	36.852	0.259	41.412	0.149
20 × 50	32.057	0.468	36.871	0.194
30 × 50	30.249	0.469	33.126	0.297
32 × 64	27.976	0.598	30.138	0.461
40 × 80	26.730	0.487	30.138	0.461

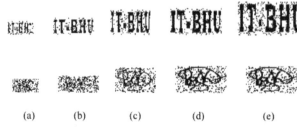

(a)   (b)   (c)   (d)   (e)

Figure 5. Extracted watermarks of different size (a) 16 × 32; (b) 20 × 50; (c) 30 × 50; (d) 32 × 64; (e) 40 × 80.

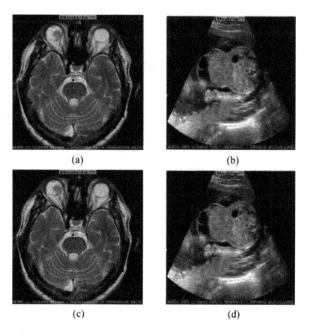

(a)   (b)

(c)   (d)

Figure 6. Original and watermarked MRI and US images (a) original MRI image (b) original US image (c) watermarked MRI image and (d) watermarked US image.

Table 4. Effect of host images.

Image type	Watermark1 (Origin centre)		Watermark2 (Doctor's Signature)	
	PSNR	Correlation	PSNR	Correlation
CT Scan	27.976	0.598	30.138	0.461
MRI	27.976	0.653	30.138	0.523
Ultrasound	27.976	0.653	30.138	0.564

extracted watermark for different medical images as shown in **Figure 7**. Effect of various wavelet filters on the proposed watermarking algorithm has also been analyzed. It can be observed from **Table 5** that the Bior 6.8 wavelet filter shows slightly better performance in terms of PSNR of the watermarked image and the correlation of extracted watermark with the original watermark. The scheme was also tested in terms of robustness of the image watermarks to JPEG compression. **Table 6** illustrates the robustness of the watermarks, which were extracted from a CT scan image after it was JPEG compressed by varying the quality factor in the range of 40 to 80. Watermarks were extracted intact after JPEG compression with different quality factors.

5. Conclusions

This paper presented a secure spread-spectrum watermarking scheme in wavelet transform domain. Performance of the scheme was tested for telemedicine applications by watermarking radiological images with sensi-

(a)   (b)   (c)

Figure 7. Extracted watermarks from different host medical images (a) CT scan; (b) MRI; (c) US image.

Table 5. Effect of wavelet filters.

Wavelet filter	Watermark1 (Origin centre)		Watermark2 (Doctor's Signature)	
	PSNR	Correlation	PSNR	Correlation
Db1 (Haar)	27.976	0.598	30.138	0.461
Db2	27.943	0.626	30.176	0.486
Db3	27.944	0.627	30.184	0.491
Bior 6.8	28.428	0.617	30.571	0.470

Table 6. Effect of JPEG compression.

Quality factor	Watermark1 (Origin centre)		Watermark2 (Doctor's Signature)	
	PSNR	Correlation	PSNR	Correlation
80	38.138	0.378	41.176	0.228
70	36.819	0.437	39.456	0.297
60	35.316	0.506	36.325	0.384
50	32.672	0.583	34.629	0.421
40	27.859	0.616	30.148	0.498

tive medical information in binary image format.

6. References

[1] H. M. Chao, C. M. Hsu and S. G. Miaou, "A Data-Hiding Technique with Authentication, Integration, and Confidentiallity for Electronic Patient Records," *IEEE Transactions on Information Technology in Biomedicine*, Vol. 6, No. 1, March 2002, pp. 46-53.

[2] U. R. Acharya, D. Anand P. S. Bhat and U. C. Niranjan, "Compact Storage of Medical Images with Patient Information," *IEEE Transactions on Information Technology in Biomedicine*, Vol. 5, No. 4, December 2001, pp. 320-323.

[3] X. Kong and R. Feng, "Watermarking Medical Signals for Telemedicine," *IEEE Transaction on Information Technology in Medicine*, Vol. 5, No. 3, 2001, pp. 195-201.

[4] G. Coatrieux, H. Maitre, B. Sankur, Y. Rolland and R. Collorec, "Relevance of Watermarking in Medical Imaging," *Proceedings of the 3rd Conference on Information Technology Applications in Biomedicine*, Arlington, 2000, pp. 250-255.

[5] K. A. Navas, S. A. Thampy and M. Sasikumar, "ERP Hiding In Medical Images for Telemedicine," *Proceedings of World Academy of Science and Technology*, Vol. 28, 2008.

[6] B. Planitz and A. Maeder, "Medical Image Watermarking: A Study on Image Degradation," *Proceedings of the Australian Pattern Recognition Society (APRS) Workshop on Digital Image Computing*, Brisbane, February, 2005, pp. 3-8.

[7] G. Coatrieux, L. Lecornu, C. Roux and B. Sankur, "A Review of Image Watermarking Applications in Healthcare," *Engineering in Medicine and Biology Society*, Vol. 1, 2006.

[8] R. C Raul, F. U. Claudia and T. B. Gershom, "Data Hiding Scheme for Medical Images," *17th International Conference on Electronics, Communications and Computers*, Cholula, 26-28 February 2007, pp. 32-32.

[9] G. C. Langelaar, I. Setyawan and R. L. Lagendijk, "Watermarking Digital Image and Video Data. A State-of-the-Art Overview," *IEEE Signal Processing Magazine*, Vol. 17, No. 5, September 2000, pp. 20-46.

[10] N: Nikolaidis and I. Pitas, "Digital Image Watermarking: An Overview," *IEEE International Conference on Multimedia Computing and Systems*, Florence, Vol. 1, June 7-11, 1999, pp. 1-6.

[11] I. J. Cox and M. L. Miller, "The First 50 Years of Electronic Watermarking," *EURASIP Journal on Applied Signal Processing*, No. 2, 2002, pp. 126-132.

[12] P. Meerwald and A. Uhl, "A Survey of Wavelet-Domain Watermarking Algorithms," *Proceedings of the SPIE Security and Watermarking of Multimedia Contents*, San Jose, Vol. 4314, 2001, pp. 505-516.

[13] S. Hajjara, M. Abdallah and A. Hudaib, "Digital Image Watermarking Using Localized Biorthogonal Wavelets," *European Journal of Scientific Research*, Vol. 26, No. 4, 2009, pp. 594-608.

[14] A. H. Paquet and R. K. Ward, "Wavelet-Based Digital Watermarking for Authentication," *Proceedings of the IEEE Canadian Conference on Electrical and Computer Engineering*, Winnipeg, Vol. 2, 2002, pp. 879-884.

[15] A. Giakoumaki, S. Pavlopoulos and D. Koutsouris, "Secure and Efficient Health Data Management through Multiple Watermarking on Medical Images," *Medical Biological Engineering & Computing*, Vol. 44, 2006, pp. 619-631.

[16] A. Giakoumaki, S. Pavlopoulos and D. Koutsouris, "Multiple Image Watermarking Applied to Health Information Management," *IEEE Transactions on Information Technology in Biomedicine*, 2006, pp. 722-732.

[17] A. Giakoumaki, S. Pavlopoulos and D. Koutsouris, "A Medical Image Watermarking Scheme Based on Wavelet Transform," *Proceedings 25th Annual International Conference of IEEE-EMBS*, Cancun, 2003, pp. 856-859.

[18] S. Dandapat, J. Xu, O. Chutatape and S. M. Krishnan, "Wavelet Transform Domain Data Embedding in a Medical Image," *Proceedings 26th Annual International Conference of IEEE-EMBS*, San Francisco, September 2004, pp. 1541-1544.

[19] J. B. Feng, I. C. Lin, C. S. Tsai and Y. P. Chu, " Reversible Watermarking: Current and Key Issues," *International Journal of Network Security*, Vol. 2, No. 3, May 2006, pp. 161-170.

[20] S. Lee, C. D. Chang and T. Kalker, "Reversible Image Watermarking Based on Integer-to-Integer Wavelet Transform," *IEEE Transaction on Information Forensics and Security*, Vol. 2, No. 3, September 2007, pp. 321-330.

[21] M. Terry, "Medical Identity Theft and Telemedicine Security," *Telemedicine and e-Health*, Vol. 15, No. 10, December 2009, pp. 1-5.

[22] F. Cayre, C. Fontaine and T. Furon, "Watermarking Security: Theory and Practice," *IEEE Transactions on Signal Processing*, Vol. 53, No. 10, October 2005, pp. 3976-3987.

[23] L. P. Freire, P. Comesana, J. R. T. Pastoriza and F. P. Gonzalez, "Watermarking Security: A Survey," *LNCS Transactions on Data Hiding and Multimedia Security*, 2006, pp. 41-72.

[24] I. J. Cox, J. Kilian, F. T. Leighton and T. Shamoon, "Secure Spread Spectrum Watermarking for Multimedia," *IEEE Transactions on Image Processing*, Vol. 6, No. 12, 1997, pp. 1673-1687.

[25] H. S. Malvar and D. A. F. Florencio, "Improved Spread Spectrum: A New Modilation Technique for Robust Watermarking," *IEEE Transactions on Signal Processing*, Vol. 51, No. 4, 2003.

[26] L. Perez-Freire and F. Perez-Gonzalez, "Spread-Spectrum Watermarking Security," *IEEE Transactions on In-*

formation Forensics and Security, Vol. 4, No. 1, 2009.

[27] G. Xuan, C. Yang, Y. Zheng, Y. Q. Shi and Z. Ni, "Reversible Data Hiding Based on Wavelet Spread Spectrum," *IEEE International Workshop on Multimedia Signal Processing*, Siena, 2004.

[28] D. Kahn, "Cryptology and the Origins of Spread Spectrum," *IEEE Spectrum*, Vol. 21, September 1984, pp. 70-80.

[29] M. Unser and A. Aldroubi, "A Review of Wavelets in Biomedical Applications," *Proceedings of the IEEE*, Vol.

84, No. 4, 1996, pp. 626-638.

[30] F. Ergun, J. Kilian and R. Kumar, "A Note on the Limits of Collusion-Resistant Watermarks," *EUROCRYPT'99 Proceedings of the* 17th *International Conference on Theory and Application of Cryptographic Techniques*, Vol. 1592, 1999, pp. 140-149.

[31] C. W. Therrien, "Decision Estimation and Classification: An Introduction to Pattern Recognition and Related Topics," Wiley, New York, 1989.

[32] MedPix™ Medical Image Database available at http://rad.usuhs.mil/medpix/medpix.html

5

A Novel Attack Graph Posterior Inference Model Based on Bayesian Network

Shaojun Zhang[1], Shanshan Song[2]
[1]*School of Information Security Engineering, Shanghai Jiao Tong University, Shanghai, China*
[2]*Information Technology Department, Guotai Junan Futures Co., Ltd, Shanghai, China*

Abstract

Network attack graphs are originally used to evaluate what the worst security state is when a concerned network is under attack. Combined with intrusion evidence such like IDS alerts, attack graphs can be further used to perform security state posterior inference (*i.e.* inference based on observation experience). In this area, Bayesian network is an ideal mathematic tool, however it can not be directly applied for the following three reasons: 1) in a network attack graph, there may exist directed cycles which are never permitted in a Bayesian network, 2) there may exist temporal partial ordering relations among intrusion evidence that cannot be easily modeled in a Bayesian network, and 3) just one Bayesian network cannot be used to infer both the current and the future security state of a network. In this work, we improve an approximate Bayesian posterior inference algorithm–the likelihood-weighting algorithm to resolve the above obstacles. We give out all the pseudocodes of the algorithm and use several examples to demonstrate its benefit. Based on this, we further propose a network security assessment and enhancement method along with a small network scenario to exemplify its usage.

Keywords: Network Security, Attack Graph, Posterior Inference, Bayesian Network, Likelihood-Weighting

1. Introduction

Network attack graphs [1-5] are widely used as a good tool to analyze network security state in comprehensive consideration of exploits, vulnerabilities, privileges, network connectivity, etc. Originally, they are built to tell what the worst scenarios are when a network is under attack. But later, it is found that security alerts can be mapped to them [6-8] and along with these observed intrusion evidence, attack graphs can also be used to assess the security state of a concerned network dynamically.

In this area, probabilistic approaches have been proposed to perform such analysis. In [9], a method which reasons about complementary intrusion evidence is presented. According to the method, security alerts generated by intrusion detection systems (IDSs) as well as reports generated by system monitoring tools can be integrated into Bayesian networks. And prior conditional probability values which denote the success rate of the corresponding attacks can be assigned to each of the evidence nodes. By doing this, uncertain or unknown intrusion evidence can be reasoned about based on verified evidence. Although quite useful in reasoning observed intrusion evidence, this method cannot tell people what attack will be executed next and with what probability.

In [10], HCPN (Hidden Colored Petri-Net) is used to depict the relationship among different steps carried out by an intruder and model intrusion actions and intrusion evidence together. The initial state of HCPN attack graph is determined by an initial probability distribution. And empirical formulas are defined to reevaluate its state after receiving each alert from the sensors (most commonly are IDSs). This method runs quite well in predicting what the next intrusion actions are. However, at reevaluating the probabilities of the graph nodes according to the alerts, the method only updates probabilities of the successor nodes of an assumed action node, which obviously contravenes our intuition that in most inference algorithms there must be backward belief propagation (*i.e.* probabilities of the predecessor nodes should also be updated).

To overcome these flaws, we firstly thought about extending the Bayesian network into a general attack graph definition to integrally model intrusion resources, actions and evidence. By exploiting Bayesian network's embedded posterior inference capability, it can not be plainer to perform attack graph-based posterior inference [11]. However, soon we found that things were not so easy. There are at least three main differences between an attack graph and a Bayesian network which obstruct this way:

- In a Bayesian network, no directed cycles are allowed. However, in a network attack graph, this restriction is not appropriate since people always want to depict potential intrusion paths succinctly.

- In a Bayesian network, there can not be any partial ordering relations among evidence nodes. However, we can often observe temporal partial ordering relations among intrusion evidence (e.g. when an ipsweep is observed before a portscan), which may indicate that some exploits happen before some others.

- At performing attack graph-based posterior inference, two questions are most often raised: 1) what is the current state of a network, and 2) what is the future state of it. Essentially this means one set of observed intrusion evidence should be used to infer two temporally different states. In Bayesian inference, this demands two prior conditional probabilistic distribution, one for current state inference and one for future state inference. Although we think it feasible to define the later one (For example we say an exploit will happen in probability 0.8 if an attacker was given enough time), it is really a disaster to define the former one (how to assess the exploit probability when the attacker has got two hours).

These obstacles almost made us give up Bayesian posterior inference. But fortunately we find a good way to overcome them—we manage to improve the likelihood-weighting algorithm (an approximate Bayesian inference algorithm) into a novel attack graph-based posterior inference algorithm. And based on this, we find a method to quantitively assess the overall security level of a concerned network and identify the most cost-effective security measures to enhance it.

The rest of this paper is organized as follows. Section 2 depicts the aforementioned posterior inference problems in details. Section 3 introduces the underlying formalized attack graph definition. Section 4 describes our improved likelihood-weighting algorithm and Section 5 gives out several examples for benefit testification. Section 6 presents our security assessment and enhancement method and Section 7 gives out an example to exemplify it. The last section concludes the paper.

2. The Primal Motives

2.1. Directed Cycles

Various models and methods have been proposed to represent multi-step network attacks and generate network attack graphs automatically. These models and methods can be roughly divided into two categories: security state enumeration and vulnerability/exploit dependency. Comparatively, the later one is more popular since it exhaustively and succinctly depicts the interdependency of security elements such as privilege, trust, vulnerability, exploit, network connectivity, etc. Representatives of this category include the approaches proposed in [2-5]. In this category, although some approaches promise that they only generate attack graphs without directed cycles, we cannot assume that all of them are generating DAG (Directed Acyclic Graph).

Here is an example to demonstrate that directed cycles sometime are useful since we want to depict the intrusion paths succinctly. Assume there are three hosts on a small network which is illustrated in **Figure 1**. Host Master has a certain vulnerability that can be exploited by the other two hosts to gain its USER privilege. On the other hand, the USER accounts on Master are mapped to a ROOT account on the other two hosts.

We can imagine that a succinct network attack graph for this network is like the one shown in **Figure 2**.

In **Figure 2** we adopt a graph notation widely used in Petri-Net. Circle s1, s2 and s3 respectively denote that the attacker has got ROOT privilege on Slave1, ROOT privilege on Slave2 and USER privilege on Master. Line a1 and a2 denote the attacker exploits the vulnerability of Master respectively from Slave1 and Slave2. Obviously, in this attack graph, there exist directed cycles.

2.2. Evidence Partial Ordering Relations

In a Bayesian network, there cannot be any partial ordering relations among observed evidence. However, at performing security posterior inference, temporal partial ordering relations among evidence nodes often provide us important cues. **Figure 3** illustrates an example which demonstrates the benefit of analyzing temporal partial ordering relations among intrusion evidence.

In **Figure 3**, we assume that the attacker initially occupies resource s_1 and her goal is to occupy s_6. The attacker can use exploit $a_1 \sim a_6$ to perform intrusion. However, exploit a_1 and a_4 will trigger alert o_1, exploit a_2 and a_3 will trigger alert o_2 and a_5 and a_6 will trigger alert o_3. Finally, during the intrusion, an evidence sequence $o_2 \rightarrow o_1 \rightarrow o_3$ is observed.

Analysis: To achieve her goal, the attacker can choose

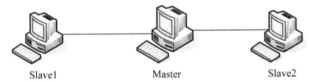

Figure 1. A small network environment.

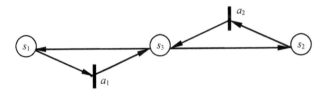

Figure 2. Attack graph for the network.

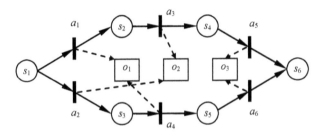

Figure 3. A simple network attack graph.

two intrusion paths:

$$\alpha.\ s_1 \to a_1 \to s_2 \to a_3 \to s_4 \to a_5 \to s_6$$

$$\beta.\ s_1 \to a_2 \to s_3 \to a_4 \to s_5 \to a_6 \to s_6$$

If we neglect all temporal partial ordering relations, then the three evidence nodes are set to **True**. And since the attack graph is symmetrical (notice there is no ordering relations between evidence nodes), using Bayesian posterior inference we can find that both intrusion paths can be chosen by the attacker. However, if we do consider temporal partial ordering relations, we can infer that only intrusion path β is chosen by the attacker, since executing intrusion path α will violate the temporal partial ordering relation $o_2 \to o_1$.

2.3. Posterior Inference for Multi-State

As we mentioned before, two questions are most often raised at performing attack graph-based posterior inference: 1) what is the current state of a network, and 2) what is the future state of it. In Bayesian inference, this means two different prior conditional probabilistic distribution should be assigned—one for current state inference and one for future state inference. If we say the assignment for the later one is tough but still practical, then it is almost infeasible to define the former one.

People may argue that Hidden Markov Model [12] or Generalized Hidden Semi-Markov Models [13] can be used to resolve this problem. But in HMM or GHSMMs, a key concept is the time instants associated with state changes. This concept is quite natural in technique areas such as speech signal processing. However in security analysis we cannot just fix a time slot for an attacker to perform actions. And even we do constrainedly figure out this slot, we still face the problem of how to define the probability of an action when the attacker is given one time slot.

Under this understanding, we decide to stick to Bayesian inference and seek if we can use one prior conditional probabilistic distribution with one set of observed intrusion evidence to infer two temporally different security states. Eventually we successfully resolve this challenge by inventing a sample reprocessing method called transientization which will be introduced in Section 4.

3. The Underlying Model

In this section, we propose a formalized network attack graph definition as the basis for attack graph-based security posterior inference.

In the early days of Internet, network attacks are often performed to demonstrate the personal skills of the attacker. They were limited to a small number of known methods such as cracking the password and exploiting the operating system vulnerabilities. But lately attacks have evolved into complex procedures which may comprise several interrelated intrusion actions. Execution of these actions incrementally changes the security state of the network, making the attacker take over more and more resources (and most commonly during the intrusion procedure the attacker will not give up resources she has already got [3]) and eventually achieve her goal. Fortunately, security devices such as IDSs will send alerts if there is an attack. Then administrators can use them to assess the real state of the network and take proper measures to compensate.

A network attack graph depicts the above three components (network resource, intrusion action and intrusion evidence) and their causal relationship. In most cases, it can exhaustively and succinctly comprises all of the potential intrusion paths. Based on the above analysis, an attack graph can formally be defined as:

Definition 1. An attack graph is a 10-tuple directed graph $AG = (S, S_0, G, A, O, E, \Delta, \Phi, \Theta, \Pi)$, where:

- $S = \{s_i | i = 1, \cdots, N_s\}$ is a finite set of resource state nodes. The value of each node variable s_i can be either **True** or **False**, denoting if a resource has been taken over by the attacker;
- $S_0 \subseteq S$ is a subset of S representing resources the attacker may initially occupy. Graphically it is the root nodes of AG;

- $G \subseteq S$ is a subset of S representing attack goals;
- $A = \{a_i | i = 1, \cdots, N_a\}$ is a finite set of intrusion action nodes. The value of each node variable a_i can be either **True** or **False**, denoting whether an intrusion action has been conducted by the attacker;
- $O = \{o_i | i = 1, \cdots, N_o\}$ is a finite set of intrusion evidence nodes. The value of each node variable o_i can be either **True** or **False**, denoting whether the evidence has been observed. Considering that in most occasions intrusion evidence will be pre-processed (e.g. fused) by the low-layer sensors so that their observation numbers are often distorted, here we only consider whether a kind of evidence has been observed, discarding its concrete observation number;
- $E = (E_1 \cup E_2 \cup E_3)$ is a finite set of edges which link nodes together. $E_1 \subseteq S \times A$ is a set of edges which denote actions can only be conducted given that all the prerequisite resources are taken over by the attacker; $E_2 \subseteq A \times S$ is a set of edges which denote actions may consequently let the attacker take over some other resources and $E_3 \subseteq A \times O$ is a set of edges which denote actions may trigger certain intrusion evidence. Generally we use $\mathbf{Pre}(n)$ and $\mathbf{Con}(n)$ to respectively denote the prerequisite nodes and consequent nodes of node n;
- $\Delta = \{\delta : (\mathbf{Pre}(a_i), a_i) \rightarrow [0,1]\}$ is the prior conditional probability distribution that an action will be conducted if its prerequisite is satisfied. In this paper, we assume that all elements of $\mathbf{Pre}(a_i)$ are in a conjunctive normal form. In other words, an action can be conducted only if all its prerequisite resources are occupied by the attacker;
- $\Phi = \{\phi : (a_i, \mathbf{Con}(a_i)) \rightarrow [0,1]\}$ is the probability distribution that an action will succeed if it is conducted. Since an action changes its consequent resource state only when it succeeds, Φ is also the probability that an action set its consequent node variables to **True**. Here we assume that for any resource node s_i if there are more than one successful actions in $\mathbf{Pre}(s_i)$, then each of them can set s_i to **True** independently;
- $\Theta = \{\theta : (a_i, o_j) \rightarrow [0,1]\}$ is the probability distribution that a type of intrusion evidence will be observed if one of its prerequisite actions is conducted. Here we also assume that for any evidence node o_j if there are more than one successful actions in $\mathbf{Pre}(o_j)$, each of them can set o_j to **True** independently;
- $\Pi = \{\pi : S \cup A \cup O \rightarrow [0,1]\}$ is the node belief distribution of AG. Here $\pi(s_i)$ denotes the probability that the attacker has taken over resource s_i;

$\pi(a_i)$ denotes the probability that action a_i has been conducted by the attacker and $\pi(o_i)$ denotes the probability that evidence o_i has been observed. Specially, Π_0 is the initial node belief distribution of AG, denoting what resources are occupied by the attacker at the very beginning. So, we can expect:

$$\pi_0(n_i) \geq 0, \ n_i \in S_0$$
$$\pi_0(n_i) = 0, \ n_i \in S_0$$

Graphically, a network attack graph follows Definition 1 is like the one illustrated in **Figure 4**.

In **Figure 4**, the attacker initially occupies resource s_1, s_2 and s_3 (with probabilities defined in Π_0). Then intrusion actions a_1, a_2 and a_3 will be conducted (with probabilities defined in Δ), and further make the attacker take over resource $s_4 \sim s_7$ (with probabilities defined in Φ). As actions being conducted, intrusion evidence $o_1 \sim o_4$ will be triggered and observed (with probabilities defined in Θ).

As mentioned before, in this paper, we are only interested in whether a type of evidence has been observed, discarding its concrete observation number. However, we can still utilize the temporal partial ordering relations among attack evidence to assist posterior inference.

Definition 2. There are two categories of evidence temporal partial ordering relations. We say:
- There is a type I temporal partial ordering relation $o_m \nearrow o_n$ if o_m is observed before o_n is observed. In other words, the first observation timepoint of o_m is earlier than the first observation timepoint of o_n.
- There is a type II temporal partial ordering relation $o_m \searrow o_n$ if o_m is never observed after o_n is firstly observed. In other words, all the observation timepoints of o_m are earlier than any of the ones of o_n.

With the above definition, the problem of network attack graph-based posterior inference can be defined as:

Given an attack graph AG, when an evidence sequence $\alpha = o_{i1} \rightarrow o_{i2} \rightarrow \cdots \rightarrow o_{ik}$ which conforms to a partial

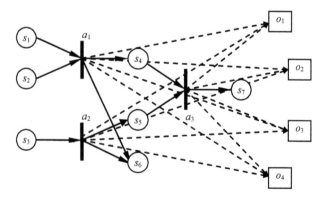

Figure 4. A typical network attack graph.

ordering relation set $\Omega = \{o_m \nearrow o_n\} \cup \{o_m \searrow o_n\}$ is observed, how to compute the corresponding graph node belief distribution sequence $\beta = \Pi_0 \Pi_1 \cdots \Pi_k$?

4. The Posterior Inference Algorithm

In this section, we propose an algorithm for resolving the above posterior inference problem. Our algorithm is mainly based on the approximate Bayesian inference algorithm—the likelihood-weighting algorithm.

A Bayesian network (or a belief network, a causal network) is a probabilistic graphical model that represents a set of variables and their probabilistic independencies. Essentially, a network attack graph following Definition 1 is a mimetic Bayesian network. However, since a Bayesian network cannot contain any directed cycle or partial ordering relation of evidence nodes, traditional Bayesian inference should not be used to perform this attack graph-based posterior inference.

To support these additional features, we manage to improve one of the approximate Bayesian network inference algorithms–the likelihood weighting algorithm [14,15] to a novel one. Likelihood weighting enhances logic sampling algorithm in that it never discards samples. It is the most commonly used simulation method for Bayesian network inference. Pseudocode of our improved algorithm is as follow:

```
ImprovedLikelihoodWeighting (AG, n, O_D, O_F, Ω, m)
Input:      AG — a network attack graph;
            n — effective sample number to generate;
            O_D — a set of observed evidence nodes;
            O_F — a set of not observed evidence nodes;
            Ω — a temporal partial ordering relation set on
O_D ∪ O_F;
            m —inference mode, 0 for future state, 1 for current
state.
Output:     Ξ — a set of effective samples.
Algorithm:  01:  Ξ←∅; i←0;
            02:  while (i<n)
            03:     w_i←1; C←∅;
            04:     for (each node variable X in AG)
            05:        X←False; F_X←∅; B_X←∅;
            06:     end for (04)
            07:     for (each node variable X∈S_0)
            08:        X←the sampling result according to Π_0;
            09:        Mark X as sampled;
            10:     end for (07)
            11:     converged←False;
            12:     while (!converged)
            13:        converged←True;
            14:        for (each node variable X=True in AG)
            15:           for (each node variable Y∈Con(X))
            16:              if (edge X→Y is not sampled) then
            17:                 if (UpdateAttackGraph(AG,X,Y)) then
            18:                    converged←False;
            19:                 end if (17)
            20:              end if (16)
            21:           end for (15)
            22:        end for (14)
            23:     end while (12)
            24:     for (each node variable X∈O_D)
            25:        X←True;
            26:        w_X←SelectEvidenceCausation(AG,X);
            27:        w_i←w_i*w_X;
            28:     end for (24)
            29:     if (m=1) then
            30:        b←Transientize(AG,O_D,O_F);
            31:     end if (29)
            32:     if (b∧PartialRelationSatisfied(AG,O_D ∪ O_F,Ω))
then
            33:        ξ_i.AG←AG; ξ_i.w←w_i;
            34:        Ξ←Ξ ∪ {ξ_i}; i←i+1;
            35:     end if (32);
            36:  end while (02)
            37:  return Ξ;
```

The 2nd line of the pseudocode is an outside loop control statement which drives the algorithm to generate n effective samples in one run. In the loop, effective samples are generated and added into a sample set Ξ which will eventually be returned.

Pseudocode 3~35 is to generate an effective sample, which could be regarded as one potential attack scenario. This procedure can be further divided into five stages:

1) Initialization (3~6). In this stage, firstly two variables w_i and C are initialized. Here w_i will be used to hold the weight of the sample and C will be used to hold the node pairs that temporally cannot be updated for their causation relationship. Then each node X in the attack graph is set to **False** and two assistant set variable F_X and B_X are initialized to empty. F_X will be used to hold the nodes whose value are set to **True** by X. B_X will be used to hold the nodes who set X to **True**. From another point of view, F_X and B_X respectively hold the forward and backward causation pointers of X.

2) Nodes sampling (7~23). In this stage, all the nodes in AG (except those nodes in O_D) will be sampled. Firstly, in line 7~10, root nodes are sampled according to the initial node belief distribution Π_0. Then, in line 11~23, AG is circularly updated until no more changes occur. In each cycle, every **True** value node X is checked out and a subfunction **UpdateAttackGraph** (for space limitation, pseudocodes of all the subfunctions are given out in An-

nex A of this paper) is called on each pair of X and its descendant node Y iff the edge $X \rightarrow Y$ is not sampled.

3) Observed evidence causation selection (24~28). In this stage, for each observed evidence node X in O_D, a subfunction **SelectEvidenceCausation** is called on X to randomly select a causation set from $\text{Pre}(X)$ to denote what set X to True. At the same time, the occurrence probability of this chosen causation set will affect the weight of the sample.

4) Transientization (29~31). If what we need to infer is the current state of the network, then the sample should be reshaped to represent a budding (not fully developed) attack scenario. The processing transientization is based on the idea that although some evidence nodes in O_F may equal to **True** in the sample, they actually represent evidence that will be observed only in the future (currently only the ones in O_D are observed). So, correspondingly, the actions that trigger the evidence also have not occurred yet. This means, in order to reshape the sample to represent current state, all these nodes should be set to **False**. In our algorithm, this processing will be performed through a subfunction **Transientize**.

5) Sample effectiveness verification (32~35). In this stage, a subfunction **PartialRelationSatisfied** is called to check whether the temporal partial ordering relations among the evidence nodes conform to the causation relations among the action nodes.

By running the algorithm, we can get a set of samples which not only have node values generated under the given probability distribution, but also definitely conform to the temporal partial ordering relations among evidence. Then, to use this sample set, a node belief computation function is defined as follow:

```
NodeBeliefComputing(AG,n,O_D,O_F,Ω,m)
Input:      AG — a network attack graph;
            n — effective sample number to generate;
            O_D — a set of observed evidence nodes;
            O_F — a set of not yet observed evidence nodes;
            Ω — a temporal partial ordering relation set on
O_D ∪ O_F;
            m —inference mode, 0 for future state, 1 for current
state.
Output:     M — a node belief metric set
Algorithm:  01:  M←∅; W←0;
            02:  Ξ←ImprovedLikelihoodWeighting(AG,n,
                              O_D,O_F,Ω,m);
            03:  for (each node variable X in AG)
            04:     N_X←0;
            05:  end for (03)
            06:  for (each sample ξ in Ξ)
            07:     for (each node variable X in ξ.AG)
```

```
08:        if (X=1) then
09:           N_X←N_X+ξ.w;
10:        end if (08)
11:     end for (07)
12:     W←W+ξ.w;
13:  end for (06)
14:  for (each node variable X in AG)
15:     M←M∪ {P_X=N_X/W};
16:  end for (14)
17:  return M;
```

By running this function, a set M will be returned which contains all the node belief values for later queries. By inputting different intrusion evidence sequences which correspond to different observation timepoints, we can get an attack graph node belief distribution sequence $\beta = \Pi_0 \Pi_1 \cdots \Pi_k$ to represent security state evolvement.

5. Node Belief Computation Examples

In order to exemplify the improved likelihood-weighting algorithm, we design and implement a Java program to perform following experiments:

5.1. Comparison with Bayesian Inference

Firstly, we use the variable elimination algorithm (a traditional Bayesian inference algorithm) to compute the posterior node belief values of the attack graph illustrated in **Figure 3**. The result is listed in **Table 1**.

In **Table 1**, different number i denotes different inference layer. In this example, $i = 0$ denotes the inference is performed before any evidence is observed, $i = 1$ denotes the inference is performed after o_2 is observed, $i = 2$ denotes the inference is performed after sequence $o_2 \rightarrow o_1$ is observed and $i = 3$ denotes the inference is performed after $o_2 \rightarrow o_1 \rightarrow o_3$ is observed.

Then we use our improved likelihood weighting algorithm to perform the same inference. The result is listed in **Table 2** (10000 effective samples without transientization) and **Table 3** (10000 samples with transientization).

Since traditional Bayesian network inference methods does not support intrusion evidence ordering, we are not surprised to see that in **Table 1**, when $i > 1$, the node belief values of intrusion path α and β are mirror symmetrical. This makes it difficult for us to judge which path has been chosen by the attacker. However, by using improved likelihood weighting algorithm, we can observe no matter in **Table 2** or **Table 3**, the node belief values of path β are all higher than path α, indicating it is more likely to have been chosen by the attacker.

Table 1. Node belief values (use traditional inference).

i	$\pi_i(s_1)$	$\pi_i(s_2)$	$\pi_i(s_3)$	$\pi_i(s_4)$	$\pi_i(s_5)$	$\pi_i(s_6)$
0	1.000	0.250	0.250	0.063	0.063	0.031
1	1.000	0.333	0.444	0.111	0.111	0.055
2	1.000	0.500	0.500	0.167	0.167	0.083
3	1.000	0.619	0.619	0.524	0.524	0.504

i	$\pi_i(a_1)$	$\pi_i(a_2)$	$\pi_i(a_3)$	$\pi_i(a_4)$	$\pi_i(a_5)$	$\pi_i(a_6)$
0	0.500	0.500	0.125	0.125	0.031	0.031
1	0.556	0.889	0.222	0.222	0.056	0.056
2	0.833	0.833	0.333	0.333	0.083	0.083
3	0.746	0.746	0.556	0.556	0.508	0.508

Table 2. Node belief values (without transientization).

i	$\pi_i(s_1)$	$\pi_i(s_2)$	$\pi_i(s_3)$	$\pi_i(s_4)$	$\pi_i(s_5)$	$\pi_i(s_6)$
0	1.000	0.247	0.259	0.060	0.063	0.028
1	1.000	0.250	0.499	0.060	0.121	0.042
2	1.000	0.392	0.606	0.092	0.202	0.071
3	1.000	0.494	0.831	0.366	0.701	0.504

i	$\pi_i(a_1)$	$\pi_i(a_2)$	$\pi_i(a_3)$	$\pi_i(a_4)$	$\pi_i(a_5)$	$\pi_i(a_6)$
0	0.498	0.503	0.122	0.132	0.031	0.029
1	0.504	1.000	0.127	0.246	0.028	0.058
2	0.792	1.000	0.190	0.405	0.044	0.101
3	0.663	1.000	0.409	0.744	0.342	0.680

Table 3. Node belief values (with transientization).

i	$\pi_i(s_1)$	$\pi_i(s_2)$	$\pi_i(s_3)$	$\pi_i(s_4)$	$\pi_i(s_5)$	$\pi_i(s_6)$
0	1.000	0.000	0.000	0.000	0.000	0.000
1	1.000	0.000	0.504	0.000	0.000	0.000
2	1.000	0.246	0.630	0.000	0.220	0.000
3	1.000	0.147	1.000	0.000	1.000	0.505

i	$\pi_i(a_1)$	$\pi_i(a_2)$	$\pi_i(a_3)$	$\pi_i(a_4)$	$\pi_i(a_5)$	$\pi_i(a_6)$
0	0.000	0.000	0.000	0.000	0.000	0.000
1	0.000	1.000	0.000	0.000	0.000	0.000
2	0.747	1.000	0.000	0.442	0.000	0.000
3	0.430	1.000	0.000	1.000	0.000	1.000

Then, to testify that our improved likelihood weighting algorithm can process attack graphs that contain directed cycles, we run the program to compute node belief values for **Figure 2**. Assuming in initial state the attacker occupies s_1 and that every other used probability is 0.5, the inference result is listed in **Table 4** (10000 effective samples, and since the graph has no evidence nodes, the result is same no matter the samples are transientized or not).

5.2. Comparison with HCPN-Based Inference

As aforementioned, in HCPN-based inference, empirical formulas are defined to reevaluate the security state of the network after intrusion evidence is observed. Comparatively, our algorithm is not dependent on any empirical formula, which makes the inference results more rational. To prove that, we modify the **Figure 3** example to the one illustrated in **Figure 5**.

Comparing with **Figure 3**, in **Figure 5** three additional nodes a_7, s_7, o_4 with the corresponding edges are added. Meanwhile, some of the action-evidence relations are modified and all the probabilities are explicitly labeled on the edges.

Similar to **Figure 3**, under the initial state the attacker whose final attack goal is also g_1 is assumed to occupy resource s_1 with probability 1.0. But during the attack, an evidence sequence $o_1 \rightarrow o_2 \rightarrow o_3 \rightarrow o_4$ is observed.

Using the HCPN-based inference method, we can get node belief values listed in **Table 5** (since HCPN only defines the belief value of resource nodes, nodes of other types are not listed).

Then we run our improved likelihood weighting inference program to perform the same computation. The result is listed in **Table 6** (10000 effective samples without transientization) and **Table 7** (10000 effective samples with transientization).

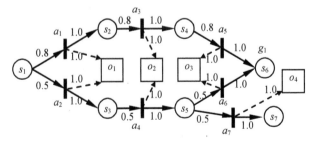

Figure 5. A network attack graph.

Table 4. Our inference result.

i	$\pi_i(s_1)$	$\pi_i(s_2)$	$\pi_i(s_3)$	$\pi_i(a_1)$	$\pi_i(a_2)$
0	1.000	0.129	0.248	0.502	0.065

Table 5. HCPN-based inference result.

i	assumed action	$\pi_i(s_1)$	$\pi_i(s_2)$	$\pi_i(s_3)$	$\pi_i(s_4)$	$\pi_i(s_5)$	$\pi_i(s_6)$	$\pi_i(s_7)$
0	-	1.0	0.0	0.0	0.0	0.0	0.0	0.0
1	a_1	1.0	0.615	0.0	0.0	0.0	0.0	0.0
	a_2	1.0	0.0	0.385	0.0	0.0	0.0	0.0
2	a_3	1.0	0.615	0.0	0.275	0.0	0.0	0.0
	a_4	1.0	0.0	0.385	0.0	0.193	0.0	0.0
3	a_5	1.0	0.615	0.0	0.275	0.0	0.109	0.0
	a_6	1.0	0.0	0.385	0.0	0.193	0.057	0.0
4	a_7	1.0	0.0	0.385	0.0	0.193	0.057	0.057

Table 6. Our inference result (without transientization).

i	$\pi_i(s_1)$	$\pi_i(s_2)$	$\pi_i(s_3)$	$\pi_i(s_4)$	$\pi_i(s_5)$	$\pi_i(s_6)$	$\pi_i(s_7)$
0	1.000	0.800	0.507	0.641	0.250	0.581	0.124
1	1.000	0.888	0.558	0.714	0.278	0.641	0.137
2	1.000	0.931	0.569	0.877	0.349	0.787	0.174
3	1.000	0.955	0.563	0.918	0.339	1.000	0.171
4	1.000	0.865	1.000	0.757	1.000	1.000	1.000

i	$\pi_i(a_1)$	$\pi_i(a_2)$	$\pi_i(a_3)$	$\pi_i(a_4)$	$\pi_i(a_5)$	$\pi_i(a_6)$	$\pi_i(a_7)$
0	0.800	0.507	0.641	0.250	0.518	0.125	0.124
1	0.888	0.558	0.714	0.278	0.574	0.141	0.137
2	0.931	0.569	0.877	0.349	0.703	0.174	0.174
3	0.955	0.563	0.918	0.339	0.890	0.227	0.171
4	0.865	1.000	0.757	1.000	0.678	0.660	1.000

We can observe that in **Table 5**, from layer 1 to 3, different actions denoting different attack paths are assumed to be conducted by the attacker. In these layers, inferred node belief values of intrusion path α are all higher than the values of path β. That is mainly due to the different probability values assigned to the two paths. In layer 4, the predominant attack path α is excluded from further consideration as o_4 can only be triggered by a_7 which is on attack path β. That judgment is quite reasonable. However, we find that most node belief values on attack path β are still not increased. It is due to the empirical formulas defined in HCPN-based inference method only update the belief values of the successor nodes of a_7 (obviously inconsistent with our intuition and what we usually see in most inference models that there should be a backward belief propagation procedure).

Table 7. Our inference result (with transientization).

i	$\pi_i(s_1)$	$\pi_i(s_2)$	$\pi_i(s_3)$	$\pi_i(s_4)$	$\pi_i(s_5)$	$\pi_i(s_6)$	$\pi_i(s_7)$
0	1.000	0.000	0.000	0.000	0.000	0.000	0.000
1	1.000	0.896	0.551	0.000	0.000	0.000	0.000
2	1.000	0.930	0.557	0.878	0.339	0.000	0.000
3	1.000	0.957	0.555	0.921	0.327	1.000	0.000
4	1.000	0.863	1.000	0.758	1.000	1.000	1.000

i	$\pi_i(a_1)$	$\pi_i(a_2)$	$\pi_i(a_3)$	$\pi_i(a_4)$	$\pi_i(a_5)$	$\pi_i(a_6)$	$\pi_i(a_7)$
0	0.000	0.000	0.000	0.000	0.000	0.000	0.000
1	0.896	0.551	0.000	0.000	0.000	0.000	0.000
2	0.930	0.557	0.878	0.339	0.000	0.000	0.000
3	0.957	0.555	0.921	0.327	0.894	0.218	0.000
4	0.863	1.000	0.758	1.000	0.674	0.668	1.000

In comparison, in **Table 6** and **Table 7**, no action is needed to be assumed to perform the inference. From layer 1 to 3, inferred node belief values of path α are all higher than the values of path β. And in layer 4, path β is confirmed by the observation of o_4, with all the belief values of that path set to 1.0 (this is the backward belief propagation we are expecting).

5.3. Algorithm Performance Evaluation

We adjust the specified number of effective samples (*i.e.* m), then record the CPU time that is used to generate the sample set. **Figure 6** illustrates three performance curves which respectively correspond to the above three examples. The hardware and software environment of the program is: Intel Core2 Duo CPU 2.00GHz, 2GB DDR2 Memory, Windows XP Professional (with Service Pack 2), Sun JDK 1.6.0_10-rc.

Figure 6 shows that for a certain attack graph, the CPU time to generate a sample set is basically proportional to the number of the samples. Through a detailed analysis it can be found that the sampling time consumption is mainly determined by two facts: 1) the node number N of the attack graph and 2) the evidence temporal partial ordering relation set Ω. According to Definition 1, in any attack graph the prerequisite node number of a single node is always below N, so we may define a constant T_{max} and use $T_{max}*N$ to denote the upper bound of the time used to process a node. And the time to generate a full sample will be less than $N*(T_{max}*N)$. On the other hand, checking against the partial ordering relation set Ω may force us to discard some generated samples. To con-

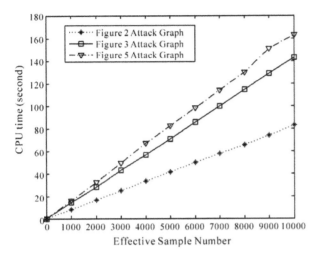

Figure 6. CPU time curves of sampling.

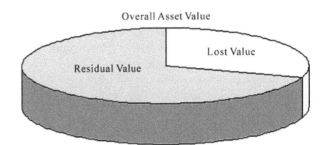

Figure 7. Components of asset value.

trol this fact, we may specify a maximal try number M. Once M samples have been generated (no matter how many effective samples are there), the program will cease sampling. In conclusion, for any attack graph, the sampling procedure can always finish in $T_{max}*M*N^2$. In other words, the algorithm has quadratic computational complexity.

6. Security Assessment & Enhancement

In this section, based on the above node belief computation algorithm, we propose a model for assessing network security level and performing security enhancement.

6.1. Security Assessment

Generally, the overall security level of a concerned network is mainly determined by three factors: 1) threat of the network, 2) vulnerability of the network and 3) influence of the potential attacks. In the previously proposed model, the former two factors have been dealt with (by IDS alerts indicating threats and network attack graph itself indicating vulnerabilities). However, we still have a problem with how to model the influence of potential attacks. In this section, we introduce a concept of asset value breakage rate to quantify it.

Asset value breakage rate is the ratio of the lost asset value to the overall asset value, illustrated in **Figure 7**. Since we often use asset CIA (confidentiality, integrity and availability) value to achieve more particular quantification, we introduce asset CIA breakage nodes into

network attack graph and extend Definition 1 into Definition 3.

Definition 3. An extended attack graph is a 12-tuple directed graph $AG = (S, S_0, A, G, O, E, \Delta, \Phi, \Theta, \Pi, P, \Upsilon)$ where $S, S_0, A, G, O, \Delta, \Phi, \Theta, \Pi$ are the same elements as defined in Definition 1 and:

- $P = (P_C \cup P_I \cup P_A)$ is a set of asset breakage nodes where P_C is a set of asset confidentiality breakage nodes, P_I is a set of asset integrity breakage nodes and P_A is a set of asset availability breakage nodes. Values of each node variable ρ_{Xi} ($X = $ C, I, A; $i = 1, \cdots, N$. where N is the total asset number) all lie in [0, 1], denoting the breakage percentage of every asset in particular aspect. Apart from that, we define a function $\lambda : P \rightarrow [0, +\infty)$ to map each asset to its overall value in confidentiality, integrity and availability. So we can use $\rho_i \times \lambda(\rho_i)$ to denote the absolute loss value of an asset in CIA.

- $E = (E_1 \cup E_2 \cup E_3 \cup E_4 \cup E_5)$ is a finite set of edges which link graph nodes together. Here E_1, E_2 and E_3 share the same definition as in Definition 1, while $E_4 \subseteq S \times P$ denotes that if the attacker gains certain resources, she will do damage to certain assets, and $E_5 \subseteq A \times P$ denotes that if the attacker executes certain actions, she will do damage to certain assets.

- $\Upsilon = \{\upsilon_1 : (s_i, \rho_j) \rightarrow [0,1], \upsilon_2 : (a_i, \rho_j) \rightarrow [0,1]\}$ is the asset breakage conductivity rate distribution where υ_1 denotes when the attacker gains a resource, how much damage will she do to an asset and υ_2 denotes when the attacker executes an action, how much damage will she do to an asset. Just like the other prior conditional probability distributions, values of Υ also lies in [0, 1] where a larger value denotes a greater potential damage.

Based on Definition 3, we can use a function $\tau(P)$ to quantify the network security level:

$$\tau(P) = \frac{\sum_{\rho \in P}(1-\rho)\lambda(\rho)}{\sum_{\rho \in P}\lambda(\rho)} = \frac{\sum_{\rho_C \in P_C}(1-\rho_C)\lambda(\rho_C) + \sum_{\rho_I \in P_I}(1-\rho_I)\lambda(\rho_I) + \sum_{\rho_A \in P_A}(1-\rho_A)\lambda(\rho_A)}{\sum_{\rho_C \in P_C}\lambda(\rho_C) + \sum_{\rho_I \in P_I}\lambda(\rho_I) + \sum_{\rho_A \in P_A}\lambda(\rho_A)}$$

In the above equation, $\tau(P)$ is the function to compute the normalized asset residual value. The right expression uses asset residual value as the numerator and asset overall value as the denominator.

Just like other network attack graph node variables, all the belief values of asset breakage nodes also can be computed by the inference algorithm in Section 4. So, by inputting different evidence sequences corresponding to different observation timepoints, eventually we can get a sequence $\tau_0 \tau_1 \cdots \tau_k$ indicating the security evolvement.

6.2. Security Enhancement

Broadly speaking, as long as a measure can help enhacing network security, it is referred to as a network security enhancement measure. In most cases, the implementation of a security enhancement measure may affect a network attack graph in two ways:

1) it changes the structure of the attack graph, or
2) it changes the conditional probability distributions of the attack graph including $\Delta, \Phi, \Theta, \Pi_0, \Upsilon$.

However, since commonly the implementation of a security enhancement measure will cut off certain intrusion paths, the resulting (enhanced) attack graph is often the sub-graph of the original attack graph. Based on this, we can always convert the above situation 1 into situation 2 by adjusting certain conditional probability.

For example, in the previous example illustrated in **Figure 2**, if the vulnerability on Master is patched, we need not generate a new attack graph, but set the conducting probability of a_1 and a_2 to 0.0.

On this basis, we introduce a security enhancement measure tuple (M, ϑ, ν):

- $M = \{m_1, \cdots, m_K\}$ is a candidate measure set.
- $\vartheta : 2^M \to 2^\Gamma$ is a function which maps a combination of measures to a rectified attack graph probability distribution $\Gamma = (\Delta, \Phi, \Theta, \Pi_0, \Upsilon)$.
- $\nu : 2^M \to R^+$ is a function which maps a combination of measures to its implementation cost.

With the above security measure tuple, we can perform the following analysis:

1) **Static Security Enhancement.** This analysis is to find the best combination of security measures to be implemented before any potential intrusion happens. A typical usage of this analysis is to enhance a network system before it is placed online. To achieve this, all candidate measure combinations need to be iterated. For each measure combination $M_C \in 2^M$, we set the probability distribution to $\Gamma' = \vartheta(M_C)$ and recompute the network normalized asset residual value τ'_0. Then the net profit of M_C is:

$$u(M_C) = (\tau'_0 - \tau_0) \times Overall\ Asset\ Value - \nu(M_C),$$

where τ_0 is the normalized asset residual value when no security measure is implemented ($M_C = \varnothing$). Finally, by sorting these measure combinations according to their net profits, we can easily choose the greatest one as the optimal enhancement solution.

2) **Dynamic Security Enhancement.** This analysis is to find the best measure combination when intrusion is happening (or has happened). To achieve this, we firstly need to use the previous inference algorithm to generate a set Ξ_T of transientized attack samples. Then we iterate all of the candidate measure combinations. For each combination $M_C \in 2^M$, we rectify the graph probability distribution to $\Gamma' = \vartheta(M_C)$. After doing this, we resample (a process same to line 11~23 of the **Improved LikelihoodWeighting** algorithm) Ξ_T according to the new distribution and get a new set Ξ_S which will be actually used to compute the network normalized asset residual value τ'_S. Then the net profit of M_C is:

$$u(M_C) = (\tau'_S - \tau_S) \times Overall\ Asset\ Value - \nu(M_C),$$

where τ_S is a normalized asset residual value when no measure is implemented ($M_C = \varnothing$). Finally, by sorting these measure combinations according to their net profits, we can easily choose the greatest one as the optimal enhancement solution.

7. Assessment & Enhancement Examples

To exemplify the above security assessment and enhancement method, in one experiment we generated an attack graph for a two tier network system. Based on it, we performed corresponding security assessment and used our enhancement method to find out optimal security enhancement measure combinations for static and dynamic security enhancement respectively.

7.1. Basic Posterior Inference

Figure 8 illustrates the topology of the two tier network. In this network, four intranet servers were connected to a switch which was further connected to the Internet by a router. A firewall was placed between the two devices to perform package filtering, besides an IDS was connected to a mirror port of the switch to monitor the outflow and inflow of the servers.

We assumed a scenario that an attacker on the Internet intends to use her personal computer to attack this network. The final goal of the attacker was to get the ROOT privilege on server3 and steal its business data.

For further analysis, we firstly need to generate a network attack graph to find out all the potential intrusion paths. So we scanned the online devices and servers and found out six vulnerabilities (listed in **Table 8**). Addi-

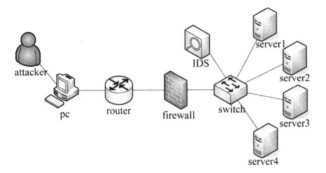

Figure 8. A two tier network system.

Table 8. Host vulnerabilities.

device	OS	application	vulnerabilities
server1	windows nt 4.0	serv-u ftp 3.0	cve-2004-0330 cve-2004-1992
server2	windows 2000	-	cve-2003-0533
server3	redhat linux 7.3	oracle 9i cvs 1.11	cve-2004-0417 cve-2004-0415
server4	redhat linux 7.3	apache 1.3.23	cve-2002-0392

tionally, we found that the firewall is configured to permit and only permit the Internet user to access intranet servers through HTTP protocol.

By importing these information into a network attack graph building system developed by us (design concept of this system mainly follows the framework proposed in [16]), we get a network attack graph shown in **Figure 9**.

In **Figure 9**, resource state nodes are represented in circles while action nodes are represented in rectangles. The top row in the figure (11 resource state nodes) includes the 6 vulnerabilities on the servers and the 5 low level privileges which can be used by anyone to access the servers. However, owes to the firewall, initially the attacker can only access server4's HTTP service and exploit the apache vulnerability (this exploitation is represented in the figure with the action node right below the top resource state node row). After that, the attacker may get the USER privilege of server4 and use this server as a stepping stone to perform further intrusion (mainly by exploiting the rest vulnerabilities listed in **Table 8**). According to **Figure 9**, to the maximum extent, the attacker can get the USER privilege of server1, server3 and server4 as well as the ROOT privilege of server2 and server3 (represented by the other 5 circles in the figure exclude the top row).

Then we should assigned conditional probability distributions to the generated graph. In this stage, we mainly used data sources such as CVSS [17] and OSVBD [18] complemented with expertise knowledge. For example, in CVSS, a score metric named *Exploitability* are defined

to indicate the difficulty for an attacker to exploit vulnerability. So we decide to use this metric to evaluate the success rate of an action by the following transformation:

$$\phi(a) = 1.0 - e^{-(\textit{Exploitability of } a)}$$

With all prior conditional probability distributions assigned, we were able to perform posterior inference according to observed intrusion evidence. As an example for exemplification, we assumed that an IDS alert sequence is observed as in **Table 9**:

By running the improved likelihood weighting algorithm, we computed node belief values for each inference layer. Due to space limitation, detailed result is not given out here. But in Annex B this security evolvement procedure is illustrated graphically. In each figure of the annex, a darker node is used to represent a greater node belief value. We see that with more evidence observed, belief values of some graph nodes increase rapidly, indicating intrution paths that are most probably chosen.

7.2. Security Assessment

Since our aim is to assess security level of the network and find out an optimal enhancement solution, we selected 5 important service assets from the network system whose CIA values are listed in **Table 10** (in thousands $US). Correspondingly, we introduced into the attack graph 15 corresponding asset breakage nodes.

Meanwhile, we quantified the asset breakage conductivity rate between these 15 nodes and the aforementioned 5 resource state nodes which represent the escalated privileges that may be gained by the attacker. The conductivity rates between them are listed in **Table 11**.

Table 9. Observed alerts.

id	exploited vulnerability	source	target
1	cve-2002-0392	pc	server4
2	cve-2003-0533	server4	server2
3	cve-2004-0417	server3	server3

Table 10. Important assets and their CIA values.

id	asset	host	$\lambda(\rho_C)$	$\lambda(\rho_I)$	$\lambda(\rho_A)$
1	ftp	server1	1	1	1
2	file	server2	50	50	50
3	database	server3	100	100	50
4	cvs	server4	10	10	10
5	apache	server4	0	10	10

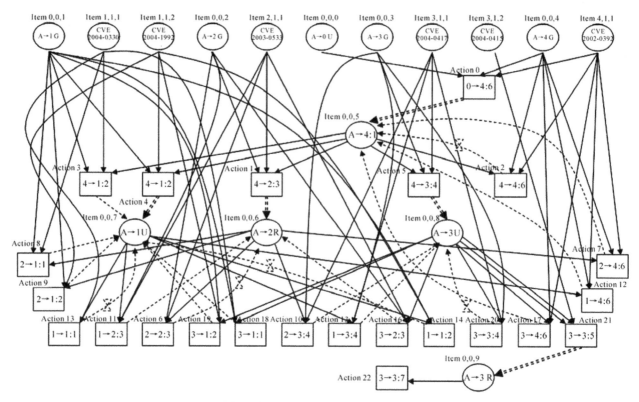

Figure 9. Attack graph of the network.

Table 11. Asset breakage conductivity rate.

	ρ_{C1}	ρ_{C2}	ρ_{C3}	ρ_{C4}	ρ_{C5}
escalated privilege	ρ_{I1}	ρ_{I2}	ρ_{I3}	ρ_{I4}	ρ_{I5}
	ρ_{A1}	ρ_{A2}	ρ_{A3}	ρ_{A4}	ρ_{A5}
	0.00	0.00	0.00	0.00	1.00
USER on server4	0.00	0.00	0.00	0.00	0.80
	0.00	0.00	0.00	0.00	0.50
	0.00	0.90	0.00	0.00	0.00
ROOT on server2	0.00	0.90	0.00	0.00	0.00
	0.00	0.50	0.00	0.00	0.00
	1.00	0.00	0.00	0.00	0.00
USER on server1	0.80	0.00	0.00	0.00	0.00
	0.50	0.00	0.00	0.00	0.00
	0.00	0.00	0.00	1.00	0.00
USER on server3	0.00	0.00	0.00	0.80	0.00
	0.00	0.00	0.00	0.50	0.00
	0.00	0.00	1.00	1.00	0.00
ROOT on server3	0.00	0.00	0.80	0.80	0.00
	0.00	0.00	0.50	0.50	0.00

After doing this, we recomputed the node belief values for each inference layer and get 2 normalized asset residual value sequences $\tau_0\tau_1\tau_2\tau_3$ listed in **Table 12** and **Table 13** (without and with transientization respectively). These sequences are graphically illustrated in **Figure 10** to reveal the evolvement of network security. In the figure we can observe that the asset residual values generated with transientization are always greater than the ones without transientization. This is reasonable since with all condition unchanged, the *current* security level of a network is always higher than its *future* security level, because from *current* timepoint to the *future* the attacker gets additional time to perform more intrusion.

7.3. Security Enhancement

Then, for enhancement, we analyzed the network system and listed 11 plainest security measures as candidates in **Table 14**. These measures include patching the vulnerabilities on the servers and disabling low level privilege accounts on them. Additionally, we identified a measure of configuring the firewall to deny all incoming access including HTTP. Costs of these security measures were also analyzed and listed in the table (in thousands $US).

By using the security enhancement methods proposed in Section 6, we eventually got all the net profit of the security measure combinations. In **Table 15** we list the

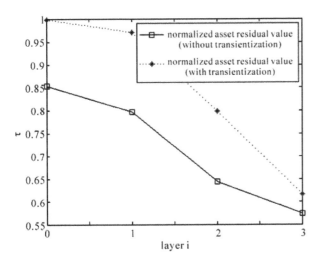

Figure 10. Evolvement of network security.

Table 12. Assessment result (without transientization).

i	0	1	2	3
$\Sigma\lambda(\rho)$	453.000	453.000	453.000	453.000
$\Sigma\rho\lambda(\rho)$	66.472	92.342	161.153	192.790
$\Sigma(1-\rho)\lambda(\rho)$	386.528	360.658	291.847	260.210
τ_i	85.33%	79.62%	64.43%	57.44%

Table 13. Assessment result (with transientization).

i	0	1	2	3
$\Sigma\lambda(\rho)$	453.000	453.000	453.000	453.000
$\Sigma\rho\lambda(\rho)$	0.909	13.548	91.443	173.655
$\Sigma(1-\rho)\lambda(\rho)$	452.091	439.452	361.557	279.345
τ_i	99.80%	97.01%	79.81%	61.67%

top 5 best security enhancement measure combinations for static security enhancement (SSE) and in **Table 16** we list the top 3 best combinations (of each inference layer) for dynamic security enhancement (DSE).

8. Conclusions

As network attack graphs are more and more widely used in real-time network security analysis, the problem of how to use observed intrusion evidence to compute attack graph node belief becomes a concerned issue. Although Bayesian network is an ideal mathematic tool for posterior inference, it can not be directly used in attack graph-based inference for the following limitations: 1) There may exist directed cycles in an attack graph, but in a Bayesian network this is not permitted. 2) There are

Table 14. Candidate security measures.

id	security measure	cost
1	patch CVE-2004-0330 on server1	0.1
2	patch CVE-2004-1992 on server1	0.1
3	patch CVE-2003-0533 on server2	5.0
4	patch CVE-2004-0417 on server3	5.0
5	patch CVE-2004-0415 on server3	1.0
6	patch CVE-2002-0392 on server4	1.0
7	disable GUEST account on server1	1.0
8	disable GUEST account on server2	50.0
9	disable GUEST account on server3	60.0
10	disable GUEST account on server4	10.0
11	add HTTP filtering rule on firewall	10.0

Table 15. Top 5 best combinations for SSE.

id	combination	cost	net gain
1	{6}	1.0	65.14
2	{1, 6}	1.1	65.04
3	{2, 6}	1.1	65.04
4	{1, 2, 6}	1.2	64.94
5	{5, 6}	2.0	64.14

Table 16. Top 3 best combinations for DSE.

layer	id	combination	cost	net gain
0	1	{1, 2, 6, 7}	2.2	40.87
	2	{1, 2, 6}	1.2	40.77
	3	{1, 2, 5, 6}	2.2	40.67
1	1	{1, 2, 3, 4}	10.2	55.20
	2	{2, 3, 4}	10.1	54.86
	3	{3, 5, 7}	7.0	54.70
2	1	{1, 2, 4, 6}	6.2	51.23
	2	{1, 2, 4}	5.2	51.23
	3	{1, 2, 4, 5}	6.2	50.73
3	1	{1, 2, 5}	1.2	11.41
	2	{1, 2, 5, 6}	2.2	11.01
	3	{1, 2, 4}	5.2	10.21

temporal partial ordering relations among intrusion evidence, but we can not use a Bayesian network to model this information. 3) A Bayesian network cannot be directly used to infer both the current and the future security state of a network. In this work, we resolve these critical problems by developing an approximate Bayesian inference algorithm—the likelihood weighting algorithm. We give out all the pseudocodes of the algorithm and use several examples to show its advantage. Essentially, we believe this algorithm is not only limited in attack graph-based analysis, but also can be applied in other techniques employing traditional Bayesian posterior inference.

Based on the algorithm and its underlying model, we further propose a novel network security assessment and enhancement method. In this paper, we use a small network system to exemplify how to use this method to quantify the overall network security level and make decisions about what security measures are most cost- effective for network security enhancement.

9. Acknowledgements

This work was supported in part by the National Natural Science Foundation of China under Grant Nos.60605019; the National High-Tech Research and Development Plan under Grant Nos.2007AA01Z473; the National Research Foundation for the Doctoral Program of Higher Education of China under Grant No.20070248002.

The authors would also like to thank all the members of Shanghai Key Laboratory for Information Security Integrated Management Technology Research.

If anyone is interested in the algorithms of this article, please feel free to contact leony7888@hotmail to get the java source codes.

10. References

[1]   O. Sheyner, J. Haines, S. Jha, et al., "Automated Generation and Analysis of Attack Graphs," Proceedings of the 2002 IEEE Symposium on Security and Privacy, Oakland, 12-15 May 2002, pp. 273-284. doi:10.1109/SECPRI.2002. 1004377

[2]   S. Jajodia, S. Noel and B. O'Berry, "Topological Analysis of Network Attack Vulnerability," Managing Cyber Threats: Issues, Approaches and Challenges, Kluwer Academic Publisher, 2004.

[3]   P. Ammann, D. Wijesekera and S. Kaushik, "Scalable, Graph-Based Network Vulnerability Analysis," Proceedings of the 9th ACM Conference on Computer & Communications Security, Washington DC, 2002, pp. 217-224.

[4]   X. Ou, S. Govindavajhala and A. Appel, "MulVAL: A Logic-Based Network Security Analyzer," Proceedings of the 14th conference on USENIX Security Symposium,

Baltimore, 31 July-5 August 2005, pp. 8-23.

[5]   R. Lippmann, K. Ingols, C. Scott, et al., "Validating and Restoring Defense in Depth Using Attack Graphs," Proceedings of the 2007 IEEE Military Communications Conference, Washington DC, 2006.

[6]   P. Ning and D. Xu, "Learning Attack Strategies from Intrusion Alerts," Proceedings of the 10th ACM Conference on Computer and Communications Security, Washington DC, October 2003.

[7]   S. Noel, E. Robertson and S. Jajodia, "Correlating Intrusion Events and Building Attack Scenarios through Attack Graph Distances," Proceedings of the 20th Annual Computer Security Applications Conference, Tucson, December 2004, pp. 350-359. doi:10.1109/SECPRI.2002. 1004377

[8]   L. Wang, A. Liu and S. Jajodia, "Using Attack Graphs for Correlating, Hypothesizing, and Predicting Intrusion Alerts," Computer Communications, Vol. 29, No. 15, 2006, pp. 2917-2933. doi:10.1016/j.comcom.2006.04.001

[9]   Y. Zhai, P. Ning, P. Iyer, et al., "Reasoning about Complementary Intrusion Evidence," Proceedings of the 20th Annual Computer Security Applications Conference, Tucson, 6-10 December 2004, pp. 39-48. doi:10.1109/ CSAC.2004.29

[10] D. Yu and D. Frincke, "Improving the Quality of Alerts and Predicting Intruder's Next Goal with Hidden Colored Petri-Net," Computer Networks, Vol. 51, No. 3, 2007, p. 632. doi:10.1016/j.comnet.2006.05.008

[11] S. Zhang, L. Li, J. Li, et al., "Using Attack Graphs and Intrusion Evidences to Extrapolate Network Security State," Proceedings of the 4th International Conference on Communications and Networking in China, Guang Zhou, 2009. doi:10.1109/CHINACOM.2009.5339841

[12] Z. Bhahramani, "An Introduction to Hidden Markov Models and Bayesian Networks," International Journal of Pattern Recognition and Artificial Intelligence, Vol. 15, No. 1, 2001, pp. 9-42. doi:10.1142/S0218001401000836

[13] F. Salfner, "Modeling Event-driven Time Series with Generalized Hidden Semi-Markov Models," Technical Report 208, Department of Computer Science, Humboldt University, Berlin, Germany, 2006.

[14] F. Jensen, "Bayesian Networks and Decision Graphs," Statistics for Engineering and Information Science, Springer, 2001.

[15] K. Korb and A. Nicholson, "Bayesian Artificial Intelligence," CRC Press, 2003. doi:10.1201/9780203491294

[16] S. Zhang, J. Li and X. Chen, "Building Network Attack Graph for Aalert Causal Correlation," Computers & Security, Vol. 27, No. 5-6, 2008, pp. 188-196. doi:10.1016/ j.cose.2008.05.005

[17] "National Institute of Standards and Technology," 2010. Common Vulnerability Scoring System. http://nvd.nist.gov/cvss.cfm

[18] "Open Security Foundation," 2010. OSVDB: The Open Source Vulnerability Database. http://osvdb.org/

Annex A: Pseudocode of Subfunctions

SF1. UpdateAttackGraph—called in ImprovedLikelihood Weighting

```
UpdateAttackGraph(AG,X,Y)
Input: AG—an attack sample
       X—an ancestor node      Y—a descendant node
Output: a boolean variable indicating if AG is updated
Alg:  01:  updated←False;
      02:  if (Y cand not sampled) then
      03:    if (for each node X' in Pre(Y) variable X'=True) then
      04:      if (for each node X' in Pre(Y)
                 IsCriticalCausation(AG,Y,X',∅)=False) then
      05:        Y←the sampling result according to δᵢ(Y);
      07:        if (Y=True) then
      08:          for (each node X' in Pre(Y))
      09:            Fₓ←Fₓ∪{Y};
      10:            Bᵧ←Bᵧ∪{X};
      11:          end for (08)
      12:          updated←True;
      13:          for (each node Z in Con(Y))
      14:            if (edge Y→Z is not sampled) then
      15:              UpdateAttackGraph(AG,Y,Z);
      16:            end if (14)
      17:          end for (13)
      18:        end if (07)
      19:        mark Y as sampled;
      20:        for (each node X' in Pre(Y))
      21:          mark edge X'→Y as sampled;
      22:        end for (20)
      23:      end if (04)
      24:    end if (03)
      25:  end if (02)
      26:  if (Y is other type node) then
      27:    if (!IsCriticalCausation(AG,Y,X,∅)) then
      28:      Y_old←Y;
      29:      y←sampling result by δ(X,Y) or φ(X,Y);
      30:      if (y=True) then
      31:        Y←True;
      32:        Fₓ←Fₓ∪{Y};
      33:        Bᵧ←Bᵧ∪{X};
      34:        updated←True;
      35:        if (Y_old=False) then
      36:          for (each node Z in Con(Y))
      37:            if (edge Y→Z is not sampled) then
      38:              UpdateAttackGraph(AG,Y,Z);
      39:            end if (37)
      40:          end for (36)
      41:        end if (35)
      42:      end if (30)
      43:      mark edge X→Y as sampled;
```

```
      44:    end if (27)
      45:  end if (26)
      46:  return updated;
```

SF2. IsCriticalCausation—called in UpdateAttackGraph and later SFs

```
IsCriticalCausation(AG,X,Y,H)
Input: AG—an attack sample
       X—a candidate causation node
       Y—a candidate affection node
       H—a set to hold historically processed nodes
Output: a boolean variable indicating if X is a critical causation of Y
Alg:  01:  if (Y is an action node) then
      02:    if (Y∈H ∨ Bᵧ=∅) then
      03:      r←False;
      04:    end if (02)
      05:    if (X∈Bᵧ ∨ (for each node Z in Bᵧ,
               IsCriticalCausation(AG,X,Z,H∪{Y})=True)) then
      06:      r←True;
      07:    else (05)
      08:      r←False;
      09:    end if (05)
      10:  end if (01)
      11:  if (Y is other type node) then
      12:    if (Y∈H 或 Bᵧ=∅) then
      13:      r←False;
      14:    end if (12)
      15:    if ({X}=Bᵧ ∨ (for each node Z in Bᵧ,
               IsCriticalCausation(AG,X,Z,H∪{Y})=True)) then
      16:      r←True;
      17:    else (15)
      18:      r←False;
      19:    end if (15)
      20:  end if (11)
      21:  return r;
```

SF3. SelectEvidenceCausation—called in ImprovedLikelihoodWeighting

```
SelectEvidenceCausation(AG,X)
Input: AG — a network attack graph
       X — an observed evidence node (whose value is True)
Output: the occurrence probability of the chosen causation set
Alg:  01:  p_Σ←0;
      02:  Φ←∅; Ψ←{Y|Y∈Pre(X)∧Y=True};
      03:  for (each non-emtpy subset ψ of Ψ)
      04:    p_ψ←∏_{Y∈ψ}θ(Y,X) * ∏_{Y∈(Ψ-ψ)}(1-θ(Y,X));
      05:    Φ←Φ∪{(ψ,p_ψ)};
```

```
06:        pΣ←pΣ+pψ;
07:    end for (03)
08:    for (each pair (ψ, pψ) in Φ)
09:        pψ←pψ / pΣ;
10:    end for (08)
11: (ψr, pψr)←chose a pair in Φ according to pψ of the pair;
12:    for (each node Z in ψ)
13:        FZ←FZ ∪ {X};
14:        BX←BX ∪ {Z};
15:    end for (12)
16:    return pψr*pΣ;
```

SF4. Transientize—called in **ImprovedLikelihood-Weighting**

```
Transientize(AG,OD,OF)
Input: AG—an attack sample OD—a set of observed evidence nodes
       OF—a set of not yet observed evidence nodes
Output: a boolean indicating AG's effectiveness after transientization
Alg:   01:    for (each node X in OF)
       02:        for (each action node Y in BX)
       03:            Y←False;
       04:            mark edge Y→X as not sampled;
       05:            BX←BX -{Y}; FY←FY -{X};
       06:            if (Y is an action node) then
       07:                mark Y as not sampled;
       08:            end if (06)
       09:            for (each node Z in BY)
       10:                mark edge Z→Y as not sampled;
       11:                BY←BY -{Z}; FZ←FZ -{Y};
       12:            end for (09)
       13:        end for (02)
       14:    end for (01)
       15:    converged←False;
       16:    while (!converged)
       17:        converged←True;
       18:        for (each non-root node in AG)
       19:            if (X is an action node) then
       20:                if (X is sampled ∧ (some node in BX is False ∨
                             X is the critical causation of some node in BX)) then
       21:                    X←False;
       22:                    mark X as not sampled;
       23:                    for (each node Y in BX)
       24:                        mark edge Y→X as not sampled;
       25:                        BX←BX -{Y}; FY←FY -{X};
       26:                    end for (23)
       27:                    converged←False;
       28:                end if (20)
       29:            else (19)
       30:                for (each node Y in BX)
       31:                    if (Y=False ∨ IsCriticalCausation(AG,X,Y,∅)) then
       32:                        mark edge Y→X as not sampled;
       33:                        BX←BX -{Y}; FY←FY -{X};
       34:                    end if (31)
       35:                end for (30)
       36:                if (BX = ∅) then
       37:                    if (X∈OD) then
       38:                        return False;
       39:                    else (37)
       40:                        X←False;
       41:                        converged←False;
       42:                    end if (37)
       43:                end if (36)
       44:            end if (19)
       45:        end for (18)
       46:    end while (16)
       47:    return True;
```

SF5. PartialRelationSatisfied—called in **Improved-LikelihoodWeighting**

```
PartialRelationSatisfied (AG,O,Ω)
Input: AG—an attack sample
       O—the evidence set of AG
       Ω—a temporal partial ordering relation set on O
Output: a boolean indicating if AG conforms to Ω (and is effective)
Alg:   01:    typeI_satisfied←True; typeII_satisfied←True;
       02:    for (each type I partial ordering relation Om ↗ On in Ω)
       03:        pairSatisfied←False;
       04:        for (each node Ai in BOm)
       05:            existJCoversI←False;
       06:            for (each node Aj in BOn)
       07:                if (IsCriticalCausation(AG,Aj,Ai,∅)) then
       08:                    existJCoversI←True;
       09:                end if (07)
       10:            end for (06)
       11:            if (!existJCoversI) then
       12:                pairSatisfied←True;
       13:            end if (11)
       14:        end for (04)
       15:        if (!pairSatisfied) then
       16:            typeI_satisfied←False;
       17:        end if (15)
       18:    end for (02)
       19:    for (each type II partial ordering relation Om ↘ On in Ω)
       20:        for (each node Ai in BOm)
       21:            for (each node Aj in BOn)
       22:                if (IsCriticalCausation(AG,Aj,Ai,∅))
       23:                    typeII_satisfied←False;
       24:                end if (22)
       25:            end for (21)
       26:        end for (20)
       27:    end for (19)
       28:    return typeI_satisfied ∧ typeII_satisfied;
```

Annex B: Graph Node Belief Evolvement

Without Sample Transientization

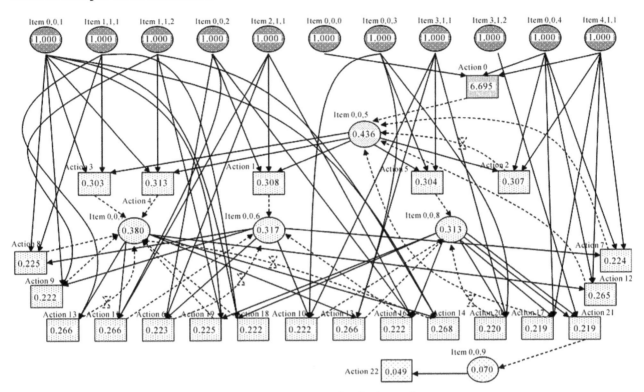

Figure 1. Layer 0-no alert is observed.

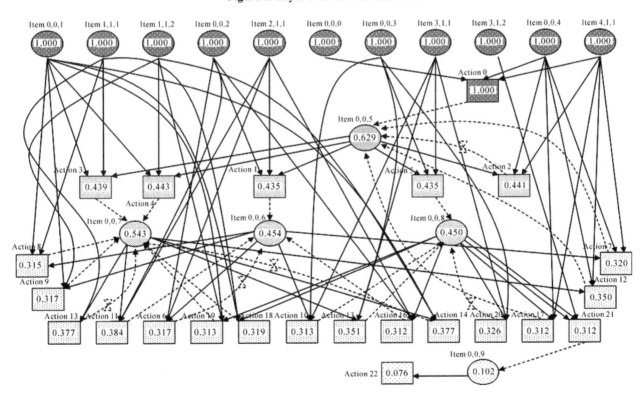

Figure 2. Layer 1–one alert is observed.

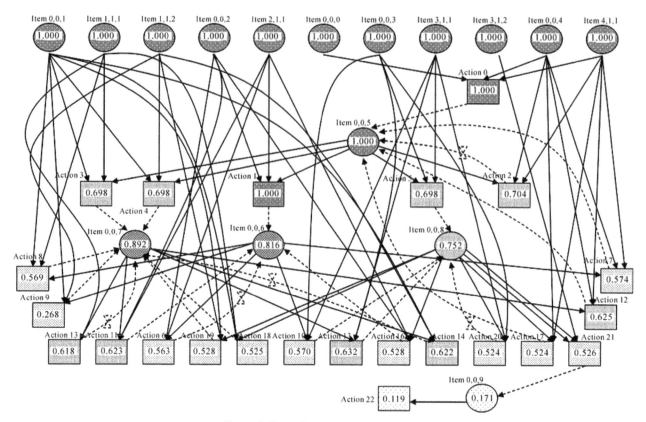

Figure 3. Layer 2–two alerts is observed.

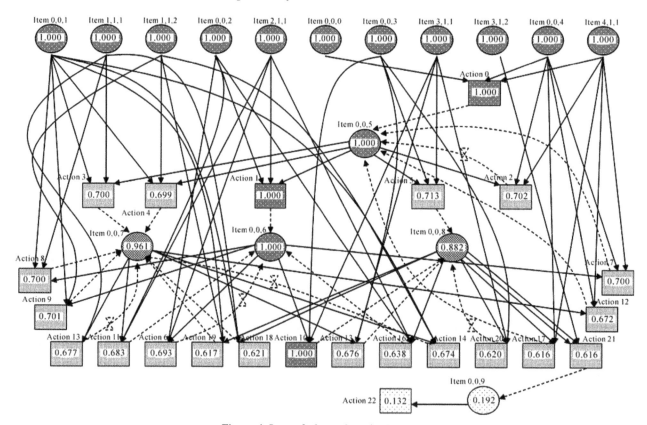

Figure 4. Layer 3-three alerts is observed.

With Sample Transientization

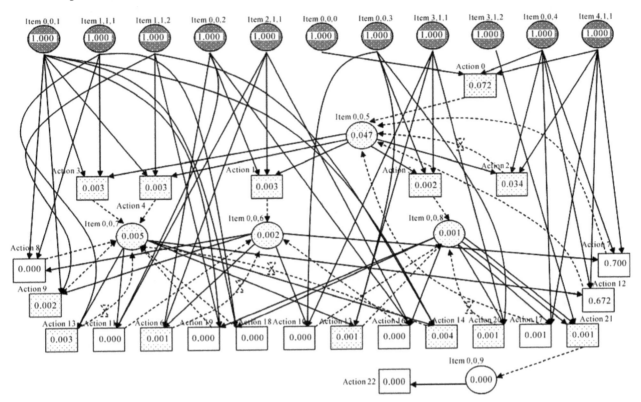

Figure 1. Layer 0-no alert is observed.

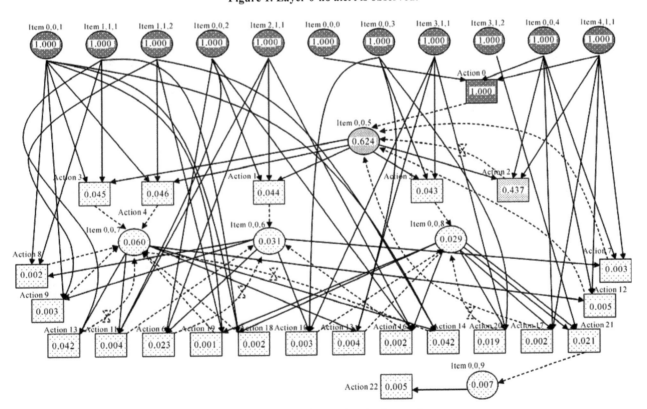

Figure 2. Layer 1—one alert is observed.

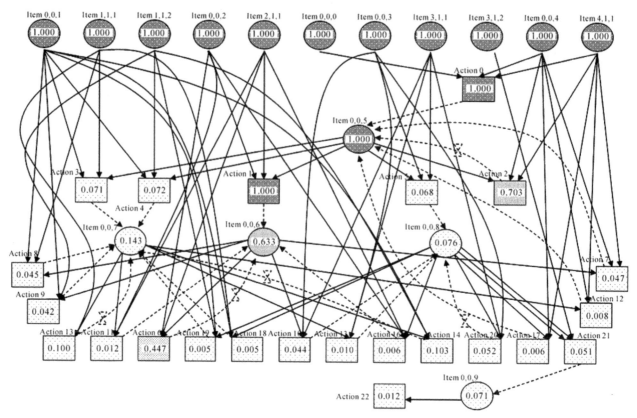

Figure 3. Layer 2–two alerts is observed.

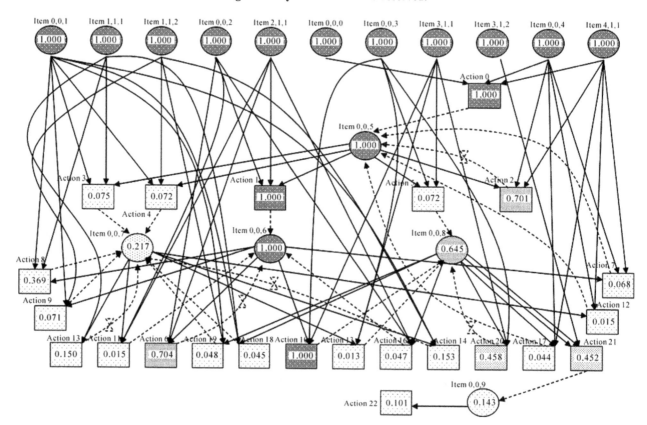

Figure 4. Layer 3–three alerts is observed.

6

SOAP-Based Security Interaction of Web Service in Heterogeneous Platforms[*]

Tao Xu, Chunxiao Yi

College of Computer Science and Technology, Civil Aviation University of China, Tianjin, China

Abstract

With the development and application of SOA technology, security issues of Web services based on heterogeneous platform have become increasingly prominent. The security of SOAP message is of great importance to Web service security. In order to solve the security issue of heterogeneous platforms, a security processing model named SIMSA (Security Interactive Model based on SOAP and Authentication) based on SOAP and authentication is proposed in this paper. By experimental verification, the model ensures the safety of SOAP message transmission and enhances the security of Web service in heterogeneous platforms.

Keywords: SOAP, Heterogeneous, Web Service, SIMSA, Security Interaction

1. Introduction

With the growth of the Service-oriented Architecture (SOA) application scale, there are hundreds of services in a large company. Different services may be deployed to platforms from different vendors, and different services installed in different locations have different access rights and security policy (encryption, signature, prevention of attacks, etc.). How to guarantee the security of services has become hot spot in foreign research institutions and scholars. IBM Tokyo Research Institute (Fumiko Satoh *et al.*) puts forward the best practice models and support tools for the specific service safety profile construction for the IBM Websphere Server according to security policy using mapping rules [1]. Microsoft Research in University of Cambridge (Karthikeyan Bhargavan *et al.*) [2] publishes a security policy configuration guidance to help developers construct the security policies of Web service according to security requirements. IBM Research Division in New York (Sam Weber *et al.*) [3] points out that there are a large number of heterogeneous platforms and different platforms have many Web Service standards and complex technologies. Even if there is a variety of "best security practices mode", it is still very difficult to ensure how to achieve the proper se-

curity.

Although SOA has solved the Web services called in heterogeneous platforms, and there are relevant security standards (WS-Security) of security information exchange between different platforms, WS-Security only gives an abstract framework to achieve security goals, including XML signatures, encryption, authentication and authorization. As for how to use them to achieve the goal of SOA security, it presents a challenge both in theoretical and technical practices [4,5].

Authentication policies and SOAP message-based security interactive study of Web services in heterogeneous platforms have been proposed in this paper. First the security feature of heterogeneous platforms is analyzed, and then the details of the security interaction model of heterogeneous platform named SIMSA is given. Combined with concrete application examples, user authentication during a Web service call as well as the safe handling of SOAP messages in heterogeneous platforms is achieved. The security model provides theoretical support for the security interacts of Web services in heterogeneous platforms and is verified by experiments. This model ensures the security interactions of Web service effectively.

2. Security Features of Heterogeneous Platform

SOA needs a wide range of interoperability between ser-

[*]This research is supported by grants from National Natural Science Foundation of China (NO. 60979011) and Tianjin Research Program of Application Foundation and Advanced Technology (NO. 09JCYBJC 02300).

vices. In the development of Web service's logic functionality, if the security features are designed, Web services will become extremely complex and service performance and scalability will be greatly reduced. In terms of the analysis on the security needs and consideration of a variety of security measures, it can not be sure whether the security components are appropriately organized and whether the system is more secure [6,7]. Security issues of Web services in SOA should be out of service functions, and the security requirements of Web services can be achieved through appropriate security configuration and mechanism. In this way, it can not only ensure the simplicity of design and call of Web services, but also can achieve the security of SOAP messaging [8,9].

An application system is usually based on a platform such as Microsoft. NET or Apache Axis. The service platform has its own security solution such as Microsoft's WSE (Web Service Enhancement) and Axis's of Rampart, etc. For the same security policy such as using certificates to sign the message, it can be achieved in the same platform for service requester to sign the message and service provider to do signature verification. If the service requester and provider are in different platforms, the security interoperability can not be guaranteed.

Each application platform has its own security mechanisms and security API. When using SOA to integrate enterprise application, services of different applications may be deployed in different application platforms and security requirements may be achieved by different security policy and platform technology. Then it needs an agent mechanism dealing with service security to package the specific realization of platform security from the logic, so that the security SOAP information of heterogeneous platform can be consistently understood and treatment.

Security processing mechanisms of Web services in heterogeneous platform provide security policy configuration and security implementation method of SOAP message [4]. Security service agents use WS-Security and other specifications to achieve the following three aspects of security requirements of SOAP message [10,11]:

• Message integrity

WS-Security takes XML signature to do digital signature for SOAP message to ensure that SOAP message passes through intermediate nodes without being tampered.

• Message confidentiality

WS-Security uses XML Encryption to encrypt the SOAP message, so that the message sender can ensure that the contents of SOAP message can be achieved by the intended recipient uniquely. In this way, even if SOAP messages are listened, listeners can not extract confiden-

tial information from the messages.

• Message authenticity

WS-Security introduces the concept of security tokens, which can represent the identity of the message sender. Combined with digital signatures, the message recipient can confirm the legitimacy and authenticity of the SOAP message sender.

3. Security Model for Heterogeneous Web Services SIMSA

Security framework and configuration strategies for heterogeneous platforms are quite different. Therefore, in order to achieve the security interaction of Web service in heterogeneous platforms, a third-party certification agency must be added. It can complete the relevant certification according to the request of the client. After the verification, client could send a request to call the Web service. To ensure the safety of service call process, both the client and Web server set the security service agent module to conduct safe handling to SOAP messages in the service interaction, including the signature and encryption of the SOAP message. The authentication module of client user is added to Web server, and only after the verification can client call the Web service. In this way, the security interactions of Web services in heterogeneous platforms can be achieved.

Combined with WS-Security specification, a security model of Web services in heterogeneous platform named SIMSA is constructed in this paper (shown in **Figure 1**). SIMSA model is mainly based on the extension of SOAP header including signature, encryption and authentication. The various components and functions of the security model are described as follows.

3.1. SIMSA Model Composition

• UDDI Server

Its main function is to store service descriptions by category. It can be a private registry, such as Capeconnect's UDDI Registry server, or it can also be a public registry, such as IBM Corporation and Microsoft's UDDI registry.

• Third-Party Certification Agency

It is used to verify the client's identity information, and only the users who pass through the authentication can send service requests to the Web server.

• WSDL Builder

It is used to describe how to use SOAP to invoke the Web service, and its function is to generate the corresponding WSDL document.

• Security Service Agent

It is the core module of the model. It is responsible for

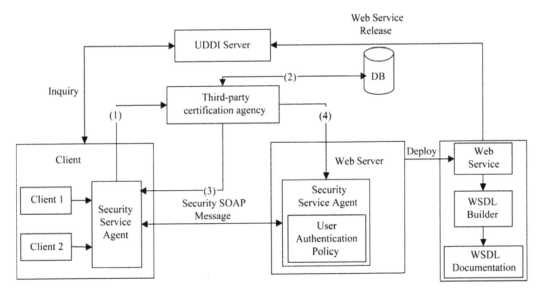

Figure 1. SIMSA Model.

the security of Web service during transmission and achieves the security requirements of the model includeing signature and encryption of the SOAP message.

- User Authentication Policy

It is also the core module of the model. It is responseble for the request verification of client's identity, and only authenticated users can call the appropriate Web service.

3.2. Third-Party Certification Agency of SIMSA Model

In order to provide reliable authentication information for the Web server, SIMSA adds a third-party certification agency. Certification agency will compare the requestor's information such as usernames, passwords and permissions and other information with that stored in the certification database (DB in **Figure 1**). It can provide users with the information needed to verify to invoke Web services. This information is encapsulated in an encrypted message, and this message will be sent to the Web server with the user's SOAP message, waiting for the server's validation. In order to formally describe the process of third-party certification agency, **Table 1** defines the parameters and function description.

The formal description of certification process in third-party certification agency is shown as follows (the following numbers correspond to that in SIMSA):

1) Client's security service agent sends user information to the third-party certification agency:

$$CSP \rightarrow AC : SOAP(IDc, PWDc, IDs) \qquad (1)$$

2) Third-party certification agency gets the user information (including user name, password, etc.) and

Table 1. Parameter description of certification.

Abbreviation	Content
AC	Third-party certification agency
CSP	Client's security service agent
SSP	Web server's security service agent
Message	The encrypted message that third-party certification agency return to the client's security service agent
Key	The encryption key that third-party certification agency uses to encrypt the Message
IDc	Client ID
IDs	Web server ID
PWDc	Client password
SOAP(Head, Body)	SOAP message
COMPARE( )	Certification agency compares requestor's information with that in the database

compares them with that in the database:

$$AC : COMPARE(IDc, PWDc) \qquad (2)$$

3) After the comparison, if properly the third-party certification agency will return a message encrypted with the *Key*, and otherwise it will reject the user's authenticcation request.

$$AC \rightarrow CSP : SOAP(Message) \qquad (3)$$

4) The third-party certification agency sends the *Key* used to encrypt the *Message* to the Web server:

$$AC \rightarrow SSP : SOAP(Key) \qquad (4)$$

3.3. Web Server's User Authentication of SIMSA Model

When the client's security service agent receives the encrypted Message that the third-party certification agency returns, the client can use the Message to invoke the Web service in the server. The SOAP message that client's security service agent sends to the Web server's security service agent includes the client ID and Message, and its formal description is:

$$CSP \rightarrow SSP : SOAP\big(Head\big(IDc, Message\big), Body\big) \quad (5)$$

When the SOAP message including the client ID and the Message reaches the Web server's security service agent, the security service agent must verify the SOAP message whether the client has the permission to call the Web service. In the process it will verify whether the ID included in the Message is the same as the client claims, if they are the same client could invoke the Web service. A user authentication policy is designed in the server's security service agent for the authentication of the client ID. The user authentication policy is shown in **Figure 2**.

The process of Web server's user authentication is:

1) Extract the *Key* used to encrypt *Message* from the SOAP message that third-party certification agency sends.

2) Extract the client ID and *Message* from the SOAP message that client sends.

3) Use the *Key* to decrypt the *Message* and extract the client ID that the *Message* contains.

4) Verify whether the ID that client claims is the same as that in the *Message*, if they are the same, the client will be allowed to call the Web service, otherwise authentication will fail.

3.4. Security Service Agent of SIMSA Model

After the user's request passes through the identity validation in the Web server, a connection is established between the Web server and client, and customers can call the Web service. In order to ensure the security of Web services exchanged between heterogeneous platforms, the SOAP messages transmitted between the server and client must be handled safely. The security service agent module of SIMSA implements these security requirements, and it achieves security interaction of end to end in message-level mainly through the security extension of SOAP message. This module is to realize the signature and encryption of SOAP message. **Figure 3** shows the security service agent module of SIMSA.

To formally descript the security interaction process of SOAP messages between heterogeneous platforms, **Table 2** defines the relevant parameters and their functions.

The simplest form of security interaction of SOAP message is that a signed and encrypted Web service request M1 is sent to the server security service agent from the client security service agent and corresponding to that the server security service agent will return a response message M2 which has been handled safely to the client security service agent. The security interaction pro-

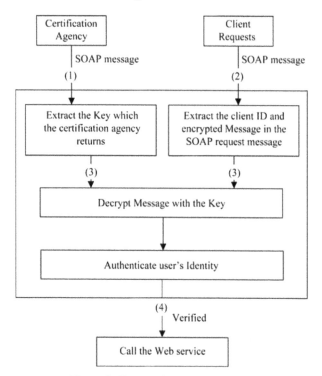

Figure 2. User Authentication Policy.

Table 2. Parameter description of security interaction in heterogeneous platform.

Abbreviation	Content
S,C	Web server and client built on different platforms
Cc	Client certificate
Cs	Server certificate
Pu(cert)	Public key of cert
Pr(cert)	Private key of cert
Mes	SOAP Message
S(Pr(cert), Mes)	Use the private key of cert to sign the Mes
Dm	The digital signature of Mes
VS(Mes, Pu(cert), Dm)	Use the public key of cert to validate the digital signature of Mes
E(Pu(cert), Mes)	Use the public key of cert to encrypt the Mes
DE(Pr(cert), Mes)	Use the private key of cert to decrypt the Mes

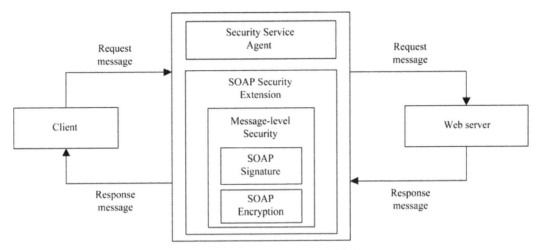

Figure 3. Security Service Agent Module.

cess of SOAP message can be formally described as:

1) Client request: encrypt and sign the request message.

$$C \rightarrow S : E\big(Pu(Cs), M_1\big), S\big(Pr(Cc), M_1\big) \qquad (6)$$

2) Server: verify the signature and decrypt the request message.

$$S : VS\big(M_1, Pu(Cc), Dm_1\big), DE\big(Pr(Cs), M_1\big) \qquad (7)$$

3) Server response: encrypt and sign the response message.

$$S \rightarrow C : E\big(Pu(Cc), M_2\big), S\big(Pr(Cs), M_2\big) \qquad (8)$$

4) Client: verify the signature and decrypt the response message.

$$C : VS\big(M_2, Pu(Cs), Dm_2\big), DE\big(Pr(Cc), M_2\big) \qquad (9)$$

4. Security Interactive Example

The user authentication module and security service agent module of the SIMSA are realized in this paper. They implement the user authentication in heterogeneous platforms and security extension of SOAP message during the process of Web service interaction.

4.1. User Authentication Implementation

The client sends the request SOAP message to the third-party certification agency. The message's format is shown in **Figure 4**, in which <authentication> shows the information required certification agency to verify; <clientID> specifies the client ID; <password> specifies client password and <serverID> specifies server ID.

The third-party certification agency queries the database to verify the client request SOAP message and after that it returns an encrypted SOAP message including the client ID and the encrypted *Message* to the client. The message's format is shown in **Figure 5**, in which <Message> contains the encrypted information.

The third-party certification agency sends the encryption key which is used to encrypt the *Message* to the Web server. The encryption key can be used to decrypt the *Message* in the user authentication security strategy when the client calls the Web service. The SOAP message's format is shown in **Figure 6**.

```
<soapenv:Header xmlns:wsa="http://www.w3.org/2005/
    08addressing">
    <authentication>
        <clientID>admin</clientID>
        <password>admin123</password>
        <serverID>server</serverID>
    </ authentication>
</soapenv:Header>
```

Figure 4. Client Request SOAP Message.

```
<soapenv:Header xmlns:wsa="http://www.w3.org/2005/
    08addressing">
    <ToClient>
        <clientID>admin</clientID>
        <Message>encrypted message...</Message>
    </ ToClient>
</soapenv:Header>
```

Figure 5. SOAP message that certification agency returned to the client.

```
<soapenv:Header xmlns:wsa="http://www.w3.org/2005/
    08addressing">
    <ToServer>
        <key>Key</key>
    </ ToServer>
</soapenv:Header>
```

Figure 6. SOAP message that certification agency returned to the server.

```
<?xml version='1.0' encoding='utf-8'?>
<soapenv:Envelopexmlns:soapenv="http://www.w3.org/2003/
05/soap-envelope">
<soaenv:Header xmlns:wsa="http://www.w3.org/2005/
08/addressing">
  <wsse:Security xmlns:wsse="http://docs.oasis-open.org
    /wss/2004/01/oasis-200401-wss-wssecurity-secext-1.0.xsd
    " soapenv:mustUnderstand="true">
  <ds:Signature>
    <ds:SignedInfo>
      <ds:CanonicalizationMethod Algorithm="http://
        www.w3.org/2001/10/xml-exc-c14n#" />
      <ds:SignatureMethod Algorithm="http://www.w3.org
        /2000/09/xmldsig#rsa-sha1" />
      <ds:Reference URI="#id-8303462">
        <ds:Transforms>
          <ds:Transform Algorithm="http://www.w3.org
            /2001/10/xml-exc-c14n#" />
        </ds:Transforms>
        <ds:DigestMethod Algorithm="http://www.w3.org
          /2000/09/xmldsig#sha1" />
        <ds:DigestValue>q0ut1qK9WER7MXSuX
        4vV4wYS3oQ=</ds:DigestValue>
      </ds:Reference>
    </ds:SignedInfo>
    <ds:SignatureValue>
      SKPKP5ICsX/lcZzCdYxk0cAsQV6Gbyau0bBJvpq
      NKL/kSyh9KvUMJIJ7i96gT46tCdexHne+LzE2CO
      1xUkBLDv8+zX049Klk++BdqiuZLF6PB/X79dqyd
      RlWYOMYuN2nMvP5Qdo3MzYOvvi2K7w3gcbiy
      euDwmWglkeR8iCqHvk=
    </ds:SignatureValue>
    <ds:KeyInfo Id="KeyId-11463270">
      <wsse:SecurityTokenReference xmlns:wsu="http://
      docs.oasis-open.org/wss/2004/01/oasis-200401-wss-
      wssecurity-utility-1.0.xsd" wsu:Id="STRId-367156">
      <ds:X509Data>
        <ds:X509IssuerSerial>
          <ds:X509IssuerName>CN=Sample Client,OU=
            Rampart,O=Apache,L=Colombo,ST=Western,
            C=LK</ds:X509IssuerName>
          <ds:X509SerialNumber>1187603652
          </ds:X509SerialNumber>
        </ds:X509IssuerSerial>
      </ds:X509Data>
      </wsse:SecurityTokenReference>
    </ds:KeyInfo>
  </ds:Signature>
  </wsse:Security>
  <wsa:To>http://10.6.233.177:8080/axis2/services/Signiture.
    signitureHttpSoap12Endpoint/</wsa:To>
    <wsa:MessageID>urn:uuid:22EC2A05BDC41A98491289
    284864538</wsa:MessageID>
  <wsa:Action>urn:echo</wsa:Action>
</soapenv:Header>
<soapenv:Body>
  <xenc:EncryptedData>
  ......
  </xenc:EncryptedData>
</soapenv:Body>
</soapenv:Envelope>
```

Figure 7. Security SOAP Message.

4.2. SOAP Message Signed and Encrypted by Security Service Agent

The SOAP message output from the server security ser-

vice agent is signed and encrypted. The signed part of the message is shown in **Figure 7**. <ds:Signature> mainly consists of three parts: <ds:SignedInfo>, <ds:Signature Value> and <ds:KeyInfo>. <ds:SignedInfo> also contains three parts including <ds:SignatureMethod>, <ds:Digest Method> and <ds:DigestValue>. <ds:SignatureMethod> indicates the algorithm that signature used; <ds:Digest Method> indicates the algorithm need to be used to generate the abstract data; <ds:DigestValue> specifies the abstract data. <ds: SignatureValue > points out the signature value. <ds:KeyInfo> shows the information of the certificate which signature uses, including the data of the X.509 certificate and the information of the certificate publisher. <soapenv:Body> contains only one element named <xenc:EncryptedData> which indicates the encrypted information. As the encrypted information is too large, the part of the information is omitted.

From **Figure 7** it can be seen that the SOAP message has been successfully signed and encrypted which ensures the security of SOAP messages transmitted between different platforms.

5. Conclusions

SOA promotes the application and integration of information technology, but the security of application and integration is much more complex. In connection with SOA application and integration practice, the security issues of Web service in the SOA architecture have been proposed. In order to solve these issues, a security interactive model of heterogeneous platform named SIMSA is designed. This model realizes security requirements during the process of calling Web services in heterogeneous platform. By making client authentication, signing and encrypting SOAP message in the process of Web service interaction in heterogeneous platform, it achieves the security interaction of Web service in heterogeneous platform, which greatly enhances Web service's security features.

6. References

[1]　F. Satoh, *et al.*, "Adding Authentication to Model Driven Security," *IEEE International Conference on Web Services* (*ICWS*), Chicago, 2006, pp. 585-594. doi:10.1109/ICWS.2006.25

[2]　K. Bhargavan, C. Fournet, *et al.*, "An Advisor for Web Services Security Policies," *Proceedings of the* 2005 *workshop on Secure web services*, New York, 2005, pp. 1-9. doi:10.1145/1103022.1103024

[3]　S. Weber, P. Austel and M. McIntosh, "A Framework for Multi-Platform SOA Security Analyses," *IEEE International Conference on Web Service*, Salt Lake City, 2007, pp. 102-109.

[4]　J. Viega, "Why Applying Standards to Web Services is

not Enough," *IEEE Security and Privacy*, Vol. 4, No. 4, 2006, pp. 25-31. doi:10.1109/MSP.2006.110

[5] Z. P. Liu, D. D. Zhou, L. Y. Xue, X. M. Chang and X. J. Song, "A Security Model of Web Service Based on SOAP," *Journal of Wuhan University* in Chinese, Vol. 52, No. 5, 2006, pp. 570-573.

[6] L. Y. Tang and S. H. Qing, "Administration of Multiple Roles in the Hybrid RBAC-DTE Policy," *Chinese Journal of Computers*, in Chinese, Vol. 29, No. 8, 2006, pp. 1419-1425.

[7] X. M. Wang and Z. T Zhao, "Role-Based Access Control Model of Temporal Object," *Acta Electronica Sinica*, in Chinese, Vol. 33, No. 9, 2005, pp. 1634-1638.

[8] W. F. Zheng, T. Xu and Q. F Gu, "Design and Implementation of Core Service in Civil Aviation Integrated Information Platform," *Computer Engineering*, In Chinese, Vol. 34, No. 21, 2008, pp. 267-269.

[9] R. Bunge, S. Chung, B. Endicott-Popovsky and D. McLane, "An Operational Framework for Service Oriented Architecture Network Security," *Proceedings of the 41st Hawaii International Conference on System Sciences*, Waikoloa, 2008, pp. 312-320.

[10] N. Bieberstein, S. Bose, M. Fiammante, K. Jones, R. Shah and Z. Ning, "Service-Oriented Architecture Guide," in Chinese, Posts & Telecom Press, Beijing, 2008, pp. 160-166.

[11] Z. P. Liu, X. M. Chang, D. D. Zhou and X. J. Song, "A Safe ID Authentication Policy in Web Service," *Journal of Computer Research and Development*, in Chinese, Vol. 43, 2006, pp. 551-555.

7

Proposed Framework for Security Risk Assessment

Zakaria I. Saleh, Heba Refai, Ahmad Mashhour
Faculty of Computer Science and Information Systems, Yarmouk University, Jordan

Abstract

Security risk assessment framework provides comprehensive structure for security risk analysis that would help uncover systems' threats and vulnerabilities. While security risk assessment is an important step in the security risk management process, this paper will focus only on the security risk assessment framework. Viewing issues that exist in a current framework, we have developed a new framework for security risk and vulnerabilities assessment by adding new components to the processes of the existing framework. The proposed framework will further enhance the outcome of the risk assessment, and improve the effectiveness of the current framework. To demonstrate the efficiency the proposed framework, a network security simulation as well as filed tests of an existing network where conducted.

Keywords: Security Risk, Vulnerabilities, Framework, Simulation

1. Introduction

The substantial usage of information and communication devices, and the increasing interconnectivity among systems and organizations, is exposing organizations for security risk and vulnerabilities, including intentional threat that would be associated to sabotage and vandalism. Therefore, there is a growing interest in applying risk analysis and risk management to eliminate security problems and protect networks.

Security Risk management is an ongoing process of identifying these risks and implementing planes to address them and risk assessment is the part of the ongoing risk management process that assigns relative priorities for mitigation plans and implementation [1]. Thus, a risk assessment framework is needed with an approach for categorizing and sharing information about the security risks of the information technology infrastructure. Furthermore, to establish useful framework for risk analysis we have to clearly identify the risks, it is not sufficient to refer to probabilities and expected values [2]. This paper will evaluate different frameworks that are being in use and then will develop an enhanced framework that will improve the outcome of the existing security risk assessment frameworks.

1.1. Overview of Vulnerabilities and Security Framework

System Vulnerabilities are defined as fault or weakness that reduces and limits system ability [3]. Assessing security risk is the initial step to evaluate and identify risks and consequences associated with vulnerabilities and provide basis for management to establish cost effective security program. The vulnerability analysis is a part of risk assessment process that focuses on methods for identifying vulnerabilities and implementing measures to mitigate the vulnerabilities, by implementing suitable protection and safeguard to maintain acceptable network security level and protect information. Many types of network attacks require a high degree of technical expertise and some may require significant financial resources to be carried successfully; however some attacks may be accomplished with few resources and little expertise.

Johnston (2004) defined a framework as structure upon or into which contents can be pit and further relates it to thoughts that are directed for a purpose. A security framework provides holistic structure for risk analysis covering both terminology on risk and vulnerabilities concepts and methodology for risk and vulnerabilities analysis for safety and security [2]. The natural of risks however, could include the possibility of threat event (e.g. flood, earthquake, and fire) that have impact on the organization's information asset as well as its physical structures [4]. In addition, the nature of information networks allows for an attack to be launched from anywhere in the world, making identifying the origins of an attack a major difficulty, if the attack is detected to start with [5].

1.2. Research Objectives

Secured networks and information systems assist organization in sharing its business in trustworthy way, helping organization to build strong relationship with customer, supplier and other business partner. Creating trust relationships through the security of information and by means of effective security controls will improve the cash flow and profitability of organization [6,7]. In addition, security risk assessment provides complete view on existing security risk and necessary security safeguard, and provides approach to security management with alternative solution for decision-making and basis for future change made in security measure [8]. Therefore, a proper and efficient security risk assessment will result in improved outcome. To prove the effectiveness of this framework I will use network security emulation to answer the following research questions, which include:

1) How effective is the proposed framework for security risk assessment?

2) Does criteria process have an impact on the security risk assessment?

3) Does the proposed security risk assessment have an impact on the security strategy development process?

1.3. Security Risk Assessment Overview

Security risk assessment is being defined as the process of evaluating security risks that is conducted identifies the required security measures [9]. The assessment is conducted at the very early stages of the system development as well as when there is change to information asset or its environment. The process includes the evaluations and analysis of all asset and processes related to the system to identifying the threat and vulnerabilities that could affect confidentiality, integrity or availability of the system, and setting required control to manage the risk [1]. Risk assessment is an essential element of risk management and to be effective, risk assessment must be an ongoing process. Depending on the purpose and the scope of security risk assessment it can be categorized into three types: (1) high level assessment that can be applied for system at design phase to identify security risks before implementation; (2) comprehensive assessment that can be used to evaluate the security risk of particular system in department to provide recommendation for improvement; (3) pre-production assessment conducted on new information system before it's rolled out or after there is major functional change [10].

1.4. Security Risk Assessment Frameworks

1) The iterative process of IT security management, which starts with assessing security risk and based on the assessment results, an appropriate security protection and safeguards would be implemented to maintain a secure protection framework as illustrated in **Figure 1** [1].

2) The national infrastructure protection plan risk management framework (NNIP-RM) is structured to promote continuous improvement to enhance critical infrastructure protection and key resource protection as shown in **Figure 2** [4].

3) Framework for information security culture, provides organizations with understanding of how to establish an information security culture to minimize risks posed by employee behavior regarding the use of information assets (**Figure 3**), where the interaction between information security components such as a policy and the behavior of employees would have an impact on the resulting information security culture [11].

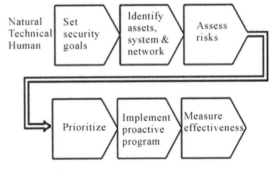

Figure 1. Security risk management process.

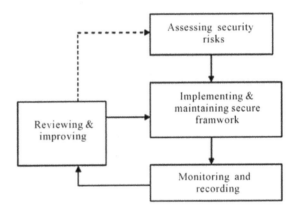

Figure 2. NIPP- RM framework.

Figure 3. Information security culture framework.

2. Research Model

Security risk and vulnerabilities assessment has many benefits and challenges associated with it. The security risk assessment should provide complete view of the existing security risk and help provide alternative solution and changes to the security measures and controls. In light of that, this research believes that none of the discussed frameworks is fully providing the desired outcome. Therefore, we propose that an enhancement is needed, which will improve the security risk assessment process, and that enhancement can be made to Ogesio [1] security risk management approach (see **Figure 1**). The approach should include two more components which will be added and placed as process 2 (Identify infrastructure vulnerabilities) and process 3 (Analyze Risks & Vulnerabilities) to the existing security risk assessment process as being illustrated in **Figure 4**.

Network infrastructure vulnerabilities are the core of all technical security issues in any information systems. The extreme importance of infrastructures to modern network systems shall be recognized. These infrastructures are complex and interdependent; therefore protecting the infrastructures is an enormous challenge. Recognizing that an organization cannot afford the costs associated with absolute protection, it is necessary to identify and prioritize the vulnerabilities in these infrastructures. These vulnerabilities can affect everything running on the network. The information infrastructure now a day is still regarded as an easy and vulnerable entry point. But discovering the threat and the likely nature of an attack — remains difficult [5]. Therefore, infrastructure vulnerabilities and infra structure evolution requires effective crisis management and preventive, strategic planning, to try and eliminate them whenever possible. This requires an evaluation of the information infrastructure, where the main operational components of the information technology infrastructure are examined for weaknesses and technology vulnerabilities. Any basic risk assessment would identify and quantify this vulnerability.

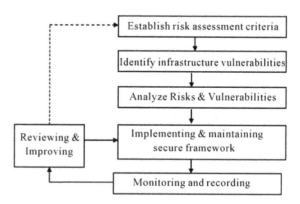

Figure 4. Proposed framework for security risk and vulnerabilities assessment.

However, establishing risk assessment criteria and then implementing & maintaining secure framework before Identify infrastructure vulnerabilities and analyze risks & vulnerabilities will not be as efficient as it would be desired.

Infrastructures vulnerabilities might arise from the common links where failures might propagate through the different systems. Thus, intrusion and disruption in one subsystem might provoke unexpected threats to other subsystem. There are four types Infrastructure threat (see **Table 1**), where attacks on the systems in all four types involve the malicious use of the information infrastructure either as a target or as a tool [12].

3. Research Method

The proposed framework effectiveness will be tested using SpiceWorks network management software version 4.7 (see **Figure 5**). SpiceWorks is a complete network management software, helpdesk, and PC inventory tools designed to manage networks in small & medium businesses. SpiceWorks gets a full and accurate scan of all network devices including Windows, Mac, and Linux machines and keep track of the network assets, run a helpdesk, monitor activity, receive reports and trouble-

Table 1. Infrastructure threat matrix [12].

Means/Tool		Target	
		Physical	Cyber
		1)	2)
	Physical	- Severing a telecom cable with a backhoe - Smashing a server with a hammer - Bombing the electric grid	- Use of electromagnetic pulse and radio-frequency weapons to destabilize electronic components
		3)	4)
	Cyber	- Hacking into a SCADA system that controls municipal sewage - "Spoofing" an air traffic control system to bring down a plane	- Hacking into a critical government network - Trojan horse in public switched network

Figure 5. Spiceworks 4.7 screenshot.

shoot network problems [13]. The software will be used to test the network of a university (for security and privacy reasons, the name of the university will remain anonymous). Using SpiceWorks, we will implement Ogesio framework process [1] and the proposed framework, test a network, and then compare the findings.

4. Data Collection and Analysis

SpiceWorks network management software was installed and to test the network and to identify infrastructure vulnerabilities and analyze risks if any found (process 2 & 3). Evaluating the major events that were taking place in the network systems by applications and other devices, the evaluation revealed a number of audit failure, warnings and errors as displayed in **Figure 6.**

The ID of the system where the audit failures occur is displayed in **Table 2** along with the source of failure, event count, and the location and the time/date in which the failures occur.

The warnings are listed in **Table 3**, along with the ID of the applications that may failure or error occur on it, source of these expected errors, the event count, the systems involved and the time/date of warning.

The security issues are listed in **Table 4**, along with the ID of the systems where the errors occur, source of errors, event count, the systems involved, and the time/date that the errors occur. In addition, **Table 4** displays

the type of security issues and the device (name or address) where the issue is identified.

Analyzing **Tables 2**, **3** and **4**, we can specify the likelihood of the events to occur by looking at the count

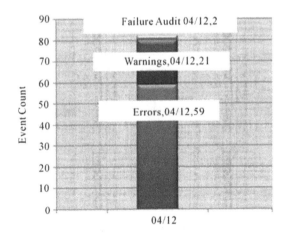

Figure 6. The major events in the network.

Table 2. Audit failure report.

ID	Sources	Count	Computers	4/12/2010
4001	SWService	2	Srvs	18:07:32

Table 3. Warnings report.

ID	Sources	Count	Computers	4/12/2010
8032	BROWSER	3	Srvs	20:59:43
8021	BROWSER	3	Srvs	20:57:19
7000	Service Control Manager	2	Srvs	20:55:22
20	Print	1	Srvs	20:12:55
7034	Service Control Manager	4	Srvs	20:08:48
7031	Service Control Manager	3	Srvs	20:03:35
7001	Service Control Manager	12	Srvs	19:51:21
7022	Service Control Manager	11	Srvs	19:51:21
7032	Service Control Manager	1	Srvs	19:15:09

Table 4. Security issues report.

ID	Sources	Count	Computers	4/12/2010
1	WinVNC4	5	Srvs	21:15:47
107	Report Server Windows Service	2	Srvs	20:54:55
18456	MSSQLSERVER	2	Srvs	20:54:53
3	SQL Browser	4	Srvs	20:54:00
1001	MS Installer	3	Srvs	20:26:15
0	System Service Model Install 3.0.0.0	10	Srvs	20:17:05
0	Net Runtime	14	Srvs	20:08:47

column that specifies how many time this event was repeated and reported. For example, we can conclude that most of the errors events have high likelihood of occurrence, and some of the warning event has high likelihood and some warnings have medium likelihood of occurrence, but the audit failure has low likelihood of occurrence because the event count is only 2.

Errors were also reported during the system test (see **Table 5**). In light of that, we need to assess the impact of the errors and warnings on the critical data assets to develop the appropriate method to manage the risks and to protect data assets. For example, an effective firewall provides the software or hardware necessary to validate and authenticate traffic and user against a security policy or set of rules to allow them to pass the private or trusted side of network. Firewall problems and issues could mean that external unauthorized people can access the private network and disclose sensitive and critical data asset.

Table 5. Reported errors type.

Device Name	Error
172.19.150.127	Permission or Firewall Problem
okhreis-pc	Permission or Firewall Problem
172.19.150.74	Permission or Firewall Problem
yu-9c2f5e2e9e4b	Permission or Firewall Problem
172.19.150.58	Permission or Firewall Problem
dr-y-aaage	Permission or Firewall Problem
drsalah	Permission or Firewall Problem

5. Conclusions

Based on the results and the findings, we conclude that the framework process is providing the desired results, where each process depends on the result of the previous one. For example, during the tests, we have identified warnings and security issues. Unless the two proposed components are added to the existing security risk assessment process as illustrated in **Figure 4** (process 2: Identify infrastructure vulnerabilities) and (process 3: Analyze Risks & Vulnerabilities) those warnings may become real issues and introduce new vulnerabilities soon or later. The only way to confirm that they will (or will not), is by identifying the vulnerabilities that each warning may have, and then analyzing the risk associated with it. Therefore, the risk analysis process depends on the result of the infrastructure vulnerabilities identification, where in this process the vulnerabilities are identified, and then the risk is analyzed based on its impact and probability of occurrence. The monitoring process is based on the result of the established risk assessment criteria, where reports are produced to indicate all alerts or warning of all possible threats. The monitoring is continuously repeated to insure the development of effective security system, and an appropriate action is taken to handle the risks associated with those threats, which should result in improving the security system. In addition, the risk assessment criteria should be based on the result of the reporting process. In other words, manager will use the report that summarize the status and performance of the security in the organization, and based on that, management will update the security system (and policy) to eliminate security weakness, and thus enhance the security system.

In light of the findings, we can conclude that the framework is effective for security risk assessment because the processes are proven to be highly interacted with each other. We also conclude that the risk assessment criteria process has appositive impact on security risk assessment, as the test results have shown in the different stages of the process. In addition, the security risk assessment process has a positive impact on the security strategic development, through continuous development of the security system to improve the security system. The security plan and strategies may specify the priorities and area of concerns as well as the degree of risk that management can accept, however, without applying the added process the system may not be as effective, as the results indicate.

6. References

[1] The Office of the Government Chief Information Officer, "Security Risk Assessment and Audit Guidelines", 2009. http://www.ogcio.gov.hk/eng/prodev/download/g51_pub

[2] T. Even, "A Unified Framework For Risk and Vulnerability Analysis Covering Both Safety and Security", *Reliability Engineering and System Safety,* Vol. 92, No. 6, 2007, pp. 745-754.

[3] G. Stoneburner, A. Goguen, A. Feringa, "Risk Management Guide for Information Technology Systems", 2002. http://csrc.nist.gov/publications/nistpubs/800-30/sp800-30f

[4] Homeland Security, "National Infrastructure Protection Plane Risk Management Framework", (2009). http://www.dhs.gov/xlibrary/assets/NIPP_RiskMgmt

[5] M. D. Cavelty, "Critical Information Infrastructure: Vulnerabilities, Threats and Responses" *Disarmament Forum ICTs and International Security*, No. 3, 2007, pp. 15-22.

[6] R. Olsson, "In Search of Opportunity Management: Is the Risk Management Process Enough?" *International Journal of Project Management*, Vol. 25, No. 8, November 2007, pp. 745-752.

[7] S. Posthumus, R. Solms, "A Framework for the Governance of Information Security", *Computer and Security*, Vol. 23, No. 8, December 2004, pp. 638-646.

[8] Akelainc, "What Risk and Vulnerability Assessment", 2009. http://www.akelainc.com/pdf_files/What%20is%20risk%20and%20vulnerability%20assessment.pdf

[9] Insight Networking, "Risk and Vulnerabilities Assessment", 2009. https://images01.insight.com/media/pdf/IN_RVA_Datasheet

[10] S. Bajpai, A. Sachdeva, J. Gupta, "Security Risk Assessment: Applying the Concept of Fuzzy Logic", *Journal of Hazardous Materials*, Vol. 173, No. 1-3, January 2010, pp.258-264.

[11] A. Veiga, J. Eloff, "A Framework and Assessment for Information Security Culture", *Computer and Security*, Vol. 29, No. 2, March 2010, pp. 196-207.

[12] Dunn Myriam, "A Comparative Analysis of Cyber security Initiatives Worldwide", *WSIS Thematic Meeting on Cybersecurity*, Geneva, 28 June-1 July 2005.

[13] SpiceWorks Inc., "SpiceWorks, IT Is Everything", April 14, 2010.

8

Proactive Security Mechanism and Design for Firewall

Saleem-Ullah Lar[1,3], Xiaofeng Liao[2], Aqeel ur Rehman[1], Qinglu Ma[1]
[1]*Department of Computer Science, Chongqing University, Chongqing, China*
[2]*Faculty of Computer Science, Senior Member IEEE, Chongqing University, Chongqing, China*
[3]*Department of Computer Science and IT, The Islamia University Bahawalpur, Pakistan*

Abstract

In this paper we have present the architecture and module for internet firewall. The central component is fuzzy controller while properties of packets are fuzzified as inputs. On the basis of proposed fuzzy security algorithm, we have figured out security level of each packet and adjust according to packets dynamic states. Internet firewall can respond to these dynamics and take respective actions accordingly. Therefore, proactive firewall solves the conflict between speed and security by providing high performance and high security. Simulation shows that if the response value is in between 0.7 and 1 it belongs to high security.

Keywords: Firewall Security, Security Evaluation, Network Security

1. Introduction

The expansion of the Internet and e-Commerce has made organizations more vulnerable to electronic threats than ever before. With the increasing quantity and sophistication of attacks on IT assets, companies have been suffering from breach of data, loss of customer confidence and job productivity degradation, all of which eventually lead to the loss of revenue. According to the 2004 CSI/FBI Computer Crime and Security survey [1], organizations that acknowledged financial loss due to the attacks (269 of them) reported $141 million lost, and this number has only grown since. Moreover, as unskilled, unmanned attacks such as worms and viruses multiply the probability of attack approaches for every organization. The question therefore shifts from whether an attack will occur, to when an attack will occur. Thus, a sound IT security plan is more important than ever, and the protection provided by current and emerging Intrusion Prevention Systems (IPS) is becoming a critical component [2-5].

IPS utilizes IDS algorithms to monitor and drop or allow traffic based on expert analysis. These devices normally work at different areas in the network and proactively monitor any suspicious activity that could otherwise bypass the firewall. IPS "firewalls" can intelligently prevent malicious traffic from entering/exiting the firewall and then alert administrators in real time about any suspicious activity that may be occurring on the network [6]. A complete network IPS solution also has the capability to enforce traditional static firewall rules and administrator-defined whitelists and blacklists.

Though IPS devices are the most resource intensive, they are still relatively high-performing due to the latest processors, software, and hardware advancements. IPS may be distributed and hardware based [7-10]. Today two categories of IPS exist: Network-based Intrusion Prevention and Host-based Intrusion Prevention. Network IPS monitors from a network segment level, and can detect and prevent both internal and external attacks. Network IPS devices separate networks in much the same fashion as firewalls. Host IPS software runs directly on workstations and servers detects and prevents threats aimed at the local host. In both cases, attack recognition is usually accomplished via two primary methods of IDS: known-attack detection, and anomalous behavior detection.

This paper focuses on fuzzy mechanism with the help of Gaussian mechanism as a member function and center of gravity procedure which is an implementation of a fuzzy inputs and outputs respectively in the model. The rest of the paper is organized as follows: Section 2 presents the challenges faced by traditional security architectures. Section 3 describes proposed firewall architecture. Section 4 explains about proposed proactive fuzzy security mechanism. Finally, Section 5 presents simulation results and concludes the paper.

2. The Challenges for Traditional Security Architecture

In fact, it is still the Firewall that plays the key role in traditional security architecture, since it controls most of the incoming and outgoing traffic of an enterprise. Essentially the firewall is almost a must-have in each enterprise. To review the challenges for the traditional architecture, undoubtedly it is necessary to address on the limitation of traditional firewalls. The inability of current firewalls may include:

1) Limited ports & performance.

2) Complicated UI configuration and policy management.

3) Scalability limitation to correspond to organization growth.

4) Unreliable network security, due to "Single Point of Defense.

5) Insufficient capability to effectively manage emerging internet applications hidden in HTTP traffic.

6) Passive security mechanism to respond network threats including network worms, Trojans and cyber-attacks.

Facing the emerging malicious codes, network worms and hybrid attacks today, traditional firewall is no longer effectively to harden your enterprise network. Traditional firewalls usually inspect the incoming traffic cautiously, and it can base on the network policies to permit, deny or drop the traffic depending on the traffic trusty or illegal. But for the outgoing traffic, unfortunately the HTTP traffic is always permitted in the enterprise network, and the firewalls are lack of the management capability to inspect the evolving internet applications which now can hide themselves in the HTTP traffic and sneak out. Thus, the enterprises gate seems secure but in fact, the security cracks have been created.

3. Proposed Firewall Architecture

A true firewall is the hardware and software that intercepts the data between the Internet and your computer. All data traffic must pass through it, and the firewall allows only authorized data to pass into the corporate network. Firewalls are typically implemented using one of four primary architectures.

- Packet Filters
- Circuit-level Gateways
- Application Proxies
- Network Address Translation

3.1. Definition

Our definition covers the state of firewall technology as a distributed security architecture placed on the data transmission path between communication endpoints. Our definition of firewall technology states that communication traffic needs to enter or leave a network security domain to be of interest to firewall technology. **Figure 1** illustrates the possible combinations for point-to-point communication. For any traffic between sender a_i and receiver b_i the definition includes traffic that traverses the protected domain $D_A (\{a_i, b_i\} \notin D_A,\ i = 1)$ and traffic that traverses networks that are not part of D_A with $a_{i\varepsilon}D_A$ and $b_i\ D_A$ (outbound traffic; $i = 2$), $a_i\ 2 = D_A$ and $b_i\ 2\ D_A$ (inbound traffic $i = 3$), or both $a_i\ 2\ D_A$ and $b_i\ 2\ D_B$ (virtual private networking between D_A and D_B; $i = 4$). Communication traffic between a_i and b_i that neither enters nor leaves a network policy domain is not subject to firewall technology.

$$\begin{bmatrix} \text{Sender} & a_i \\ \text{Receiver} & b_i \end{bmatrix} i\varepsilon\{1,2,3,4\}$$

$$a_i \varepsilon D_A \left(\{a_i, b_i\} \notin D_A,\ i = 1 \right)$$

Fuzzy agent is the basic element in this architecture specific attack or a particular phase of an attack. It consists of three components; fuzzy Context, exponential moving average module and fuzzy inference engine shown in **Figure 2**. Fuzzy context represents the problem domain *i.e.* normal profile of network in reference to particular intrusion. Exponential moving average module adapts the fuzzy context according to current network conditions and traffic patterns, while fuzzy inference engine actually classifies an event using fuzzy knowledge base and real-time inputs. Fuzzy context is a key component of the fuzzy agent, which consists of rules and membership functions. Context generation and evolution module constructs optimized rules and membership functions for current network. Fuzzy rules can be expressed in terms of simple if-then statements with higher interpretability score. Let the fuzzy sets for fuzzy input variables are low, medium and high. The membership functions of each linguistic fuzzy set in terms of boundary parameters are describe by Equations (1)-(2). The boundary parameters are functions of evolved parameters as defined in Equation (5) and moving average

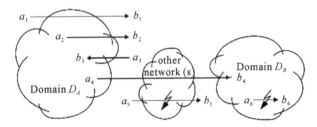

Figure 1. Communication traffic governed by firewall technology between senders and receivers.

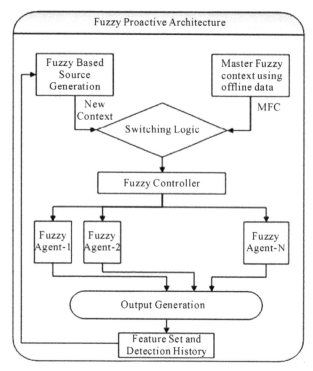

Figure 2. Architecture of a fuzzy typical approach.

modules output. Member-ship functions contract or expand linearly according to network history depending upon exponential moving average modules output. This helps in adjusting the attack threshold value at that particular interval while evolved parameters set the normal and not-normal class boundaries.

Fuzzy inference engine that is third component of fuzzy agent, classifies the real-time input as normal or malicious using fuzzy knowledge base. It basically accomplishes three functions (fuzzification, fuzzy inference, defuzzification) based on Mumdani principle [11]. In fuzzification, a crisp input *i.e.* a record from feature set is mapped to fuzzy sets to determine the membership degree. The inference engine evaluates applicable rules and their degree of matching to generate consequent rules. The defuzzification function aggregates the consequent rules and using centroid method, generates one crisp output, which determines the class of input record [11].

3.2. Controller

Proposed mechanism is employed in the controller which is the core module this firewall. The controller has the functionality to integrate with the arrival packets (inputs) applied rules, and fuzzy logic to measure the security level of arriving packets. Using these values controller has to do following main tasks to process the connections accordingly.

1) Filtration
2) Dynamic Monitoring

3.3. Dynamic Packet Filtering

Dynamic packet filtering is a firewall and routing capability that provides network packet filtering based not only on packet information in the current packet, but also on previous packets that have been sent. For example without dynamic packet filtering, a connection response may be allowed to go from the internet to the secure part of the network. Dynamic packet filtering would consider whether a connection was started from inside the secure part of the network and only allow a connection response from the internet if the packet appeared to be a response to the request.

Dynamic packet filtering filters packets based on:

1) Administrator defined rules governing allowed ports and IP addresses at the network and transport layers of the OSI network model.

2) Connection state which considers prior packets that have gone through the firewall.

3) Packet contents including the application layer contents

Static packet filtering only filters packets based on administrator defined rules governing allowed ports and IP addresses at the network and transport layers of the OSI network model as mentioned in item 1 above. Therefore dynamic packet filtering also called state-full inspection which provides additional capabilities including inspection of packet contents up to the application layer and consideration of the state of any connections.

Dynamic packet filtering provides a better level of security than static packet filtering since it takes a closer look at the contents of the packet and also considers previous connection states.

3.4. Network Address Translation

NAT is a very important aspect of firewall security. It conserves the number of public addresses used within an organization, and it allows for stricter control of access to resources on both sides of the firewall. Most modern firewalls are state full—that is, they are able to set up the connection between the internal workstation and the Internet resource. They can keep track of the details of the connection, like ports, packet order, and the IP addresses involved. This is called keeping track of the state of the connection. In this way, they are able to keep track of the session composed of communication between the workstation and the firewall, and the firewall with the Internet. When the session ends, the firewall discards all of the information about the connection. It is suggested to design network using RFC-1918 [12] that never advertised outside from the intranet. The mapping is dynamic so it is difficult to guess either two connections with the same IP actually come from the same or different hosts.

3.5. Security Rules and Policies

Allowing or denying services or connections between networks defined by security policies and rules.

4. Proactive Fuzzy Security Mechanism

Saniee Abadeh [13] presents combined fuzzy logic and genetic algorithm to evolve fuzzy rules, optimize membership functions to detect new anomalies. While our proposed proactive firewall security mechanism which is employed in the fuzzy controller is different and explained as follows.

4.1. Proactive Control

Since the state of packets in the networks is constantly varying, its security level is also changeable. Previous secure user may initiate malicious attack or disobey the security rules. So the fields of "attack times" are used to record the times of disobeying security rules. Accordingly, the source or destination security values will be adjusted to respond to its varying security state. When the source and destination security vary from 1 to 0, the overall security level of the connection smoothly vary accordingly. Therefore, the output can reflect the changes of packets status. Different methods and security policies are used for 1148 different kinds of connections and policies of control over them are adjusted according to their varying states. So, the firewall is fuzzily adaptive and proactive.

4.2. Source Generation

Figure 3 describe Input generation based on source and destination security values employed in fuzzy controller. Range of input is [0, 1] and value is directly proportional to security level. We have defined Gaussian member function for the source security, which is represented as

$$\mu_S\left(s, c, \sigma\right) = e^{\frac{(s-c)^2}{2\sigma^2}} \quad 0 \leq S \leq 1 \tag{1}$$

μ_{Sl}, μ_{Sm} and μ_h denoted as Low, Medium, and High security levels for the source member function respectively depending on parameters σ and c.

$$\mu_D\left(D, c, \sigma\right) = e^{\frac{(D-c)^2}{2\sigma^2}} \quad 0 \leq D \leq 1 \tag{2}$$

μ_{Dl}, μ_{Dm} and μ_{Dh} denoted as Low, Medium, and High security levels for the destination member function respectively.

4.3. Applied Rules and Regulations

For our system we have defined the rules as shown in the **Figure 3**, while fuzzy applied relations for the applied rules are as follows.

    Rule **1** IF source = low and destination = low THEN security = low

    Rule **2** IF source = low and destination = medium THEN security = low

    Rule **n** IF source = high or destination = high THEN security = high

Mathematically we can define applied relations as,

For Rule 1: $\mu_{R1} = \mu_{S1} \cap \mu_{D1} \cap \mu_{Z1}$

For Rule n: $\mu_{Rn} = \mu_{Sn} \cap \mu_{Dn} \cap \mu_{Zn}$

So we can write that,

$$\mu_R = \mu_{R1} \cap \mu_{R2} \cap \mu_{Rn} \tag{3}$$

Therefore,

$$Z = \left(S * D\right) \cdot R \tag{4}$$

and

$$\mu\left(z\right) = \bigcup\left[\mu_S \cap \mu_D \cap \mu_R\right] \tag{5}$$

We defined above rules just to cope up with the issue of input space up to maximum possible effort. Since process mostly requires non-fuzzy values, so defuzzification process is necessary to implement this is described in next section. For low priority based trusted packets both application level and dynamic packet monitor are used providing high security, while filtration takes place for highly trusted packets. It is fuzzily adaptive and proactive in a sense that its characteristics and packet status are fuzzified and its output reflects the packet dynamic status (**Figure 4**).

4.4. Destination Generation

We have defined member function for destination output which is obtained from Equation (5) as,

$$Z_0 = \frac{\int_z z\mu\left(z\right)\mathrm{d}z}{\int_z \mu\left(z\right)\mathrm{d}z}$$

The above equation used is based on center of gravity method.

Figure 5 shows the characteristics and security level designed for output generation based on the rules and relations described earlier.

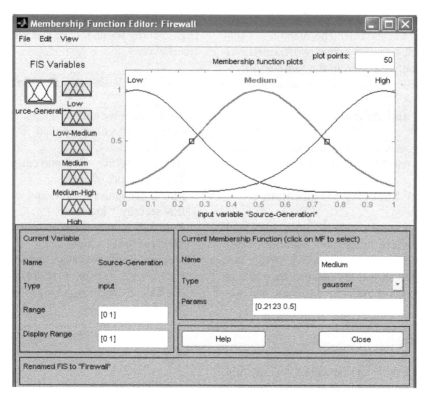

Figure 3. Input members function generation.

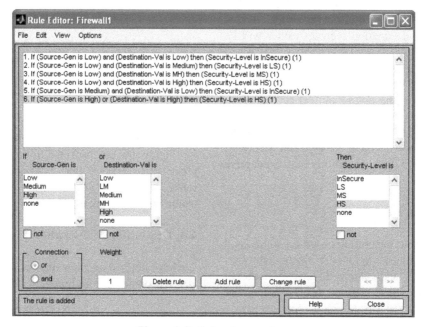

Figure 4. Defining fuzzy rules.

5. Simulation and Analysis

This section describes the experimental results and performance evaluation of the proposed system. The proposed system is implemented in MATLAB (7.0.1). Based on above defined procedure our simulation results described in the following figures. **Figure 6** describes the value generated by source and destination with its security level based on the defined rules. We can see that values on both sides are almost directly proportional which reflects the level of the security

The fuzzy rules given to the fuzzy system is done

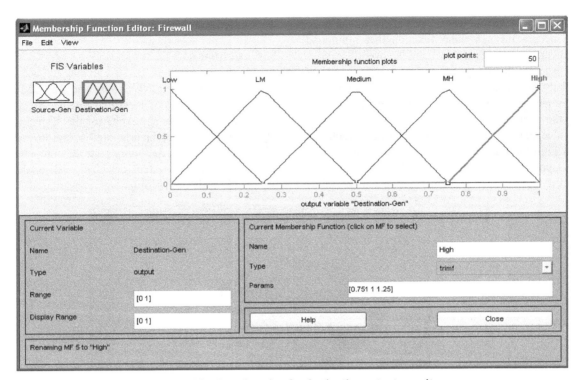

Figure 5. Members function for destination output security.

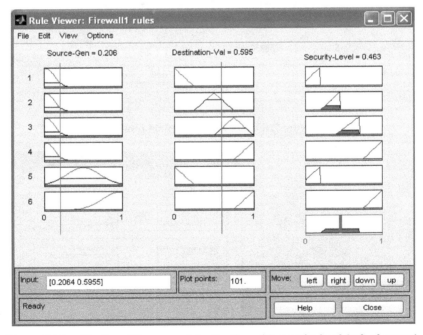

Figure 6. Visualization of Source and destination with security level (rule observer).

manually by analyzing intrusion behavior. Some time it is very difficult to generate fuzzy rules manually due to the fact that the input data is huge and also having more attributes. But, a few of researches are available in the literature for automatically identifying of fuzzy rules in recent times. Motivated by this fact, we make use of mining methods to identify a better set of rules.

Table 1 and **Figure 7** shows the clear view about the security level for each connection.

Various control method used to monitor and control the connection according to its security level. Therefore firewall is proactive, intelligent and remains secure and provide high performance.

A smoothly varying surface can provide the value of

overall security level for each connection. It has been observe deeply through ramp function that input and output security varies from 0 to 1 and the overall security level also varies smoothly, and we can get the status of the packets from the output generation. The ramp function is an elementary unary real function, easily computable as the mean of its independent variable and its absolute value and it is derived by the look of the graph.

From **Figures 8** and **9** we can see that as source generated value increases or decreases it has clear effect on the security level and a particular action will be taken

place based on the results.

6. Conclusions

In this work, fuzzy based system was designed to evaluate the threat level of identified threats, because it is impossible to provide assurance for the system and justify security measures incorporated unless the system is analyzed during the designing state of computer based systems. With this system designed, risk analysis has been made easier to perform.

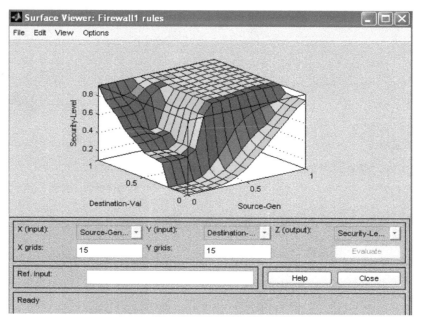

Figure 7. Surface level view (final result).

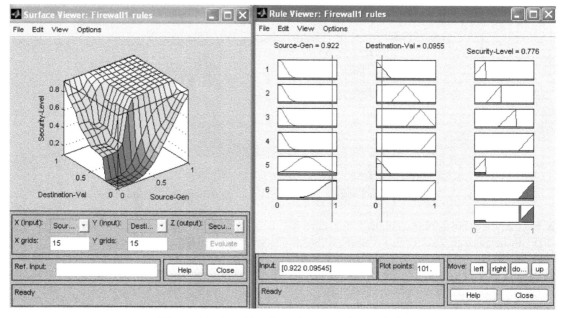

Figure 8. Rule and surface viewer (high security).

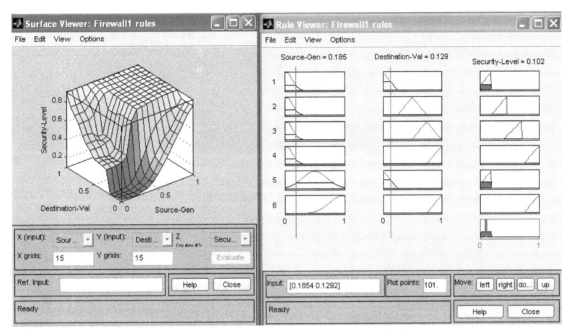

Figure 9. Rule and surface viewer (low security).

Table 1. Security level for each connection.

Output Value -$\mu(z)$	Security Level	Action Taken for Connection
>0 and <0.2	Insecure	Denied
>0.2 and <0.4	Low Security	Dynamic Monitoring and Auditing
>0.4 and <0.7	Medium Security	Dynamic Monitoring and Filtering
>0.7 and <1	High Security	Only Filter

Overall security level and methods to control packets and connections can be adjusted as per network dynamic status. It resolves the issues between security and speed providing high security and high performance. It is fuzzily adaptive and intelligent and has flexibility with a high degree of performance.

7. Future Work

For further research, this system designed can be redesigned using object orientated programming language and other models like DREAD and SWOT model can be used.

8. References

[1] CSI/FBI, "Computer Crime and Security Survey," 2004. http://i.cmpnet.com/gocsi/db_area/pdfs/fbi/FBI2004.pdf

[2] C. Baumrucker, J. Burton, S. Dentler, *et al.*, "Cisco Security Professional's Guide to Secure Intrusion Detection Systems," Syngress Publishing, Burlington, 2003.

[3] C. Endorf, E. Schultz and J. Mellander, "Intrusion Detection & Prevention," McGraw-Hill, Boston, 2004.

[4] "Technical Overview of The Bouncer," http://www.cobrador.net/docs/whitepaper.pdf

[5] M. Barkett, "Intrusion Prevention Systems," NFR Security, Inc., 2004. http://www.nfr.com/resource/downloads/SentivistIPS-WP.pdf

[6] K. Xinidis, K. G. Anagnostakis and E. P. Markatos, "Design and Implementation of a High Performance Network Intrusion Prevention System," *Proceedings of the 20th International Information Security Conference (SEC 2005)*, Makuhari-Messe, Chiba, 30 May-1 June 2005.

[7] T. Sproul and J. Lockwood, "Wide-Area Hardware-Accelerated Intrusion Prevention Systems (WHIPS)," *Proceedings of the International Working Conference on Active Networking (IWAN)*, Lawrence, 27-29 October 2004.

[8] D. Sarang, K. Praveen, T. S. Sproull and J. W. Lockwood, "Deep Packet Inspection Using Parallel Bloom Filters," *IEEE Micro*, Vol. 24, No. 1, 2004., pp. 52-61.

[9] D. V. Schuehler, J. Moscola and J. W. Lockwood, "Architecture for a Hardware-Based, TCP/IP Content-Processing System", *IEEE Micro*, Vol. 24, No. 1, 2004, pp. 62-69.

[10] H. Song and J. W. Lockwood, "Efficient Packet Classification for Network Intrusion Detection Using FPGA," *Proceedings of the International Symposium on Field-Programmable Gate Arrays (FPGA'05)*, Monterey, 20-22 February 2005.

[11] J. Yen and R. Langari, "Fuzzy Logic: Intelligence, Control and Information," Prentice Hall, Upper Saddle River, 1999.

[12] http://tools.ietf.org/html/rfc1918

[13] M. S. Abadeh, J. Habibi and C. Lucas, "Intrusion Detection Using a Fuzzy Genetics-Based Learning Algorithm," *Journal of Network and Computer Applications*, Vol. 30, No. 2007, 2007, pp. 414-428.

9

Tanimoto Based Similarity Measure for Intrusion Detection System

Alok Sharma, Sunil Pranit Lal[*]

Faculty of Science, Technology and Environment, University of the South Pacific, Suva, Fiji

Abstract

In this paper we introduced Tanimoto based similarity measure for host-based intrusions using binary feature set for training and classification. The k-nearest neighbor (kNN) classifier has been utilized to classify a given process as either normal or attack. The experimentation is conducted on DARPA-1998 database for intrusion detection and compared with other existing techniques. The introduced similarity measure shows promising results by achieving less false positive rate at 100% detection rate.

Keywords: Intrusion Detection, kNN Classifier, Similarity Measure, Anomaly Detection, Tanimoto Similarity Measure

1. Introduction

Intrusion detection is an important area in the field of computers and security, and in the recent years it has generated considerable interest in the research community. The intrusion detection system (IDS) can be subdivided into two main categories namely, signature-based detection and behavior-based detection. In this paper we focus on behavior-based detection which is also known as anomaly detection. An important feature of anomaly detection is that it can detect unknown attacks. Behavior modeling can be done by either modeling the user-behavior or process. The system call data is one of the most common types of data used for modeling process behavior. Host-based anomaly detection systems mostly focus on system call sequences with the assumption that a malicious activity results in an abnormal trace. Such data can be collected by logging the system calls using operating system utilities e.g. Linux strace or Solaris Basic Security Module (BSM). In this framework, it is assumed that the normal behavior can be profiled by a set of patterns of sequence of system calls. Any deviation from the normal pattern is termed as intrusion in this framework. An intrusion detection system needs to learn the normal behavior patterns from the previously collected data and this is normally accomplished by data mining or machine learning techniques. The problem of intrusion detection thus boils down to a supervised classification problem to identify anomalous sequences, which are measurably different from the normal behavior. The system call sequences of normal instances are used as the training set. Though anomaly-based IDS can detect unknown attacks, it suffers from having unacceptable false-positive rate [1]. This is because of the fact that it is hard to perfectly model a normal behavior. Unlike the traditional pattern recognition approach for classification, the aim in the present context is not only to achieve high accuracy rate but also to minimize the false positive rate. In recent years, a lot of research activities in anomaly detection focus on learning process behaviors and building the profiles with system call sequences as data sources.

Various machine learning techniques such as Support Vector Machines [2] and Neural Network [3] have been proposed for designing intelligent intrusion detection systems. Interested readers are directed to Tsai *et al.* [4] for a comprehensive overview on this subject. In this paper we use the kNN classification scheme [5-7] as an efficient means for intrusion detection. In carrying out the classification, it is a common practice to use features represented as frequency of system calls observed. While this approach has produced outstanding results [7], we are more interested in reducing the computational cost associated with classification task. Instead of representing features as frequency, which involves repetitive counting, we only consider absence or presence of a system call and represent it as a single bit of data. Needless to say binary representation consumes less storage space compared to integer representation. To this end, we propose a Tanimoto binary similarity measure, and empirically evaluate and compare its performance. To the best of authors' knowledge the result is better than other binary similarity schemes for intrusion detection reported in literature.

2. A Brief Description of the Preceding Work

In this section we briefly describe the research work on behavior-based intrusion detection procedures. Denning [8] did a pioneering work on behavior-based intrusion detection. In this approach profiles of subjects are learnt and statistical methods are used to compute deviations from the normal behavior. Lane and Brodly [9] propose another approach for capturing a user's behavior. A database of sequences of UNIX commands that normally a user issues, is maintained for each user. Any new command sequence is compared with this database using a similarity measure. Forrest *et al.* [10,11] introduce a simple anomaly detection method based on monitoring the system calls invoked by active and privileged processes. The profile of normal behavior is built by enumerating all fixed length of unique and contiguous system calls that occur in the training data, and unmatched sequences in actual detection are considered abnormal. A similar approach is followed by Lee *et al.* [12], but they make use of a rule learner RIPPER, to form the rules for classification. Lee and Stolfo [13] use data mining approach to study a sample of system call data to characterize the sequences contained in normal data by a small set of rules. In monitoring and detection, the sequences violating those rules are treated as anomalies [14]. Warrender *et al.* [15] propose Hidden Markov Model (HMM) method for modeling and evaluating invisible events based on system calls. It is believed that the entire sequence of system calls in a process need not exhibit intrusive behavior, but few subsequences of very small lengths may possess the intrusive characteristics. Rawat *et al* [16] showed using rough set technique that the intrusive behavior in a process is very localized. Sharma *et al.* [7] introduce kernel based similarity measure for host-based intrusions. They have used kNN classifier to classify a process as either normal or abnormal.

Most of the IDSs that model the behavior of processes in terms of subsequences, take fixed-length, contiguous subsequences of system calls. One potential drawback of this approach is that the size of the database that contains fixed-length contiguous subsequences increases exponentially with the length of the subsequences. Wespi *et al.* [17] propose a variable length subsequence approach. Asaka *et al.* [18] develop another approach based on the discriminant method in which an optimal classification surface is first learned from samples of the properly labeled normal and abnormal system call sequences. Wang *et al.* [19] develop another Principle Component Analysis based method for anomaly intrusion detection with less computation efforts. Tandon and Chan [20] propose to consider system calls arguments and other parameters, along with the sequences of system calls. They make use of the variant of a rule learner LERAD (Learning Rules for Anomaly Detection).

In order to detect the deviation of anomalous system call sequences from the normal set of sequences, Liao and Vemuri [5] used a similarity measure based on the frequencies of system calls used by a program (process), rather than the temporal ordering. Their approach draws an analogy between text categorization and intrusion detection, such that each system call is treated as a word and a set of system calls generated by a process as a document. They used a '*bag of system calls*' representation. Liao and Vemuri [5,21] adopted this representation to profile the behavior according to the trace of each process independently and a kNN method is used for classification. In this method, each system call is treated as a word and a collection of system calls during the execution of a process is treated as a document. The system call trace of a process is converted into a vector and cosine similarity measure is used to calculate the similarity among processes. In another study [22] by the same group, the Robust Support Vector Machine (RSVM) is applied to anomaly-based IDS. Recently, the emphasis of this RSVM study is on exhibiting the effectiveness of the method in the presence of noisy data. Rawat *et al.* [6] propose anomaly-based IDS. A new similarity measure called binary weighted cosine (BWC) is proposed and it is shown that by kNN classifier with the new measure, one can reduce the false positive rate substantially without sacrificing the detection rate. The authors have shown that by defining appropriate similarity measures, the detection by simple kNN can be as efficient as the sophisticated classification techniques like SVMs. Sharma *et al.* [7] propose a very efficient anomaly based IDS. They have introduced kernel based similarity measure and showed that it can capture similarity at very accurate level. They have used kNN as their classification scheme. The success of any such classification is hinged on two important aspects the similarity measure and the classification scheme.

3. Notations and Descriptions

In the remaining discussion $S = \{s_1, s_2, s_3, \cdots, s_m\}$ denotes a set of unique system calls where $m = |S|$ is the number of system calls. The training set X is defined as a set of labeled sequences $\{< Z_i, c_i > | Z_i \in S^*; c_i \in \{0, 1\}\}$ where Z_i is an input sequence of system calls or a process, c_i is a corresponding class label denoting 0 for "normal" label and 1 for "intrusion" label and S^* is the set of all finite strings of symbol of S. In this representation, the ordering information of adjacent system calls in the input sequence is not considered to be significant and only the frequency of each system call is preserved. Given the data set X, the goal of the learning algorithm is to find a classifier $h: S^* \rightarrow \{0, 1\}$ that maximizes detection rate and minimizes false positive rate.

The vector-space model of Information Retrieval (IR) is also often used to represent the set of processes. A process is depicted as a binary vector to represent the occurrences of system call. The value 1 represents the occurrences of a system call in a process and its absence is represented by 0. Thus we define Zb_i the binary representation of Z_i, where the entries of Zb_i is 1, if the corresponding system call is present, and 0, otherwise.

4. Tanimoto Similarity Measure

The concept of Tanimoto coefficient [23], is presented here for binary similarity. It is an extension of Jacquard coefficient, which is a binary similarity measure. Given two vectors of binary features, Zb_i and, Zb_j the binary Tanimoto coefficient is represented as

$$BT(Z_i, Z_j) = T(Zb_i, Zb_j) = \frac{Zb_i \cdot Zb_j}{\|Zb_i\|^2 + \|Zb_j\|^2 - Zb_i \cdot Zb_j} \quad (1)$$

where $\| \bullet \|$ is the Euclidean norm.

The Jacquard and Tanimoto coefficients have been extensively applied in several fields ranging from studying the diversity of species in ecosystem [24], to measuring similarity between chemical compounds [25]. In this paper we experiment using Tanimoto coefficient to measure the similarity between processes represented as binary features.

5. Binary Tanimoto Weighted Cosine (BTWC) Similarity Measure

In order to define BTWC similarity measure, we first define cosine similarity measure [5]. The cosine similarity measure $\lambda(Z_i, Z_j)$ between any two processes Z_i and Z_j is defined as follows.

$$CosSim(Z_i, Z_j) = \lambda(Z_i, Z_j) = \frac{Z_i . Z_j}{\| Z_i \| . \| Z_j \|} \quad (2)$$

The motive behind multiplying binary Tanimoto and $CosSim$ is that $CosSim(Z_i, Z_j)$ measures the similarity

based on the frequency and binary Tanimoto is the weight associated with Z_i and Z_j. In other words, binary Tanimoto tunes the similarity score $CosSim(Z_i, Z_j)$ according to the number of similar and dissimilar system calls between the two processes. The BTWC similarity measure can be given as

$$BTWC(Z_i, Z_j) = T(Zb_i, Zb_j) \times CosSim (Z_i, Z_j) \quad (3)$$

Therefore, the similarity measure BTWC takes frequency and the number of common system calls into consideration while calculating similarity between two processes.

6. K-Nearest Neighbors with the Similarity Measures

The kNN classifier is a generalized form of NN classifier. In this approach the behavior of a new process is classified by collecting the majority of k closest training processes. The average of these majority k measures is computed which is compared with the threshold value to determine if the process is normal or attack. The pseudo code of kNN procedure with similarity measure is as follows.

Let the training set X has n processes such that $Z_j \in X$. Let P be any new process.

for $j = 1$ to n
    $sm_j = similarity\_measure(P, Z_j)^1$;
end
$sm_k = find\_top\_k(sm_j)$;
$avg = average(sm_k)$;
if avg > threshold
    P = 'normal'
else
    P = 'attack'
end

7. An Illustration

In this section, we analyze the proposed scheme with the help of an example. To illustrate, consider two training processes Z_1 and Z_2 associated with 10 unique system call S. Let also consider a test process Z to measure the similarity with the training processes. The processes and the unique system call set S are defined as follows:

S = {auditon, chdir, close, creat, kill, login,

mkdir, stat, su, sysinfo}

Z_1 = {login, stat, stat, stat, stat, auditon,

auditon, auditon, auditon}

---

[1]In place of *similarity_measure*, equation 1 or 3 will be used.

$Z_2 = \{$login, close, su, sysinfo, stat, chdir,

chdir, mkdir, creat, kill$\}$

$Z = \{$login, auditon, auditon, stat, mkdir,

close, close, creat, kill$\}$

To find the similarity between a test and train processes, we observe that there are only three common system calls between Z and Z_1. However, there are six common system calls between Z and Z_2. This inferred that there is more similarity between Z and Z_2. Therefore, hypothetically $\mathrm{Sim}(Z, Z_2) > \mathrm{Sim}(Z, Z_1)$, where Sim is any similarity measure function. Computing the similarity score between these processes using $CosSim$, binary Tanimoto and BTWC similarity measures, we get,

$$CosSim(Z, Z_1) = 0.6276 \quad CosSim(Z, Z_2) = 0.5604$$
$$\mathrm{BT}(Z, Z_1) = 0.4286 \quad \mathrm{BT}(Z, Z_2) = 0.6000$$
$$\mathrm{BTWC}(Z, Z_1) = 0.2690 \quad \mathrm{BTWC}(Z, Z_2) = 0.3363$$

According to $CosSim$ similarity measure, Z is more similar to Z_1 than to Z_2, since $CosSim(Z, Z_1) > CosSim(Z, Z_2)$. However, this contradicts with the hypothesis. On the other hand, using binary Tanimoto and BTWC similarity measures, Z appeared to be more similar to Z_2 than to Z_1, since $\mathrm{BT}(Z, Z_2) > \mathrm{BT}(Z, Z_1)$ and $\mathrm{BTWC}(Z, Z_2) > \mathrm{BTWC}(Z, Z_1)$. The similarity scores measured by binary Tanimoto and BTWC validate the hypothesis. Therefore, it is more likely that by using these two techniques, better results for intrusion detection problem can be achieved.

In order to see the application of kNN classifier with binary Tanimoto and BTWC similarity measures, let us assume a third training process Z_3, such that $\mathrm{BT}(Z, Z_3) = 0.5$ and $\mathrm{BTWC}(Z, Z_2) = 0.3$. Suppose the threshold for binary Tanimoto is $\theta_{\mathrm{BT}} = 0.58$ and for BTWC is $\theta_{\mathrm{BTWC}} = 0.32$. If the classification procedure to label a process Z into either as attack or normal is conducted by comparing the highest similarity score then by binary Tanimoto the process will be classified as normal since, $\mathrm{BT}(Z, Z_2) = 0.6 > \theta_{\mathrm{BT}}$ and by BTWC it will also be classified as normal since, $\mathrm{BTWC}(Z, Z_2) = 0.3363 > \theta_{\mathrm{BTWC}}$. This could give statistically unstable results as the classification is dominated by a single training process (with the highest similarity score). A better classification scheme would be to evaluate the average of top k scores to arrive to the labeling of processes. If $k = 2$ then for binary Tanimoto using kNN classifier the average of top 2 similarity scores would be $avg < \theta_{\mathrm{BT}}$. This means that the process Z is now classified as an attack since, $avg < \theta_{\mathrm{BT}}$. In a similar way, process Z will be classified as an attack for BTWC using kNN classifier since, $avg = 0.3181 < \theta_{\mathrm{BTWC}}$. Therefore binary Tanimoto and BTWC similarity measures with kNN classifier are

expected to give statistically stable results by comparing the average similarity measure of top k processes.

8. Experimentation

In order to perform experimentation we use BSM audit logs from the 1998 DARPA data [26] for training and testing of our algorithm. This is the same data set used in previous research efforts [5-7] and thus it enables us compare the results. There are 50 unique system calls in the training data. All the 50 system calls are shown in **Table 1**.

In this dataset about 2000 normal sessions reported in the four days of data and the training data set consists of 606 unique processes. There are 412 normal sessions on the fifth day and we extract 5285 normal processes from these sessions. We use these 5285 normal processes as testing data. In order to test the detection capability of our method, we considered 54 intrusive sessions as test data. **Table 2** lists these attacks. A number in the beginning of the name denotes the week and day followed by the name of the session (attack).

Table 1. List of 50 unique system calls.

access, audit, auditon, chdir, chmod, chown, close, creat, execve, exit, fchdir, fchown, fcntl, fork, fork1, getaudit, getmsg, ioctl, kill, link, login, logout, lstat, memcntl, mkdir, mmap, munmap, oldnice, oldsetgid, oldsetuid, oldutime, open, pathdonf, pipe, putmsg, readlink, rename, rmdir, setaudit, setegid, seteuid, setgroups, setpgrp, setrlimit, stat, statvfs, su, sysinfo, unlink, vfork

Table 2. List of 54 attacks used in test data.

1.1_it_ffb clear,	1.1_it_format_clear,	2.2_it_ipsweep,
2.5_it_ftpwrite,	2.5_it_ftpwrite_test,	3.1_it_ffb_clear,
3.3_it_ftpwrite,	3.3_it_ftpwrite_test,	3.4_it_warez,
3.5_it_warezmaster,		4.1_it_080520warezclient,
4.2_it_080511warezclient,		4.2_it_153736spy,
4.2_it_153736spy_test,		4.2_it_153812spy,
4.4_it_080514warezclient,	4.4_it_080514warezclient_test,	
4.4_it_175320warezclient,		4.4_it_180326warezclient,
4.4_it_180955warezclient,		4.4_it_181945warezclient,
4.5_it_092212ffb,		4.5_it_141011loadmodule,
4.5_it_162228loadmodule,		4.5_it_174726loadmodule,
4.5_it_format,	5.1_it_141020ffb,	5.1_it_174729ffb_exec,
5.1_it_format,		5.2_it_144308eject_clear,
5.2_it_163909eject_clear,	5.3_it_eject_steal,	5.5_it_eject,
5.5_it_fdformat,	5.5_it_fdformat_chmod,	6.4_it_090647ffb,
6.4_it_093203eject,	6.4_it_095046eject,	6.4_it_100014eject,
6.4_it_122156eject,	6.4_it_144331ffb,	test.1.2_format,
test.1.2_format2,	test.1.3_eject,	test.1.3_httptunnel,
test.1.4_eject,	test.2.1_111516ffb,	test.2.1_format,
test.2.2_xsnoop,	test.2.3_ps, test.2.3_ps_b,	test.2.5_ftpwrite,
test.2.4_eject_a,	test.2.2_format1	

An intrusive session is said to be detected if any of the processes associated with this session is classified as abnormal. Thus detection rate is defined as the number of intrusive sessions detected, divided by the total number of intrusive sessions. We perform the experiments with $k = 5$.

In **Tables 3-6** we show Liao-Vemuri scheme [5], BWC scheme [6], BTWC scheme and binary Tanimoto scheme respectively for $k = 5$. In the tables, the first column represents the threshold values used in the experiments. The second column depicts the false positives rates and the third column depicts the detection rate.

It can be seen from **Table 3** that for Liao-Vemuri scheme the false positive rate is very high (25.8%) at a detection rate of 100%. It can be observed from **Table 4** that BWC is a better technique than Liao-Vemuri as it provides lesser false positive rate (4.65%) at a detection rate of 100%. However, this false positive rate (4.65%) still may not be acceptable. The BTWC scheme (**Table 5**) gives better performance by getting false positive rate of 4.1% at 100% detection. Next, the binary Tanimoto scheme performs the best by giving 3.7% false positive rate at a detection rate of 100%. **Table 7** summarizes the results obtained in **Tables 3-6**. It can be seen the binary

Table 3. Liao-vemuri scheme.

Threshold	False Positive Rate	Detection Rate
0.52	0.0000	0.3519
0.89	0.0009	0.7593
0.99	0.0096	0.9630
0.995	0.2575	1.0000

Table 4. Binary weighted cosine scheme.

Threshold	False Positive Rate	Detection Rate
0.52	0.0000	0.3704
0.86	0.0095	0.9444
0.90	0.0238	0.9815
0.90099	0.0465	1.0000

Table 5. BTWC scheme.

Threshold	False Positive Rate	Detection Rate
0.52	0.0000	0.3704
0.86	0.0348	0.9630
0.88	0.0401	0.9630
0.889	0.0411	1.0000

Table 6. Binary tanimoto scheme.

Threshold	False Positive Rate	Detection Rate
0.52	0.0000	0.3519
0.86	0.0312	0.9630
0.92	0.0369	0.9630
0.9219	0.0369	1.0000

Table 7. Summary: false positive rate at 100% detection rate for all the schemes.

Method	False Positive Rate	Detection Rate
Liao-Vemuri	25.75%	100.0%
BWC	4.7%	100.0%
BTWC	4.1%	100.0%
Binary Tanimoto	3.7%	100.0%

Tanimoto scheme is better than other schemes. The advantage of this scheme is that it utilizes only binary data which has lesser computing and managing requirements.

The receiver operating characteristic (ROC) curve is also depicted in **Figure 1**. It provides a comparison between the techniques. The ROC curve is a graph between the attack detection rate and false positive rate. It can be seen in the figure that binary Tanimoto converges to 100% detection rate faster than other three schemes. The curve of BTWC scheme is better than binary Tanimoto for smaller values of false positive rate. However, it converges slower to 100% detection rate than binary Tanimoto scheme. Nonetheless, the benchmark is to obtain lowest false positive rate at 100% detection rate and the proposed schemes are outperforming other similarity measures.

9. Conclusions

The Tanimoto based similarity measure schemes have been introduced in this work. It was observed that these schemes produced better results than other techniques. The best result obtained by Tanimoto scheme was 3.7% at the detection rate of 100%. To the best of the authors' knowledge the performance of the proposed technique is better than any previously documented result using binary similarity measure in the area of intrusion detection.

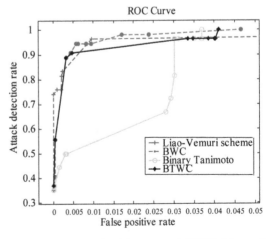

Figure 1. ROC curve for Liao-vemuri, BWC, binary tanimoto and BTWC schemes.

It is worth highlighting that a binary representation of features captures less detailed information about a process compared with features represented as frequency. Even with this limitation, we obtained good results, which gives validity to our proposed approach.

10. Acknowledgements

The authors would like to thank the reviewers and the Editor for providing constructive comments about the paper.

11. References

[1] T. Lane and C. E. Brodley, "Temporal Sequence Learning and Data Reduction for Anomaly Detection," *In Proceedings of 5th ACM Conference on Computer & Communication Security*, San Francisco, November 3-5, 1998, pp. 150-158.

[2] Y. Yi, J. Wu and W. Xu, "Incremental SVM Based on Reserved Set for Network Intrusion Detection," *Expert Systems with Applications*, Vol. 38, No. 6, 2011, pp. 7698-7707.

[3] G. Wang, J. Hao, J. Ma and L. Huang, "A New Approach to Intrusion Detection Using Artificial Neural Networks and Fuzzy Clustering," *Expert Systems with Applications*, Vol. 37, No. 9, 2010, pp. 6225-6232.

[4] C. F. Tsai, Y. F. Hsu, C. Y. Lin and W. Y. Lin, "Intrusion Detection by Machine Learning: A Review," *Expert Systems with Applications*, Vol. 36, No. 10, 2009, pp. 11994-12000.

[5] Y. Liao and V. R. Vemuri, "Use of K-Nearest Neighbor Classifier for Intrusion Detection," *Computers & Security*, Vol. 21, No. 5, 2002, pp. 439-448.

[6] S. Rawat, V. P. Gulati, A. K. Pujari and V. R. Vemuri, "Intrusion Detection Using Text Processing Techniques with a Binary-Weighted Cosine Metric," *Journal of Information Assurance and Security*, Vol. 1, 2006, pp. 43-50.

[7] A. Sharma, A. K. Pujari and K. K. Paliwal, "Intrusion Detection Using Text Processing Techniques with a Kernel Based Similarity Measure," *Computers & Security*, Vol. 26, No. 7-8, 2007, pp. 488-495.

[8] D. E. Denning, "An Intrusion-Detection Model," *In Proceedings of the 1986 IEEE Symposium on Security and Privacy (SSP '86)*, IEEE Computer Society Pressm, 1990, pp. 118-133.

[9] T. Lane and C. E. Brodly. "An Application of Machine Learning to Anomaly Detection," *In Proceeding of the 20th National Information System Security Conference*, Baltimore, MD, 1997, pp. 366-377.

[10] S. Forrest, S. A. Hofmeyr, A. Somayaji and T. A. Long-staff, "A Sense of Self for Unix Processes," *Proceedings of the 1996 IEEE Symposium on Research in Security and Privacy*, Los Alamos, 1996, pp.120-128.

[11] S. Forrest, S. A. Hofmeyr and A. Somayaji, "Computer Immunology," *Communications of the ACM*, Vol. 40, No. 10, 1997, pp. 88-96.

[12] W. Lee, S. Stolfo and P. Chan. "Learning Patterns from Unix Process Execution Traces for Intrusion Detection," *In Proceedings of the AAAI97 Workshop on AI Methods in Fraud and Risk Management*, AAAI Press, Menlo Park, 1997, pp. 50-56.

[13] W. Lee and S. Stolfo, "Data Mining Approaches for Intrusion Detection," *Proceedings of the 7th USENIX Security Symposium*, Usenix Association, 1998, pp.79-94.

[14] E. Eskin, A. Arnold, M. Prerau, L. Portnoy and S. Stolfo, "A Geometric Framework for Unsupervised Anomaly Detection: Detecting Intrusions in Unlabeled Data," Applications of Data Mining in Computer Security, Kluwer Academics Publishers, Berlin, 2002, pp. 77-102.

[15] C. Warrender, S. Forrest and B. Pearlmutter, "Detecting Intrusions Using System Calls: Alternative Data Models," *Proceedings of 1999 IEEE Symposium on Security and Privacy*, Oakland, 1999, pp. 133-145.

[16] S. Rawat, V. P. Gulati and A. K. Pujari, "A Fast Host-Based Intrusion Detection System Using Rough Set Theory," *Computer Science*, Vol. 3700, No. 2005, 2005, pp. 144-161.

[17] A. Wespi, M. Dacier and H. Debar, "Intrusion Detection Using Variable-Length Audit Trail Patterns," *Proceedings of the Third International Workshop on the Recent Advances in Intrusion Detection (RAID'2000)*, Toulouse, No. 1907, 2000.

[18] M. Asaka, T. Onabuta, T. Inove, S. Okazawa and S. Goto, "A New Intrusion Detection Method on Discriminant Analysis," *IEICE Transaction on Information and Systems E84D*, Vol. 5, 2001, pp. 570-577.

[19] W. Wang, X. Guan and X. Zhang, "A Novel Intrusion Detection Method Based on Principle Component Analysis in Computer Security," *Proceedings of the International IEEE Symposium on Neural Networks*, Dalian, *Lecture Notes in Computer Science*, Vol. 3174, No. 2004, 2004, pp. 657-662.

[20] G. Tandon and P. K. Chan, "Learning Useful System Call Attributes for Anomaly Detection," *Proceedings of the 18th International Florida Artificial Intelligence Research Society (FLAIRS) Conference*, Clearwater Beach, 2005, pp. 405-410.

[21] Y. Liao and V.R. Vemuri, "Using Text Categorization Techniques for Intrusion Detection," *Proceedings USE NIX Security 2002*, San Francisco, 2002, pp. 51-59.

[22] H. Wenjie, Y. Liao and V.R. Vemuri, "Robust Support Vector Machines for Anomaly Detection in Computer Security," *In International Conference on Machine Learning*, Los Angeles, 2003.

[23] T. T. Tanimoto, "IBM Internal Report 17th," November 1957. http://en.wikipedia.org/wiki/Jaccard_index for details.

[24] J. A. Wallwork, "The Distribution and Diversity of Soil Fauna," Academic Press, London. 1976.

[25] P. Willett, "Chemical Similarity Searching," *Journal of Chemical Information and Computer Sciences*, Vol. 38,

1998, pp. 983-996.

[26] DARPA 1998 Data, "MIT Lincoln Laboratory," 2007. http://www.ll.mit.edu/IST/ideval/data/data index.html

10

An Authentication Method for Digital Audio Using a Discrete Wavelet Transform

Yasunari Yoshitomi, Taro Asada, Yohei Kinugawa, Masayoshi Tabuse
Graduate School of Life and Environmental Sciences, Kyoto Prefectural University, Kyoto, Japan

Abstract

Recently, several digital watermarking techniques have been proposed for hiding data in the frequency domain of audio files in order to protect their copyrights. In general, there is a tradeoff between the quality of watermarked audio and the tolerance of watermarks to signal processing methods, such as compression. In previous research, we simultaneously improved the performance of both by developing a multipurpose optimization problem for deciding the positions of watermarks in the frequency domain of audio data and obtaining a near-optimum solution to the problem. This solution was obtained using a wavelet transform and a genetic algorithm. However, obtaining the near-optimum solution was very time consuming. To overcome this issue essentially, we have developed an authentication method for digital audio using a discrete wavelet transform. In contrast to digital watermarking, no additional information is inserted into the original audio by the proposed method, and the audio is authenticated using features extracted by the wavelet transform and characteristic coding in the proposed method. Accordingly, one can always use copyright-protected original audio. The experimental results show that the method has high tolerance of authentication to all types of MP3, AAC, and WMA compression. In addition, the processing time of the method is acceptable for everyday use.

Keywords: Authentication, Audio, Copyright Protection, Tolerance to Compression, Wavelet Transforms

1. Introduction

Recent progress in digital media technology and distribution systems, such as the Internet and cellular phones, has enabled consumers to easily access, copy, and modify digital content, such as electric documents, images, audio, and video. Therefore, techniques to protect the copyrights for digital data and prevent unauthorized duplication or tampering are urgently needed.

Digital watermarking (DW) is a promising method of copyright protection for digital data. Several studies have investigated audio DW [1-12]. Two important properties of audio DW are inaudibility of DW-introduced distortion, and robustness to signal processing methods, such as compression. In addition to these properties, the data rate and complexity of the DW have attracted attention when discussing the performance of a DW.

We have attempted to develop a method in which 1) the DW can be sufficiently extracted from the watermarked audio, even after compression, and 2) the quality of the audio remains high after embedding the DW. However, there is generally a tradeoff between these two properties. Therefore, we focus on this tradeoff and attempt to overcome this critical difficulty by optimizing the positions of the DW in the frequency domain. Recently, digital audio distributed over the Internet and cellular phone systems is often modified by compression, which is one of the easiest and most effective ways to defeat a DW without significantly deteriorating the quality of the audio.

In previous research, we simultaneously improved both the extraction performance of the DW and the quality of the DW-contained audio by developing a multipurpose optimization problem for deciding the positions of the DW in the frequency domain and obtaining a near-optimum solution for the problem using a discrete wavelet transform (DWT) and a genetic algorithm (GA) for realizing high tolerance to MP3 compression, which is the most popular compression technique [13,14]. Our method enabled us to embed the DW in an almost optimal manner within any digital audio. However, obtaining the near-optimum solution was very time consuming. In the present study, to overcome this issue essentially, we have developed an authentication method for digital audio to protect the copyrights. In contrast to the DW, no additional information is inserted into the original audio by the proposed method, and the digital audio is authenticated using features extracted using the DWT and characteristic coding of the proposed method. This paper presents an analysis of the performance of the method.

2. Wavelet Transform

The original audio data $s_k^{(0)}$, which is used as the level-0 wavelet decomposition coefficient sequence, where k denotes the element number in the data, are decomposed into the multi-resolution representation (MRR) and the coarsest approximation by repeatedly applying the DWT. The wavelet decomposition coefficient sequence $s_k^{(j)}$ at level j is decomposed into two wavelet decomposition coefficient sequences at level $j+1$ by using (1) and (2):

$$s_k^{(j+1)} = \sum_n \overline{p_{n-2k}} s_n^{(j)} \tag{1}$$

$$w_k^{(j+1)} = \sum_n \overline{q_{n-2k}} s_n^{(j)} \tag{2}$$

where p_k and q_k denote the scaling and wavelet sequences, respectively, and $w_k^{(j+1)}$ denotes the development coefficient at level $j+1$. The development coefficients at level J are obtained using (1) and (2) iteratively from $j=0$ to $j=J-1$. **Figure 1** shows the process of multi-resolution analysis by DWT.

In the present study, we use the Daubechies wavelet for the DWT, according to the references [14,15]. As a result, we obtain the following relation between p_k and q_k:

$$q_k = (-1)^k p_{1-k} \tag{3}$$

We select the Daubechies wavelet because we compared the results by the proposed method with those by our retorted method [13,14], where the Daubechies wavelet was used for the DW.

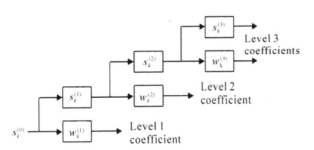

Figure 1. Multi-resolution analysis by the DWT.

3. Proposed Authentication Algorithm

It is known that the histogram of the wavelet coefficients of each domain of the MRR sequences has a distribution which is centered at approximately 0 when the DWT is performed on audio data, as shown in **Figure 2** [13]. In the present study, the above phenomenon is exploited for the authentication of the audio signal. The procedure is described below.

3.1. Selective Coding

3.1.1. Setting of Parameters
For the coding of the audio, we obtain the histogram of the wavelet coefficients V at the selected level of an MRR sequence (see **Figure 3**). Like the DW techniques for images [15,16] and digital audio [13,14], we set the following coding parameters:

The values of $Th(minus)$ and $Th(plus)$ (see **Figure 3**) are chosen such that the non-positive wavelet coefficients (S_m in total frequency) are equally divided into two groups by $Th(minus)$, and the positive wavelet coefficients (S_p in total frequency) are equally divided into two groups by $Th(plus)$. Next, the values of $T1$, $T2$, $T3$, and $T4$, the parameters for controlling the authentication precision, are chosen to satisfy the following conditions:

1) $T1 < Th(minus) < T2 < 0 < T3 < Th(plus) < T4$.

2) The value of S_{T1}, the number of wavelet coefficients in $(T1, Th(minus))$, is equal to S_{T2}, the number of wavelet coefficients in $[Th(minus), T2)$. In short, $S_{T1} = S_{T2}$.

3) The value of S_{T3}, the number of wavelet coefficients in $(T3, Th(plus)]$, is equal to S_{T4}, the number of wavelet coefficients in $(Th(plus), T4)$. In short, $S_{T3} = S_{T4}$.

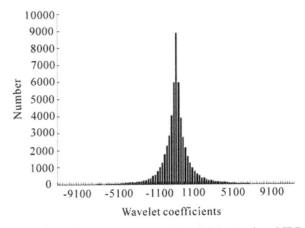

Figure 2. Histogram of the wavelet coefficients of an MRR sequence at level 3 (jazz) [13].

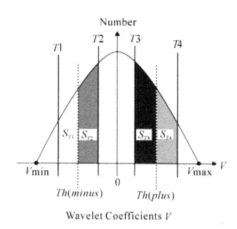

Figure 3. Schematic diagram of the histogram of MRR wavelet coefficients.

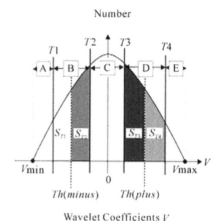

Figure 4. Five sets (A, B, C, D, and E) are described by a histogram of wavelet coefficients V of an MRR sequence for the assignment of a bit.

4) $S_{T1}/S_m = S_{T3}/S_p$.

In the present study, the values of both S_{T1}/S_m and S_{T1}/S_p are set to 0.3, which was determined experimentally.

3.1.2. Domain Segmentation in a Wavelet Coefficient Histogram

In preparation of a coding for authentication, the procedure separates the wavelet coefficients V of an MRR sequence into five sets (hereinafter referred to as A, B, C, D, and E), as shown in **Figure 4**, using the following criteria:

- $A = \left\{ V \middle| V \in V^{SC}, V \leq T1 \right\}$,

- $B = \left\{ V \middle| V \in V^{SC}, T1 < V < T2 \right\}$,

- $C = \left\{ V \middle| V \in V^{SC}, T2 \leq V \leq T3 \right\}$,

- $D = \left\{ V \middle| V \in V^{SC}, T3 < V < T4 \right\}$,

- $E = \left\{ V \middle| V \in V^{SC}, T4 \leq V \right\}$,

where V^{SC} is the set of wavelet coefficients in the original audio file.

3.1.3. Selective Coding Algorithm

The wavelet coefficients of an MRR sequence are coded according to the following rules, in which V_i denotes one of wavelet coefficients:

When $V_i \in C$, flag f_i is set to be 1, and bit b_i is set to be 0.

When $V_i \in (A \cup E)$, flag f_i is set to be 1, and bit b_i is set to be 1.

When $V_i \in (B \cup D)$, flag f_i is set to be 0, and bit b_i is set to be 0.5.

For the authentication of the digital audio, we use a code C (hereinafter referred to as an original code), which is the sequence of b_i defined above. For the coding and authentication, we assign a sequence number and a flag for each wavelet coefficient. The flag $f_i = 1$ for a V_i means that the V_i is assigned a bit ($b_i = 0$ or 1) for a coding. The flag $f_i = 0$ for a V_i provides that the V_i is not assigned a bit of 0 or 1: b_i is externally set to be 0.5 as an arbitrary constant and the value of b_i does not influence the performance of the proposed method described in Section 3.2. The exclusion of all V_i belonging to the sets B and D, where the magnitude of the V_i are intermediate, from the objects for coding is a novel feature of the present study.

3.2. Authentication

3.2.1. Setting of Parameters

We authenticate not only an original digital audio file but also a signal-processed version. Compression, one example of signal processing, is often applied to digital audio for the purposes of distribution via the Internet or for saving on a computer. Through the same procedure as described in Section 3.1, we applied the DWT to digital audio and obtained a histogram of wavelet coeffcients V' at the same level of the DWT as that of the coding for the original audio file, which is described in Section 3.1. Then, we set the authentication parameters as follows:

The values of $Th'(minus)$ and $Th'(plus)$ (see **Figure 5**) are chosen such that the non-positive wavelet coefficients (S_m' in total frequency) are equally divided into two groups by $Th'(minus)$, and the positive wavelet coefficients (S_p' in total frequency) are equally divided into two groups by $Th'(plus)$. Next, the values of $T1'$, $T2'$, $T3'$, and $T4'$, the parameters for controlling the authentication precision, are chosen to satisfy the following conditions:

1) $T1' < Th'(minus) < T2' < 0 < T3' < Th'(plus) < T4'$.

2) The value of S'_{T1}, the number of wavelet coefficients in $(T1', Th'(minus))$, is equal to S'_{T2}, the number of wavelet coefficients in $[Th'(minus), T2')$. In short, $S'_{T1} = S'_{T2}$.

3) The value of S'_{T3}, the number of wavelet coefficients in $(T3', Th'(plus)]$, is equal to S_{T4}, the number of wavelet coefficients in $(Th'(plus), T4')$. In short, $S'_{T3} = S'_{T4}$.

4) $S'_{T1}/S'_m = S'_{T3}/S'_p$.

In the present study, the values of both S'_{T1}/S'_m and S'_{T3}/S'_p are set to be 0.3, the same as the settings used for the coding for the original audio file, which is described in Section 3.1.

3.2.2. Domain Segmentation in a Wavelet Coefficient Histogram

In the preparation of a coding for authentication, the procedure separates the wavelet coefficients V' of an MRR sequence into three sets (hereinafter referred to as F, G, and H), as shown in **Figure 5**, using the following criteria:

- $F = \{V' | V' \in V'^{AC}, V' < Th'(minus)\}$,

- $G = \{V' | V' \in V'^{AC}, Th'(minus) \leq V' \leq Th'(plus)\}$,

- $H = \{V' | V' \in V'^{AC}, Th'(plus) < V'\}$,

where V'^{AC} is the set of wavelet coefficients of the a target audio file for making the code for authentication.

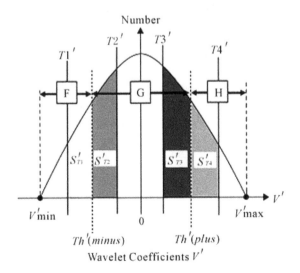

Figure 5. Three sets (F, G, and H), indicated on the histogram, of MRR wavelet coefficients used for the authentication.

3.2.3. Authentication Algorithm

The wavelet coefficients of an MRR sequence are coded according to the following rules, in which V'_i denotes one of wavelet coefficients:

When $f_i = 1$ and $V'_i \in G$, bit b'_i is set to be 0.

When $f_i = 1$ and $V'_i \in (F \cup H)$, bit b'_i is set to be 1.

When $f_i = 0$, bit b'_i is set to be 0.5.

When $f_i = 0$, b'_i is externally set to be 0.5 as an arbitrary constant and the value of b_i does not influence the performance of the proposed method described below.

For the authentication of the digital audio, we use the code C' (hereinafter referred to as an authentication code), which is the sequence of b'_i defined above. The authentication ratio AR (%) is defined by the following:

$$AR = \frac{100 \sum_{i=1}^{N} f_i \left(1 - |b_i - b'_i|\right)}{\sum_{i=1}^{N} f_i} \qquad (4)$$

where N is the number of wavelet coefficients assigned flags in the coding for the original audio file, which is described in Section 3.1. According to (4), the values of neither b_i nor b'_i influence the value of AR in the case that $f_i = 0$, which provides that the corresponding V'_i is not assigned a bit of 0 or 1 for the coding for the original audio file.

For using the proposed method, we need store flags f_i and an original code C of each audio file whose copy right we should protect. In calculating (4) for the authentication of an original audio file, we do not use an original audio file but the flags f_i and the original code C of the original audio file.

4. Experiment

In this section, we describe computer experiments and their results for evaluating the performance of the proposed method.

4.1. Method

The experiment was performed in the following computational environment: the personal computer was a Dell Dimension 8300 (CPU: Pentium IV 3.2 GHz; main memory: 2.0 GB); the OS was Microsoft Windows XP; the development language was Microsoft Visual C++ 6.0.

Five music audio files, which were composed of the first entries in the five genre categories: classical, jazz, popular, rock, and hiphop in the music database RWC for research purpose [17], were copied from CDs onto a personal computer as WAVE files with the following specifications: 44.1 kHz, 16 bits, and monaural. For each music audio file selected from the database, one 10-second clip of music audio (hereinafter referred to as an original music audio clip) was extracted starting at 1 minute from the beginning of the audio file and saved on a personal computer. In addition, for each of the five music audio files mentioned above, several 10-second audio clips were extracted by shifting the start-time 1 second at a time from the beginning of the audio file and were saved on a personal computer for use in evaluating the performance of the proposed method. For the purpose of evaluating the tolerance of authentication to compression, MP3, AAC, and WMA compression systems were each used to compress the original music audio clip to bit rates of 64, 96, and 128 kbps. The process of the experiment was as follows: obtain the code of the original WAVE file, compress the file by MP3, AAC, and WMA, and then convert the compressed files into the WAVE files used for the authentication.

For the DWT, we use Daubechies wavelets. Level 8 was chosen as the standard for the DWT based on an analysis of preliminary experiments, and this level was used for most of the experiments. The influence of the level of the DWT on the authentication ratio was also analyzed as part of the experiments.

Instead of the Dell Dimension 8300 (CPU: Pentium IV 3.2 GHz; main memory: 2.0 GB), Dell Dimension DXC051 (CPU: Pentium IV 3.0 GHz, memory: 1.0 GB) is used only for the comparison with the reported study [13,14].

4.2. Results and Discussion

4.2.1. Authentication Process

Table 1 illustrates the process of authentication of audio clips. The jumps in the wavelet coefficient number, such as from 573 to 578, indicate that the intervening wavelet coefficients belong to either the set B or D, which are out of assignment of a bit to 0 or 1 for the coding for the original music audio clip. The authentication ratio AR defined by (4) was $(6/7) \times 100$ in the case of **Table 1**, where the bits of the music audio clip after MP3 compression were equal to those of the original music except for wavelet coefficient number 579.

4.2.2. Robustness to Compression

Whenever we applied the proposed method to the five original music audio clips, the authentication ratio was 100%. When we applied it to several music clips compressed by MP3, AAC, and WMA, the authentication ratio was at or near 100% (**Table 2**).

4.2.3. Authentication Ratios for Other Non-Signal-Processed Music Audio Clips

The purpose of authentication is to protect the copyright

Table 1. Authentication process (hiphop).

Wavelet coefficients No.	Original		After MP3 compression (128kbps)		Bit correspondence
	set	bit	set	bit	
572	C	0	G	0	Yes
579	C	0	F	1	No
580	C	0	G	0	Yes
584	C	0	G	0	Yes
588	E	1	H	1	Yes
589	C	0	G	0	Yes
590	C	0	G	0	Yes

Table 2. Authentication tolerance to compression (%).

Compression Method	Bit rate (kbps)	Classical	Jazz	Popular	Rock	Hiphop
MP3	128	99.86	99.86	99.86	100	99.57
	96	99.86	100	99.86	100	99.86
	64	99.72	99.72	99.86	100	98.28
AAC	128	100	100	100	100	97.55
	96	99.86	100	99.86	100	100
	64	100	100	99.14	99.72	99.00
WMA	128	100	100	100	100	100
	96	100	100	100	100	100
	64	100	99.86	100	100	100

(%)

on audio data. When the music audio file targeted for being authenticated was different from that used for making the code of the original music audio clip, the authentication ratios AR defined by (4) were about 50% (more precisely, they fell in the range 44.09 to 55.62%), which was about half of the authentications ratios when authenticating the same clip as the original music audio clip (100% in all cases in this experiment; see **Table 3**). An authentication ratio of 50% corresponds to the value in the case that randomly generated bits are used for b_i and/or b_i' in (4). Accordingly, the proposed method distinguishes an original music audio clip from each of the other four used in this experiment.

Using the original code obtained from the original music audio clip, which was the 10-second clip extracted staring at 1 minute from the beginning of each of the five music audio files, we calculated the authentication ratio to the 10-second clips extracted by shifting the start-time for the clip 1 second at a time. For each of the original music audio clips, the authentication ratio was 100% when an original code was used as the authentication code (**Figure 6**). In **Figure 6**, the point 60 seconds on the horizontal axis corresponds to the case that the original code is used as the authentication code. Not including these cases, the authentication ratio for jazz, popular, and rock music audio fell mostly in the 40 to 60% range. In contrast, the authentication ratio for classical and hiphop varied according to the start time. Not including the case of using the original code for the authentication code, the highest authentication ratio was 93.95%, which was ob-

Table 3. Authentication ratio (%) in all combinations of original and authentication.

		Original				
		Classical	Jazz	Popular	Rock	Hiphop
Authentication	Classical	100	44.22	47.98	52.89	53.61
	Jazz	55.62	100	49.86	51.01	46.54
	Popular	44.09	53.89	100	49.57	52.88
	Rock	47.69	50.86	49.42	100	48.13
	Hiphop	48.41	50.43	47.55	51.44	100

(%)

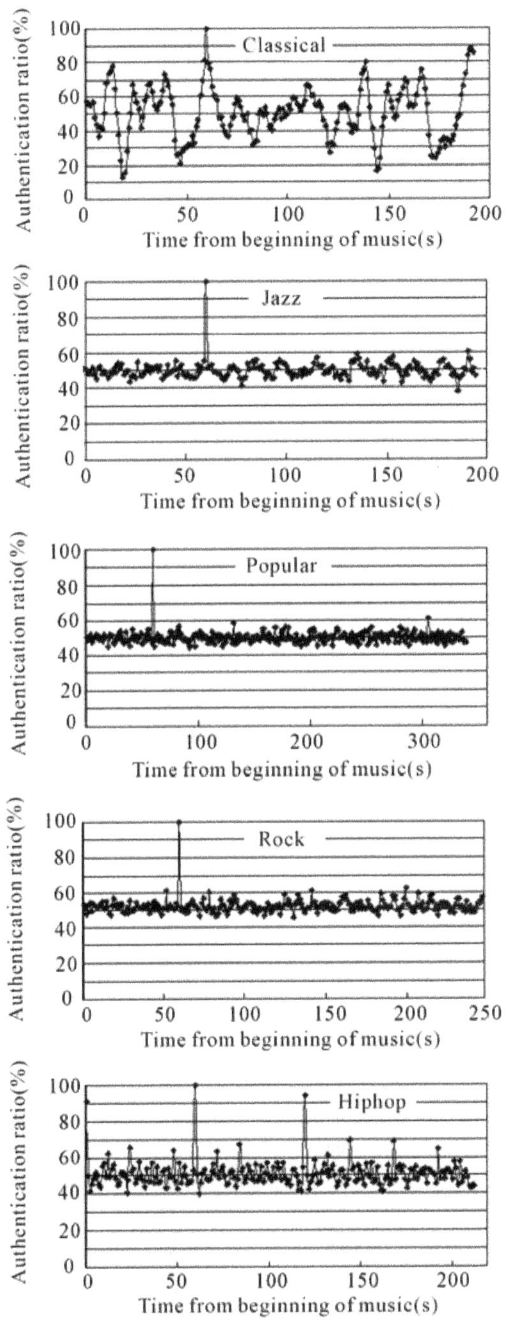

Figure 6. Authentication ratios using clips shifted 1 second at a time for each of the five selected audio clips.

served for hiphop. Accordingly, the threshold of the authentication ratio for judging authentication of an original music audio clip should be about 95%. As the authentication ratios to music clips extracted from the music audio files, from which the original music audio clip were obtained, stayed under 95% (again, excluding the cases of using the identical clip), we conclude that the probability of getting an authentication ratio above 95% would be small if we applied the proposed method to other music selected from the database. In other words, we propose that music audio be judged as authenticated when the file gives an authentication ratio of 95% or higher for a certain clip taken from a music audio file. When we used 95% as a threshold for the authentication ratio, both the false negative and positive rates for the authentication of the music audio clip were zero in the both cases shown in **Table 3** and **Figure 6**.

4.2.4. Influence of DWT Level on Authentication Ratio

All authentication ratios described above were obtained using a DWT at level 8. The tolerances of the authentication ratio to signal processing by MP3, AAC, and WMA at DWT levels of 2 to 8 with bit rates of 128, 96, and 64 kbps are shown for each bit rate in **Tables 4-6**, respectively. The authentication ratio does not noticeably change at bit rates of from 64 to 128 kbps. The authentication ratio tends to be slightly higher with increases in the DWT level of the original coding, which is the same as that of the authentication coding. For DWT levels of 7 or 8, the authentication ratio exceeds 95% for all settings of MP3, AAC, and WMA compression tested. The lowest authentication ratio, 94.57%, occurred for DWT level 6 applied to the hiphop audio clip compressed by AAC with a bit rate of 128 kbps. The number of data of the original music audio clip, which is treated as the amount of data at DWT level 0, was 441,000. The number of wavelet coefficients of MRR sequences was reduced by half for an increase of DWT level by one, meaning that the number of 0 or 1 bits in both the original and the authentication coding was also reduced by half.

4.2.5. Comparison with Watermarking

There is generally a tradeoff between 1) the tolerance of the DW to signal processing, such as compression, and 2) the quality of the music audio after embedding the DW. In other words, to improve the first property tends to cause a deterioration of the second property. We had overcome this critical difficulty of the DW by optimizing the positions of the DW in the frequency domain [13,14], [18-20]. However, it took much time to get the condition for embedding the DW by the reported method.

Figure 7 shows the relationship between the quality of music audio and the detection rate of the DW after MP3 compression, using the jazz clip as the original music au-

Table 4. Authentication ratio (%) of music audio compressed by MP3, AAC, and WMA at DWT levels of 2 to 8 with a bit rate of 128 kbps.

(1) Classical			
DWT level	Signal processing		
	MP3	AAC	WMA
2	99.07	99.41	99.99
3	99.67	99.69	100
4	99.99	99.9	100
5	99.98	99.98	100
6	100	100	100
7	100	100	100
8	99.86	100	100

(2) Jazz			
DWT level	Signal processing		
	MP3	AAC	WMA
2	98.63	99.33	99.95
3	99.64	99.8	100
4	99.97	99.99	100
5	100	100	99.98
6	100	100	100
7	100	100	99.93
8	99.86	100	100

(3) Popular			
DWT level	Signal processing		
	MP3	AAC	WMA
2	92.78	95.08	99.95
3	95.05	98.5	100
4	97.37	99.7	99.99
5	98.53	99.98	100
6	99.71	100	100
7	100	100	100
8	99.86	100	100

(4) Rock			
DWT level	Signal processing		
	MP3	AAC	WMA
2	94.2	95.88	99.81
3	96.72	98.79	99.98
4	98.89	99.85	100
5	99.64	99.98	100
6	100	100	99.96
7	100	100	100
8	100	100	100

(5) Hiphop			
DWT level	Signal processing		
	MP3	AAC	WMA
2	95.65	61.31	99.6
3	96.27	72.89	99.69
4	96.85	84.3	99.69
5	98.19	91.64	99.89
6	99.67	94.57	100
7	99.93	96.67	100
8	99.57	97.55	100

(%)

Table 5. Authentication ratio (%) of music audio compressed by MP3, AAC, and WMA at DWT levels of 2 to 8 with a bit rate of 96 kbps.

(1) Classical			
DWT level	Signal processing		
	MP3	AAC	WMA
2	95.95	98.76	99.96
3	96.92	99.08	99.99
4	97.89	99.48	100
5	98.53	99.64	100
6	99.53	99.78	100
7	99.71	100	100
8	99.71	99.86	100

(2) Jazz			
DWT level	Signal processing		
	MP3	AAC	WMA
2	96.48	98.62	99.97
3	98.42	99.39	100
4	99.79	99.95	100
5	100	99.98	99.98
6	100	100	100
7	100	100	99.93
8	100	99.86	100

(3) Popular			
DWT level	Signal processing		
	MP3	AAC	WMA
2	85.61	89.7	99.62
3	94.74	94.7	99.9
4	97.43	98.4	99.85
5	98.79	99.42	99.98
6	99.89	100	100
7	99.86	100	100
8	99.86	100	100

(4) Rock			
DWT level	Signal processing		
	MP3	AAC	WMA
2	89.79	92.56	99.33
3	95.37	96.3	99.78
4	98.58	98.94	99.98
5	99.69	99.8	100
6	99.96	99.89	99.96
7	100	100	100
8	100	100	100

(5) Hiphop			
DWT level	Signal processing		
	MP3	AAC	WMA
2	92.76	94.86	99.46
3	94.13	96.16	99.54
4	95.38	97.43	99.6
5	97.01	98.84	99.84
6	98.91	99.67	100
7	99.57	99.93	100
8	99.86	100	100

(%)

Table 6. Authentication ratio (%) of music audio compressed by MP3, AAC, and WMA at DWT levels of 2 to 8 with a bit rate of 64 kbps.

(1) Classical		
DWT level	Signal processing		
	MP3	AAC	WMA
2	98.18	98.08	99.88
3	98.87	98.51	99.96
4	99.54	99	99.98
5	99.91	98.73	100
6	99.96	99.13	100
7	99.93	99.42	100
8	99.86	100	100

(2) Jazz		
DWT level	Signal processing		
	MP3	AAC	WMA
2	92.41	97.23	99.85
3	95.45	98.45	100
4	98.39	99.54	100
5	99.93	99.95	99.98
6	100	99.89	100
7	100	99.86	99.93
8	99.71	100	100

(3) Popular		
DWT level	Signal processing		
	MP3	AAC	WMA
2	73.87	81.86	96.73
3	87.94	90.43	99.44
4	95.21	96.02	99.42
5	98.26	97.77	99.84
6	99.78	98.8	100
7	100	99.57	100
8	99.86	99.14	100

(4) Rock		
DWT level	Signal processing		
	MP3	AAC	WMA
2	82.67	88.43	96.12
3	91.55	93.67	99.14
4	97.09	97.56	99.69
5	99.4	98.91	99.95
6	99.93	99.17	99.96
7	100	99.35	100
8	100	99.71	100

(5) Hiphop		
DWT level	Signal processing		
	MP3	AAC	WMA
2	82.13	92.95	97.86
3	86	94.35	98.85
4	89.31	95.82	98.78
5	92.62	96.7	99.31
6	97.43	97.9	99.86
7	98.48	98.26	99.86
8	98.27	98.99	99.86

(%)

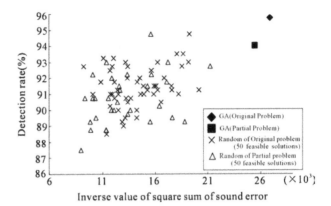

Figure 7. Relationship between sound quality after embedding the DW and detection rate of the DW [13].

dio clip and 96-kbps MP3 compression [13]. The same original music audio clip was also used in the present experiment. In order to achieve a high detection rate of the DW and high quality of the original music audio clip after embedding the DW, the reported method using a genetic algorithm was effective, as shown in **Figure 7**. In the present study, the authentication ratio for the same original music audio clip as that used for getting the results of **Figure 7** was 100%, and a deterioration in the quality of the original music audio clip did not occur, which corresponds to an infinite value on the horizontal axis shown in **Figure 7**.

Moreover, it took 2.41×10^4 to 3.20×10^4 s and 1.59×10^2 to 1.85×10^3 s (with the personal computer referred to as PC2), respectively, to embed the DW using as the formula of the optimization problem the original problem and the partial problem (which had a much smaller search space) [14], while it took 2.05×10^{-1} to 2.10×10^{-1} s (with the personal computer referred to as PC2) and 2.03×10^{-1} to 2.19×10^{-1} s (with the personal computer referred to as PC1) for one coding for an original music audio clip in the present study (**Table 7**). In the reported study [13,14], the experiment was performed in the following computation environment: the personal computer was a Dell Dimension DXC051 (CPU: Pentium IV 3.0 GHz; main memory: 1.0 GB), which is referred to as PC2 in **Table 7**; the OS was Microsoft Windows XP; the development language was Microsoft Visual C++ 6.0. The average time for one coding for an original music audio clip was less than 10^{-5} times that to embed the DW using as the formula of the optimization problem the original problem, and less than 10^{-3} times that to embed the DW using as the formula of the optimization problem the partial problem in the reported study. In addition, no deterioration in quality of the original music audio clip ever occurred using the proposed method. These two factors strongly suggest that the proposed method is far superior to the reported method.

Table 7. Comparison of time(s) to obtain a coding of the proposed method or to embed the DW using as the formula of the optimization problem the original problem and the partial problem of the reported study [14].

	Coding		DW	
			Original problem	Partial problem
	PC1	PC2	PC2	PC2
Classical	2.19×10^{-1}	2.05×10^{-1}	3.20×10^{4}	1.04×10^{3}
Jazz	2.03×10^{-1}	2.06×10^{-1}	2.52×10^{4}	5.12×10^{2}
Popular	2.19×10^{-1}	2.10×10^{-1}	2.41×10^{4}	1.85×10^{3}
Rock	2.19×10^{-1}	2.08×10^{-1}	2.44×10^{4}	2.02×10^{2}
HipHop	2.19×10^{-1}	2.08×10^{-1}	2.78×10^{4}	1.59×10^{2}
Average	2.16×10^{-1}	2.07×10^{-1}	2.67×10^{4}	7.53×10^{2}

PC1: Dell Dimension 8300 (CPU: Pentium IV 3.2 GHz; main memory: 2.0 GB); PC2: Dell Dimension DXC051 (CPU: Pentium IV 3.0GHz; main memory: 1.0 GB).

5. Conclusions

We have developed an authentication method for music audio using a DWT. When we applied this method to five original music audio clips, the authentication ratio was 100%. Moreover, for music audio data compressed by MP3, AAC, or WMA, the authentication ratio was always at or near 100%. We used flags for distinguishing the wavelet coefficients used for storing a 0 or 1 bit of the original and authentication coding from other coefficients. The method never deteriorated the quality of the original music audio because it does not change it. When a level 8 DWT was used, which was the standard in this experiment, the mean time for the coding for the original music audio clip was 2.16×10^{-1} s and that for the authentication was 2.22×10^{-1} s for a 10-second original music audio clip. We propose that a music audio file should be judged to be authenticated when the file gives a 95% or higher authentication ratio for a certain clip taken from the music audio file.

For using the proposed method, we need to store in a data base 1) flags used for selective coding, and 2) an original code of each audio file whose copy right we should protect. In calculating the authentication ratio for the authentication of an original audio file, we do not need an original audio file but 1) the flags, and 2) the original code of the original audio file.

6. References

[1] D. Kirovski and H. S. Malvar, "Spread-Spectrum Water-marking of Audio Signals," *IEEE Transactions on Signal Processing*, Vol. 51, No. 4, 2003, pp. 1020-1033.

[2] K. Yeo and H. J. Kim, "Modified Patchwork Algorithm: A Novel Audio Watermarking Scheme," *IEEE Transactions on Speech and Audio Processing*, Vol. 11, No. 4, 2003, pp. 381-386.

[3] S. Wu, J. Huang, D. Huang and Y. Q. Shi, "Efficiently Self-synchronized Audio Watermarking for Assured Audio Data Transmission," *IEEE Transactions on Broadcasting*, Vol. 51, No. 1, 2005, pp. 69-76.

[4] X. Y. Wang and H. Zhao, "A Novel Synchronization Invariant Audio Watermarking Scheme Based on DWT and DCT," *IEEE Transactions on Signal Processing*, Vol. 54, No. 12, 2006, pp. 4835-4840.

[5] S. Xiang and J. Huang, "Histogram-based Audio Water-marking against Time-Scale Modification and Cropping Attacks," *IEEE Transactions on Multimedia*, Vol. 9, No. 7, November 2007, pp. 1357-1372.

[6] S. Kirbiz, A. N. Lemma, M. U. Celik and S. Katzenbeis-ser, "Decode-Time Forensic Watermarking of AAC Bit-streams," *IEEE Transactions on Information Forensics and Security*, Vol. 2, No. 4, 2007, pp. 683-696.

[7] D. J. Coumou and G. Sharma, "Insertion, Deletion Codes with Feature-Based Embedding: A New Paradigm for Watermark Synchronization with Applications to Speech Watermarking," *IEEE Transactions on Information Forensics and Security*, Vol. 3, No. 2, 2008, pp. 153-165.

[8] S. Xianga, H. J. Kimb and J. Huanga, "Audio Water-marking Robust against Time-Scale Modification and MP3 Compression," *Signal Processing*, Vol. 88, No. 10, 2008, pp. 2372-2387.

[9] X. Y. Wang, P. P. Niu and H. Y. Yang, "A Robust, Digital-audio Watermarking Method," *IEEE Multimedia*, Vol. 16, No. 3, 2009, pp. 60- 69.

[10] N. K. Kalantari, M. A. Akhaee, S. M. Ahadi and H. Amindavar, "Robust Multiplicative Patchwork Method for Audio Watermarking," *IEEE Transactions on Audio, Speech and Language Processing*, Vol. 17, No. 6, 2009, pp. 1133-1141.

[11] X. Y. Wanga, P. P. Niub and H. Y. Yangb, "A Robust Digital Audio Watermarking Based on Statistics Charac-teristics," *Pattern Recognition*, Vol. 42, No. 11, 2009, pp. 3057-3064.

[12] K. Yamamoto and M. Iwakiri, "Real-Time Audio Wa-termarking Based on Characteristics of PCM in Digital Instrument," *Journal of Information Hiding and Multimedia Signal Processing*, Vol. 1, No. 2, 2010, pp. 59-71.

[13] S. Murata, Y. Yoshitomi and H. Ishii, "Optimization of Embedding Position in an Audio Watermarking Method Using Wavelet Transform," *Autumn Research Presentation Forums of ORSJ*, Japanese, October 2007, pp. 210-211.

[14] S. Murata, "Optimization of Embedding Position in an Audio Watermarking Method Using Wavelet Transform," Master's Thesis, Osaka University, Suita, Japanese, 2006, pp. 53.

[15] D. Inoue and Y. Yoshitomi, "Watermarking Using Wavelet Transform and Genetic Algorithm for Realizing High Tolerance to Image Compression," *Journal of the IIEEJ*, Vol. 38, No. 2, March 2009, pp. 136-144.

[16] M. Shino, Y. Choi and K. Aizawa, "Wavelet Domain Digital Watermarking Based on Threshold-Variable Decision," Technical Report of IEICE, DSP2000-86, Japanese, Vol. 100, No. 325, September 2000, pp. 29-34.

[17] M. Goto, H. Hashiguchi, T. Nishimura and R. Oka, "RWC Music Database: Database of Copyright-Cleared Musical Pieces and Instrument Sounds for Research Purposes," *Transactions of IPSJ*, Japanese, Vol. 45, No. 3, March 2004, pp. 728-738.

[18] M. Tanaka and Y. Yoshitomi, "Optimization Problem for Embedding Position in an Audio Watermarking Based on Logarithmic Amplitude Modification for Realizing High Tolerance to MP3 Compression," *Autumn Research Presentation Forums of ORSJ*, Japanese, September 2006, pp. 70-71.

[19] M. Tanaka and Y. Yoshitomi, "Digital Audio Watermarking Method with MP3 Tolerance Using Genetic Algorithm," *Proceedings of 11th Czech-Japan Seminar on Data Analysis and Decision Making Under Uncertainty*, Sendai, September 2008, pp. 81-85.

[20] R. Tachibana, "Capacity Analysis of Audio Watermarking Based on Logarithmic Amplitude Modification against Additive Noise," *IEICE Transactions on Fundamentals of Electronics, Communications and Computer Sciences*, Japanese, Vol. J86-A, No. 11, November 2003, pp. 1197-1206.

11

Effective and Extensive Virtual Private Network

Tarek S. Sobh, Yasser Aly

Information Systems Department, Egyptian Armed Forces, Cairo, Egypt

Abstract

A Virtual Private Network (VPN) allows the provisioning of private network services for an organization over a public network such as the Internet. In other words a VPN can transform the characteristics of a public which may be non-secure network into those of a private secure network through using encrypted tunnels. This work customized a standard VPN to a newly one called EEVPN (Effective Extensive VPN). It transmits a small data size in through a web based system in a reasonable time without affecting the security level. The proposed EEVPN is more effective where it takes small data transmission time with achieving high level of security. Also, the proposed EEVPN is more extensive because it is not built for a specific environment.

Keywords: Virtual Private Network, Network Security, Secure Data Transmission

1. Introduction

Connecting to the internet using Virtual Private Networks (VPNs) [1,2] achieves a great security transmission over the internet to the users.

Most computer systems today have 3 major lines of defense: access control, intrusion detection and prevention, and data encryption. In addition, Access control and intrusion detection [3,4] are not helpful against compromising of the authentication module. If a password is weak and has been compromised, access control and intrusion detection cannot prevent the loss or corruption of information that the compromised user was authorized to access, and also it is not helpful when the intruder uses the system and software bugs to compromise the integrity, confidentiality, or availability of resources [5,6].

To improve security solution, this work introduces a customized Effective and Extensive Virtual Private Networks called (EEVPN). The proposed EEVPN used to secure war game as a web based system. It is more effective because it is faster than other VPNs where it takes less transmission time. Here we achieved this result after comparing the proposed model results with the corresponding Cisco VPN and IBM VPN results over the same data transmission.

This paper is structured as follows: Section 2 explains VPN basic definitions and some related work. Section 3 introduces the proposed model idea and implemented algorithm. Section 4 explains the experimental results and finally Section 5 contains conclusion.

2. Virtual Private Networks

VPNs reduce remote access costs by using public network resources. Compared to other solutions, including private networks, a VPN is inexpensive [7].

A VPN uses data encryption and other security mechanisms to prevent unauthorized users from accessing data, and to ensure that data cannot be modified without detection as it flows through the Internet [8,9]. It then uses the tunneling process to transport the encrypted data across the Internet. Tunneling is a mechanism for encapsulating one protocol in another protocol as shown in **Figure 1**.

2.1. VPN Architectures

A VPN consists of four main components: 1) a VPN client, 2) a Network Access Server (NAS), 3) a tunnel terminating device or VPN server, 4) a VPN protocol. In a typical access VPN connection, a remote user (or VPN client) initiates a PPP connection with the ISP's NAS via the public switched telephone network (PSTN) [10,11]. An NAS is a device that terminates dial-up calls over analog (basic telephone service) or digital (ISDN) circuits [8]. The NAS is owned by the ISP, and is usually implemented in the ISP's POP. After the user has been authenticated by the appropriate authentication method, the NAS directs the packet to the tunnel that connects both the NAS and the VPN server. The VPN server may reside in the ISP's POP or at the corporate site, depending on the VPN model that is implemented.

The VPN server recovers the packet from the tunnel, unwraps it, and delivers it to the corporate network. **Figure 2** illustrates VPN architecture. There are four tunneling protocols used to establish VPNs, and three are extensions of the Point-to-Point Protocol (PPP) [5,6,10,11]: 1) Point-to-Point Tunneling Protocol (PPTP). 2) Layer 2 Forwarding (L2F). 3) Layer 2 Tunneling Protocol (L2TP). 4) IP Security (IPSec) Protocol Suite. In this Section we will discuss IPSec with some details because IPSec can work with IP4 and IP6.

IPSec provides cryptography-based protection of all data at the IP layer of the communications stack. It provides secure communications transparently, with no changes required to existing applications [12,13].

IPSec protects network traffic data in three ways [12, 13]: 1) Authentication: The process by which the identity of a host or end point is verified. 2) Integrity checking: The process of ensuring that no modifications were made to the data while in-transit across the network. 3) Encryption: The process of "hiding" information while in-transit across the network in order to ensure privacy.

2.3 Commercial VPNs

Many companies produced a lot of VPNs deals with dif-

ferent data sizes. On the other hand a few works that deal with small data sizes especially less than 1 MB, because it is a special purpose for specific application such as War Game which needs high security with low time transmission.

Here we will discuss two popular VPN commercial products Cisco VPN and IBM VPN. There are different VPN products from both Cisco and IBM such as Cisco's VPN 3000 Concentrator, Cisco VPN client 3.0, Cisco Easy VPN and IBM eNetwork. Cisco's VPN (Virtual Private Network) 3000 Concentrator solution utilizes advanced PKI technology that enables mobile and remote users to securely transfer sensitive information in fully encrypted format [www.Cisco.com].

With eToken, there is only one password to remember. Users can take their authentication keys and digital certificates with them wherever they go, on a key chain or in their pocket. Full two-factor authentication can easily be implemented from any computer that runs the Cisco VPN client 3.0 via Microsoft's CAPI interface when communicating with a Cisco VPN 30XX Concentrator Series [www.Cisco.com].

Cisco Easy VPN, a software enhancement for existing Cisco routers and security appliances, greatly simplifies VPN deployment for remote offices and teleworkers. Based

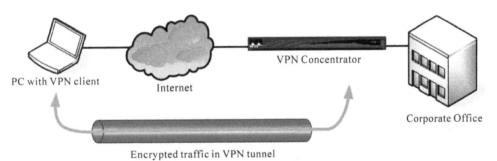

Figure 1. VPN Implementation [9].

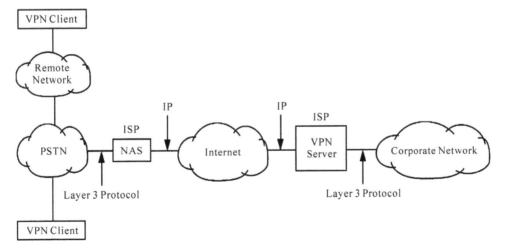

Figure 2. VPN Architecture [13].

on the Cisco Unified Client Framework, Cisco Easy VPN centralizes VPN management across all Cisco VPN devices thus reducing the complexity of VPN deployments [www.Cisco.com].

Cisco Easy VPN enables an integration of VPN remotes-Cisco routers, Cisco ASA & PIX Security Appliances, Cisco VPN concentrators or software clients-within a single deployment with a consistent policy and key management method thus simplifying remote side administration [www.Cisco.com].

eNetwork is IBM's VPN Solutions [www.IBM.com]. Here we explain briefly the implementation of eNetwork VPN and describe its value. It is based on IPSec. However, given the multitude of network environments and business needs, all scenarios have not been addressed in this section.

IBM added-value while many VPN solutions today consist only of firewalls, IBM eNetwork VPN solutions will also encompass multi-platform VPN-enabled clients and servers, routers, and management functions [www.IBM.com]. The advantages of IBM VPN solutions are: scalability; flexibility of VPN function placement; and the ability to have secure IP tunnels all the way from the client to IBM servers, where the majority of critical corporate data resides today. Also, IBM VPN solutions can be customized to be as secure or as flexible as required. It provides capabilities that can link your IT assets with Web technology to build secure e-business solutions [www.IBM.com].

2.4. War Games and VPN

War game is a simulated battle between two or more opposing fighting sides [3,4,14]. In most cases, there are two fighting sides and they are represented by the red and blue colors. Each side has its own goals to achieve at the expense of the other side, considering each side capabilities, organization, weapons, and tactical experience of management armed forces during the battle. In addition, environmental conditions such as battle terrain nature, battle timing, weather, surrounding environment must be considered. In addition to the fighting sides, one more side representing the arbitrator must be existed in the war game system. The arbitrator side is responsible of monitoring the fighting sides and evaluates their decisions.

Although it may be possible to play some forms of war games without the use of any prepared materials, most war games require a set of tools to keep track of and display data, force locations and movements, and interactions between opposing units. We have different instrumentality of war games [3,4]:
- Manual games, which represented by simple tools:

maps, charts, notebook of data, and orders of battles, perhaps a set of written rules and procedures and all decisions are man-made.
- Computer-assisted games use machines ranging from desktop personal computers to very large mainframes. The machines are used to keep track of the force positions, their movement, weapon capabilities, and other critical, data-intensive pieces of information.
- Rand Corporation (fully automated) has been in the forefront of an effort to extend the role of the computer beyond that of capable assistant or sometimes opponent. This game is carried out completely on a computer, although usually with human intervention to issue orders.

The integrated software components for implementing web based war games system of each side include: 1) Operating system component 2) Database component 3) GIS component.

Securing web based war games system is very important. The main task is to achieve a high level of security to the web based war game system [5] and controlling its sides' behaviors. Since the entire network packets are going from or to the side LAN must be passed through the gateway computer, the security process is activated on the gateway computer. Encryption/decryption module is responsible of doing two tasks [14,15]. The first task is encrypting each network packet before going out from the side LAN to the web. The second is decrypting each network packet coming from the web before entering the side LAN. This is why we use a VPN for securing web based war games system. The main task of VPN here is to achieve a high level of security to the web based war games system and controlling its sides' behaviors.

3. Proposed Model

As shown in **Figure 3**, this work provides three levels of security to secure the web based war game system in the following manner:

Access control module: the access control is applied to our web based war game system using two access control mechanisms. The first mechanism is the server operating system access control mechanism. This mechanism is applied to the war game system resources (directories, files, printers ...etc). The second mechanism is the DBMS access control mechanism and it is applied to the war game system database.

Virtual Private Network security module: this module is responsible of doing two tasks. The first task is encrypting each network packet before going out from the side LAN to the web. The second is decrypting each network packet coming from he web before entering the

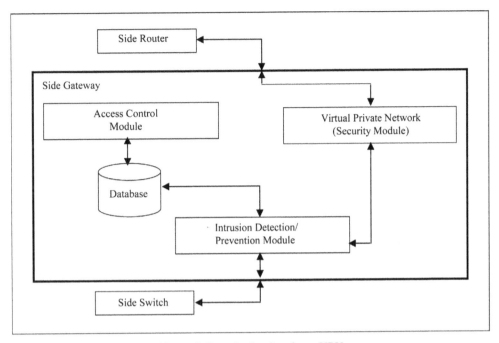

Figure 3. Security levels using a VPN.

side LAN.

Intrusion detection/prevention module: this module is responsible of checking each incoming network packet and test if it represents a normal or intrusive behavior. If the packet represents a normal behavior, the intrusion detection module forwards it to its destination; otherwise, an alarm is given to the system administrator and the packet will be blocked.

Some encryption schemes can be proven secure on the basis of the presumed hardness of a mathematical problem. Some times the secure encryption schemes it has a mathematical meaning, and there are multiple different other definitions. The proposed model use a public-key cryptography as a part from encryption schemes of VPN but it is used within our context in which the scheme will be deployed securely as shown in **Figure 3**. We customized both PPTP and IPSec for our EEVPN by erasing many overheads from them which are only needed for keeping security at large transmission time (*i.e.* large data size), so we became faster without affecting security.

EEVPN is very easy to configure and install. It is basically a wrapper for sending packets over an SSL (Ver. 3.0) connection. It supports public key encryption using client & server certificates (SSLv3). We have used a bit different approach here (*i.e.* we haven't used amvpn-keytool). **Figure 4** traces the path taken by a packet as it travels over the SSL3 tunnel created by EEVPN.

Each layer of protocol adds some bytes of overhead. This fact is illustrated in **Figure 4**. Since EEVPN just acts like a wrapper program to send packets over an SSL

connection, no overhead is introduced by the EEVPN program itself. However the underlying SSL layer does add some headers. Also, we put up small ssl-timeline details about SSL handshake procedure, along with introduction to using ssldump, which is very useful to capture SSL sessions.

Figure 4 shows that the EEVPN layer produces two packets, a short packet of 29 bytes is generated with the normal packet of 152 bytes, for an input of length 128 bytes. We have found this behavior even for other wrappers like Stunnel. However, at this point, we are not yet sure as to why the shorter packet is generated and what it contains.

EEVPN does not provide mechanism to achieve compression (*i.e.* EEVPN does not support any compression mechanisms). Also no option is provided which can allow a user to select a cipher suite. The cipher suite IN USE, can be only be found out by taking the SSLdump of the session.

We conducted a series of experiments with random packet sizes and measured the packet length on the wire. The experimental results can be accessed here from the results one can conclude that EEVPN solution adds an average of 155 bytes of overhead to the data.

EEVPN uses the cryptographic functions provided by your SSL implementation plugin. Hence, if someone needs to add his own algorithm, he has to look for plug-in support in the SSL implementation that he is using or built his own code.

Currently, we are using open SSL implementation of SSL, which AFAIK does not yet support any plug-in

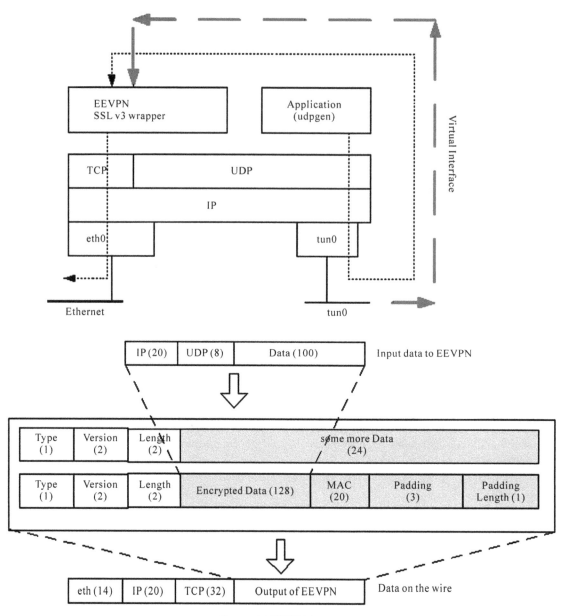

Figure 4. EEVPN layers.

algorithms to be used. However there is always the option of patching the source code itself with new algorithms and recompile the code.

The PPP-over-SSL solution for forming VPN is highly scalable. For example if a company has 'N' different sites, then it would be necessary to have O(N^2) point-topoint PPP-over-SSH links and each site will have to maintain an entry in the routing table for (N-1) other sites. It is clear a full mesh will be necessary in this case, as the complexity of maintaining any other network infrastructure will be prohibitively high.

Here the proposed EEVPN algorithm is embedded in a war game system [14] as a web based system to be one of the defense lines for securing the war game data over the public network the Internet as shown in **Figure 5**.

In our example we can now execute a war game as a web based application system in a secured manner because we will be sure from achieving authentication, integrity, and confidentiality.

[We used Microsoft visual basic 6.0 enterprise edition to design and execute the security test program]

It includes identifying the remote IP address and using encryption for data transmitted or decryption for data received.

If we send the data from side to another side without using the encryption mechanism in VPN (*i.e.* without making check for encryption), there is a possibility for hackers to get the data, modify it, or destroy it.

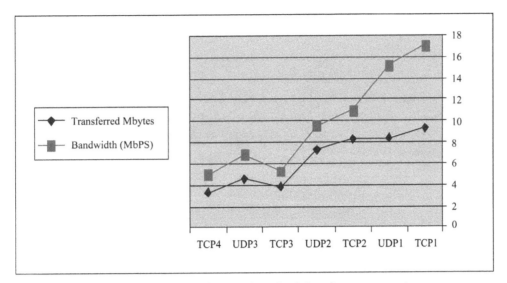

Figure 5. Hardware implementation of web based war game system.

But if we use the encryption mechanism in VPN (*i.e.* check for encryption) the data transmitted will not be understudiedable for anyone else the specific recipient how has the specific IP address, and has the decryption capability due to VPN security checks.

When the transmitted data has been received to the destination side that has the capability to decrypt the data and understand it, otherwise it will not be understandable data if not choosing VPN decryption mechanism.

Algorithm for testing security (Encryption & Decryption)

```
Sub data send
        Read (data)
        If check encryption sending is true then send en-
crypt (data)
                Else send (data)
End Sub
Sub load port
                Local port = value
        Remote port = value
End Sub
Sub data arrive
        If check decryption receiving is true then receive
decrypt (data)
                Else receive (data)
End Sub
Sub encrypt (string)
        Loop i from 1 to length (string)
            encrypt = encrypt & key(i)
End Sub
Sub decrypt (string)
        Loop i from 1 to length (string)
            decrypt = decrypt & key(i)
End Sub
```

4. Experimental Results

Our objective is to measure & compare security level, transmission time for our created VPN with respect to other VPNs, via web based application. Measurements for transmission time with respect to data packet size:

In order to keep everything isolated, we created a new user/group (avpn/zvpn) on client (a) and server (z) using Linux command line, also passwordless login was created using SSH.

A series of tests [15-18] were run to determine the effects of a VPN connection on wireless network performance. In particular, we were interested in the performance "hit" one might take when accessing a VPN via a wireless connection (we tested a wired connection for comparison). All tests were performed using Iperf and CMPmetrics as trusted benchmarks. The First test was done using a PPTP VPN connection. The second test was done using the Cisco IPSec client for Windows 2000. The range of nodes used is between 100 and 1500 nodes.

4.1. Proposed EEVPN and Cisco VPN Results

Table 1 is a summary result of IPSec client test in case of using Cisco VPN for both plain and encrypted wireless traffic. **Table 2** is a summary result of PPTP test for plain and encrypted traffic in case of wireless connection and traditional wired traffic.

Table 3 is a summary result of proposed EEVPN with IPSec client test for both plain and encrypted wireless traffic. **Table 4** is a summary result of proposed EEVPN with PPTP test for plain and encrypted traffic in case of wireless connection and traditional wired traffic.

Figures 6-9 show another representation of the experimental output results of the above tables.

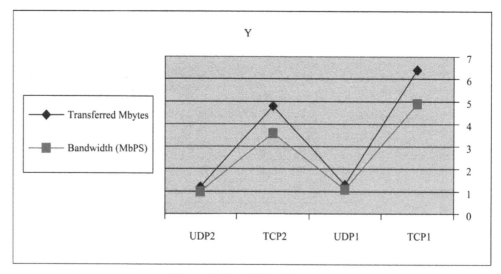

Figure 6. Cisco IPSec client test.

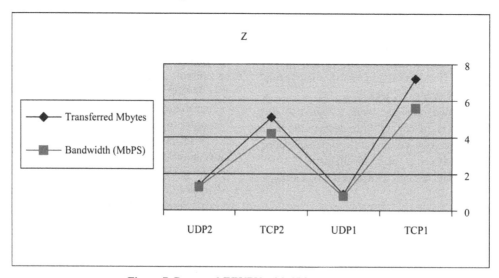

Figure 7. Proposed EEVPN with IPSec client test.

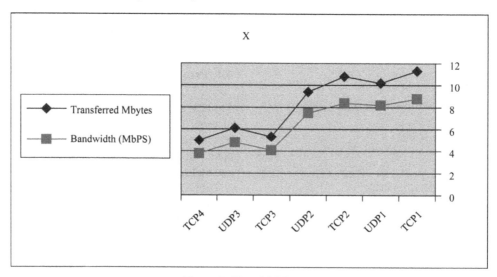

Figure 8. Cisco PPTP test.

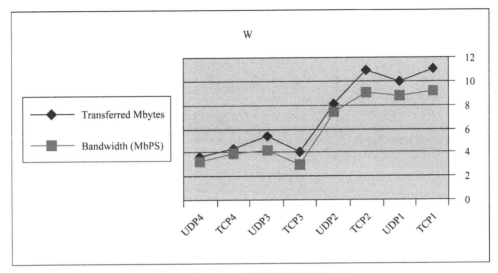

Figure 9. Proposed EEVPN PPTP test.

Table 1. IPSec client test in case of using Cisco VPN.

Test#	Protocol	Bytes (KB) transferred	Bandwidth (Mbps)
1	TCP	640	4.9
(non-encrypted wireless)	UDP	130	1.1
2	TCP	480	3.6
(encrypted wireless)	UDP	120	1.0

Table 3. Proposed EEVPN with IPSec client test.

Test#	Protocol	Bytes (KB) transferred	Bandwidth (Mbps)
1	TCP	720	5.6
(non-encrypted wireless)	UDP	90	0.8
2	TCP	510	4.2
(encrypted wireless)	UDP	140	1.3

Table 2. Cisco PPTP test.

Test#	Protocol	Bytes (KB) transferred	Bandwidth (Mbps)
1	TCP	1130	8.8
(non-encrypted wired)	UDP	1020	8.2
2	TCP	1080	8.4
(encrypted wired)	UDP	940	7.5
3	TCP	530	4.1
(non-encrypted wireless)	UDP	610	4.8
4	TCP	500	3.8
(encrypted wireless)	UDP	470	3.8

Table 4. Proposed EEVPN with PPTP test.

Test#	Protocol	Bytes (KB) transferred	Bandwidth (Mbps)
1	TCP	1110	9.2
(non-encrypted wired)	UDP	1000	8.8
2	TCP	1090	9.1
(encrypted wired)	UDP	810	7.4
3	TCP	410	3.0
(non-encrypted wireless)	UDP	540	4.2
4	TCP	430	3.9
(encrypted wireless)	UDP	360	3.2

4.2. Proposed EEVPN and IBM VPN Results

Table 5 is a summary result of IPSec client test in case of using IBM VPN for both plain and encrypted wireless traffic. **Table 6** is a summary result of PPTP test for plain and encrypted traffic in case of wireless connection and traditional wired traffic.

Figures 10-13 show another representation of the experimental output results of the above tables.

We can notice for the above figures that smaller values transferred we have better bandwidth in EEVPN than CISCO and IBM VPN, but in higher values transferred

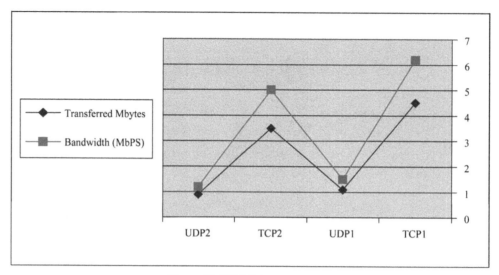

Figure 10. IBM IPSec client test.

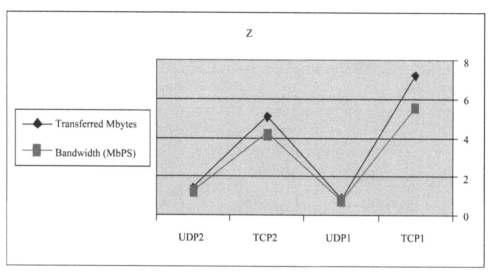

Figure 11. Proposed EEVPN with IPSec client test.

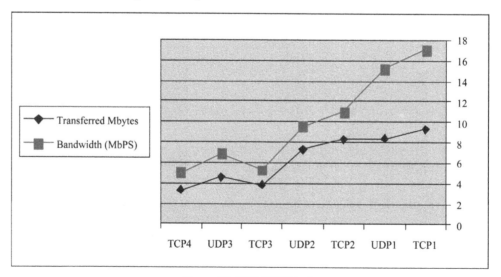

Figure 12. IBM PPTP test.

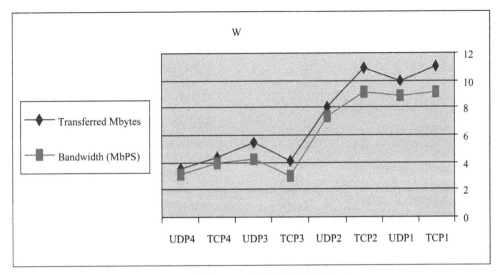

Figure 13. Proposed EEVPN PPTP test.

Table 5. IPSec client test in case of using IBM VPN.

Test#	Protocol	Bytes (KB) transferred	Bandwidth (Mbps)
1	TCP	620	4.5
(non-encrypted wireless)	UDP	150	1.1
2	TCP	500	3.5
(encrypted wireless)	UDP	120	0.9

Table 6. IBM PPTP test.

Test#	Protocol	Bytes (KB) transferred	Bandwidth (Mbps)
1	TCP	1710	9.3
(non-encrypted wired)	UDP	1520	8.4
2	TCP	1100	8.3
(encrypted wired)	UDP	960	7.3
3	TCP	530	3.8
(non-encrypted wireless)	UDP	690	4.6
4	TCP	500	3.3
(encrypted wireless)	UDP	490	3.5

we have better bandwidth in CISCO and IBM VPN than EEVPN.

Comparing results ensures that low transmission time is for EEVPN.

We can say that if we will transfer smaller values of bytes, it is better to use EEVPN, like in our implementa-tion in which we secured a war game, we will deal with smaller values of bytes, keeping high security level which we tested using our program & trying to hack messages during data transmission to ensure data integrity & con-fidentiality.

5. Conclusions

This work customized a standard Virtual Private Net-works (VPN) to a newly one called EEVPN (Effective Extensive VPN). In fact we need to transmit a small data size in our example war game as a web based system in a fastest way without affecting the security level. From the experimental results the proposed EEVPN is faster with losing to the security level.

The proposed EEVPN is more effective because it is faster than other VPNs in sending small data size; where it takes small data transmission time, achieving high lev-el of security. Also, the proposed EEVPN is more exten-sive because it is not built for a specific environment, which makes the customization of the VPN is very diffi-cult, so it can be installed at any environment which is faster and more secured than many other VPNs like CISCO VPN and IBM VPN incase of transmitting small data size (*i.e.* less than 1 MB).

We plan in the near future to implement some tech-niques in order to enhance quality of streaming over VPN.

6. References

[1] D. L. Clark, "IT Manger's Guide to Virtual Private Net-works," McGraw-Hill, New York, 1999.

[2] S. Badr, "Security Architecture for Internet Protocols,"

Ph.D. Thesis, Military Technical College, Cairo, 2001.

[3] A. Farouk, "Intrusion Detection in a War a Game Web Based Application," Master of Science Thesis, Ain Shams University, Cairo, 2004.

[4] A. E. Taha, "Secured Access Control in Web Based War Game Application," Master of Science Thesis, Ain -Shams University, Cairo, Egypt, October 2002.

[5] N. Malheiros, E. Madeira, F. L. Verdi and M. Magalhaesb, "Managing Layer 1 VPN Services," *Optical Switching and Networking*, Vol. 5, No. 4, 2008, pp. 196-218. doi:10.1016/j.osn.2008.02.002

[6] P. Juste, D. Wolinsky, P. Boykin, M. Covington and R. Figueiredo, "SocialVPN: Enabling Wide-Area Collaboration with Integrated Social and Overlay Networks," *Computer Networks*, Vol. 54, No. 12, August 2010, pp. 1926-1938. doi:10.1016/j.comnet.2009.11.019

[7] A. G. Yay1ml1, "Selective Survivability with Disjoint Nodes and Disjoint Lightpaths for Layer 1 VPN," *Optical Switching and Networking*, Vol. 6, No. 1, 2009, pp. 3-9. doi:10.1016/j.osn.2008.05.002

[8] C. Xenakis, C. Ntantogian and I. Stavrakakis, "A Networkassisted Mobile VPN for Securing Users Data in UMTS," *Computer Communications*, Vol. 31, No. 14, 2008, pp. 3315-3327. doi:10.1016/j.comcom.2008.05.018

[9] M. N. Ismail and M. T. Ismail, "Analyzing of Virtual Private Network over Open Source Application and Hardware Device Performance," *European Journal of Scientific Research*, Vol. 28, No. 2, 2009, pp: 215-226.

[10] R. Bolla, R. Bruschi, F. Davoli and M. Repetto, "Hybrid Optimization for QoS Control in IP Virtual Private Net-

works," *Computer Networks*, Vol. 52, No. 3, 2008, pp. 563-580. doi:10.1016/j.comnet.2007.10.006

[11] S. Gold, "Pirate Bay Develops Anonymous VPN User Protection," *Infosecurity*, Vol. 6, No. 3, 2009, pp. 8. doi:10.1016/S1754-4548(09)70045-2

[12] D. Forte *et al.*, "SSL VPN and Return on Investment: A Possible Combination," *Network Security*, Vol. 10, No. 10, 2009, pp. 17-19. doi:10.1016/S1353-4858(09)70112-6

[13] T. Rowan, "VPN Technology: IPSEC vs SSL," *Network Security*, Vol. 2007, No. 12, December 2007, pp. 13-17. doi: 10.1016/S1353-4858(07)70104-6

[14] J. F. Dunnigan, "Wargames Handbook: How to Play and Design Commercial and Professional Wargames," Writer's Club Press, 2000.

[15] Y. Dakroury, I. A. El-ghafar and A. Taha, "Secured Web-Based War Game Application Using Combined Smart Certificate and Secure Cookies Techniques," *Proceeding of the 1st IEEE International Symposium on Signal Processing and Information Technology*, Cairo, December 2001, pp. 447-453.

[16] Downloading rpm's for VPN, http://sourceforge.net/projects

[17] G. F. Luger, "Artificial Intelligence Structures and Strategies for Complex Problem Solving," 4th Edition, Addison Wesley, New York, 2001.

[18] K. Heller, K. Svore, A. Keromytis and S. Stolfo, "One Class Support Vector Machines for Detecting Anomalous Window Registry Accesses," *3rd IEEE Conference and Data Mining Workshop on Data Mining for Computer Security*, Florida, November 2003.

12

New Approach for Fast Color Image Encryption Using Chaotic Map

Kamlesh Gupta[1]*, Sanjay Silakari[2]
[1]*Department of Computer Science, Jaypee University of Engineering and Technology, Guna, India*
[2]*Department of Computer Science, Rajiv Gandhi Technical University, Bhopal, India*

Abstract

Image encryption using chaotic maps has been established a great way. The study shows that a number of functional architecture has already been proposed that utilize the process of diffusion and confusion. However, permutation and diffusion are considered as two separate stages, both requiring image-scanning to obtain pixel values. If these two stages are mutual, the duplicate scanning effort can be minimized and the encryption can be accelerated. This paper presents a technique which replaces the traditional preprocessing complex system and utilizes the basic operations like confusion, diffusion which provide same or better encryption using cascading of 3D standard and 3D cat map. We generate diffusion template using 3D standard map and rotate image by using vertically and horizontally red and green plane of the input image. We then shuffle the red, green, and blue plane by using 3D Cat map and standard map. Finally the Image is encrypted by performing XOR operation on the shuffled image and diffusion template. Theoretical analyses and computer simulations on the basis of Key space Analysis, statistical analysis, histogram analysis, Information entropy analysis, Correlation Analysis and Differential Analysis confirm that the new algorithm that minimizes the possibility of brute force attack for decryption and very fast for practical image encryption.

Keywords: Chaotic Map, 3D Cat Map, Standard Map, Confusion and Diffusion

1. Introduction

With the fast development of image transmission through computer networks especially the Internet, medical imaging and military message communication, the security of digital images has become a most important concern. Image encryption, is urgently needed but it is a challenging task because it is quite different from text encryption due to some intrinsic properties of images such as huge data capacity and high redundancy, which are generally difficult to handle by using conventional techniques. Nevertheless, many new image encryption schemes have been suggested in current years, among which the chaos-based approach appears to be a hopeful direction.

General permutation-diffusion architecture for chaos-based image encryption was employed in [1,2] as illustrated in **Figure 1**. In the permutation stage, the image pixels are relocated but their values stay unchanged. In the diffusion stage, the pixel values are modified so that a minute change in one-pixel spreads out to as many pixels as possible. Permutation and diffusion are two different and iterative stages, and they both require scanning the image in order to gain the pixel values. Thus, in the encryption process, each round of the permutation-diffusion operation requires at least twice scanning the same image.

In this paper, we generate diffusion template using 3D standard map and rotated image by using vertically and horizontally red and green plane of the input image. We then shuffle the red, green, and blue plane by using 3D

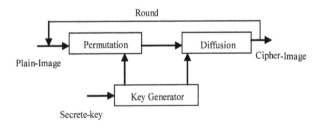

Figure 1. Permutation and diffusion based image cryptosystem.

Cat map and standard map. Finally the Image is encrypted by performing XOR operation on the shuffled image and diffusion template. The objectives of this new design includes: 1) to efficiently extract good pseudorandom sequences from a cascading of 3D cat and standard map for color image and 2) to simultaneously perform permutation and diffusion operations for fast encryption.

The rest of this paper is organized as follows: Section 2 focuses on the efficient generation of pseudorandom sequences. In Section 3, proposed algorithm is described in detail. Section 4 presents simulation results and performance analyses. In Section 5, conclusions and future work.

2. Efficient Generation of Pseudorandom Sequences

The generation of pseudorandom is based on two cascaded chaotic maps behave as a single chaotic map in present case. The 3D cat map & 3D standard map are taken for encryption. The pseudorandom matrix generated by this method is given below. (The explanation for pseudorandom sequences generation is given in Section 3).

3. Proposed Algorithm

The proposed algorithm are divided into several stages

Table 1. Generation of pseudorandom values by proposed method.

'FC'	'EE'	'C4'	'D1'	'E6'	'D3'	'E8'	'E9'	'EA'	'CB'	'EA'	'ED'
'D7'	'EC'	'D9'	'EE'	'5'	'FF'	'16'	'17'	'9'	'EF'	'FF'	'1B'
'26'	'9'	'A'	'E2'	'FA'	'2'	'FC'	'F5'	'1C'	'2F'	'1E'	'1F'
'2D'	'33'	'10'	'26'	'0'	'28'	'11'	'2A'	'4'	'17'	'15'	'F8'
'19'	'38'	'15'	'2B'	'3F'	'1E'	'19'	'41'	'2A'	'1C'	'1D'	'45'
'3C'	'40'	'10'	'33'	'47'	'44'	'58'	'37'	'5A'	'35'	'5C'	'3F'
'5F'	'41'	'51'	'5E'	'31'	'54'	'24'	'61'	'35'	'27'	'28'	'47'
'4D'	'6C'	'4F'	'6E'	'45'	'42'	'56'	'71'	'3A'	'59'	'3C'	'5B'
'63'	'89'	'74'	'6D'	'49'	'6F'	'69'	'61'	'6B'	'5D'	'6D'	'6E'
'8F'	'62'	'7B'	'64'	'89'	'66'	'7F'	'8C'	'53'	'54'	'64'	'9F'
'80'	'72'	'A6'	'74'	'99'	'67'	'7D'	'7E'	'9D'	'AD'	'80'	'81'
'87'	'97'	'89'	'99'	'9A'	'9B'	'9C'	'BB'	'70'	'AE'	'72'	'73'
'A2'	'A3'	'BF'	'A5'	'B5'	'A7'	'C2'	'9A'	'A6'	'C5'	'A8'	'9E'
'9D'	'BC'	'B2'	'90'	'AC'	'A1'	'AE'	'AF'	'A0'	'C8'	'C9'	'A3'
'CE'	'CF'	'DF'	'C1'	'BC'	'C3'	'E2'	'CE'	'CF'	'E5'	'E6'	'D1'
'E7'	'F7'	'CE'	'DB'	'D8'	'DD'	'DA'	'BD'	'DC'	'C5'	'E4'	'B1'

and explained below.

3.1. Diffusion Template

According to the proposal the diffusion template must have the same size as main image. Let the main image have m number of rows n number of columns then the diffusion template is created as follows

$$(i,j,k) = \text{round}\left(\frac{255}{n} \times j\right) \qquad (1)$$

where $1 \le i \le m$, $1 \le j \le n$ and $1 \le k \le 3$.

Equation (1) form the matrix with all rows filled with linearly spaced number in between 0 to 255. The sequence is randomized by 3D standard map in discrete form as given below.

The 3D standard map randomizes the pixels by reallocating it in new position by utilizing its property of one to one mapping. **Figure 2** shows the final diffusion template by using 3D standard map.

$$i' = (i+j)\bmod m \qquad (2)$$

$$j' = \left[j + k + K1 \times \sin\left(i \times \frac{c}{2 \times pi}\right)\right]\bmod n \qquad (3)$$

$$k'\left[k + K1 \times \sin\left(i \times \frac{p}{2 \times pi}\right) + K2 \times \sin\left(j \times \frac{p}{2 \times pi}\right)\right]\bmod p \qquad (4)$$

where the $K1$, $K2$ are the integers, $p = 3$ for the case of color image and i', j', k' shoes the transformed location of i, j, k.

$$I'_{\text{diff}}(i',j',k') = I'_{\text{diff}}(i,j,k).$$

3.2. Image Encryption

Step 1. The main image is divided into three separate images I_R, I_G and I_B as follows

$$I_R(x,y) = I(x,y,1) \quad I_G(x,y) = I(x,y,2)$$
$$I_B(x,y) = I(x,y,3)$$

where $1 \le x \le m$ and $1 \le y \le n$.

Step 2. The Red and Green image are transform verti-

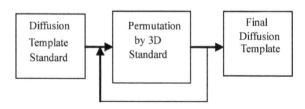

Figure 2. Diffusion template.

cally and horizontally respectively. The blue image remains same and reconstructs the new image.

$$I_R'(x,y) = I_R\left[\left(x+\frac{m}{2}\right)\right]\bmod m, y$$

$$I_G'(x,y) = I_R\left[x\left(y+\frac{n}{2}\right)\right]\bmod n$$

$$I_B'(x,y) = I_B(x,y) \quad I_{\text{new}}(x,y,1) = I_R'(x,y)$$
$$I_{\text{new}}(x,y,2) = I_G'(x,y) \quad I_{\text{new}}(x,y,3) = I_B'(x,y).$$

Step 3. Perform the first level confusion by using 2D cat map. Slice the plane normal to R, G, B Planes by

$$I'_{\text{new}}(i,j,k) = I'_{\text{SRGB}}(j',k') = I_{\text{new}}(i,j,k)$$
where $1 \le i \le m$, $1 \le j \le n$ and $1 \le k \le 3$.

$$j' = (j + r_x + r_y + p \times k)\bmod m$$

$$k' = (q \times j + r_y + (p \times q + 1) \times k)\bmod n$$

where j' and k' are obtained by 2D cat map and p and q are integer > 0 and r_x, r_y are offset integer such that $0 \le r_x \le m$, $0 \le r_y \le n$.

Step 4. Generate Final confusion stage by two cascade 3D maps first by cat map then by standard map. So the transformation of location (i, j, k) into (i'', j'', k'') is performed by following equations.

$$i' = \Big[\big((1 + a_x a_z b_y)\times i + a_z \times j$$
$$+ (a_y + a_x \times a_z + a_x \times a_y \times a_z \times b_y)\times k\big)\Big]\bmod m$$

$$i' = \Big[(b_z + a_x \times b_y + a_x \times a_z \times b_y \times b_z)\times i + (a_z \times b_z + 1)$$
$$\times j + (a_y \times a_z + a_x \times a_y \times a_z \times b_y \times b_z + a_x \times a_z \times b_y$$
$$+ a_y \times b_y + 1)\times k\Big]\bmod n$$

$$k' = \Big[(a_x \times b_x \times b_y + b_y)\times i + b_x \times j$$
$$+ (a_x \times a_y \times b_x \times b_y + a_x \times b_x + a_y \times b_y + 1)\times k\Big]\bmod p$$

$$i'' = \Big[(i' + k')\Big]\bmod m$$

$$j'' = \left[\left((i' + j') + K1 \times \sin\left(i'' \times \frac{n}{2 \times pi}\right)\right)\right]\bmod n$$

$$k'' = \left[k' + K1 \times \sin\left(i'' \times \frac{p}{2 \times pi}\right)\right.$$
$$\left. + K2 \times \sin\left(j + \frac{p}{2 \times pi}\right)\right]\bmod p$$

$$I_{\text{con}}f(i'',j'',k'') = I'(i,j,k)$$

where a_x, a_y, a_z, b_x, b_y, b_z and $K1$, $K2$ are integers > 0.

Each confusion step is followed by diffusion obtained

by EXOR operations performed between each pixels of I_{conf} and diffusion I_{diff}. The proposed image encryption architecture is given in **Figure 3**.

$$I_{\text{encp}} = I_{\text{conf}} \oplus I_{\text{diff}}.$$

3.3. Key Generation Process

The proposed method has a large number of variables which can be used as key parameters but to avoid the exceptionally large key and decreased key sensitivity, the parameter which does not having great affects on encryption are avoid or scaled. The selected key parameters and their length are given below

Step 1. Diffusion template shuffling $\mathbf{D_s}$ = 8 bits.

Step 2. Diffusion template offset value $\mathbf{D_x D_y D_z}$ = 8 + 8 + 2 = 18 bits.

Step 3. Diffusion template variables $\mathbf{D_{k1} D_{k2}}$ = 8 + 8 = 16 bits.

Step 4. Sliced RGB plane Shuffling = $\mathbf{S_s}$ = 8 bits.

Step 5. Sliced RGB plane offset values $\mathbf{S_x S_y}$ = 8 bits.

Step 6. Sliced RGB Plane Variables $\mathbf{S_p S_q}$ = 8 + 8 = 16 bits.

Step 7. Final Confusion shuffling $\mathbf{C_s}$ = 8 bits.

Step 8. Confusion offset of cat map $\mathbf{C_x C_y C_z}$ = 8 + 8 + 2 = 18 bits.

Step 9. Confusion cat map variables $\mathbf{C_a C_b}$ = 8 + 8 = 16 bits.

Step 10. Confusion offset of standard map $\mathbf{C_x' C_y' C_z'}$ = 8 + 8 + 2 = 18 bits.

Step 11. Confusion standard map variables $\mathbf{C_{k1} C_{k2}}$ = 8 + 8 = 16 bits.

Final key structure

$$\mathbf{D_s D_x D_y D_z D_{k1} D_{k2} S_s S_x S_y S_p S_q}$$
$$\mathbf{C_s C_x C_y C_z C_a C_b C_x' C_y' C_z' C_{k1} C_{k2}}$$

Total bits = 8 + 18 + 16 + 8 + 8 + 16 + 8 + 16 + 16 + 18 + 16 = 148 bits.

3.4. Image Decryption

Step 1. Generate the diffusion template in same way as in encryption section.

Step 2. Re-transformation of location is done by two cascaded 3D maps firstly by standard map then by cat map.

So the re-transformation of location (i'', j'', k'') into (i, j, k) is performed by following equations

$$i' = \Big[(i'' + k'')\Big]\bmod m$$

$$j' = \left[i'' + j'' + k1 \times \sin\left(i' \times \frac{n}{2 \times pi}\right)\right]\bmod n$$

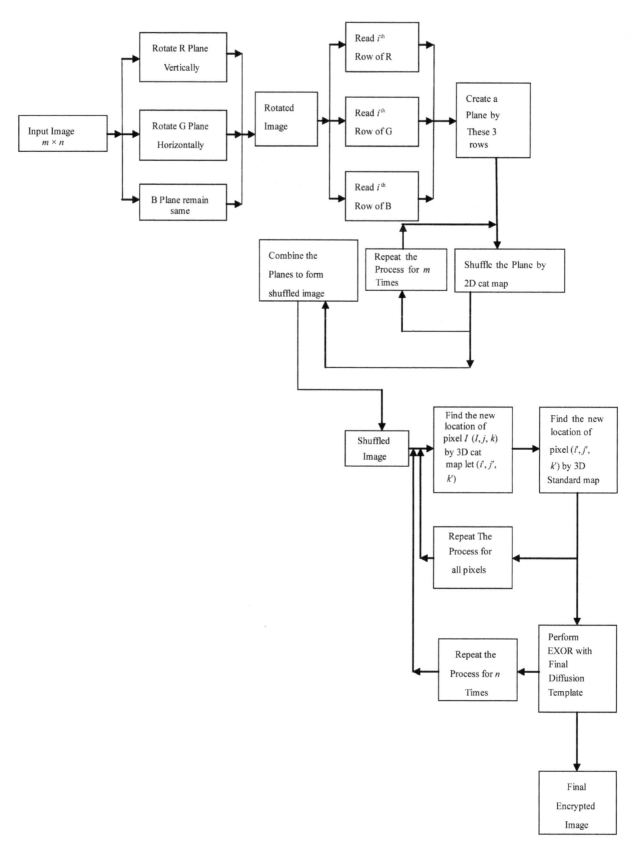

Figuer 3. Image encryption by using confusion and diffusion.

$$k' = \left[k'' + k1 \times \sin\left(j' \times \frac{n}{2 \times pi} \right) + k2 \times \left(j' \times \frac{n}{2 \times pi} \right) \right] \bmod p$$

$$i = \left[\left(1 + a_x a_z b_y \right) \times i' + a_z \times j' + \right.$$
$$\left. \left(a_y + a_x \times a_z + a_x \times a_y \times a_z \times b_y \right) \times k' \right] \bmod m$$

$$i = \left[\left(b_z + a_x \times b_y + a_x \times a_z \times b_y \times b_z \right) \times i' + \left(a_z \times b_z + 1 \right) \right.$$
$$\times j' + \left(a_y \times a_z + a_x \times a_y \times a_z \times b_y \times b_z + a_x \times a_y \times b_y \right.$$
$$\left. + a_x \right) \times k' \right] \bmod n$$

$$k = \left[\left(a_x \times b_x \times b_y + b_y \right) \times i' + b_y \times j' + \right.$$
$$\left. \left(a_x \times a_y \times b_x \times b_y + a_x \times b_x + a_y \times b_y + 1 \right) \times k' \right] \bmod p$$

$$I_{\text{retransf}}(i,j,k) = I_{\text{encp}}(i,j,k)$$

where a_x, a_y, a_z, b_x, b_y, b_z and $K1$, $K2$ are integers > 0.

Each confusion step is followed by diffusion obtained by EXOR operations performed between each pixels of I_{retrnsf} and diffusion I_{diff}

$$I'_{\text{dencp}} = I_{\text{retrnsf}} \oplus I_{\text{diff}}.$$

Step 3. Performing inverse of First level confusion. Slicing the plane normal to R, G, B Planes

$$I'_{\text{SRGB}}(j,k) = I'_{\text{dencp}}(i,j,k)$$

for each value of i, j changed from 0 to m, k changed from 0 to 3.

De-shuffling the sliced plane

$$I_{\text{DRGB}}(j,k) = I'_{\text{SRGB}}(j,k)$$

where j' and k' are obtained by 2D cat map given below

$$j' = \left(j + r_x + r_y + p \times k \right) \bmod m$$

$$k' = \left(q \times j + r_y + \left(p \times q + 1 \right) \times k \right) \bmod n$$

where p and q are integers > 0, and r_x, r_y are offset integers such that $0 \leq r_x \leq m$ and $0 \leq r_y \leq n$.

Recombining the planes for forming 3D matrix for next operation

$$I'(i,j,k) = I'_{\text{DRGB}}(j,k).$$

Step 4. Re-rotating the image planes

Dividing main image into three separate images I_R, I_G and I_B as follows

$$I_R(x,y) = I'(x,y,1) \quad I_g(x,y) = I'(x,y,2)$$
$$I_B(x,y) = I'(x,y,3)$$

where $1 \leq x \leq m$ and $1 \leq y \leq n$.

Scrolling the red plane vertically

$$I_R(x,y) = I_R\left[\left(x + \frac{m}{2} \right) \bmod m, y \right].$$

Scrolling the green plane horizontally

$$I_G(x,y) = I_R\left[x\left(y + \frac{n}{2} \right) \bmod n \right].$$

Blue plane remain intact.

$$I_B(x,y) = I_B(x,y).$$

Step 5. Next recombination of planes are performed to form final decrypted image

$$I_{\text{final}}(x,y,1) = I_R(x,y) \quad I_{\text{final}}(x,y,2) = I_G(x,y)$$
$$I_{\text{final}}(x,y,3) = I_B(x,y)$$

4. Performance Analysis

4.1. Key Space Analysis

The strong point of the proposed algorithm is the generation of the permutation sequence with the chaos sequence. The key space should also be suitably large to make brute-force attack not feasible. In the proposed algorithm, we use 148 bit key (37 Hex number) is used. It has been observed in **Figures 4(a)** and **(b)** that with slightly varying the initial condition of the chaotic sequence. It has been almost impossible to decrypt the image.

4.2. Statistical Analysis

It is well known that passing the statistical analysis on cipher-text is of crucial importance for a cryptosystem actually, an ideal cipher should be strong against any statistical attack. In order to prove the security of the proposed image encryption scheme, the following Statistical tests are performed.

4.2.1. Histogram Analysis

To prevent the access of information to attackers, it is important to ensure that encrypted and original images do not have any statistical similarities. The histogram analysis clarifies that, how the pixel values of image are distributed. A number of images are encrypted by the encryption schemes under study and visual test is performed.

An example is shown in **Figure 5**. In **Figure 5** shows histogram analysis on test image using proposed algorithm. The histogram of original image contains great sharp rises followed by sharp declines as shown in **Figure 5** and the histograms of the encrypted images for different round as shown in **Figures 5(a)-(f)** have uniform distribution which is significantly different from original image and has no statistical similarity in ap-

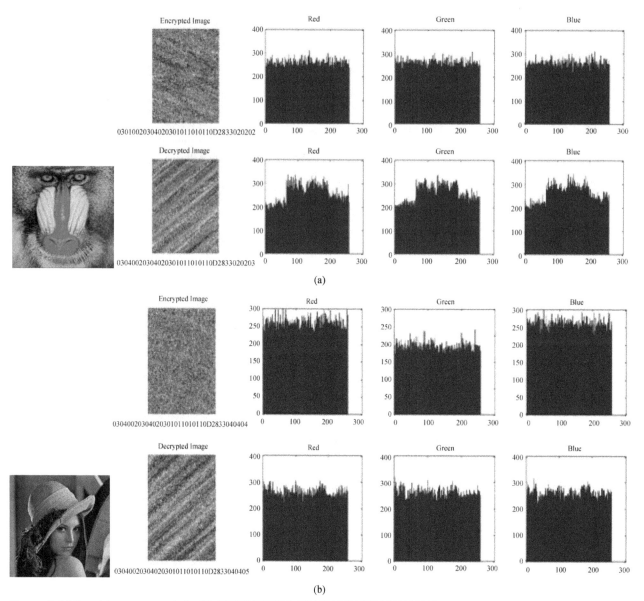

Figure 4. (a) Input image encrypted with 0304002030402 0301011010110D2833020202 and Decrypted by 0304002030402030-1011010110D2833020203; (b) Input lenna image encrypted with 0304002030402030101101010110D2833040404 and Decrypted by 0304002030402030101101010110D2833040405.

pearance. So, the surveyed algorithms do not provide any clue for statistical attack. The encrypted image histogram, approximated by a uniform distribution, is quite different from plain-image histogram.

4.2.2. Correlation Analysis

There is a very good correlation among adjacent pixels in the digital image [3]. Equation (5) is used to study the

Correlation between two adjacent pixels in horizontal, vertical and diagonal orientations. This is shown in **Figure 6**.

x and y are intensity values of two neighboring pixels in the image and N is the number of adjacent pixels selected from the image to calculate the correlation. 1000 pairs of two adjacent pixels are selected randomly from image to test correlation. The correlation coefficient be-

$$c_r = \frac{N\sum_{j=1}^{N}\left(x_j \times y_j\right) - \sum_{j=1}^{N} x_j \times \sum_{j=1}^{N} y_j}{\sqrt{\left(N\sum_{j=1}^{N} x_j^2 - \left(\sum_{j=1}^{N} x_j\right)^2\right) \times \left(N\sum_{j=1}^{N} y_j^2 - \left(\sum_{j=1}^{N} y_j\right)^2\right)}} \qquad (5)$$

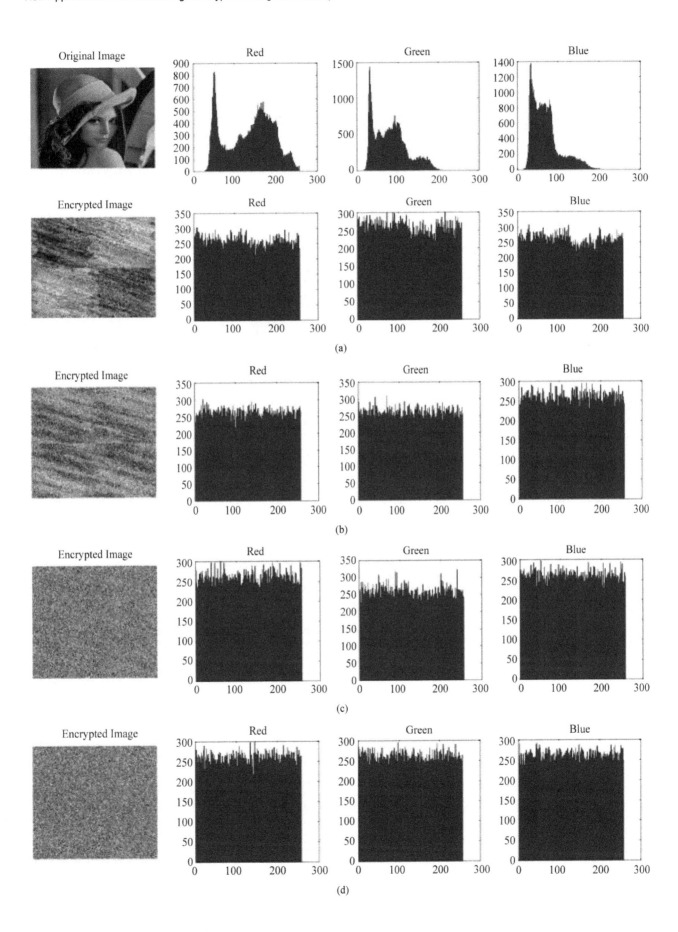

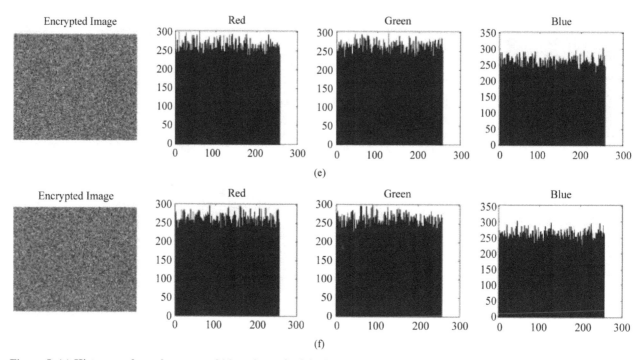

(e)

(f)

Figure 5. (a) Histogram for red, green and blue plane of original and encrypted image for $R = 1$; (b) Histogram for red, green and blue plane of encrypted image for $R = 2$; (c) Histogram for red, green and blue plane of encrypted image for $R = 4$; (d) Histogram for red, green and blue plane of encrypted image for $R = 8$; (e) Histogram for red, green and blue plane of encrypted image for $R = 16$; (f) Histogram for red, green and blue plane of encrypted image for $R = 32$.

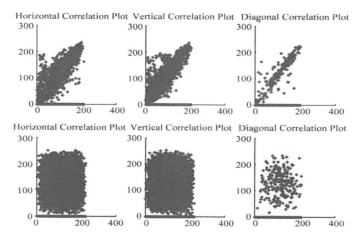

Figure 6. Correlation for horizontal, vertical and diagonal.

tween original and cipher image is calculate in **Table 6**.

4.3. Key Space Analysis

Key space size is the total number of different keys that can be used in the cryptography. Cryptosystem is totally sensitive to all secret keys. A good encryption algorithm should not only be sensitive to the cipher key, but also the key space should be large enough to make brute-force attack infeasible. The key space size for initial conditions and control parameters is over than 2^{148}. Apparently, the key

space is sufficient for reliable practical use.

4.4. Differential Analysis

In general, a desirable characteristic for an encrypted image is being sensitive to the little changes in plain-image (e.g. modifying only one pixel). Adversary can create a small change in the input image to observe changes in the result. By this method, the meaningful relationship between original image and cipher image can be found. If one little change in the plain-image can cause a significant change in the cipher-image, with respect to diffusion and confusion, then the differential attack actually loses its efficiency and becomes almost useless. There are three common measures were used for differential analysis: MAE, NPCR and UACI. Mean Absolute Error (MAE). The bigger the MAE value, the better the encryption security. NPCR means the Number of Pixels Change Rate of encrypted image while one pixel of plain-image is changed. UACI which is the Unified Average Changing Intensity, measures the average intensity of the differences between the plain-image and Encrypted image.

Let $C(i, j)$ and $P(i, j)$ be the color level of the pixels at the ith row and jth column of a $W \times H$ cipher and plain-image, respectively. The MAE between these two images is defined in

$$\text{MAE} = \frac{1}{W \times H} \sum_{j=1}^{W} \sum_{i=1}^{H} |c(i, j) - p(i, j)|. \qquad (6)$$

Consider two cipher-images, $C1$ and $C2$, whose corresponding plain-images have only one pixel difference.

The NPCR of these two images is defined in

$$\text{NPCR} = \frac{\sum_{i,j} D(i, j)}{W \times H} \times 100\% \qquad (7)$$

where W and H are the width and height of the image and $D(i, j)$ is defined as

$$D(i, j) = \begin{cases} 0, & \text{if } C1(i, j) = C2(i, j) \\ 1, & \text{if } C1(i, j) \neq C2(i, j) \end{cases}.$$

Another measure, UACI, is defined by the following formula:

$$\text{UACI} = \frac{1}{W \times H} \sum_{i,j} \left[\frac{c1(i, j) - c2(i, j)}{255} \right] \times 100\%. \qquad (8)$$

Tests have been performed on the encryption schemes on a 256-level color image of size 256×256 shown in **Figures 5(a)-(f)**. The MAE, NPCR and UACI experiment result is shown in **Tables 4** and **2**. The **Tables 3** and **5** compare the result of Yong previous related work based on chaotic map and our. Results obtained from NPCR show that the encryption scheme's sensitivity to little changes in the input image is under 0.01%. According to the UACI estimation result, the rate influence due to one pixel change is very low. The results

demonstrate that a swiftly change in the original image will result in a negligible change in the ciphered image.

4.5. Information Entropy Analysis

It is well known that the entropy $H(m)$ of a message source m can be measured by

$$H(m) = \sum_{i=0}^{m-1} p(m_i) \log \frac{1}{p(m_i)} \qquad (9)$$

where M is the total number of symbols $m_i \in m$; $p(m_i)$ represents the probability of occurrence of symbol mi and log denotes the base 2 logarithm so that the entropy is expressed in bits. For a random source emitting 256 symbols, its entropy is $H(m) = 8$ bits. This means that the cipher-images are close to a random source and the proposed algorithm is secure against the entropy attack. The test result on different image for different round is defined in **Table 7**.

4.6. Speed Analysis

Apart from the security consideration, some other issues on image encryption are also important. This includes the encryption speed for real-time processes. In general, encryption speed is highly dependent on the CPU/MPU structure, RAM size, Operating System platform, the programming language and also on the compiler options. So, it is senseless to compare the encryption speeds of two ciphers image.

Without using the same developing atmosphere and optimization techniques. Inspire of the mentioned difficulty, in order to show the effectiveness of the proposed image encryption scheme over existing algorithms. We

Table 2. NPCR, UACI and Entropy for key sensitivity test.

Lenna Error Image	$R = 2$	$R = 3$	$R = 4$
NPCR	99.5966593424	99.6098836263	99.651082356
UACI	52.5394813687	51.6816741344	50.603535970
Entropy	7.99913068980	7.99912231127	7.9991865161
Baboon Error Image			
NPCR	99.6103922526	99.5905558268	99.599711100
UACI	46.9998348460	47.8581327550	48.719709807
Entropy	7.99901078968	7.99905756543	7.9991734549

Table 3. Comparison of NPCR and UACI with Yong Wong et al.

Name of image		$R = 1$		$R = 2$		$R = 3$	
		Our	Yong Wang et. al	Our	Yong Wang et. al	Our	Yong Wang et. al
Airplane	NPCR	**99.62**	97.621	99.60	99.637	99.62	99.634
	UACI	**33.19**	32.909	33.10	33.575	33.35	33.580

Table 4. NPCR and UACI for different round on different color image.

Image		$R = 1$	$R = 2$	$R = 3$	$R = 4$	$R = 8$	$R = 10$	$R = 16$	$R = 32$
Baboon	NPCR	99.55	99.57	99.59	99.59	99.61	99.60	99.60	99.61
	UACI	37.17	38.68	39.00	38.78	38.69	38.88	39.03	38.89
	MAE	71.65	74.52	75.29	75.18	75.23	75.37	75.34	75.50
Lenna	NPCR	99.63	99.64	99.59	99.62	99.62	99.61	99.62	99.59
	UACI	28.87	27.51	27.33	27.42	27.43	27.64	27.51	27.37
	MAE	80.84	77.24	77.46	77.58	77.76	77.84	77.67	77.54
Pepper	NPCR	99.62	99.62	99.58	99.58	99.63	99.62	99.62	99.62
	UACI	38.05	38.26	37.99	38.03	38.34	38.20	38.33	38.11
	MAE	75.20	74.68	74.27	74.48	74.89	74.62	74.62	74.61
Airplane	NPCR	99.62	99.60	99.59	99.62	99.63	99.61	99.59	99.60
	UACI	33.19	33.10	33.35	33.27	33.329	33.28	33.32	33.31

Table 5. The round number of scanning-image, permutation and diffusion to achieve NPCR > 0.996 and UACI > 0.287.

	NPCR	UACI	No. of Round for Confusion and Diffusion
Our	>0.996	>0.287	1
Ref. [3]	>0.996	>0.333	2
Ref. [4]	>0.996	>0.333	18
Ref. [5]	>0.996		5
Ref. [6]	>0.996	>0.333	6
Ref. [7]	>0.996	>0.333	6

evaluated the performance of encryption schemes with an un-optimized MATLAB 7.0 code. Performance was measured on a machine with Intel core 2 Duo 2.00 GHz CPU with 2 GB of RAM running on Windows XP. The time for encryption and decryption is measured for different round is shown in **Tables 8** and **9**.

4.7. FIPS 140 Testing

We also show that our proposed algorithm pass the FIPS 140-2 randomness tests. There are four tests: Mono-bit, Poker, Runs tests and Long run tests. Each of the tests was designed to test the randomness of a sample sequence length of 20,000 bits as follows:

4.7.1. The Monobit Test

1) Calculate x which is the number of ones in the 20,000 bit stream.

2) The test is passed if $9725 < x < 10{,}275$.

4.7.2. The Poker Test

1) Divide the 20,000 bit stream into 5000 contiguous 4 bit segments. Count and store the number of occurrences of each of the 16 possible 4 bit values. Denote $g(i)$ as the number of each 4 bit value i where 0 - 15.

2) Calculate x by

$$X = \frac{16}{5000} \sum_{i=0}^{15} g(i)^2 - 5000 \qquad (10)$$

3) The test is passed if $2.16 < x < 46.17$.

4.7.3. The Runs Test

1) A run represents a maximal sequence of consecutive bits of all ones or all zeros. The incidences of runs of all lengths in the sample stream should be counted and stored.

2) The test is passed if the number of runs is each within the corresponding interval specified below **Table 10**.

4.7.4. The Long Run Test

1) Find the longest run in the 20,000 bits.

2) If the length of the longest run in the bit stream of 20,000 bit (both of one and zero) is smaller than 26, the test is passed.

Table 6. Correlation coefficient for plain and cipher image.

Images	Correlation coefficient of plain image			Correlation coefficient of Cipher image		
	Horizontal	Vertical	Diagonal	Horizontal	Vertical	Diagonal
Baboon	0.8646	0.8293	0.8114	0.004	0.007	0.037
Lena	0.9156	0.8808	0.8603	0.001	0.006	0.091
Pepper	0.9376	0.9364	0.8935	0.005	0.006	0.023

Table 7. Entropy test for different color image.

Image	$R=1$	$R=2$	$R=3$	$R=4$	$R=8$	$R=10$	$R=16$	$R=32$	Yong Wang et al. [7]
				Our Scheme					
Baboon	7.9988	7.9990	7.9991	7.9992	7.9990	7.9990	7.9990	7.9991	-
Lenna	7.9981	7.9991	7.9991	7.9992	7.9991	7.9990	7.9990	7.9990	7.9990
Pepper	7.9987	7.9991	7.9991	7.9989	7.9989	7.9992	7.9992	7.9992	7.9990
Airplan	7.9989	7.9989	7.9991	7.9991	7.9991	7.9991	7.9991	7.9992	-
Boat	7.9986	7.9992	7.9991	7.9990	7.9990	7.9990	7.9991	7.9991	-

Table 8. Encryption time in second for different round.

Image	$R=1$	$R=2$	$R=3$	$R=4$	$R=8$	$R=10$	$R=16$	$R=32$
				Our Scheme				
Baboon	0.510	0.87	1.20	1.56	2.94	3.65	5.73	11.24
Lenna	0.521	0.87	1.197	1.561	2.933	3.662	5.697	11.225
Pepper	0.521	0.87	1.197	1.561	2.933	3.662	5.697	11.225
Airplan	0.521	0.87	1.197	1.561	2.933	3.662	5.697	11.225
Boat	0.521	0.87	1.197	1.561	2.933	3.662	5.697	11.225

Table 9. Decryption time in second for different round.

Image 256 × 256	$R=1$	$R=2$	$R=3$	$R=4$	$R=8$	$R=10$	$R=16$	$R=32$
				Our Scheme				
Baboon	0.43	0.77	1.12	1.470	2.85	3.55	5.62	11.17
Lenna	0.429	0.77	1.137	1.471	2.869	3.548	5.618	11.20
Pepper	0.430	0.78	1.139	1.472	2.869	3.549	5.619	11.22
Airplan	0.429	0.77	1.137	1.471	2.869	3.548	5.618	11.20
Boat	0.434	0.722	1.065	1.414	2.807	3.523	5.594	11.15

We need to change the testing algorithm to suit to image data so we randomly chose 100 streams of 20,000 consecutive bits from the ciphered images of image A. Then we find statistics of the randomly chosen 100 streams for each test and compared them to the acceptance ranges. **Table 11** show the numbers of the samples among 100 randomly chosen samples, which passed the Mono-bit, Poker, Long run tests and run tests.

5. Conclusions

This paper presents a technique which replaces the traditional preprocessing complex system and utilizes the basic operations like confusion, diffusion which provide same or better encryption using cascading of 3D standard and 3D cat map. We generate diffusion template using 3D standard map and rotate image by using vertically and horizontally red and green plane of the input image. We then shuffle the red, green, and blue plane by using 3D Cat map and standard map. Finally the Image is encrypted by performing XOR operation on the shuffled image and diffusion template. Completion of the design, both theoretical analyses and experimental tests have been carried out, both confirming that the new cipher

Table 10. FIPS-140 test range.

Length of the run	1	2	3	4	5	≥6
Required interval	2315 - 2685	1114 - 1386	527 - 723	240 - 384	103 - 209	103 - 209

Table 11. FIPS-140 test P = pass, F = fail.

Name of image		$R = 1$	$R = 2$	$R = 3$	$R = 4$	$R = 8$	$R = 10$	$R = 16$	$R = 32$
Baboon	runs	10P, 10P	11P, 12P	13P, 15P	12P, 14P	15P, 11P	12P, 12P	16P, 12P	17P, 14P
	pocker	374.7F	9.8944P	15.443P	12.985P	13.644P	8.678P	12.556P	12.556P
	mono	10082P	9975P	9969P	9952P	9990P	10031P	9913P	10032P
Lenna	runs	10P, 11P	13P, 15P	13P, 15P	17P, 13P	12P, 12P	13P, 13P	15P, 20P	12P, 12P
	pocker	317.4F	24.30P	14.022P	8.9920P	18.227P	21.856P	11.558P	18.752P
	mono	9956P	10025P	10103P	9967P	9938P	10054P	9900P	10112P
Pepper	runs	12P, 16P	13P, 15P	12P, 13P	12P, 14P	12P, 13P	13P, 13P	13P, 11P	14P, 14P
	pocker	138.41F	13.196P	12.057P	13.337P	18.227P	20.454P	10.227P	27.929P
	mono	10085P	9982P	10001P	9967P	10048P	9994P	9913P	10036P
Airplan	runs	12P, 10P	14P, 13P	17P, 23P	12P, 14P	14P, 13P	15P, 12P	12P, 13P	12P, 11P
	pocker	880.25F	30.016P	13.504P	12.134P	16.761P	20.108P	12.800P	9.568P
	mono	10030P	10075P	9975P	9996P	9940P	10071P	9946P	9973P

possesses high security and fast encryption speed. In conclusion, therefore, the new cipher indeed has excellent potential for practical image encryption applications.

6. References

[1]   G. Chen, Y. Mao and C. K. Chui, "A Symmetric Image Encryption Scheme Based on 3D Chaotic Cat Maps," *Chaos Solitons & Fractals*, Vol. 21, No. 3, 2004, pp. 749-761.

[2]   D. Xiao, X. Liao and P. Wei, "Analysis and Improvement of a Chaos-Based Image Encryption Algorithm," *Chaos Solitons & Fractals*, Vol. 40, No. 5, December 2007.

[3]   Y. Wanga, K.-W. Wong, X. F. Liao and G. R. Chen, "A New Chaos-Based Fast Image Encryption Algorithm," *Applied Soft Computing*, Vol. 11, No. 1, 2011, pp. 514-522.

[4]   Z. Guan, F. Huang and W. Guan, "Chaos-Based Image Encryption Algorithm," *Physics Letters A*, Vol. 346, No. 1-3, 2005, pp. 153-157.

[5]   S. Lian, J. Sun and Z. Wang, "A Block Cipher Based on a Suitable Use of the Chaotic Standard Map," *Chaos Solitons & Fractals*, Vol. 26, No. 1, 2005, pp. 117-129.

[6]   K. W. Wong, B. S. Kwok and W. S. Law, "A Fast Image Encryption Scheme Based on Chaotic Standard Map," *Physics Letters A*, Vol. 372, No. 15, 2008, pp. 2645-2652.

[7]   Y. Mao, G. Chen and S. Lian, "A Novel Fast Image Encryption Scheme Based on 3D Chaotic Baker Maps," *International Journal of Bifurcation and Chaos*, Vol. 14, No. 10, 2004, pp. 3613-3624.

13

McAfee SecurityCenter Evaluation under DDoS Attack Traffic

Sirisha Surisetty, Sanjeev Kumar
Network Security Research Lab, Department of Electrical/Computer Engineering,
The University of Texas-Pan American, Edinburg, USA

Abstract

During the Distributed Denial of Service (DDoS) attacks, computers are made to attack other computers. Newer Firewalls now days are providing prevention against such attack traffics. McAfee SecurityCenter Firewall is one of the most popular security software installed on millions of Internet connected computers worldwide. "McAfee claims that if you have installed McAfee SecurityCentre with anti-virus and antispyware and Firewall then you always have the most current security to combat the ever-evolving threats on the Internet for the duration of the subscription". In this paper, we present our findings regarding the effectiveness of McAfee SecurityCentre software against some of the popular Distributed Denial Of Service (DDoS) attacks, namely ARP Flood, Ping-flood, ICMP Land, TCP-SYN Flood and UDP Flood attacks on the computer which has McAfee SecurityCentre installed. The McAfee SecurityCentre software has an in built firewall which can be activated to control and filter the Inbound/Outbound traffic. It can also block the Ping Requests in order to stop or subside the Ping based DDoS Attacks. To test the McAfee Security Centre software, we created the corresponding attack traffic in a controlled lab environment. It was found that the McAfee Firewall software itself was incurring DoS (Denial of Service) by completely exhausting the available memory resources of the host computer during its operation to stop the external DDoS Attacks.

Keywords: Distributed Denial of Service (DDoS) Attack, McAfee Firewall, NonPaged Pool Allocs, ARP Flood, Ping-Flood, ICMP Land, TCP-SYN Flood, UDP Flood Attack

1. Introduction

Firewall is one of the most popular security software installed on millions of Internet connected computers worldwide. Today's PCs need the protection provided by a firewall to ensure the safety of both personal data, inbound and outbound traffic. Having a firewall, benefits the user and the PC by shielding them from the attacks of malicious users, would be the general thinking of a common PC user. Are these Personal Firewalls, which are provided by the most popular Antivirus companies to protect your system, safe? This is the question that we are trying to answer in this paper by evaluating the effectiveness of these personal firewalls. We know that the Firewall plays a vital role in defending against DDoS attacks. Sometimes they will cause some overhead while they are defending against the DDoS attacks. In this paper we will study the overhead, if any, caused by the McAfee

SecurityCenter software firewall in defending the system against the Denial of Service attacks namely ARP Flood, Ping Flood, ICMP LAND, TCP-SYN Flood and UDP Flood attacks. We considered one attacks per layer, *i.e.*, from Layer-2 to Layer-4 in the TCP/IP suite.

"McAfee claims that it's security products use the award-winning technology and if you have installed McAfee SecurityCentre with anti-virus and anti-spyware and Firewall then you always have the most current security to combat the ever-evolving threats on the Internet for the duration of the subscription" [1]. There are different types of Distributed Denial of Service (DDoS) attacks and they exhaust resources of a victim computer differently such as processor, memory or bandwidth resources. The famous websites like e-Bay, e-Trade, Yahoo, Twitter and Facebook were also the victims of these DDoS attacks [2,3]. Recently, efforts have been made to increasingly deploy security systems such as Firewalls and IPS (Intrusion Prevention Systems) to provide security against DDoS attacks. However, most recent DDoS attacks during July 4th, Independence Day weekend in 2009, on South Korean and US government websites convey the fact that even Firewalls and IPS, commonly deployed in the network, do not always help in defending against the DDoS Attacks [4,5]. In this July 4th, 2009 attack, the websites of a number of US and South Korean government agencies crashed and their computers experienced continuing problems since the cyber attack was launched. Not only Firewalls and IPSs the service packs released also are not able to prevent the attacks completely [6].

Some of the DDoS attacks are the Ping Flood Attack, ICMP Land Attack, TCP-SYN Attack, ARP Flood Attack and UDP Flood Attack. All of these can cause Denial of service by storming the host with the respective attack traffic. Some of them are used to bring down the host in a Local Area Network where as some can bring down a host in internet that can be a web server or Internet root servers itself [7]. To evaluate the performance of McAfee SecurityCenter's Personal Firewall against such DDoS attacks, we experimented with so called and commercially promoted, secure computer system, namely Apple's iMac with Windows XP-SP2 operating system. We also compared the performance of McAfee SecurityCenter when the iMac platform is deploying Windows XP-SP2 with that of a DELL Inspiron 530 desktop built with Vista Business and McAfee SecurityCentre with Personal Firewall and 2 GB of RAM. We consider attacks at Layer-2, Layer-3 and Layer-4 in the TCP/IP suite in this paper. The rest of the paper is organized as follows: Section 2 provides the information about experimental setup. In Section 3 we present experiments to evaluate effect of different attacks on the McAfee SecurityCenter. Section 4 is conclusion followed by Section 5 as Acknowledgment and Section 6 as references.

2. Experimental Setup

The experimental setup was used to simulate the network condition as shown in **Figure 1**. All of the DDoS attacks were simulated in controlled lab environment of Networking Research Lab of Electrical/Computer Engineering here at the University of Texas-Pan American, by making multiple computers send a barrage of corresponding attack traffic to the Victim computer up to a maximum speed of 1000 Mbps/1 Gbps. We stressed out the McAfee personal firewall installed on an Apple iMac with Windows XP-SP2 operating system at the same transmission rate but changing the load at every step starting from 10 Mbps to 100 Mbps in steps of 10 Mbps

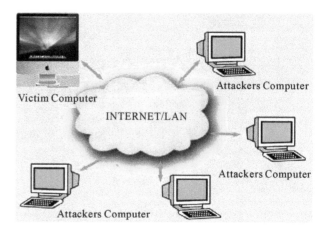

Figure 1. Distributed denial of service (DoS) attack.

and from 100 Mbps to 1 Gbps in steps of 100 Mbps. Each load is transmitted for 10 minutes duration. The victim computer is an Apple iMac with Windows XP-SP2 installed in it with McAfee SecurityCenter and also a DELL Inspiron 530 Desktop Computer with McAfee SecurityCenter.

The parameters of performance evaluation considered for this experiment were the Processor utilization and the NonPaged Pool Allocations in the main memory. NonPaged Pool allocs are those pages that can never be paged out of the system as these are Kernel functions and device drivers that in particular require real memory and should be present always for execution of a process [8,9]. During the experiment, the needed performance metric values were logged by the system under attack for analysis purposes by using some of the system activity commands. The logs were the performance counters available in the system. The Ping Flood, Smurf Attack, ICMP Land, TCP-SYN Flood, ARP Flood and UDP Flood attacks are performed on McAfee under that was installed on Windows XP and the results are as shown in Section 3.

3. Experimental Evaluation under Different DDos Attacks

In this section the background on different DDoS attacks that we consider for this experimentation are discussed and the results per each DDoS attacks are explained. The description of the results starts from the order of layers *i.e.*, from lower layer (layer-2) (ARP Attack) to higher layers (layer-4) (UDP Flood) in the TCP/IP suite.

3.1. ARP Flood Attack

Address Resolution Protocol (ARP) is used in Local Area networks to resolve IP addresses into hardware MAC addresses. It is a very basic and essential protocol used to communicate in LAN either by gateway or by any host. The ARP request message consists of the IP address of the host, IP and hardware MAC address of the initiator who wish to communicate and broadcasts that within the LAN. All the hosts in the LAN receives the ARP request but only the host who has that IP will respond and unicast the initiator its hardware MAC (Medium Access Control) address. Also the ARP cache table of receiver host will be updated with the corresponding IP-MAC addresses for further communication with the initiator [10]. Attackers take advantage of this protocol and try to flood the end host with ARP Requests and the host ultimately ends up in replying to those requests and updating its cache table and gets busy with this task. With a flood of such requests, resource starvation usually happens on the host computer. Those resources can be either processor consumption or memory. One general way of DDoS is to storm the host with a barrage of ARP requests thereby incurring a DDoS attack on the host while being consumed in replying to all the requests it receives and exhausts the system resources. ARP-based flooding attack is a Layer-2 attack.

ARP Flood Attack on McAfee SecurityCenter

In this case the ARP flood was sent to iMac with Windows XP-SP2 operating system, with windows Firewall OFF and McAfee Personal Firewall ON. The processor utilization due to this ARP-based flooding attack is shown below in **Figure 2**. The upper line shows the maximum processor utilization, the middle line shows the average procesor utilization and the bottom line shows the minimum processor utilization of Windows XP with McAfee SecurityCenter for ARP-based flooding attack traffic. It can be observed that the average processor utilization was just 50% even for maximum attack load of 1Gbps. In this case we can say that the system with McAfee Firewall was able to sustain tha attack.

3.2. Ping Flood Attack

Ping is a type of ICMP message that is used to know the reachability of a host. Based on RFC 0792 [11], ICMP Echo request must be replied with an ICMP Echo Reply message. Attackers take advantage of this protocol and try to flood the end host with Ping Requests and the host ultimately replies to those requests and hence consumes the computer resources. With a flood of such requests, resource starvation usually happens on the host computer. The attacker, generally, spoofs the source IP and sends a barrage of Ping requests to the victim computer. The victim computer incurs Denial of Service while being consumed in replying to all the requests it receives. This Ping Flood Attack is a Layer-3 attack in the TCP/IP suite. One of the earlier work shows that a simple Ping attack can make the target host busy in processing the ping requests consuming 100% of the CPU utilization [12].

Ping Flood Attack on McAfee SecurityCenter

Ping Flooding traffic is sent to the iMac deploying Windows XP-SP2 with McAfee SecurityCenter. When the attack was started the simply froze after a while giving a BSoD (Blue Screen of Death). When restarted the system displayed the message on the screen as shown in **Figures 3** and **4**. After restarting the system again 1Gbps of traffic is sent to it and again the system behaved in the same manner giving the BSoD. **Figures 5** and **6** show the Pool NonPaged bytes and Allocs for this time. The processor utilization was just 50% on an average. The default mode of McAfee firewall is to block the incoming ping requests as shown in **Figure 7** above. We have not opted for "Allow ICMP ping requests", so we assume that the ICMP ping requests are not allowed and hence system will be safe. But just after start of the attack, the system froze showing the BSoD and then it can be observed from the **Figures 5** and **6** that it has just taken 8 seconds for the system to hang up before giving the BSoD and the Pool Nonpaged Allocation have grown exponentially. After the

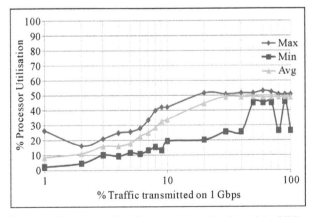

Figure 2. Processor utilization (on a logarithmic scale) of iMac deploying windows XP OS with McAfee SecurityCenter firewall under ARP attack.

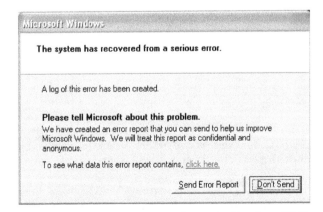

Figure 3. System error message after restarting from BSoD.

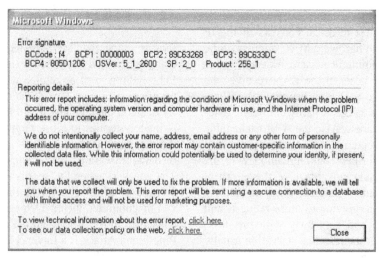

Figure 4. System error message after restarting from BSoD.

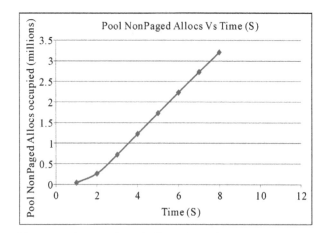

Figure 5. NonPaged pool allocs for 1 Gbps of ping traffic when McAfee firewall was in default mode.

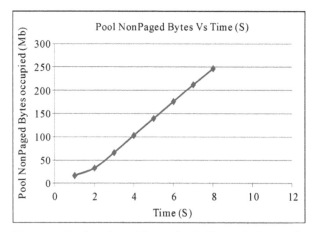

Figure 6. NonPaged pool bytes for 1 Gbps of ping traffic when McAfee firewall was in default mode.

restart we collected the "dump files" and analyzed them for the possible reasons. The main reason for this BSoD was some module named "mfehidk.sys" that was cor-

rupting the stack, as can be known from the "Bug check Analysis". The process "mfehidk.sys" is the Host Intrusion Detection Link Driver belongs to the software McAfee, Inc [13]. From this we can know that the reason for BSoD on windows XP-SP2 with McAfee Security-Center was the McAfee Host Intrusion Detection Link Driver.

We tried the Ping attack one more time with the option "Allow ICMP ping requests" in **Figure 7** checked, that is we are allowing the attack now. This time the computer ran smoothly, *i.e.*, the system did not crash and the processor utilization is as shown in **Figure 8** below:

From **Figure 8** it can be seen that the average processor utilization was just 50% for 1 Gbps of traffic and the system was working properly withour freezing up. The option "Allow ICMP ping requests", as shown in **Figure 7**, tells us that the defaut mode is set to block the attack on the system, but the McAfee Firewall was unable to block it and created a Denial of Service on the host system itself by creating an exception in the memory and freezing the system resulting in the BSoD, but when we are allowing the attack, by checking the option "Allow ICMP ping requests", the system was safe with 50% of processor utilization. We observed the similar condition in other computer with Vista operating system.

The Ping attack was performed to see the performance of latest DELL Inspiron 530 desktop built on Intel Core 2 Quad 2.4 Ghz processor with Vista Business and McAfee SecurityCentre 9.3 with Personal Firewall 10.3 and 2 GB of RAM.

We consider here 2 cases

Case I: McAfee Firewall was activated and was allowing incoming ICMP Echo Requests.

Case II: McAfee Firewall was activated and was blocking Incoming ICMP Echo Requests.

The results in each case are detailed below:

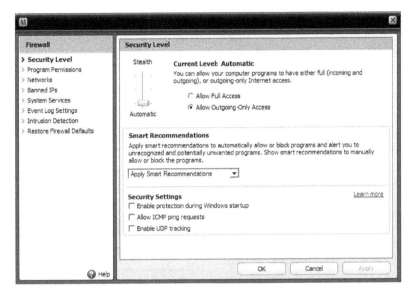

Figure 7. Default setting in McAfee firewall showing the options to allow/disallow ping and UDP traffic.

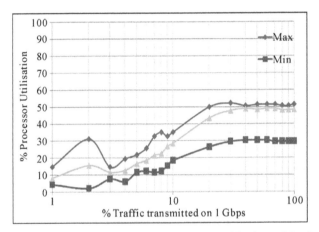

Figure 8. Processor utilization (on a logarithmic scale) of iMac deploying windows XP OS with McAfee SecurityCenter firewall under ping attack with allowing ICMP ping requests.

Case I:

This is the case where McAfee Firewall was activated and it was allowing Incoming ICMP Echo Request packets. Ping attack traffic is sent to the Victim computer in the range of 10% to 100% over 100 Mbps Ethernet medium.

The NonPaged Pool allocs and Bytes allocated were found as shown in **Figures 9** and **10**. The data was logged using the performance counters in windows operating system and is plotted.

Case II:

This is the case where McAfee Firewall is activated while blocking the Inbound ICMP Echo request packets. Generally the results similar to case I were anticipated. But the system became non-responsive after 2.5 minutes of launching the attack with 100 Mbps of Ping attack traffic in the Fast Ethernet medium. System had to be

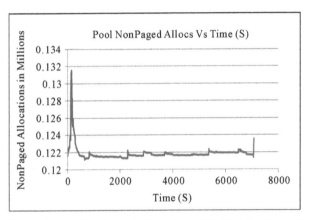

Figure 9. NonPaged pool allocation with McAfee firewall activated and allowing incoming echo request.

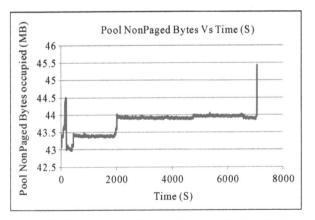

Figure 10. NonPaged pool bytes allocated with McAfee firewall activated and allowing incoming echo request.

restarted and the load of the attack traffic was reduced. To understand the system behavior the attack traffic was reduced to 1 Mbps. It was found that even with 1 Mbps of Ping attack traffic the system froze, and was not responding after 3 hours of launching the attack.

Figures 11 and **12** show that the NonPaged pool allocs and NonPaged pool bytes occupancy in main memory due to 1Mbps of Ping traffic sent to the victim computer. It is observed that while McAfee firewall was defending the victim computer against the Ping attack; the generated NonPaged allocs consumed the entire memory resource of the victim computer which resulted in the Denial of Service attack. As no other Applications were running it was clear that McAfee itself was causing the Denial of Service attack by creating NonPaged allocs.

Figure 13 shows the Processor utilization and Memory occupancy just before the system hangs up. We can observe that the processor utilization was low and it is 34% where the entire RAM was consumed that resulted in the Denial of Service attack. This flaw that we discovered with McAfee Firewall was observed on more than one type of computer platform. We observed the same problem on XP-SP2 operating system as well as Windows Vista Ultimate 32-bit operating system. The same flaw is discovered in McAfee SecurityCentre 2010 also.

When it was installed in Vista the McAfee was consuming the entire main memory and caused the Denial of Service (DoS), whereas in XP-SP2 it was resulting in system freeze and BSoD. The reason for this is well explained in [14], where it says that: "Prior to Vista, the memory manager on 32-bit Windows calculates how much address space to assign each type at boot time. Its formulas take into account various factors, the main one being the amount of physical memory on the system. The amount it assigns to NonPaged pool starts at 128 MB on a system with 512 MB and goes up to 256 MB for a system with a little over 1 GB or more. The memory manager in 32-bit Windows Vista and later, doesn't carve up the system address statically; instead, it dynamically assigns range to different types of memory according to changing demands. However, it still sets a maximum for NonPaged pool that's based on the amount of physical memory, either slightly more than 75% of physical memory or 2 GB, whichever is smaller". This can be verified with **Figure 6** for XP where the system froze and displayed BSoD after the NonPaged bytes occupied reached nearly 250MB and **Figure 12** for Vista shows that all the available main memory, *i.e.*, nearly 1.6 GB (75% of 2 GB) out of available 2 GB of RAM is consumed.

3.3. ICMP Land Attack

This is another Layer-3 attack where the ICMP ping request packet is spoofed with destination IP host/port address same as source's. When a barrage of such Land

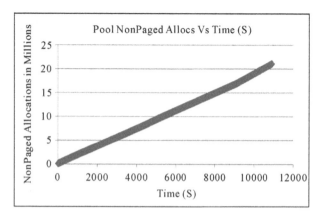

Figure 11. NonPaged pool allocs for 1 Mbps of ping traffic when McAfee firewall was activated and was configured to block ping attack traffic.

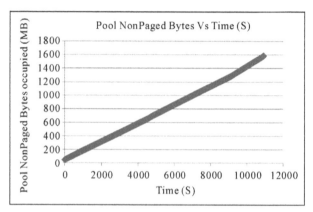

Figure 12. Pool NonPaged bytes in main memory for 1 Mbps of ping attack traffic when McAfee firewall was activated and was configured to block ping attack traffic.

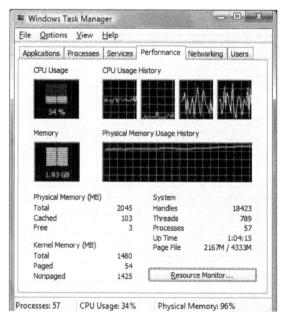

Figure 13. CPU and memory utilization just before the system hang up.

attack packets were sent the host becomes busy in replying to itself and results in system lockup. This vulnerability was found in Windows XP with SP2 service pack and also Windows Server 2003 with firewall turned off. These systems are found vulnerable for the LAND attack, which caused a temporary Denial of Service (DoS) that lasts for 15 to 30 seconds. In case of windows Server 2003 not only the server but also all workstations on the network froze [15]. A similar testing was done on Windows XP, Vista and Apple's Leopard OS, where it was found that the Windows Vista has crashed at ICMP Land attack load of 30 Mbps [16].

ICMP LAND Attack on McAfee SecurityCenter

As shown in **Figure 14** above the Average processor utilization recorded for ICMP Land attacks was nearly 70% at 1 Gbps and the attack ran smoothly and the system was working normally without giving any of the effects described in case of ping attack.

3.4. TCP-SYN Flood Attack

TCP flood attack is Layer-3 attacks, which is most popular denial of Service attack that exhausts the system resources and brings many serious threats to the entire network. The host retains many half open connections and there by exhausts its memory and processor utilization. The Transmission Control Protocol (TCP) that is built on IP has a three-way handshake process for any connection establishment. When a client initiates the TCP connection, it send a SYN packet to the server and then the server responds with an SYN-ACK packet and stores the request information in memory stack. After receiving the SYN-ACK packet the client should confirm the request by sending an ACK packet. When the server receives the ACK packet it checks in the memory stack to see whether this packet corresponds to previously received SYN. If it is, then the connection is established between the client and the server and data transfer can be started. This is the Three-way handshake method used to establish a connection using TCP protocol. In TCP-SYN Flood attack, the attacker sends a barrage of SYN packets with spoofed IP address to the server and the server stores that information in the memory stack, sends the SYN-ACK and waits for the final ACK from the attacker. But the attacker will not send the ACK so such connections will be left in the memory stack. This process consumes considerable memory as well as processor utilization of the server. If large amounts of SYN attack packets were sent then a Denial of Service attack can be launched on the victim. There are many methods suggested to fight against this TCP-SYN attack [17-19]. Service packs and some firewalls have also been evalu-

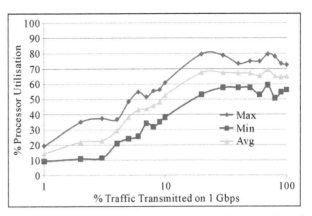

Figure 14. Processor utilization (on a logarithmic scale) of the iMac computer deploying XP-SP2 OS, with McAfee Firewall at default settings due to ICMP Land attack.

ated to measure their effectiveness in mitigating the DoS [20-22] attacks.

TCP-SYN Attack on McAfee SecurityCenter

TCP-SYN flood is Layer-4 Denial of Service attack. TCP-SYN attack traffic is sent to the iMac deploying WindowsXP-SP2 with McAfee Firewall at default settings and there is no option to avoid the TCP-SYN attack. After we started the TCP-SYN attack, the system froze giving us the BSoD again, as in the case of Ping attack. The processor utilization was just 50% for 1 Gbps of traffic and the Pool NonPaged Allocs and Bytes were plotted as shown in the **Figures 15** and **16**. These are very much similar to the case where Ping attack was done and the reason was the same. McAfee Firewall is creating NonPaged allocations that are growing unboundedly in the main memory and cannot be paged out. The operating system cannot allocate more than the assigned memory so it is causing in system freeze and resulting in BSoD. It can be observed that it took 8 seconds for the system to freeze from the **Figures 15** and **16**.

3.5. UDP Flood Attack

DDoS attack using the UDP packets is called UDP Flood attack. UDP Flood attack is a Layer-4 attack. Specialists have discovered the UDP Flood vulnerabilities during the year 1998-2000 in many systems including Microsoft products. In UDP Flood attack a barrage of UDP packets are sent to the victim computer either on specified ports or on random ports. The victim computer processes the incoming data to determine which application it has requested on that port and in case of absence of requested application on that port, the victim sends a "ICMP Destination Unreachable "message to the sender, which is generally a spoofed IP. If such a barrage of requests were sent then it results in Denial of Service on the victim

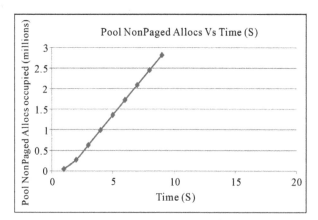

Figure 15. NonPaged Pool Allocs for 1 Gbps of TCP-SYN Flood when McAfee Firewall was in default mode.

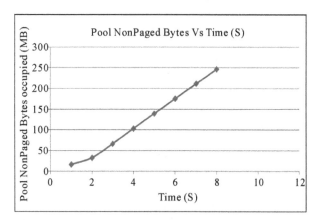

Figure 16. NonPaged Pool Bytes occupied for 1 Gbps of TCP-SYN Flood when McAfee Firewall was in default mode.

computer as the victim will become busy in processing those packets and sending ICMP Destination Unreachable messages. UDP flood attacks may also depletes the bandwidth of network around the victim's system. For example, by sending UDP packets with spoofed return addresses, a hacker links one system's UDP character-generating (chargen) service to another system's UDP echo service. As the chargen service keeps generating and sending characters to the other system, whose echo service keeps responding, UDP traffic bounces back and forth, preventing the systems from providing services [21].

UDP Flood Attack on McAfee SecurityCenter

The system froze in this case also giving us the same BSoD and the "dump crash files" are analyzed and found out to be the same reason as in case of Ping and TCP-SYN attacks. McAfee is causing unbounded growth of NonPaged pool allocation that's filling up the memory and hence resulting in system BSoD.

In case of UDP Flood attack even with the option

"Allow UDP Tracking", as shown in **Figure 7**, checked the system still freezes and results in BSoD.

4. Conclusions

Our experiments with real attack traffic show that McAfee firewall is able to defend against some attack traffic but not others. We can observe that McAfee is able to defend ARP-based flood and ICMP Land Attacks but was not able to defend other attacks and became the reason of Denial of service by itself on the host, which it has to protect. The possible reasons for the unbounded growth of Nonpaged pool Allocations were:

- Unexpected driver code path.
- Intermediate returns from functions that allocated the NonPaged pool memory (memory leaks).
- Bug fixes or work arounds, that added a new piece of code to allocate, but forgot to disallocate.
- Unexpected sequence of hardware Events/Behavior that called the buggy ISRs (Interrupt Service Routine).
- Mis-communication between modules of driver and or OS components.

ARP-based flooding attack usually happens in the LAN as it is a Layer-2 attack. McAfee SecurityCentre is allowing ARP attack as it mainly concentrates on internet based flooding attacks. In case of PING, TCP-SYN and UDP Flood attacks, the attack packets are coming from different IP addresses that are usually spoofed and McAfee may be allocating more Nonpaged memory for defending these types of attacks per each packet it receives and as there will be lot of hosts attacking, it's creating a lot of NonPaged allocs and trying to occupy the RAM, thereby creating BSoD in XP and system get freeze due to RAM unavailability in Vista. This is because in the ICMP land, the attack packets are crafted as if they are originating from one IP address, that is usually its own IP, so it's not creating more processes and hence is not creating any Denial of Service by itself on the host.

5. Acknowledgements

This work was supported in part by the funding from U.S. National Science Foundation, Grant No: 0521585.

6. References

[1] McAfee Claim, 2009.
     http://us.mcafee.com/root/landingpages/affLandPage.asp?
     affid=0&lpname=14229&cid=41183

[2] Latest DDoS Attack on Twitter, 2010.
     http://status.twitter.com/post/157191978/ongoing-denial-of-service-attack

[3] Latest DDoS Attack on Twitter and Facebook, 2010.
     http://www.techcrunch.com/2009/08/06/ddos-attacks-cru

sh-twitter-hobble-facebook

[4]   US, South Korean Websites under Attack, 2010.
      http://government.zdnet.com/?p=5093

[5]   US Government Sites Bombarded by Botnet, 2010.
      http://news.techworld.com/security/118814/us-governme
      nt-sites-bombarded-by-botnet/

[6]   S. Kumar, M. Azad, O. Gomez and R. Valdez, "Can Mi-
      crosoft's Service Pack 2 (SP2) Security Software Prevent
      Smurf Attacks?" *Proceedings of the Advanced Interna-
      tional Conference on Telecommunications (AICT'06)*, Le
      Gosier, 19-22 February 2006.

[7]   S. Gaudin, "DoS Attack Cripples Internet Root Servers,"
      2010.
      http://www.informationweek.com/news/internet/showArt
      icle.jhtml?articleID=197003903

[8]   NonPaged Allocations in Microsoft Windows, 2010.
      http://technet.microsoft.com/en-us/library/cc778082(WS.
      10).aspx

[9]   Information on Pool Resources, 2010.
      http://blogs.technet.com/askperf/archive/2007/03/07/mem
      ory-management-understanding-pool-resources.aspx

[10] D. C. Plummer, "Ethernet Address Resolution Protocol,"
      IETF Network Working Group, RFC-826, 2010.
      http://www.ietf.org/rfc/rfc826.txt

[11] J. Postel, "Internet Control Message Protocol," IETF
      Network Working Group, RFC-792, 2010.
      http://tools.ietf.org/html/rfc0792

[12] S. Kumar, "PING Attack—How Bad Is It?" *Computers &
      Security Journal*, Vol. 25, No. 5, July 2006, pp. 332-337.

[13] Information about Mfehidk.Sys File, 2010.
      http://www.file.net/process/mfehidk.sys.html

[14] NonPaged Pool Allocation in Windows, 2010.
      http://blogs.technet.com/markrussinovich/archive/2009/0
      3/26/3211216.aspx

[15] Possible LAND Attack Vulnerability Affects Windows
      XP and 2003, 2010.
      HTTP://articles.techrepublic.com.com/5100-10878_11-5
      611467.html

[16] S. Raj, V. Hari and S. Kumar, "Performance of Windows
      XP, Windows Vista and Apple's Leopard Computers un-
      der a Denial of Service Attack," 2010 *4th International
      Conference on Digital Society, (ICDS* 2010), St. Maarten,
      10-16 February 2010.

[17] P.-E. Liu and Z.-H. Sheng, "Defending against TCP-SYN
      Flooding with a New Kind of SYN-Agent," *International
      Conference on Machine Learning and Cybernetics*, Vol.
      2, 12-15 July 2008, pp. 1218-1221.

[18] Shakhov, V. Vladimir and H. Choo, "On Modeling Coun-
      teraction against TCP SYN Flooding," 21*st International
      Conference on Information Networking, ICOIN* 2007,
      Estoril, 23-25 January 2007.

[19] W. Chen, D.-Y. Yeung and P.-E. Liu, "Defending Against
      TCP SYN Flooding Attacks under Different Types of IP
      Spoofing," *International Conference on Networking Sys-
      tems and International Conference on Mobile Communi-
      cations and Learning Technologies, ICN/ICONS/MCL* 2006,
      Morne, 23-29 April 2006, p. 38.

[20] S. Kumar and E. Petana, "Mitigation of TCP-SYN At-
      tacks with Microsoft's Windows XP Service Pack2 (SP2)
      Software," *7th International Conference on Networking,
      IEEE*, Cancun, 13-18 April 2008.

[21] F. Lau, S. H. Rubin, M. H. Smith and L. Trajkovic, "Dis-
      tributed Denial of Service Attacks," *IEEE International
      Conference on Systems, Man, and Cybernetics*, Nashville,
      8-11 October 2000, pp. 2275-2280.

[22] S. Surisetty and S. Kumar, "Is McAfee SecurityCen-
      ter/Firewall Software Providing Complete Security for
      your Computer?" *4th International Conference on Digital
      Society, (ICDS* 2010), St. Maarten, 10-16 February 2010.

14

Audio Watermarking Using Wavelet Transform and Genetic Algorithm for Realizing High Tolerance to MP3 Compression

Shinichi Murata[1], Yasunari Yoshitomi[2], Hiroaki Ishii[3]
[1]*Panasonic Corporation, Kadoma, Osaka, Japan*
[2]*Graduate School of Life and Environmental Sciences, Kyoto Prefectural University, Kyoto, Japan*
[3]*School of Science and Technology, Kwansei Gakuin University, Sanda, Hyogo, Japan*

Abstract

Recently, several digital watermarking techniques have been proposed for hiding data in the frequency domain of audio signals to protect the copyrights. However, little attention has been given to the optimal position in the frequency domain for embedding watermarks. In general, there is a tradeoff between the quality of the watermarked audio and the tolerance of watermarks to signal processing methods, such as compression. In the present study, a watermarking method developed for a visual image by using a wavelet transform was applied to an audio clip. We also improved the performance of both the quality of the watermarked audio and the extraction of watermarks after compression by the MP3 technique. To accomplish this, we created a multipurpose optimization problem for deciding the positions of watermarks in the frequency domain and obtaining a near-optimum solution. The near-optimum solution is obtained by using a genetic algorithm. The experimental results show that the proposed method generates watermarked audios of good quality and high tolerance to MP3 compression. In addition, the security was improved by using the characteristic secret key to embed and extract the watermark information.

Keywords: Audio Watermarking, Genetic Algorithm, Optimization, Wavelet Transforms, Secret Key

1. Introduction

Recent progress in digital media and digital distribution systems, such as the Internet and cellular phones, has enabled us to easily access, copy, and modify digital content, such as electric documents, images, audio, and video. Under these circumstances, techniques to protect the copyrights of digital data and to prevent unauthorized duplication or tampering of these data are strongly desired.

Digital watermarking (DW) is a promising method for the copyright protection of digital data. Several studies have investigated audio DW [1-12]. Currently, digital audio clips distributed over the Internet or cellular phone systems are often modified by compression, which is one of the easiest and most effective ways to overcome DW without significantly deteriorating the quality of the audio. Two important properties in audio DW are the inaudibility of the distortion due to DW, and the robustness against signal processing methods, such as compression. In addition to these properties, the data rate and the complexity of DW have attracted attention when discussing the performance of DW.

We developed a method in which 1) a digital watermark can be sufficiently extracted from watermarked audio, even after compression, and 2) the quality of the audio remains high after embedding the digital watermark. However, there generally is a trade-off relation between these two properties.

In the present study, we improved both the extraction of digital watermarks and the quality of the watermarked audio by developing a multipurpose optimization problem for deciding the positions of digital watermarks in the frequency domain and obtaining a near-optimum solution by using a discrete wavelet transform (DWT) and a genetic algorithm (GA) [13,14] for realizing high tolerance to compression by MP3, which is the most popular compression technique. The proposed method enables us to embed digital watermarks in a near-optimum manner for each audio file. In addition, the security of the watermarked audio is improved by using a characteristic secret key to embed and extract digital watermarks.

2. Wavelet Transform

Original audio data $s_k^{(0)}$ is used as the level-0 wavelet decomposition coefficient sequence, where k denotes the element number in the data. The data is decomposed into the multi-resolution representation (MRR) and the coarsest approximation by repeatedly applying a DWT. The wavelet decomposition coefficient sequence $s_k^{(j)}$ at level j is decomposed into two wavelet decomposition coefficient sequences at level $j+1$ by (1) and (2):

$$s_k^{(j+1)} = \sum_n \overline{p_{n-2k}} s_n^{(j)}, \tag{1}$$

$$w_k^{(j+1)} = \sum_n \overline{q_{n-2k}} s_n^{(j)}, \tag{2}$$

where p_{n-2k} and q_{n-2k} denote the scaling and wavelet sequences, respectively, and $w_k^{(j+1)}$ denotes the development coefficient at level $j+1$. The development coefficients at level J are obtained by using (1) and (2) iteratively from $j=0$ to $j=J-1$. **Figure 1** shows the process of a multi-resolution analysis by DWT.

The signal is re-composed by using (3) repeatedly from $j=J-1$ to $j=0$.

$$s_n^{(j-1)} = \sum_k \left[p_{n-2k} s_k^{(j)} + q_{n-2k} w_k^{(j)} \right] \tag{3}$$

In the present study, we use the Daubechies wavelet for DWT. As a result, we obtain the following relation between p_{n-2k} and q_{n-2k}:

$$q_k = (-1)^k p_{1-k} \tag{4}$$

3. Wavelet Domain Digital Watermarking Based on Threshold-Variable Decision

It is known that the histogram of the wavelet coefficients of each domain of MRR sequences has a distribution that is centered at approximately 0 when DWT is performed on a natural visual image [15]. For an audio clip, we also found the same phenomena. **Figure 2** shows an example of an audio histogram.

In the present research, the technique [15] for exploiting the above phenomena on a natural image for embedding a digital watermark on the wavelet coefficients of MRR sequences is applied to audio DW. The procedure is described below.

3.1. Embedment of Watermark Information

3.1.1. Setting of Parameters
For the watermarking of an audio clip, we obtain the histogram of the wavelet coefficients V at the selected level of MRR sequences. **Figure 3** shows a schematic diagram of the histogram of the wavelet coefficients V of an MRR sequence. As with the DW techniques for images [15,16], we set the following watermarking parameters:

The values of $Th(\text{minus})$ and $Th(\text{plus})$ (see **Figure 3**) are chosen such that the non-positive wavelet coefficients (S_m in total frequency) are equally divided into two groups by $Th(\text{minus})$, and the positive wavelet coefficients (S_p in total frequency) are equally divided into two groups by $Th(\text{plus})$. Next, the values of $T1$, $T2$, $T3$, and $T4$, which are the parameters for controlling the embedment strength, are chosen to satisfy the following conditions:

1) $T1 < Th(\text{minus}) < T2 < 0 < T3 < Th(\text{plus}) < T4$.

2) The value of S_{T1}, the number of wavelet coefficients in $(T1, Th(\text{minus}))$, is equal to S_{T2}, the number of wavelet coefficients in $[Th(\text{minus}), T2)$. In short, $S_{T1} = S_{T2}$.

3) The value of S_{T3}, the number of wavelet coefficients in $(T3, Th(\text{plus})]$, is equal to S_{T4}, the number of

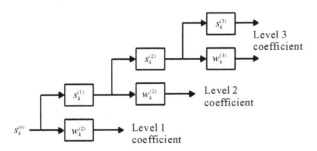

Figure 1. Multi-resolution analysis by the DWT.

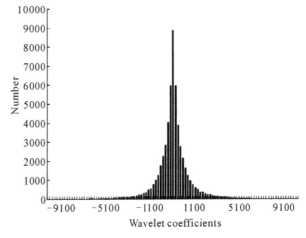

Figure 2. Histogram of the wavelet coefficients of an MRR sequence at level 3 (jazz).

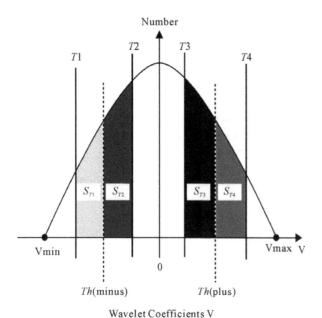

Figure 3. Schematic diagram of the histogram of MRR wavelet coefficients.

wavelet coefficients in $(Th(\text{plus}), T4)$. In short, $S_{T3} = S_{T4}$.

4) $S_{T1}/S_m = S_{T3}/S_p$.

In the present study, the values of both S_{T1}/S_m and S_{T3}/S_p are set to 0.2, which was determined experimentally.

3.1.2. Embedment of Watermark Information

The wavelet coefficients of MRR are rewritten according to the following rules in embedding digital watermark. Here, V_i denotes one of the wavelet coefficients.

1) In the case that bit W_i in watermark W is 0,
   when $V_i < T2$, V_i is changed to $T2$.
   when $V_i > T3$, V_i is changed to $T3$.
   when $T2 \leq V_i \leq T3$, V_i is kept.
2) In the case that bit W_i in watermark W is 1,
   when $T1 < V_i \leq 0$, V_i is changed to $T1$.
   when $0 < V_i < T4$, V_i is changed to $T4$.
   when $V_i \leq T1$ or $V_i \geq T4$, V_i is kept.

The wavelet coefficient V_i is set in the range of $T2 \leq V_i \leq T3$ when bit W_i in watermark W is 0, whereas the DWT coefficient V_i is set in the range of $V_i \leq T1$ or $V_i \geq T4$ when bit W_i in watermark W is 1. The frequency of the change of V_i toward the inside is expected to be approximately equal to the change toward the outside when the number of 0 bits is approximately the same as the number of 1 bits.

3.1.3. Generation of Watermarked Audio

The inverse DWT (IDWT) is performed to wavelet coefficients V_i' embedded with the watermark to obtain the

audio with the watermark.

3.2. Detection of the Watermark

3.2.1. Presumption of Parameters

The watermarked audio, which may be modified by signal processing methods, such as MP3 compression, is converted into wavelet coefficients. The wavelet coefficient in the region where the watermark information is embedded is denoted as V''.

For the histogram of V'', the two parameters $Th'(\text{minus})$ and $Th'(\text{plus})$, which correspond to $Th(\text{minus})$ and $Th(\text{plus})$ for the histogram of V before embedding the watermark, are obtained in the same manner as that for $Th(\text{minus})$ and $Th(\text{plus})$, mentioned in Section 3.1.1. $Th'(\text{minus})$ and $Th'(\text{plus})$ can be used as presumptive values for $Th(\text{minus})$ and $Th(\text{plus})$, respectively, because the distribution of the histogram of V'' is expected to be approximately the same as that of V before embedding the watermark.

The watermarked audio can undergo certain types of audio processing, including compression, such that the difference between the distribution of the histogram of V'' after audio processing and that of V before embedding the watermark is not negligible. In such a case, it may not be persuasive that $Th'(\text{minus})$ and $Th'(\text{plus})$ can be used as presumptive values for $Th(\text{minus})$ and $Th(\text{plus})$, respectively.

3.2.2. Detection of Watermark Information

When the wavelet coefficient V_i'' is in the range of $Th'(\text{minus}) \leq V_i'' \leq Th'(\text{plus})$, the corresponding bit W_i'' in measured watermark W'' is judged to be 0. When the DWT coefficient V_i'' is in the range of $V_i'' < Th'(\text{minus})$ or $V_i'' > Th'(\text{plus})$, the corresponding bit W_i'' in the measured watermark W'' is judged to be 1.

The detection rate $d(x)$ (%) is defined as the percentage of correspondence between the bit W_i in watermark W and the corresponding bit W_i'' in measured watermark W''.

4. Use of the Secret Key

When we embed a digital watermark by using the partial problem described in Section 5, the watermark is produced by using a secret key $S(\gamma)$, which is composed of a row of γ integers randomly selected once or less per integer in the integer range from 1 to N, as shown in the example below ($\gamma = 400$), where γ is the number of bits of the watermark and N is the total number of wavelet coefficients that are candidates embedded with DW.

$$S(400) = (271, 72, 39, 990, 524, 88, \cdots, 1011, 688, 312) \tag{5}$$

Each value and order of numbers in $S(\gamma)$ indicate the position of each bit of the digital watermark in the DW region. Here, the position in the region is expressed as a one-dimensional coordinate. For example, the first number, 271, and the second number, 72, in $S(400)$ mean that the first and second bits of the watermark are set for the wavelet coefficients at the coordinates of 271 and 72 in the DW region, respectively.

As described in Section 3.1.2, the selected wavelet coefficient in the target region is changed according to the value of each bit of the digital watermark, the secret key, and the shift value k of the coordinate, which is described in Section 5. The value of each bit of the digital watermark and the secret key decide an initial bit pattern in the positions in the DW region.

The DW positions of the wavelet coefficients decided by secret key $S(4)$ presented below in (6) are simply demonstrated in **Figure 4**.

$$S(4) = (271, 72, 39, 990) \tag{6}$$

The coordinate shift is performed by generating $S'(\gamma)$ such that the shift value is added to all values of the elements in $S(\gamma)$. For example, it is assumed that the shift value is 10. As a result,

$$S'(4) = \{281, 82, 49, 1000\} \tag{7}$$

The DW positions of the wavelet coefficients decided by secret key $S'(4)$ described in (7) are simply demonstrated in **Figure 5**.

5. Optimal Watermarking Problem

Because our approach of DW optimization is on the first and challenging stage, we formulate the problem in a simple way on the viewpoint of optimization problem. Therefore, in the present study, we formulate the optimization problem as minimization for distortion. We can also formulate the problem using the constraint of keeping distortion less than the masking threshold. Such more elaborate approach is our next target.

To minimize the error $e(x)$ caused by watermarking and to maximize the detection rate $d(x)$ (%) of digital watermark after compression by the MP3 technique under a restriction condition on $d(x)$, an optimum watermarking problem is formulated as follows:

$$P \text{ Minimize } e(x), \tag{8}$$

$$\text{Maximize } d(x), \tag{9}$$

$$\text{Subject to } d(x) > a, \tag{10}$$

$$e(x) = \sum_{i=1}^{N} (y_i - y_i')^2, \tag{11}$$

Case WCV level 3

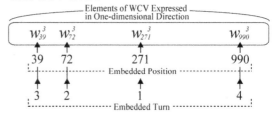

Figure 4. The DW positions of wavelet coefficients decided by secret key. $S(4) = (271, 72, 39, 990)$ in the case of DWT level 3.

Case WCV level 3 $k=10$

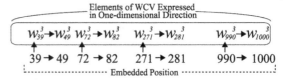

Sample Key $S(4) = \{271, 72, 39, 990\}$
New Key $S'(4) = \{281, 82, 49, 1000\}$

Figure 5. The DW positions of wavelet coefficients decided by secret key. $S'(4) = \{281, 82, 49, 1000\}$ obtained from $S(4) = (271, 72, 39, 990)$ by using the shift value $k = 10$ in the case of DWT level 3.

$$\sum_{i=1}^{N} x_i = R, \tag{12}$$

$$x = (x_1, x_2, \cdots, x_N), \tag{13}$$

$$x_i \in \{0, 1\}, \tag{14}$$

where y_i, y_i' denote the values of the i-th sound data before and after embedding the digital watermark, respectively; N denotes the total number of wavelet coefficients at the DWT level selected for embedment; a, R are constants; and x_i is a 0 - 1 variable that decides the embedment of the watermark on the corresponding wavelet coefficient, where 1 denotes an embedment and 0 denotes a non-embedment.

When the number of wavelet coefficients that are possible targets for digital watermark embedment becomes larger, the solution space of P becomes larger, with the result that a search for an optimal or near-optimal solution is time-consuming or difficult. Accordingly, we define the partial problem P as follows:

$$P' \text{ Minimize } e(s), \tag{15}$$

$$\text{Maximize } d(s), \tag{16}$$

$$\text{Subject to } d(s) > a, \tag{17}$$

$$e(s) = \sum_{i=1}^{N} (y_i - y_i')^2, \tag{18}$$

$$x_{i+s} = c_i, \tag{19}$$

$$\sum_{i=1}^{N} c_i = R , \qquad (20)$$

$$\boldsymbol{c} = \left(c_1, c_2, \cdots, c_N \right) , \qquad (21)$$

$$\boldsymbol{x} = \left(x_1, x_2, \cdots, x_N \right) , \qquad (22)$$

$$c_i \in \{0,\ 1\} , \qquad (23)$$

$$x_i \in \{0,\ 1\} , \qquad (24)$$

where s is an integer variable ranging from 0 to $N-1$; c_i is a 0 - 1 constant that decides the digital watermark embedment on the corresponding wavelet coefficient, where 1 denotes an embedment and 0 denotes a non-embedment, and y_i, y_i', N, a, R, x_i are the same as those described for P. We prepare a random initial pattern for $\boldsymbol{c} = \left(c_1, c_2, \cdots, c_N \right)$ to solve P'.

For getting the detection rate $\mathrm{d}(\boldsymbol{x})$, we use the watermark, the wavelet transformation level, and the (near-)optimum solution for P or P' as input data to the decoder for the proposed method.

In the present study, we use DWT. However other optimal watermarking problems can be formulated using other transforms as shown in our previous study [17,18] where discrete Fourier transform and a watermarking method proposed in the reported study [19] were used.

6. GA Approach

GA is one of the most acknowledged methods for near-optimization. We presume that P and P' might have many locally optimum solutions. According to our experiences, GA was fairly effective for searching the acceptable near-optimum solutions for many discrete optimization problems even when many locally optimum solutions could exist. We use GA in the present study because we have much more successful experiences on GA application to optimization problems than those on other methods. Other acknowledged techniques such as tabu search [20] for solving discrete optimization problems could be other options for solving P and P'.

The GA, which is based on biological evolution, has been applied for solving the optimization problem. The solution of the optimization problem is expressed as a genotype. In each generation, there is a population composed of several individuals identified by their genotypes. The basic idea of GA is that if the number of better individuals is increased by generation updating, an optimum or approximately optimum solution, as expressed by an individual, will eventually be obtained. Chromosome composed of genes is string specifying an individual. For the generation updating, crossover and mutation are performed. The crossover takes two parent strings and generates two offspring strings. The mutation changes selected strings in a random way. In the references [13,14], the GA is explained in detail.

In this section, we explain our approach for obtaining near-optimum solutions for P and P' by using a GA.

6.1. Coding

The GA coding for Experiment 1, described below, is performed as follows.

A gene is expressed by a bit of value 0 or 1. Accordingly, each chromosome is composed of a row of bits. The total number of bits is m, in which n bits of the higher ranks are associated with the level of DWT and $(m-n)$ subordinate bits are associated with the shift value s, described for P' in the binary expression (**Figure 6**).

When an individual associated with a level that actually does not exist in a list of levels used for DWT is generated in the GA process, the individual is judged to have a fatal gene and is deleted, and a new individual is generated.

The GA coding for Experiment 2, described below, is performed as follows.

A gene is expressed by a bit of value 0 or 1 for P. Accordingly, each chromosome is composed of a row of bits. The total number of bits is k. Each bit is assigned to each DWT coefficient for possible embedment of the watermark (**Figure 7**). The value of 1 for a bit means that the corresponding DWT coefficient is selected as an object of watermarking, whereas 0 denotes non-embedment for the corresponding DWT coefficient.

A gene is also expressed by a bit of value 0 or 1 for P'. Accordingly, each chromosome is composed of a row of bits. The total number of bits is l. The chromosome expresses shift value s described in P' in the binary expression (**Figure 8**).

1011010...0101

Level   Shift value

000:Level 1 **001**:Level 2 **010**:Level 3 **011**:Level 4
100:Level 5 **101**:Level 6 **110**:Level 7 **111**:Level 8

Figure 6. Schematic diagram of a chromosome structure in Experiment 1 for P'.

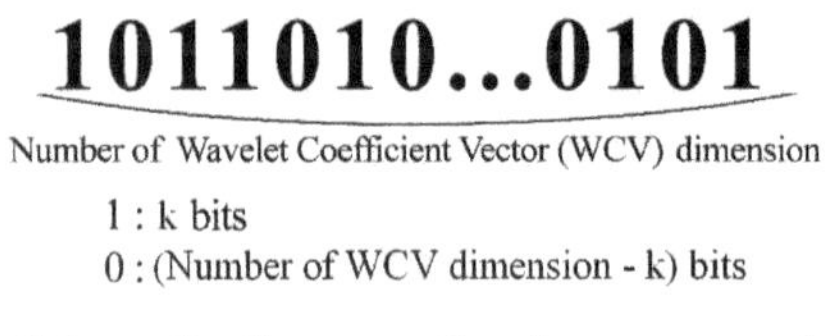

1011010...0101

Number of Wavelet Coefficient Vector (WCV) dimension

1 : k bits

0 : (Number of WCV dimension - k) bits

Figure 7. Schematic diagram of a chromosome structure in Experiment 2 for P.

1100...1001
Shift value

Figure 8. Schematic diagram of a chromosome structure in Experiment 2 for *P'*.

6.2. Strategy

For *P*, a one-point crossover and a mutation by the exchange(s) of pairs of 0 and 1 on a chromosome are used, while for *P'* a two-point crossover and a one-point mutation are used. The fitness function $f = (d - a + 1)/e$ is used for both *P* and *P'*, where *d*, *a*, and *e* were introduced in Section 5.

7. Numerical Experiments

In this section, we describe our computer experiments and the results for evaluating the performance of the proposed method.

7.1. Method

The experiment was performed in the following computational environment: the personal computer was a Dell Dimension DXC051 (CPU: Pentium IV 3.0 GHz; main memory: 1.0 GB); the OS was Microsoft Windows XP; the development language was Microsoft Visual C++ 6.0.

For DWT, we use Daubechies wavelets, which were successfully used in related research on DW techniques for images [16]. Moreover, a string composed of 400 randomly generated bits is used as the watermark information.

Five music audio files, composed of the first entry in five genre categories (classical, jazz, popular, rock, and hiphop) in the research music database RWC [21], were copied from CDs onto the personal computer as WAVE files with the following specifications: 44.1 kHz, 16 bits, and monaural. For each music audio file selected from the database, one 10-sec clip of the music audio (hereafter referred to as the original music audio clip) was extracted starting at 1 minute from the beginning of the audio file and saved on a personal computer. The watermarked music audio clip was produced by embedding a digital watermark on the original audio clip by the proposed method.

In Experiment 1, where the near-optimum solutions for *P'* were obtained by using GA to evaluate the tolerance of watermarking to compression, MP3, AAC, and WMA compression systems were each used to compress the watermarked music audio clip to bitrates of 64, 96, and 128 kbps. The bitrate of 32 kbps was also used for MP3. Moreover, for *P'*, the fitness function value of the near-optimum solutions obtained with GA was compared with the fitness function values of the feasible solutions at the initial generation.

In Experiment 2, the near-optimum solutions for *P* and *P'* were obtained by using GA, and the performances of those solutions were compared with respect to the calculation times for getting those solutions, the quality of the watermarked music audio clip, and the detection rate of the watermarks after compression by the MP3 technique. Moreover, for *P* and *P'*, the near-optimum solutions obtained by using GA were compared with the solutions produced by random generation of individual, neglecting the restrictions (10) for *P* and (17) for *P'*, with respect to the quality of the watermarked music audio clip, and the detection rate of the watermarks after compression by the MP3 technique.

7.2. Procedure

The procedure in the experiment is as follows.
Step 1:
First, an initial population consisting of several individuals is generated. In the process of generating an initial population having a given number of individuals, the individual that does not meet the restriction or that has a fatal gene is deleted as soon as it is produced, and a new individual is generated. If all individuals generated in 300 continuous trials do not meet the restriction or have at least one fatal gene, the procedure is terminated. When an initial population having a given number of feasible individuals is generated, go to Step 2.
Step 2:
The embedment of digital watermark according to the condition decided by each individual, the sound compression with the MP3 technique and the detection of digital watermark after MP3 decoding are performed, and then the fitness is calculated. When the generation is final, the procedure is terminated. Otherwise, go to Step 3.
Step 3:
The roulette strategy for selection, crossover, and mutation are performed. Go to Step 2.

The near-optimum solution, which is defined as the solution having the highest fitness through all generations, is obtained by repeating the process from Steps 2 to 3 until the given final generation.

7.3. Conditions

Table 1 shows the conditions of the GA strategy. In addition to the conditions shown in **Table 1**, the lower bound of the detection rate *a*, described by the restriction conditions (10) and (17), was set to 90. **Table 2** shows

Table 1. Conditions of the GA strategy.

Exp. No.	Problem	Population size	Generation loop	Crossover rate	Mutation rate
1	P'	30	100	0.6	0.1
2	P'	30	100	0.6	0.1
	P	50	200	0.6	0.2

Table 2. Conditions of chromosome structure in GA.

Exp. No.	Problem	Parameter values
1	P'	$m = 19, n = 3$
2	P'	$l = 16$
	P	$k = 400$

the conditions of the chromosome structure in GA (k, l, m, n are introduced in Section 6).

For Experiment 1, 32 and 64 kbps were used as the bitrates of the MP3 compression and DWT levels ranging from one to eight were selected as the search range. For Experiment 2, 96 kbps was used as the bitrate of the MP3 compression for level 3 of DWT, and 32 kbps was used for levels 4 to 6 of DWT.

For Experiment 1, we obtained the segmental-signal-to-quantization-noise ratio (hereafter referred to as SNR_{seg}), as defined by (25) and (26).

$$SNR_j = 10 \log_{10} \left\{ \sum_{r=1}^{N_j} y_{j,r}^2 \bigg/ \sum_{r=1}^{N_j} \left(y_{j,r} - y'_{j,r} \right)^2 \right\}, \quad (25)$$

$$SNR_{seg} = \frac{1}{N_f} \sum_{j=1}^{N_f} SNR_j, \quad (26)$$

where $y_{j,r}, y'_{j,r}$ denote the values of the r-th sound data of frame j before and after embedding the digital watermark, respectively, and N_j, N_f denote the number of sound data at frame j and the number of frames to be measured for SNR_{seg}, respectively. In the present study, we used 209 ms as the time length of one frame. When calculating SNR_{seg}, we excluded the frame with $SNR_j = \infty$, which means there is no change of all values of the sound data of frame j. An audio frame size of 209 ms is adopted for comparison with results obtained by our previous watermarking method [17,18], where the frame size was decided in the relation to the condition of watermarking.

7.4. Results and Discussions

7.4.1. Experiment 1

In this subsubsection, to examine the performance of the proposed method in Experiment 1, the fitness function

value of the near-optimum solution for the partial problem P' is first compared with that obtained from 30 feasible solutions generated at random for the partial problem P'. Next, the tolerances of watermark obtained by the proposed method to compression by MP3, AAC, and WMA are shown, and the time to obtain the near-optimum solution for the partial problem P' is shown to check the practicability of the proposed method.

Each DWT level obtained as an element composed of a chromosome of the near-optimum solution by GA was 4 for classical and jazz, 5 for rock and hiphop, and 6 for popular music for 32 kbps of the bitrate condition of MP3, while the DWT level for 64 kbps as the bitrate condition of MP3 was 3 for classical, jazz, and rock music, 4 for popular, and 5 for hiphop.

As shown in **Figures 9-13**, GA successfully found a good solution considered as the near-optimum solution for each case. **Table 3** shows the tolerance of watermark to the compression. **Table 4** shows the time to obtain a near-optimum solution. For the MP3 bitrate condition of 32 and 64 kbps in the process of GA, the average detection rate after compression by MP3 with the bitrate of 32 to 128 kbps was 98.39% and 93.88%, respectively, and the average time to obtain the near-optimum solution was 5.94×10^2 and 3.78×10^2 sec, respectively. As a condition for obtaining the high tolerance of watermark to MP3 compression, 32 kbps was better than 64 kbps. However, it took more time to obtain the near-optimum solution for the MP3 bitrate condition for 32 kbps than the time for 64 kbps. Moreover, for the MP3 bitrate condition of 32 kbps and 64 kbps in the process of GA, the average detection rate after compression by AAC with the bit rate of 64 to 128 kbps was 93.71% and 84.62%, respectively, and that by WMA with the bitrate of 64 to 128 kbps was 98.33% and 95.07%, respectively. As shown in **Table 5**, SNR_{seg} after embedding the watermark on the condition of the near-optimum solution obtained by the proposed method was 69.7 to 78.6 dB. These values suggest that noise due to the watermarking was difficult to perceive.

7.4.2. Experiment 2

In this subsubsection, to examine the performance of the proposed method in Experiment 2, the performances of the near-optimum solutions for the original problem P and the partial problem P' and those obtained from the solutions generated at random for the original problem P and the partial problem P' are compared with respect to the detection rates of the watermarks after MP3 compression and by the errors of the watermarking. Next, the times to obtain the near-optimum solution for the original problem P and the partial problem P' are shown to check the practicability of the proposed method.

As shown in **Figures 14** to **18**, GA successfully found a good solution considered as the near-optimum solution in each case for the original problem P and the partial problem P'. Moreover, the near-optimum solution for the original problem P had better performance as a condition for embedding watermarks than that for the partial problem P'. However, the time to obtain the near-optimum solution for the original problem P was approximately 2 to 200 times, compared with that for the partial

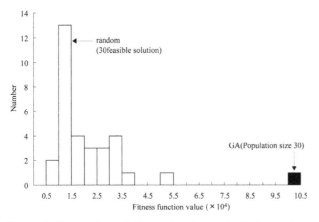
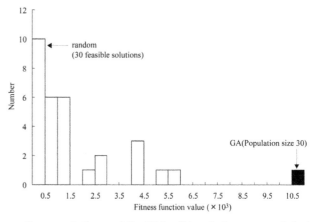

Figure 9. Comparison of fitness function value between the near-optimum solution and the 30 feasible solutions generated at random (Experiment 1, music file: classical). Left figure: MP3 bit rate; 32 kbps. Right figure: MP3 bit rate; 64 kbps.

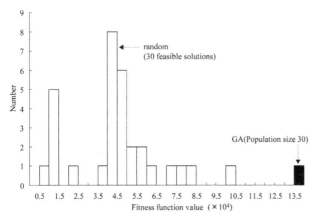
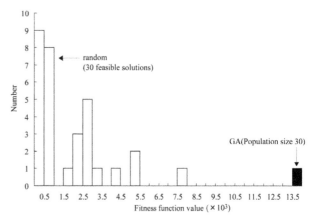

Figure 10. Comparison of fitness function value between the near-optimum solution and the 30 feasible solutions generated at random (Experiment 1, music file: jazz). Left figure: MP3 bit rate; 32 kbps. Right figure: MP3 bit rate; 64 kbps.

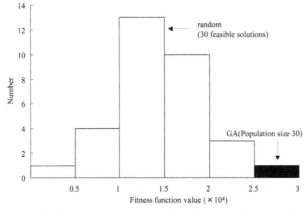
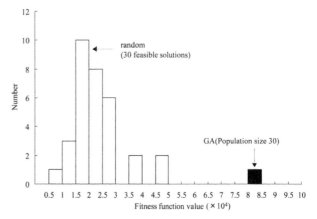

Figure 11. Comparison of fitness function value between the near-optimum solution and the 30 feasible solutions generated at random (Experiment 1, music file: popular). Left figure: MP3 bit rate; 32 kbps. Right figure: MP3 bit rate; 64 kbps.

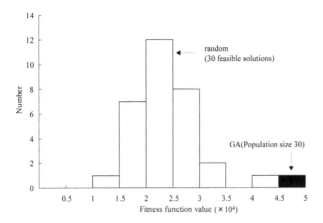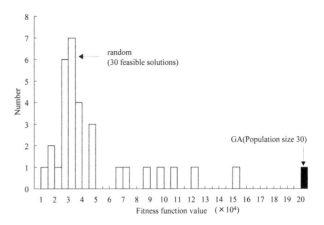

Figure 12. Comparison of fitness function value between the near-optimum solution and the 30 feasible solutions generated at random (Experiment 1, music file: rock). Left figure: MP3 bit rate; 32 kbps. Right figure: MP3 bit rate; 64 kbps.

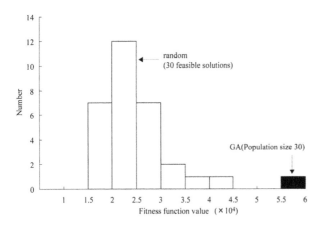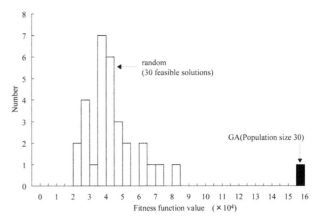

Figure 13. Comparison of fitness function value between the near-optimum solution and the 30 feasible solutions generated at random (Experiment 1, music file: hiphop). Left figure: MP3 bit rate; 32 kbps. Right figure: MP3 bit rate; 64 kbps.

problem P' (**Table 6**). Practically, the watermarking decided by a near-optimum solution for the partial problem P' is recommended. In addition, an initial solution for the partial problem P' can be considered to be a secret key. Therefore, the partial problem P' has an advantage over the original problem P from the viewpoint of watermarking security.

7.4.3. Comparison with Another Technique

For making the technical level of the proposed method clear, we compared the results by the proposed method with those by our retorted method [17,18]. In our reported study, another optimal watermarking problem was formulated using discrete Fourier transform and a watermarking method proposed in the reported study [19]. In our reported study, a string composed of 92 randomly generated bits was used as the watermark information, the same clips as used in the present study were used, and SNR_{seg} was measured using the same condition as that used in the present study. **Table 7** shows the toler-

ance of watermark to the compression in using our reported method. Comparing **Table 7** with **Table 3**, it is clear that the proposed method had higher tolerance to compression by each of MP3, AAC, and MWA than that by our reported study. As shown in **Table 8**, SNR_{seg} after embedding the watermark on the condition of the near-optimum solution obtained by our reported method was 36.8 to 52.2 dB. Although the amount of watermark information used in the present study was more than 4 times to that of our reported study, the proposed method realized lower noise than that by our reported method (**Tables 5** and **8**).

7.4.4. Discussion for Practical Setup

It takes much time to apply our technique to a song of 3 - 5 minutes as one clip. For practical usage of our approach, we will select some short clips of 10 second, for example. Then, we will use our approach to each short clip. The methodology for effective selections of short clips in a song is our next target.

Table 3. Watermarking tolerance to compression measured by detection rate (%) in Experiment 1.

(a) MP3 bitrate as GA condition: 32 kbps

Compression		Classical	Jazz	Popular	Rock	Hiphop
Method	Bitrate (kbps)					
MP3	128	99.75	99.75	99.5	99.25	99.25
	96	99.75	99.75	99.5	99.25	99.25
	64	99.25	99.25	98.25	97.25	98.25
	32	93.75	93.5	98.25	97.25	97.75
AAC	128	99	99	98.25	97	97.25
	96	89.75	91.15	95.25	94.5	93.25
	64	87.25	87	92.5	93	91.5
WMA	128	99.75	99.75	99.5	99.75	99.25
	96	98.75	97.75	99.5	98.75	99
	64	98.25	95.5	97.25	96	96.25
						(%)

(b) MP3 bitrate as GA condition: 64 kbps

Compression		Classical	Jazz	Popular	Rock	Hiphop
Method	Bitrate (kbps)					
MP3	128	100	100	99.25	100	98.25
	96	99.25	99.25	98.75	97.75	97.5
	64	95.5	95.5	95.25	92	96.25
	32	80.25	80.25	88.5	75.5	88.5
AAC	128	95.25	95.25	93.5	87.75	96.25
	96	80.25	80.25	87	74.75	91.5
	64	77.75	77.75	80.25	67.25	84.5
WMA	128	100	99	99.75	97.75	98.5
	96	97.75	93	96.25	92.75	94.75
	64	94.25	89	94	89	90.25
						(%)

Table 4. Time (sec.) to obtain a near-optimum solution in Experiment 1.

MP3 bitrate	32 kbps	64 kbps
Classical	4.02×10^2	3.98×10^2
Jazz	4.20×10^2	2.70×10^2
Popular	1.16×10^3	3.93×10^2
Rock	4.67×10^2	3.17×10^2
HipHop	5.19×10^2	5.12×10^2

Table 5. SNR_{seg} [dB] after embedding a watermark on the condition of near-optimum solution obtained by the proposed method in Experiment 1.

MP3 bitrate	32 kbps	64 kbps
Classical	70.1	73.2
Jazz	76.3	78.6
Popular	69.7	73.9
Rock	72.9	78.1
HipHop	73.6	71.1

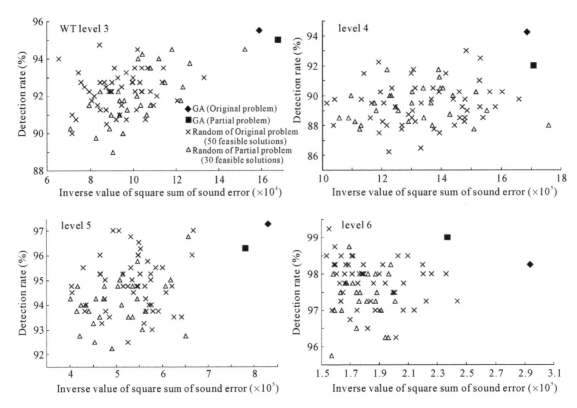

Figure 14. Comparison between the near-optimum solutions and the solutions generated at random (Experiment 2, music file: classical).

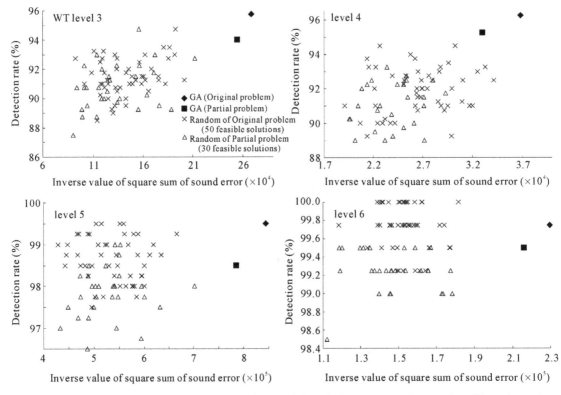

Figure 15. Comparison between the near-optimum solutions and the solutions generated at random (Experiment 2, music file: jazz).

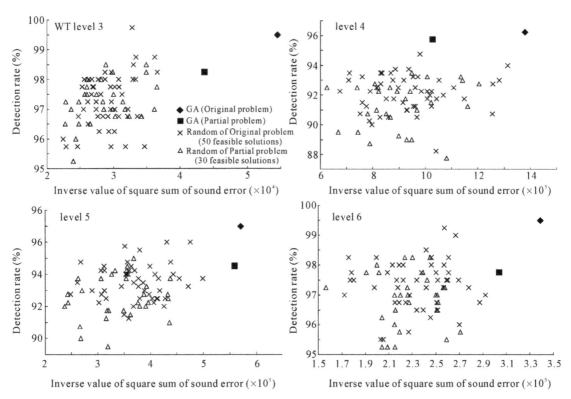

Figure 16. Comparison between the near-optimum solutions and the solutions generated at random (Experiment 2, music file: popular).

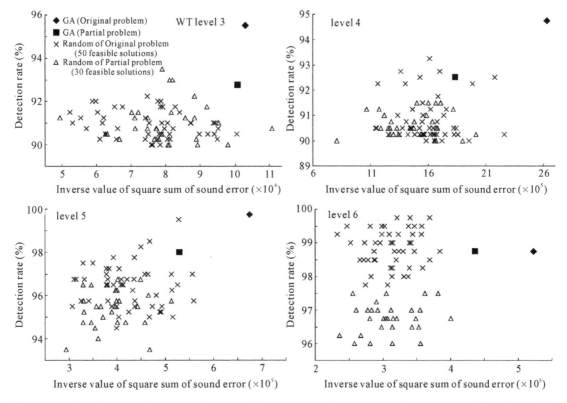

Figure 17. Comparison between the near-optimum solutions and the solutions generated at random (Experiment 2, music file: rock).

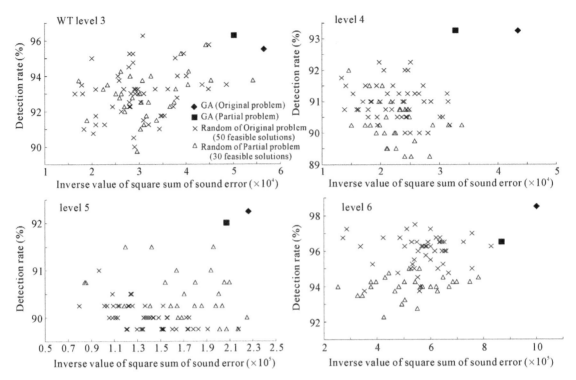

Figure 18. Comparison between the near-optimum solutions and the solutions generated at random (Experiment 2, music file: hiphop).

It is difficult to model the compression attack in general. In this paper, the framework of watermark optimization is shown on the viewpoint of realizing good quality and high tolerance to MP3 compression. Because MP3 compression is one of the easiest attacks to watermark, we have selected it as an example. In addition, the high tolerance of watermark by the proposed method to each of AAC and WMA compression, which are representative audio compression techniques, is also shown in this paper.

8. Conclusions

A method for embedding digital watermark using DWT and GA to realize high tolerance to compression by MP3 is proposed. The proposed method enables us to embed digital watermark in a near-optimum manner for each music audio clip. Moreover, the near-optimum solution for the original problem P and partial problem P', and the initial pattern of digital watermark for P' are used as secret keys in extracting the digital watermark. The experimental results show that the proposed method generates watermarked audio of good quality and high tolerance to MP3 compression.

9. Acknowledgements

The authors would like to thank Associate Professor H. Okuhara of the Graduate School of Osaka University for his valuable advice on this research. The authors would also like to thank Associate Professor M. Tabuse of Kyoto Prefectural University for his valuable support of this research.

10. References

[1]   D. Kirovski and H. S. Malvar, "Spread-Spectrum Watermarking of Audio Signals," *IEEE Transactions on Signal Processing*, Vol. 51, No. 4, April 2003, pp. 1020-1033.

[2]   I.-K. Yeo and H. J. Kim, "Modified Patchwork Algorithm: A Novel Audio Watermarking Scheme," *IEEE Transactions on Speech and Audio Processing*, Vol. 11, No. 4, July 2003, pp. 381-386.

[3]   S. Wu, J. Huang, D. Huang and Y. Q. Shi, "Efficiently Self-Synchronized Audio Watermarking for Assured Audio Data Transmission," *IEEE Transactions on Broadcasting*, Vol. 51, No. 1, March 2005, pp. 69-76.

[4]   X. Y. Wang and H. Zhao, "A Novel Synchronization Invariant Audio Watermarking Scheme Based on DWT and DCT," *IEEE Transactions on Signal Processing*, Vol. 54, No. 12, December 2006, pp. 4835-4840.

[5]   S. Xiang and J. Huang, "Histogram-Based Audio WaterMarking against Time-Scale Modification and Cropping Attacks," *IEEE Transactions on Multimedia*, Vol. 9,

No. 7, November 2007, pp. 1357-1372.

[6]   S. Kirbiz, A. N. Lemma, M. U. Celik and S. Katzenbeisser, "Decode-Time Forensic Watermarking of AAC Bitstreams," *IEEE Transactions on Information Forensics and Security*, Vol. 2, No. 4, December 2007, pp. 683-696.

[7]   D. J. Coumou and G. Sharma, "Insertion, Deletion Codes with Feature-Based Embedding: A New Paradigm for Watermark Synchronization with Applications to Speech Watermarking," *IEEE Transactions on Information Forensics and Security*, Vol. 3, No. 2, June 2008, pp. 153-165.

[8]   S. Xianga, H. J. Kimb, and J. Huanga, "Audio Watermarking Robust against Time-Scale Modification and MP3 Compression," *Signal Processing*, Vol. 88, No. 10, October 2008, pp. 2372-2387.

[9]   X. Y. Wang, P. P. Niu and H. Y. Yang, "A Robust, Digital-Audio Watermarking Method," *IEEE Multimedia*, Vol. 16, No. 3, July 2009, pp. 60-69.

[10] N. K. Kalantari, M. A. Akhaee, S. M. Ahadi and H. Amindavar, "Robust Multiplicative Patchwork Method for Audio Watermarking," *IEEE Transactions on Audio, Speech, and Language Processing*, Vol. 17, No. 6, August 2009, pp. 1133-1141.

[11] X. Y. Wanga, P. P. Niub and H. Y. Yangb, "A Robust Digital Audio Watermarking Based on Statistics Characteristics," *Pattern Recognition*, Vol. 42, No. 11, November 2009, pp. 3057-3064.

[12] K. Yamamoto and M. Iwakiri, "Real-Time Audio Watermarking Based on Characteristics of PCM in Digital Instrument," *Journal of Information Hiding and Multimedia Signal Processing*, Vol. 1, No. 2, April 2010, pp. 59-71.

[13] D. Goldberg, "Genetic Algorithm in Search, Optimization, and Machine Learning," Addison-Wesley, Reading, Boston, 1989.

[14] J. H. Holland, "Adaptation in Natural and Artificial Systems," The University Michigan Press, Ann Arbor, 1975, and MIT Press, Cambridge, 1992.

[15] M. Shino, Y. Choi and K. Aizawa, "Wavelet Domain Digital Watermarking Based on Threshold-Variable Decision," *Technical Report of IEICE*, DSP2000-86, in Japanese, Vol. 100, No. 325, September 2000, pp. 29-34.

[16] D. Inoue and Y. Yoshitomi, "Watermarking Using Wavelet Transform and Genetic Algorithm for Realizing High Tolerance to Image Compression," *Journal of the Institute of Image Electronics Engineers of Japan*, Vol. 38, No. 2, March 2009, pp. 136-144.

[17] M. Tanaka and Y. Yoshitomi, "Digital Audio Watermarking Method with MP3 Tolerance Using Genetic Algorithm," *Proceedings of the* 2006 *IEICE General Conference*, Tokyo, 21 March 2006, p. 182.

[18] M. Tanaka and Y. Yoshitomi, "Digital Audio Watermarking Method with MP3 Tolerance Using Genetic Algorithm," *Proceedings of* 11*th Czech-Japan Seminar on Data Analysis and Decision Making under Uncertainty*, Sendai, 15-17 September 2008, pp. 81-85.

[19] R. Tachibana, "Capacity Analysis of Audio Watermarking Based on Logarithmic Amplitude Modification against Additive Noise," *IEICE Transactions on Fundamentals of Electronics, Communications and Computer Sciences*, in Japanese, Vol. J86-A, No. 11, November 2003, pp. 1197-1206.

[20] F. Glover, "Future Paths for Integer Programming and Links to Artificial Intelligence," *Computers and Operations Research*, Vol. 13, No. 5, May 1986, pp. 533-549.

[21] M. Goto, H. Hashiguchi, T. Nishimura and R. Oka, "RWC Music Database: Database of Copyright-Cleared Musical Pieces and Instrument Sounds for Research Purposes," *Transactions of IPSJ*, in Japanese, Vol. 45, No. 3, March 2004, pp. 728-738

15

A Comparative Study of Related Technologies of Intrusion Detection & Prevention Systems

Indraneel Mukhopadhyay[1], Mohuya Chakraborty[1], Satyajit Chakrabarti[2]
[1]*Department of Information Technology, Institute of Engineering & Management, Kolkata, India*
[2]*Institute of Engineering & Management, Kolkata, India*

Abstract

The rapid growth of computer networks has changed the prospect of network security. An easy accessibility condition causes computer networks to be vulnerable against numerous and potentially devastating threats from hackers. Up to the moment, researchers have developed Intrusion Detection Systems (IDS) capable of detecting attacks in several available environments. A boundlessness of methods for misuse detection as well as anomaly detection has been applied. Intrusion Prevention Systems (IPS) evolved after that to resolve ambiguities in passive network monitoring by placing detection systems on the line of attack. IPS in other words is IDS that are able to give prevention commands to firewalls and access control changes to routers. IPS can be seen as an improvement upon firewall technologies. It can make access control decisions based on application content, rather than IP address or ports as traditional firewalls do. The next innovation is the combination of IDS and IPS known as Intrusion Detection and Prevention Systems (IDPS) capable of detecting and preventing attacks from happening. This paper presents an overview of IDPS followed by their classifications and applications. A new signature based IDPS architecture named HawkEye Solutions has been proposed by the authors. Authors have presented the basic building blocks of the IDS, which include mechanisms for carrying out TCP port scans, Traceroute scan, ping scan and packet sniffing to monitor network health detect various types of attacks. Real time implementation results of the system have been presented. Finally a comparative analysis of various existing IDS/IPS solutions with HawkEye Solutions emphasizes its significance.

Keywords: Advances of Network Security, Intrusion Detection System, Intrusion Prevention System, HawkEye Solutions

1. Introduction

The Internet is a worldwide network of interconnected computers enabling users to share information along multiple channels. A computer connected to the Internet is able to access information from a vast array of available servers and other computers by moving information from them to former computer's local memory. Common uses of the Internet are Email, World Wide Web, remote access, collaboration, streaming media and file sharing. But nowadays malfunctions on the Web are increasing. There are computer investment frauds, cyber crimes, financial crimes, phishing scams, chatting (masquerading) and crimes associated which share trading on Web. Network Security consists of the provisions made in an underlined computer network infrastructure and policies adopted by the Network Administrator to protect the network and network accessible resources from unauthorized access, consistent and continuous monitoring and measurement of its effectiveness combined together.

In the last few years networking revolution has finally come of age due to changing nature of Internet computing. However complete prevention of breaches of security is unrealistic. Intrusion detection is the process of monitoring the events occurring in a computer system/ network and analyzing them for signs of possible attacks, which can lead to violations or imminent threats of violation of computer security policies, of the organization. An intrusion detection system (IDS) is software that automates the intrusion detection process. An intrusion prevention system (IPS) is software that has all the capabilities of an intrusion detection system and can also attempt to stop possible incidents. IDS and IPS technologies offer many of the same capabilities, and administrators can usually disable prevention features in IPS products, causing them to function as IDSs. The combination of IDS and IPS known as Intrusion Detection and Prevention Systems (IDPS) is capable of detecting and preventing attacks from happening. This paper presents an overview of IDPS followed by their classifications and applications. A new signature based IDPS architecture named HawkEye Solutions has been proposed by the authors.

1.1. Meaning of IDS/IPS

IDS generally do not react against occurred attacks and usually have the state of informing administrator for occurrence of an intrusion and have several methods for detecting attacks. Monitoring and analyzing network activities, finding vulnerable parts in network and integrity testing of sensitive and important data are few examples of IDS operations for intrusions detection [1]. Incidents have many causes, malware, attackers gaining unauthorized access to systems, and authorized users of systems who misuse their privileges or attempt to gain additional privileges for which they are not authorized. Many incidents are malicious in nature; many are not. IPS on the other hand is software that has all the capabilities of IDS and can attempts to stop possible incidents. Accordingly, for brevity the term Intrusion Detection and Prevention Systems (IDPS) is used throughout the rest of this article to refer to both IDS and IPS technologies.

1.2. IDPS Components

Typical components of IDPS and their functionalities are [2]:
- Sensor/Agent: Monitors and analyzes network activity. The term sensor is used for IDPS that monitor networks, including network-based, wireless, and network behavior analysis technologies. The term agent is used for host-based IDPS technologies.
- Database Server: Used as a repository for event information recorded by the sensors or agents processed by the management server.
- Management Server: Centralized device that receives; analyzes and manages event information from the sensors/agents. It identifies events that the sensors/agents cannot.
- Console: Provides an interface for the users and administrators. Console software is typically in-

stalled onto standard computers providing both administration and monitoring capabilities.

IDPS are differentiated by the types of events that they can recognize and the methodologies that they use to identify incidents. IDPS typically perform the following functions:
- Recording Information: Event information is usually recorded locally, and might also be sent to separate systems such as centralized logging servers, security information and event management solutions, and enterprise management systems.
- Notifying Security Administrators: Alerts or alarms occur when any of the following like-e-mails, web pages, messages on the IDPS user interface, SNMP traps, syslog messages, and user-defined programs, are detected by the system. A simple notification message includes basic information regarding an event; administrators need to access the IDPS Console for additional information in order to neutralize them.
- Producing Reports: Summarized reports of the monitored events and/or action taken by the administrator based on the details of the particular events.

1.3. Types of IDPS

IDPS perform extensive logging of data that is related to detected events in the network. These data can then be used to confirm the validity of alerts, investigate incidents, and correlate events between the IDPS and other logging sources [2].
- Host-Based: Monitors the characteristics of a single host and the events occurring within that host for suspicious activity. Examples of the types of characteristics a host-based IDPS might monitor are network traffic, system logs, running processes, application activity, file access and modification, and system configuration changes. Host-based are deployed on critical hosts such as publicly accessible servers and servers containing sensitive information.
- Network-Based: Monitors network traffic for particular network segments or devices and analyzes the network and application protocol activity to identify suspicious activity. It can identify many different types of events of interest. It is mostly deployed at a boundary between networks, virtual private network servers, remote access servers, and wireless networks.
- Hybrid: Both host-based as well as network-based IDPS may be used simultaneously.
- Network Behavior Analysis (NBA): Examines net-

work traffic to identify threats that generate unusual traffic flows, such as distributed denial of service attacks, certain forms of malware, and policy violations. NBA systems are most often deployed to monitor flows of the internal networks, and are also sometimes deployed where they can monitor flows between an organization's internal networks and external.

The organization of the paper is as follows. After the introduction in Section 1, different techniques of intrusion detection is discussed in Section 2. Section 3 deals with various types of analysis techniques performed by IDPS. Section 4 highlights the related works that act as a motivation for the proposed signature based IDPS architecture called HawkEye Solutions, whose architecture is shown in Section 5. Working principle and features of HawkEye Solutions are presented in Sections 6 and 7 respectively. Snapshots of real time implementation results are shown in Section 8. In Section 9 a comparative analysis of various existing IDS/IPS solutions is made with HawkEye Solutions that emphasizes its significance. Section 10 deals with issues and challenges faced by an IDPS environment. Finally the article is concluded in Section 11 with some highlights on future works.

2. Techniques of Intrusion Detection

Many of the techniques used in attempting to detect intrusion are reviewed here in this section. The most common ones are summarized below.

- Artificial Neural Networks (ANNs): Can be trained to recognize arbitrary patterns in input data, and associate such patterns with an outcome, which can be a binary indication of whether an intrusion has occurred [3].
- State Transition Tables: Describe a sequence of actions an intruder does in the form of a state transition diagram. When the behavior of the system matches those states, an intrusion is detected [4].
- Genetic Algorithms (GAs): Mimic the natural reproduction system in nature where only the fittest individuals in a generation will be reproduced in subsequent generations, after undergoing recombination and random change. The application of GAs in IDS research appeared as early as 1995, and involves evolving a signature that indicates intrusion [5]. A related technique is the Learning Classifier System (LCS), where binary rules are evolved, that collectively recognizes patterns of intrusion.
- Bayesian Network: A set of transition rules are represented as probabilistic interdependencies in a graphical model. Each node contains the state of random variable and a conditional probability table, which determine the probabilities of the node in a state, given a state of its parent [6]. An advantage of the approach is that it can deal with incomplete data.
- Fuzzy Logic: A set of concepts and approaches designed to handle vagueness and imprecision. A set of rules can be created to describe a relationship between the input variables and the output variables, which may indicate whether an intrusion has occurred. Fuzzy logic uses membership functions to evaluate the degree of truthfulness [7].

3. Types of Analysis Techniques

IDPS implementation uses a single technique or a combination of two techniques among the commonly used are:

- Code Analysis: Aims at identifying malicious activity by analyzing attempts to execute code. For example, code-behavior analysis can first execute code in a virtual environment and compare its behavior to profiles or rules; buffer overflow detection identifies typical sequences of instructions that attempt to perform stack and heap buffer overflows.
- Network Traffic Analysis and Filtering: Analyses network, transport and application layer protocols and include processing for common applications. Sensors/Agents often include a host-based firewall that can restrict incoming and outgoing traffic for the system.
- File System Monitoring: Includes a number of methods, such as file integrity checking, file attribute checking; these two methods can only determine after-the-fact if the file has been changed. Some sensors/agents typically those who use a small library the transparently intercepts, are able to monitor all attempts to access critical files and stop attempts that are suspicious. The current attempt is compared against a set of policies regarding file access and blocked if the type of access that has been requested (read-write-execute) contradicts a policy.
- Log Analysis: Some sensors/agents can identify malicious activity by monitoring and analyzing system and application logs, which contain information e.g., shutting down the system, starting a service, application startup and shutdown, failures, configuration changes.
- Network Configuration Monitoring: Sensors are able to monitor a host's current network configuration and detect changes to it. For example, network interfaces being placed in promiscuous mode, ad-

ditional TCP or UDP ports or unusual protocols being used could indicate that the host has already been compromised and is being configured for use in future attacks or for transferring data.

- Process Status Monitoring: Some host-based IDPSs can monitor the status of the processes and services running on a host; when they detect that one has stopped, they restart automatically. This provides protection against some forms of malware which can sometimes disable antivirus software and the like.

- Network Traffic Sanitization: This protection is usually implemented by appliance-based IDPSs. Sanitization of traffic may rebuild all requests and responses directed to the host or coming from it, thus neutralizing certain unusual activity, particularly in packet headers and application protocol headers. It can also reduce the amount of reconnaissance the attackers can perform on the host, by hiding OS fingerprints and application error messages.

- Signature Based: Based on pattern matching. A dictionary of known fingerprints is used and run across a set of input. This dictionary contains a list of known bad signatures, such as malicious network payloads or the file contents of a worm executable. This database of signatures is the key to the strength of the detection system, and its prowess is a direct result of its speed. It uses network payload signatures, as is used in network intrusion detection systems [8]. The detection methods used performs an evaluation of packet contents received from the network, typically using passive capture techniques. This can include matching signatures based on payload contents measured by string comparisons, application protocol analysis, or network characteristics. Lists of unacceptable patterns are compared against a list of network traffic and alerts are issued when a match is found. The biggest drawback to signature-based detection methods is that they are reactionary; they rarely can be used to detect a new worm.

- Anomaly Based: In this model, computer behavior is studied extensively under normal operating conditions [9]. On compromise by a worm, virus, or attacker, the system's behavior is expected to change. A monitoring system can detect these changes and respond accordingly [10]. In this way, the host is able to adapt to its normally changing behavior while remaining responsive to new threats. While such a system would prove to be nearly infinitely adaptive the biggest challenge is the long training time required to develop a reliable baseline

of behavior. This assumes that no anomalies occur during this period.

4. Related Works

Easy accessibility condition in wireless networks causes more vulnerability against wired networks. The level of vulnerability has made it mandatory to adopt security policies in wireless networks more now than before. In centralized-IDPS, the analysis of data is performed at a fixed number of locations. But in distributed-IDPS the analysis of data is performed at a number of locations that is commensurate to number of available systems in the network. In ad-hoc-based wireless networks we are forced to use distributed-IDPS because we cannot set of fixed locations/hosts for using centralized IDS [11]. Recently, new methods appear in distributed-IDS categories known as Grid Intrusion Detection system, which uses Grid Computing to detect intrusion packets [12].

Distributed intrusion detection is an ideal approach to the detection of worm activities. As worms spread on the network from host to host, they will quickly cover a large network if left unchecked. As such, a disconnected set of network-IDS monitors will generate an increasing number of alerts. However, with no central infrastructure, the larger picture of a spreading worm will be difficult to gain at an early enough time to contain the spread of the worm [13].

Design of a robust security system should fulfill the objectives of security like authenticity, confidentiality, integrity, availability & non-repudiation. IDPS contains modules to detect intrusion, filtering intrusion, trace-back of intrusion origin, and prevention mechanism for theses intrusions. This security system needs the robust automated auditing and intelligent reporting mechanism and robust prevention techniques. The system should be divided into three sub-systems:

- Intrusion Detection System
- Backtracking of Intrusion Source
- Prevention Techniques

The components of the intrusion detection and prevention system are shown in **Figure 1**. The rule based intelligent intrusion detection and prevention model contains a scheduler to prepare schedule to check different logs for possible intrusions, and detectors to detect normal or abnormal activity. If activity is normal then standard alarming and reporting would be executed.

If abnormal activity is found then the rule engine checks the rule to detect intrusion point and type of intrusion. The model also contains an expert system to detect source of intrusion and suggests best possible prevention technique and suitable controls for different intrusions. This model also uses security audit as well as

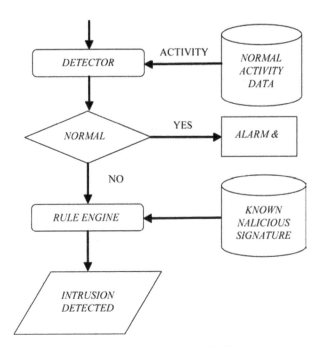

Figure 1. Components of IDPS.

alarming and reporting mechanisms. The malicious activity database is stored for future intrusion detection. To detect the source by tracking, backward chaining approach is used. The rules are defined and are stored in the Rule Engine of the system. Intrusion points & types are passed to the expert system. Expert system evaluates that data with known malicious activity database and detects the source using backward chaining approach. After detecting source, system suggests the different prevention techniques. For this robust security system the authors use intelligent models like expert system.

Expert systems are the most common form of Artificial Intelligence applied today in intrusion detection system. An expert system consists of a set of rules that encode the knowledge of a human "expert". These rules are used by the system to make conclusions about the security-related data from the intrusion detection system. Expert system permits the incorporation of an extensive amount of human experience into a computer application and then utilizes that knowledge to identify activities that match the defined characteristics of misuse and attack. Expert system detects intrusions by encoding intrusion scenarios as a set of rules. These rules replicate the partially ordered sequence of actions that include the intrusion scenario. Some rules may be applicable to more than one intrusion scenario. Rule-based programming is one of the most commonly used techniques for developing expert systems. Rule based analysis relies on sets of predefined rules that can be repeatedly applied to a collection of facts and that are provided by an administrator, automatically created by the system or both. Facts repre-

sent conditions that describe a certain situation in the audit records or directly from system activity monitoring & rules represent heuristics that define a set of actions to be executed in a given situation & describe known intrusion scenario(s) or generic techniques. The rule then *fires*. It may cause an alert to be raised for a system administrator. Alternatively, some automated response, such as terminating that user's session, block user's account will be taken. Normally, a rule firing will result in additional assertions being added to the fact base. They, in turn, may lead to additional rule-fact bindings. This process continues until there are no more rules to be fired. Consider the intrusion scenario in which two or more unsuccessful authentication attempts are made in a period of time shorter than it would take a human to present biometric info in the login information at biometric sensor. If the rule or rules for this scenario fire, then suspicion level of specific user can get increased. The system may raise an alarm or report 'freeze action' to the named user's account. Account freeze would be entered into the fact database.

The model suggested in this paper is useful to detect the intrusion and also contains an expert system to detect source of intrusion and suggests best possible prevention technique and suitable controls for different intrusions. This model also uses security audit as well as alarming and reporting mechanisms. The malicious activity database is stored for future intrusion detection. To detect the source by tracking, backward chaining approach is used. The rules are defined and are stored in the Rule engine of the system. The intelligent model uses AI and expert system is backbone of this system.

5. Architecture of HawkEye Solutions

The architecture of HawkEye Solutions is focused on performance, simplicity, and flexibility. The architecture comparison between standard IDPS and HawkEye Solutions is shown in **Figure 2**. **Figure 2(a)** shows the standard IDPS Architecture and **Figure 2(b)** shows HawkEye Solutions Architecture.

The different components of HawkEye Solutions are:
- Sensors/agents monitor and analyze activities.
- Management server is a centralized device which receives and manages information from the sensors or agents.
- Database server is a repository for event information recorded by sensors, agents, and/or management servers.
- Console provides an interface for IDPS's users and administrators.
- Demilitarized Zone (DMZ) works as the primary filter, which has the normal security software's

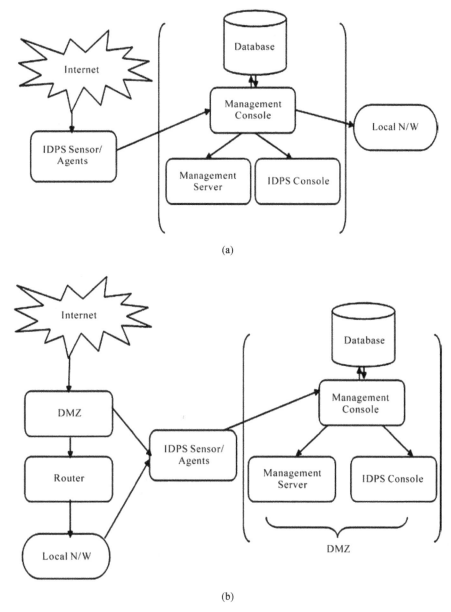

Figure 2. Standard IDPS vs. HawkEye solutions architecture. (a) Standard IDPS architecture; (b) HawkEye solutions architecture.

loaded, but for a network it does not mean that the network is safe from attacks. So IDPS is implemented in both the DMZ and also in the network where the sensors/agents monitor attacks. In normal IDPS the DMZ is not available.

Till date research on IPS dealt with the level of threat-risk assessment on the attacked asset based via Hidden Markov Model (HMM) and Fuzzy Risk Assessment [14]. But work must be done to deal with real data with better HMM model. Kalman filter and its integration with agents/sensors could be a good option [15], in this direction the authors have simulated a DoS attack and then used a Kalman Filter to detect foreign intrusion in the network. The filter worked on the data provided by the network router. In the simulation it was seen that due to the use of Kalman Filter with the increase in the number of observations, higher was the estimation accuracy. Kalman filter showed a stabilized oscillation around a constant positive value. It proved that the illegitimate scan activities are mainly caused by a worm infection. If the illegitimate scan traffic is caused by non-worm noise, the traffic does-not grow exponentially, and the estimated value of infection rate would either fluctuate without any point or band of convergence, or it would oscillate around zero.

6. Working Principle of HawkEye Solutions

This section deals with the working principle of Hawk-Eye Solutions. The various steps followed by HawkEye Solutions are as follows:

- An event record is created. This occurs when an action happens; such as packets of data transmitting in the network or even a file is opened or a program is executed like the text editor like Microsoft Word. The record is written into a file that is usually protected by the operating system trusted computing base.
- The target agent transmits the file to the command console. This happens at predetermined time intervals over a secure connection.
- The detection engine, configured to match patterns of misuse, processes the file.
- A log is created that becomes the data archive for all the raw data that will be used in prosecution.
- An alert is generated. When a predefined pattern is recognized, such as access to a mission critical file, an alert is forwarded to a number of various subsystems for notification, response, and storage.
- The security flag/message are sent *i.e.* notified.
- A response is generated. The response subsystem matches alerts to predefined responses or can take response commands from the security officer. Responses include reconfiguring the system, shutting down a target, logging off a user, or disabling an account.
- The alert is stored. The storage is usually in the form of a database. Some systems store statistical data as well as alerts.
- The raw data is transferred to a raw data archive. This archive is cleared periodically to reduce the amount of disk space used.
- Reports are generated. Reports can be a summary of the alert activity.
- Data forensics is used to locate long-term trends and behavior is analyzed using both the stored data in the database and the raw event log archive.

The flow diagram of the steps discussed above is shown in **Figure 3**. The lifecycle of an event recorded through the proposed architecture is advantageous as everything hap-pens in real-time. The disadvantage is that the end users suffer from system performance degradation.

7. Features of HawkEye Solutions

This section describes the various features of HawkEye

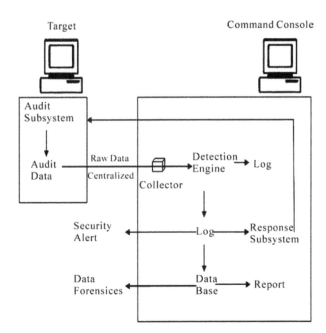

Figure 3. Flow diagram of working principle of HawkEye Solutions.

Solutions that has been developed viz., Ping Scan, Trace Route Scan, TCP Scan and Packet Sniffing.

7.1. Ping Scan

The Internet Ping command bounces a small packet off a domain or IP address to test network communications, and then tells how long the packet took to make the round trip [16]. The Ping command is one of the most commonly used utilities on the Internet by both people and automated programs for conducting the most basic network test, which is to test whether one computer can reach another computer on the network, and if so the time it takes. It works by sending a small packet of information containing an ICMP ECHO_REQUEST to a specified computer, which then sends an ECHO_REPLY packet in return [17].

7.2. Trace Route Scan

The Trace Route scan traces the network path of Internet routers that packets take as they are forwarded from your computer to a destination address. The "length" of the network connection is indicated by the number of Internet routers in the trace route path. Trace routes can be useful to diagnose slow network connections. For example, if one can usually reach an Internet site but it is slow today, then a trace route to that sites should show you one or more hops with either long times or marked with "*" indicating the time was really long.

7.3. TCP Scan

The process of scanning TCP ports involves probing each and every port for a specific domain name to check the status of the ports so as to determine which ports are open, closed or dropped. It will enable the network administrator to also view the services by which the concerned domain name is connected with the host computer [18,19].

7.4. Packet Sniffing

A Sniffer is a program that eavesdrops on the network traffic by grabbing information traveling over a network. A packet sniffer, sometimes referred to as a network monitor or network analyzer, can be used legitimately by a network or system administrator to monitor and troubleshoot network traffic. Using the information captured by the packet sniffer an administrator can identify erroneous packets and use the data to pinpoint bottlenecks and help maintain efficient network data transmission.

In its simple form a packet sniffer simply captures all of the packets of data that pass through a given network interface. Typically, the packet sniffer would only capture packets that were intended for the machine in question. However, if placed into promiscuous mode, the packet sniffer is also capable of capturing packets traversing the network regardless of destination.

8. Implementation Results

This section provides the real time implementation results of HawkEye Solutions for trace route scan and abnormal packet detection through its packet sniffing utility.

Figure 4 shows the screenshot of trace route scan. On selecting the Trace Route Scan option, a textbox appears on the right hand panel that requests the user to enter the IP address or URL of the destination to be traced. The output consists of 3 columns corresponding to each router or hop. Each of the 3 columns is a response from the concerned router in terms of how long it took (each hop is tested 3 times). The result of the scan is shown in the output text box and is automatically saved into the log file ScanTrace.txt. **Figure 5** shows the screenshot of packet sniffing utility. On selecting the Packet Sniffer option and on clicking the Start button, the sniffing of packets starts with the packet details and data of each packet shown instantaneously. The information shown in the figure includes the details of Ethernet header, IP header and TCP/UDP header [20]. The packet sniffer also detects the abnormal packets (if any) and the cause for the abnormality for individual packets. The screenshot of the result is shown in **Figure 6**. These are displayed

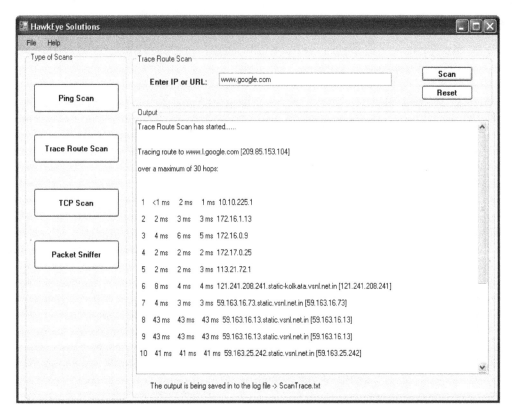

Figure 4. Screenshot of trace route scan of HawkEye solutions.

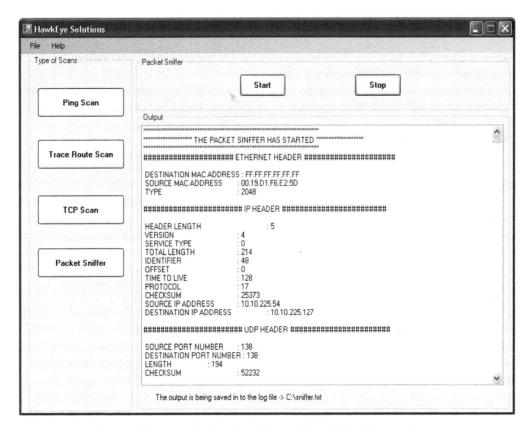

Figure 5. Screenshot of packet sniffing utility of HawkEye solutions.

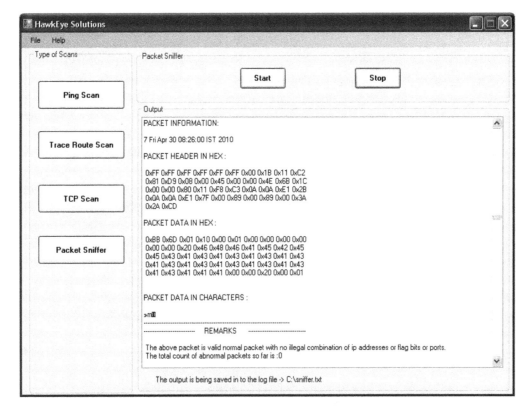

Figure 6. Screenshot of abnormal packet detection by HawkEye solutions.

along with the total count of abnormal packets discovered up to that instant. The data contained in the packet is displayed in the hexadecimal and string format. The result of the scan is shown in the output text box and is automatically saved into the log file sniffer.txt.

9. Comparative Analysis

A comparative analysis of HawkEye Solutions with other signature-based IDS/IPS solutions like Snort Inline, Strataguard, IntruPro IPS, and Packet Alarm [21] is made. **Table 1** shows the comparative analysis chart vis-à-vis design parameters that include IDS as well as IPS. The table clearly indicates that HawkEye Solutions at it stands today is able to meet some of the design parameters that are not met by IntruPro IPS like personalized rule creation and vulnerabilities scanner.

Features of HawkEye Solutions which scores over other available IDS/IPS are:

- Capturing packets, organized by TCP or UDP threads.
- Passively monitoring network.
- Packet viewing and logging in Hex-format.
- Detection of abnormal packet on comparison with benchmark ones and stating cause of abnormality. In case of abnormality the Source IP address can be traced.

The Ping Scan and Packet Sniffing utility the user has a chance of detecting an IP Spoofing. Detected IP can be blocked.

10. Issues and Challenges

Majority of the past research employed analysis was based on data sourced from audit trails, system calls and network traffic. In the network traffic, most research studies looked at the packet header for analysis. Some other research analyzed the payload. Analyzing the packet header is prone to IP address spoofing, while analyzing the payload is prone to data encryption. Several papers also presented the kernel as a data source [22]. IDS assume that signatures of the malware would remain unchanged during the malware's lifetime at present. But if the malware code mutates then the detector (IDS/IDPS) cannot recognize the signature until the new signature has been integrated with its database [23].

11. Conclusions

It is not realistic to accept that IDPS should be capable of detecting all attacks and also prevent them from happening. Perfect detection and prevention is simply not an attainable goal given the complexity and rapid evolution in both attacks and systems. Nowadays even malware developers are creating self mutating worms, which are very hard to detect even for an IDPS. In this article a new type of signature based IDPS–HawkEye Solutions has been discussed which can detect abnormal packets, blocks

Table 1. Comparison of different IDS with HawkEye solutions vis-à-vis design parameters.

Design Parameters	Performance Analysis of various IDS/IPS				
	Snort Inline (IDS)	Strata Guard (IDS)	IntruPro (IPS)	HawkEye Solutions (IDS)	Packet Alarm (IDS)
Anomalies Detection.	√	√	√	√	√
Firewall Inclusion					
IP Tunnels Inspection					
IPv6 Support		√			
Protection against DoS Attack			√	√	√
Personalized Rule Creation	√			√	
Automatic Rules Actualization	√		√	√	
Vulnerabilities Scanner				√	√
Multi-sensor Management		√	√		√
Secure Management (SSH/HTTPS)		√			√
Remote Management		√	√	√	√
Reports Generation		√	√	√	

attacking IP addresses and generates reports. Much work is yet to be done on this solution that should fulfill monitoring of network traffic, creation of per-flow packet traces and adaptive learning of intrusion, inclusion of firewall. It should be able to capture a wide variety of hard-to-see protocol-bug-based attacks, SYN Flood, Land, Teardrop, Smurf and whatever has not been invented yet.

12. References

[1]   S. Northcutt and J. Novak, "Network Intrusion Detection: An Analyst's Handbook," 2nd Edition, New Riders Publishing, Berkeley, 2000.

[2]   K. Scarfone and P. Mell, "Guide to Intrusion Detection and Prevention Systems (IDPS)," *NIST Special Publication*, February 2007, pp. 800-94

[3]   A.-S.Mohammad and Z. Mohammad, "Efficacy of Hidden Markov Models over Neural Networks in Anomaly Intrusion Detection," 30*th Annual International Computer Software and Applications Conference*, Chicago, 2006, pp. 325-332.

[4]   K. Ilgun, R. A. Kemmerer and P. A. Porras, "State Transition Analysis: A Rule-based Intrusion Detection Approach," *IEEE Transactions on Software Engineering*, Vol. 21, No. 3, March 1995, pp. 181-199. doi:10.1109/32. 372146

[5]   M. Crosbie and E. Spafford, "Applying Genetic Programming to Intrusion Detection," *GECCO '96 Proceedings of the First Annual Conference on Genetic Programming* 1996..

[6]   F. Jemili, M. Zaghdoud and M. B. Ahmed, "A Framework for an Adaptive Intrusion Detection System using Bayesian Network," *IEEE Intelligence and Security Informatics*, May 2007, pp. 66-70. doi:10.1109/ISI.2007. 379535

[7]   A. El-Semary, J. Edmonds, J. Gonzalez and M. Papa, "A Framework for Hybrid Fuzzy Logic Intrusion Detection Systems," 14*th IEEE International Conference on Fuzzy Systems*, May 2005, pp. 325-330. doi:10.1109/FUZZY. 2005.1452414

[8]   R. Bace and P. Mell, "Intrusion Detection Systems," 2001. http://csrc.nist.gov/publications/nistpubs/800-31/sp800-3 1.pdf

[9]   S. Forrest, *et al.*, "A Sense of Self for UNIX Processes," *Proceeding of* 1996 *IEEE Symposium on Research in Security and Privacy*, 1996, pp. 120-128.

[10]   J. O. Kephart, *et al.*, "Blueprint for a Computer Immune System," *Proceedings* 1997 *Virus Bulletin International Conference*, San Francisco, 1-3 October 1997.

[11]   A. Abraham, *et al.* "Fuzzy Online Risk Assessment for Distributed Intrusion Prediction and Prevention Systems," 10*th International Conference on Computer Modeling and Simulation, UKSim/EUROSim*, Cambridge, 2008, pp. 216-223.

[12]   F. Y. Leu, J. C. Lin, M. C. Li, C. T. Yang and P. C. Shih, "Integrating Grid with Intrusion Detection," *Proceedings of* 19*th International Conference on Advanced Information Networking and Applications*, 2005, pp. 304-309.

[13]   Jose Nazario, "Defense and Detection Strategies Against Internet Worms," Artech House, London, 2004

[14]   A. Abraham *et al.* "DIPS: A Framework for Distributed Intrusion Prediction and Prevention Systems Using Hidden Markov Model and Online Fuzzy Risk Assessment," *Proceedings of* 3*rd International Symposium on Information Assurance and Security*, Manchester, 29-31 August 2007, pp. 183-188.

[15]   I. Mukhopadhyay, *et al.*, "Implementation of Kalman Filter in Intrusion Detection System," *Proceeding of International Symposium on Communications and Information Technologies*, Vientiane, 21-23 October 2008.

[16]   RFC 791, "Internet Protocol," http://www.faqs.org/rfcs/ rfc791.html

[17]   "Assigned Internet Protocol Numbers," 17 May 2010. http://www.iana.org/assignments/protocol-numbers/protocol-numbers. xml,

[18]   Version of the Internetwork General Protocol, 27 June 2007.   http://www.isi.edu/in-notes/iana/assignments/version-numbers

[19]   RFC 793, "Transmission Control Protocol," http://www. faqs.org/rfcs/rfc793.html

[20]   RFC 768, "User Datagram Protocol," http://www.faqs. org/rfcs/rfc768.html

[21]   E. Guillen, D. Padilla and Y. Colorado, "Weakness and Strength Analysis over Network-Based Intrusion Detection and Prevention System," *IEEE Latin-American Conference on Communications*,   2009.

[22]   K. Byung-Joo and K. Il-Kon, "Kernel Based Intrusion Detection System," *Proceedings of* 4*th Annual ACIS International Conference on Computer and Information Science*, Jeju Island, 14-16 July 2005, pp. 13-18. doi:10.1109/ICIS.2005.78

[23]   Danilo Bruschi, Lorenzo Martignoni and Martia Monga, "Code Normalization for Self-Mutating Malware," *IEEE Security & Privacy*, Vol. 5, No. 2, 2007. pp 46-54.

16

A Comparison of Link Layer Attacks on Wireless Sensor Networks

Shahriar Mohammadi[1], Reza Ebrahimi Atani[2], Hossein Jadidoleslamy[3]
[1]*Department of Industrial Engineering, K. N. Tossi University of Technology, Tehran, Iran*
[2]*Department of Computer Engineering, University of Guilan, Rasht, Iran*
[3]*Department of Information Technology, Anzali International Branch, The University of Guilan, Rasht, Iran*

Abstract

Wireless sensor networks (WSNs) have many potential applications [1,2] and unique challenges. They usually consist of hundreds or thousands of small sensor nodes such as MICA2, which operate autonomously; conditions such as cost, invisible deployment and many application domains, lead to small size and resource limited sensors [3]. WSNs are susceptible to many types of link layer attacks [1] and most of traditional network security techniques are unusable on WSNs [3]; This is due to wireless and shared nature of communication channel, untrusted transmissions, deployment in open environments, unattended nature and limited resources [1]. Therefore security is a vital requirement for these networks; but we have to design a proper security mechanism that attends to WSN's constraints and requirements. In this paper, we focus on security of WSNs, divide it (the WSNs security) into four categories and will consider them, include: an overview of WSNs, security in WSNs, the threat model on WSNs, a wide variety of WSNs' link layer attacks and a comparison of them. This work enables us to identify the purpose and capabilities of the attackers; furthermore, the goal and effects of the link layer attacks on WSNs are introduced. Also, this paper discusses known approaches of security detection and defensive mechanisms against the link layer attacks; this would enable IT security managers to manage the link layer attacks of WSNs more effectively.

Keywords: Wireless Sensor Network, Security, Link Layer, Attacks, Detection, Defensive Mechanism

1. Introduction

Advances in wireless communications have enabled the development of low-cost and low-power WSNs [1]. WSNs have many potential applications [1,2] and unique challenges. They usually are heterogeneous systems contain many small devices, called sensor nodes, that monitoring different environments in cooperative; *i.e.* sensors cooperate to each other and compose their local data to reach a global view of the environment; sensor nodes also can operate autonomously. In WSNs there are two other components, called "aggregation points" and "base stations" [4], which have more powerful resources than normal sensors. As shown in **Figure 1**, aggregation points collect information from their nearby sensors, integrate them and then forward to the base stations to process gathered data. Limitations such as cost, invisible deployment and variety of application domains, lead to requiring small size and resource limited (like energy, storage

and processing) sensors [3]. WSNs are vulnerable to many types of attacks and due to unsafe and unprotected nature of communication channel [5-7], untrusted and broadcast transmission media, deployment in hostile environments [1,2], automated nature and limited resources, most of security techniques of traditional networks are impossible in WSNs; therefore, security is a vital and complex requirement for these networks. It is necessary to design an appropriate security mechanism for these networks [2,8], which attending to be WSN's constraints. This security mechanism should cover different security dimension of WSNs, include confidentiality, integrity, availability and authenticity. The main purpose of this paper is presenting an overview of different link layer attacks on WSNs and comparing them together. In this paper, we focus on security of WSNs and classify it into four categories, as follows:
- An overview of WSNs,
- Security in WSNs include security goals, security

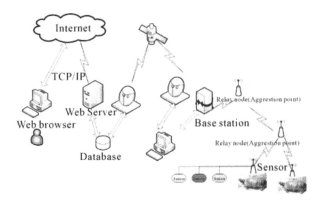

Figure 1. WSN's architecture.

obstacles and security requirements of WSNs.

- The threat model on WSNs,
- A wide variety of WSN's link layer attacks and comparing them to each other, include classification of WSN's link layer attacks based on threat model and compare them to each other based on their goals, results, strategies, detection and defensive mechanisms;

This work makes us enable to identify the purpose and capabilities of the attackers; also, the goal, final result and effects of the attacks on the WSNs. We also state some available approaches of security detection and defensive mechanisms against these attacks to handle them. The rest of this paper is organized as follows: in Section 2 an overview of WSNs is presented. Section 3 is mainly focused on the security issues in WSNs. Section 4 considers the threat model in WSNs. Section 5 includes definitions, strategies and effects of link layer attacks on WSNs. WSNs' link layer attacks is considered in Section 6 and finally conclusion are drawn in Section 7.

2. Overview of WSNs

In this section, we present an outline of different aspects of WSNs, such as definition, characteristics, applications, constraints and challenges.

2.1. Definition and Suppositions of WSNs

A WSN is a heterogeneous system consisting of hundreds or thousands of low-cost and low-power tiny sensors to monitor and gather real-time information from deployment environment [8-10]. Common functionality of WSNs are broadcasting and multicasting, routing, forwarding and route maintenance. The sensor's components are: sensor unit, processing unit, storage/memory unit, power supply unit and wireless radio transceiver; these units are communicating to each other, as shown in **Figure 2**. The existing components on WSN's architecture

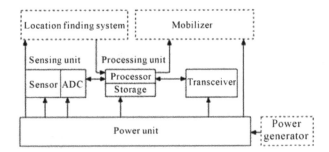

Figure 2. WSN's node architecture.

include sensor nodes (motes or field devices that are sensing data), network manager, security manager, aggregation points, base stations (access point or gateway) and user/human interface. Besides, there are two approaches in WSN's communication models containing hierarchical WSN versus distributed [8] and homogeneous WSN versus heterogeneous [8]. Some of the common suppositions of these networks are:

- Insecure radio links [6,10,11],
- Packet injection and replay [6,10],
- Non tamper resistant [11],
- Many normal sensor nodes (high-density) and low malicious nodes,
- Powerful attackers (laptop-class) [11,12].

2.2. WSNs Characteristics and Weakness

Most important characteristics of WSNs are:

- Constant or mobile sensors (mobility).
- Resource limited sensors [5,13] (limited range radio communication, energy, computational capabilities [5]), low reliability, wireless communication [5] and immunity.
- Dynamic/unpredictable WSN's topology and self-organization [5,14].
- Ad-hoc based networks [10,15] and hop-by-hop communication (multi-hop routing) [14,16,17].
- Non-central management, autonomously and infra-structure-less [10].
- Open/hostile-environment nature [10,11] and high density.

2.3. WSN's Applications

In general, there are two kinds of applications for WSNs: monitoring and tracking [10]. Therefore, some of the most common applications of these networks are: military, medical, environmental monitoring [3,8,10], industrial, infrastructure protection [3,10], disaster detection and recovery, agriculture, intelligent buildings, law enforcement, transportation and space discovery (as shown in **Figure 3(a)** and **3(b)**).

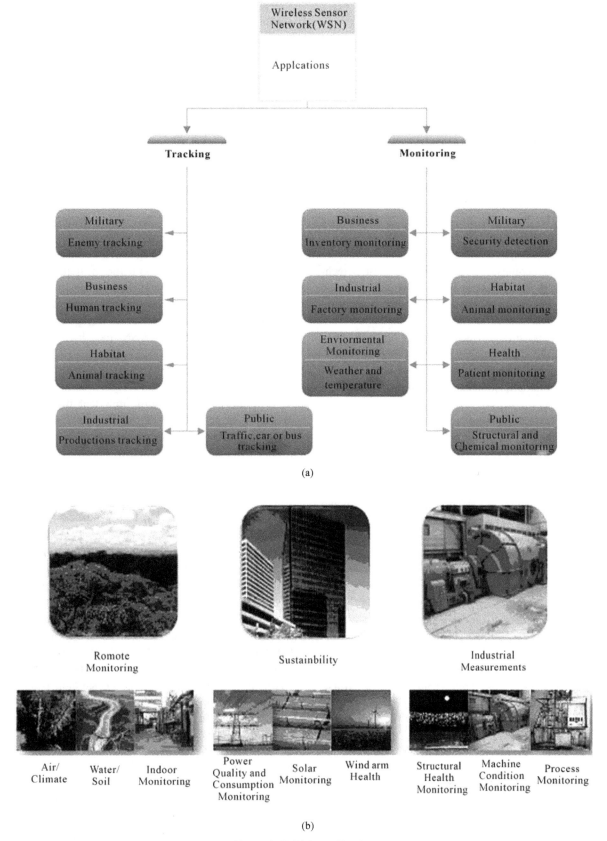

(a)

(b)

Figure 3. WSN's applications.

2.4. Vulnerabilities and Challenges of WSN

WSNs are vulnerable to many kinds of attacks; some of the most important reasons are:
- Theft (reengineering, compromising and replicating),
- Limited capabilities [18,19] (DoS attacks risks, constraint in using encryption),
- Random deployment (hard preconfiguration) [18, 7].
- Unattended nature [7,14,15,18].

In continue this section states most common challenges and constraints in WSNs; include:
- Deployment on open/dynamic/hostile environments [7,12,15] (physical access, capture and node des-truction);
- Insider attacks;
- Inapplicable/unusable traditional security techni-ques [3,7,19] (due to limited devices/resources, deploying in open environments and interaction with physical environment);
- Ad-hoc based deployment [12,15] (dynamic structure and topology, self-organization);
- Resource scarcity/hungry [5,7,20] (low and expensive communication/computation/processing resources);
- Devices with limited capabilities [21,22], pervasi-veness (privacy worries), wireless (medium) [5,7, 18] and mobility;
- Unreliable communication [5,7] (connectionless packet-based routing ⇨ unreliable transfer, channel broadcast nature ⇨ conflicts, multi-hop routing and network congestion and node processing ⇨ Latency);
- Unattended operation [6,12] (Exposure of physical attacks, managed remotely, no central management point);
- Increased attacks' risks and vulnerabilities [7], new attacks, increased tiny/embedded devices, multi-hopping routing (selfish) [14];
- Immense/large scale (high density, scalable security mechanism requirement);
- Redesigning security architectures (distributed and self-organized);

3. Security in WSNs

Now, intrusion techniques in WSNs are increasing; also there are many methods to disrupt these networks. In WSNs, data accuracy and network health are necessary; because these networks usually use on confidential and sensitive environments. There are three security key points on WSNs, including system (integrity, availability), source (authentication, authorization) and data (integrity, confidentiality). Necessities of security in WSNs are:
- Correctness of network functionality;
- Unusable typical networks protocols [3,15];
- Limited resources [5,7,23];
- Untrusted nodes [5,12,15];
- Requiring trusted center for key management [15], to authenticate nodes to each other [24], preventing from existing attacks and selfishness [23,25] and extending collaboration;

3.1. Why Security in WSNs?

Security in WSNs is an important, critical issue, necessa-ry and vital requirement, due to:
- WSNs are vulnerable against security attacks [7, 26] (broadcast and wireless nature of transmission medium);
- Nodes deploy on hostile environments [7,12,15] (unsafe physically);
- Unattended nature of WSNs [6,12];

3.2. Security Issues

This section states the most important discussions on WSNs; it is including key establishment, secrecy, authentication, privacy, robustness to DoS attacks, secure routing and node capture [18,15].

3.3. Security Services

There are many security services on WSNs; but some of their common are including encryption and data link layer authentication [12,15,20,23], multi-path routing [15,14, 23,24], identity verification, bidirectional link verification [14,15,24] and authenticated broadcasts. As **Figure 4** shows, the most important dimensions of security in WSNs are including security goals, obstacles, constraints, security threats, security mechanisms and security classes; however, this paper considers only star spangled parts/ blocks to classify and compare WSNs' link layer attacks based on them; i.e. security threats (including availability, authenticity, integrity and confidentiality) and security classes (containing interruption, interception, modification and fabrication); as shown in **Table 1**.

4. Threat Model in WSNs

There are many classes of WSNs' attacks based on nature and goals of attacks or attackers; but, in this section we present and compare their most important classes (called threat model of WSNs).

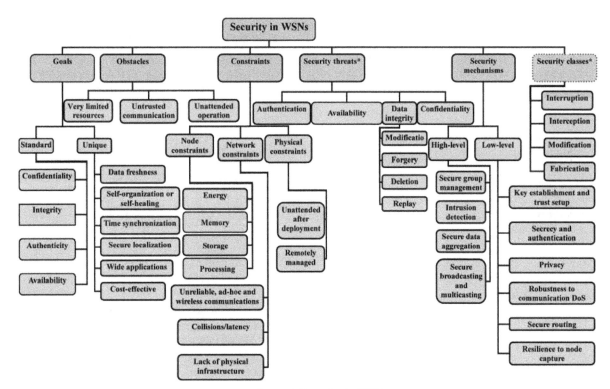

Figure 4. Security in WSNs.

Table 1. WSN's link layer attacks classification based on WSNs' threat model.

Attacks/features	Security class[1]	Attack threat[2]	Threat model[3]		
			Attacker location	Attacking device	Attacks on WSN's protocols
Node outage	Modification	Availability, integrity	External	Both	Active
Link layer jamming	Modification	Availability, integrity	External	Both	Active
Collision	Modification	Availability, integrity	External	Both	Active
Resource Exhaustion	Modification	Availability, integrity	External	Both	Active
Traffic manipulation	Modification	Availability, integrity	External	Both	Active
Unfairness	Modification	Availability, integrity	External	Both	Active
Acknowledge spoofing	Fabrication, modification	Integrity, authenticity	Both	Both	Active
Sinkhole	Modification, fabrication	Availability, integrity, authenticity	Both	Both	Active
Eavesdropping	Interception	Confidentiality	External	Both	Passive
Impersonation	Interception, fabrication, modification,	Availability, integrity, confidentiality, authenticity	External	Both	Active
Wormholes	Fabrication, interception	Confidentiality, authenticity	External	Both	Active
Desynchronization	Modification, fabrication	Availability, authenticity	External	Both	Active
Denial of Service (DoS) attacks	Interruption, interception, modification, fabrication	Availability, integrity, confidentiality, authenticity	Both	Both	Active

[1]Security class: the nature of attacks; include interruption, interception, modification and fabrication;
[2]Attack threat: security service attacked; threaten/affected security dimension; include confidentiality, integrity, authenticity and availability;
[3]Threat model: based on attacker location or access level (internal/insider or external/outsider), based on attacking devices (mote-class or laptop-class and based on damage/attacks on WSN protocols include active attacks (availability (packet drop or resource consumption), integrity (information modification) and authenticity (fabrication)), passive attacks (confidentiality (interception));

4.1. Attacks based on Damage/Access Level

In this subsection is presented the classifications of WSNs' link layer attacks based on their damage level or attacker's access level, including:

4.1.1. Active Attacker
This kind of attacker does operations, such as:
- Injecting faulty data into the WSN;
- Impersonating [3,10];
- Packet modification [15];
- Unauthorized access, monitor, eavesdrop and modify resources and data stream;
- Creating hole in security protocols [12];
- Overloading the WSN;

Some of the goals and effects of these attacks are:
- The WSN functionality disruption;
- The WSN performance degradation;
- Sensor nodes destruction;
- Data alteration;
- Inability in use the WSN's services;
- Obstructing the operations or to cut off certain nodes from their neighbors;

4.1.2. Passive Attacker
Passive attacker may do the following functions;
- Attacker is similar to a normal node and gathers information from the WSN;
- Monitoring and eavesdropping [3,12] from communication channel by unauthorized attackers;
- Naturally against privacy;

The goals and effects of this kind of attacker include:
- Eavesdropping, gathering and stealing information;
- Compromised privacy and confidentiality requirements;
- Storing energy by selfish node and to avoid from cooperation;
- The WSN functionality degradation;
- Network partition by non-cooperate in operations;

4.2. Attacks based on Attacker Location

Attacker can be deployed inside or outside the WSN; if the attacker be into the WSN's range, called insider (internal), and if the attacker is deployed out of the WSN's range, called outsider (external). This subsection presented and classified the WSNs' link layer attacks based on attackers' location, including:

4.2.1. External Attacker (Outsider)
Some of the most common features of this type of attacks are:
- External to the network [3,15] (from out of the WSN range);

- Device: Mote/Laptop class;
- Committed by illegally parties [3,9];
- Initiating attacks without even being authenticated;

Some of the common effects of these attacks are:
- Jamming the entire communication of the WSN;
- WSN's resources consumption;
- Triggering DoS attacks;

4.2.2. Internal Attacker (Insider)
The meaning of insider attacker is:
- Main challenge in WSNs;
- Sourced from inside of the WSN and access to all other nodes within its range [2,3,9];
- Authorized node in the WSN is malicious/compromised;
- Executing malicious data or use of cryptography contents of the legitimate nodes [12,15];
- Legitimate entity (authenticated) compromising a number of WSN's nodes;

Some of most important goals of these attacks type are:
- Access to cryptography keys or other WSN codes;
- Revealing secret keys;
- A high threat to the functional efficiency of the whole collective;
- Partial/total degradation/disruption;

4.3. Attacks based on Attacking Devices

Attackers can use different types of devices to attack to the WSNs; these devices have different power, radio antenna and other capabilities. There are two common categories of them, including:

4.3.1. Mote-class Attacker
Mote-class attacker is every one that using devices similar to common sensor nodes; this means,
- Occurring from inside the WSN;
- Using WSN's nodes (compromised sensor nodes) or access to similar nodes/motes (which have similar functionality as the WSN's nodes) [9,10];
- Executing malicious codes/programs;

Mote-class attacker has many goals, such as:
- Jamming radio link;
- Stealing and access to cryptography keys;

4.3.2. Laptop-class Attacker
Laptop-class attacker is every one that using more powerful devices than common sensor nodes, including:
- Main challenge in WSNs;
- Using more powerful devices by attacker, thus access to high bandwidth and low-latency communication channel;
- Traffic injection [3];

- Passive eavesdrop [15] on the entire WSN by a single laptop-class device;
- Replacing legitimate nodes;

Laptop-class attackers have many effects on WSNs, for example:

- Launching more serious attacks and then lead to more serious damage;
- Jamming radio links on the WSN entirely (by using more powerful transmitter);
- Access to high bandwidth and low-latency communication channel;

4.4. Attacks based on Function (Operation)

Link layer attacks in WSNs have been classified into three types, based on their main functionality; this subsection presented them, include:

4.4.1. Secrecy

Its definition and techniques are:

- Operating stealthy on the communication channel;
- Eavesdropping [5,12];
- Packet replay, spoofing or modification;
- Injecting false data into the WSN [2,8];
- Cryptography standard techniques can prevent from these attacks;

Goals and effects of this kind of attacks are:

- Passive eavesdrop;
- Packet replication, spoofing or modification;

4.4.2. Availability

This class of attacks known as Denial of Services (DoS) attacks; which leads to WSNs' unavailability, degrade the WSNs' performance or broken it. Some of the most common goals and effects of this attacks' category are including:

- Performance degradation;
- The WSN's services destruction/disruption;
- The WSN useless/unavailable;

4.4.3. Stealthy

This kind of attacks is operating stealthy on the communication channel; such as:

- Eavesdropping [3,10,12];
- False data injection into the WSN;

The most important effects of these attacks are including:

- Partial/entire degradation/disruption the WSN's services and functionality;

As shown in **Table 2**, damage level of link layer attacks on WSNs can be high (serious effect on the WSN) or low (limited effect on the WSN); besides, the attackers identification can be easy (possible), medium or hard (impossible), depending on that kind of attack; also the

attackers' presence or attacks' effects can be explicit (serious damage) or implicit (for example, eavesdropping).

5. Definitions, Strategies and Effects of Link Layer Attacks on WSNs

WSNs are designed in layered form; this layered architecture makes these networks susceptible and lead to da-mage against many kinds of attacks. For each layer, there are some attacks and defensive mechanisms. Thus, WSNs are vulnerable against different link layer attacks, such as DoS attacks, Collision, unfairness and other attacks to link layer protocols [3,15]; WSNs are susceptible to link layer attacks. Attackers can gain access to transmission media, create radio interference, prevent from legitimate sensor nodes to communicate/transmit (access to the com-munication channel) or launch DoS attacks against link layer. Now, in **Table 3** is presented the definitions of link layer attacks on WSNs, and then it classified and compared them to each others based on their strategies and effects.

6. Comparison Link Layer Attacks on WSNs

WSNs are vulnerable against link layer attacks. Therefore, we have to use some techniques to protect data accuracy, network functionality and its availability. As a result, we require establishing security in WSNs with attention to requirements and limitations of these networks.

Table 2. Threat model of WSNs.

Attack category/ features	Types	Damage level[4]	Ease of identify[5]	Attacker presence[6]
Based on damage level	Active attacker	High	Easy	Explicit
	Passive attacker	Low	Hard	Implicit
Based on attacker location	External (outsider)	Low	Medium	Implicit
	Internal (insider)	High	Hard	Implicit
Based on attacking devices	Mote-class attacker	Low	Hard	Implicit
	Laptop-class attacker	High	Easy	Explicit
Based on attack function	Secrecy	High	Hard	Implicit
	Availability	High	Hard	Both
	Stealthy	High	Hard	Implicit

[4]Damage level: high (serious or more damage than other type) and low (limitary);
[5]Ease of identify attackers: easy (possible), medium (depending on attack type) and hard (impossible or not as easy to prevent as other ones);
[6]Attacker presence or attack's effect: explicit (more powerful attacker, then more serious damage/harm) and implicit;

Table 3. Link layer attacks on WSNs (classification and comparison based on strategies and effects).

Attack/criteria	Attack definition	Attack techniques	Attack effects
Node outage	• Stopping the functionality of WSN's components, such as a sensor node or a cluster-leader;	• Physically ; • Logical;	• Stop nodes' services; • Take over/compromise the partial/entire the WSN and prevent from some communication; • Impossibility reading gathered information; • Launching other attacks;
Link layer jamming	• Finding data packet and to jam it[1];	• Looking at the probability distribution of the inter-arrival times between all types of packets; • This attack can be applied on S-MAC, B-MAC and L-MAC protocols [1];	• Colliding packets during transmission; • Exhausting nodes' resources; • Confusion;
Collision	• Message transmission by two nodes on a same frequency [1,5], simultaneously; • There are 2 types collision: environmental and probabilistic collision;	• Environmental collision; • Probabilistic collision; • Verifying and isolate radio transmissions; • Change packet's fields; • Alter the ack message;	• Interferences [1]; • Data/control packets corruption/cripple [1]; • Discarding packets; • Energy exhaustion; • Cost effective;
Resource Exhaustion	• Repeated collisions and continuous retransmission until the sensor node death [1];	• Continuously retransmission; • Interrogation attack (RTS/CTS); • Message modification; • Ack corruption/change;	• Resources exhaustion; • Compromise availability;
Traffic manipulation	• Regular monitoring transmissions and computing some parameters based on affected MAC protocol carefully ⇨ time adjustment ⇨ transmitting messages just at the moment when normal nodes do so; • Similar to Collision attack;	• Regular monitoring the communication channel and computing require parameters; • Misusing from the wireless nature of communications in WSNs; • Disobeying the coordination rules of MAC schemes in use; • Collision attack techniques; • Unfairness attack techniques; • Continuously collisions and unfairness;	• Excessive packet collisions; • Artificially increased contention; • Decreasing signal quality and network availability; • Aggressively competition for channel usage; • Break the protocols' operations; • Unfair bandwidth usage; • Degradation of the WSN performance; • Traffic distortion; • Effects of collision and unfairness attacks; • Confusion;
Unfairness	• Partial DoS attack; • Using other attacks such as collision and exhaustion continuously;	• Intermittent application of collision and exhaustion attacks; • Misusing/abusing a cooperative MAC-layer priority mechanism; • Continuously request to access to channel by attacker;	• Decrease utility and efficiency of services; • Nodes' hungry to channel access; • Limiting access to channel and undermine communication channel capacity;
Acknowledge spoofing	• An adversary can spoof link layer acknowledgements (ACKs) of overheard packets [11];	• ACKs replication; • Forging/spoofing link layer ACKs of neighbor nodes;	• False view/information of the WSN; • Launch selective forwarding attack; • Packet loss/corruption;
Sinkhole	• A special selective forwarding attack; • More complex than blackhole attack; • Attracting [5,6] or draw the all possible network traffic to a compromised node by placing a malicious node closer to the base station [17] and enabling selective forwarding; • Centralizing traffic into the malicious node [13]; • Possible designing another attack during this attack; • Sinkhole detection is very hard;	• Luring [3] or compromising nodes [11]; • Tamper with application data along the packet flow path (selective forwarding); • Receiving traffic and altering or fabricating information [17]; • Identity spoofing for a short time; • Using the communication pattern; • Creating a large sphere of influence; • Based on used routing protocol: MintRoute or MultiHopLQI protocol;	• Luring and to attract almost all the traffic; • Triggering other attacks, such as eavesdropping, trivial selective forwarding, blackhole and wormhole; • Usurp the base station's position; • Message modification; • Information fabrication and packet dropping; • Suppressed messages in a certain area; • Routing information modification/fake; • Resource exhaustion;

Eavesdroping[7]	• Detecting the contents of communication by overhearing/stealthy attempt to data;	• Interception; • Abusing of wireless nature of WSNs' transmission medium; • Using powerful resources and strong devices, such as powerful receivers and well designed antennas;	• Launching other attacks (wormhole, black-hole); • Extracting sensitive WSN information; • Delete the privacy protection and reducing data confidentiality;
Impersonaion[8]	• Malicious node impersonates a cluster leader and lures nodes to a wrong position; • Impersonating a node within the path of the data flow of attacker's interest by modifying routing data or implying itself as a trustworthy communication partner to neighboring nodes in parallel;	• The WSN reconfiguration; • Access to encryption keys and authentication information; • Man-in-the-middle attack and fake MAC addresses; • Node replication [26]; • Physical access to the WSN; • False or malicious node attack techniques; • Sybil attacks techniques; • Misdirection/misrouting; • Modifying routing information; • Luring/convince nodes;	• Routing information modification; • False sensor readings; • Making network congestion or collapse; • Disclose secret keys; • Network partition; • False and misleading messages generated; • Resources exhaustion; • Degrade the WSN performance; • Invasion; • Carrying out further attacks to disrupt operation of the WSN; • Confusion and taken over the entire WSN;
Wormholes	• Tunneling [5,11] and replicating messages from one location to another through alternative low-latency links [1,3], that connect two or more points (nodes) of the WSN with fast communication medium [14] (such as Ethernet cable, wireless communication or optical fiber), by colluding two active nodes (laptop-class attackers [3]) in the WSN, by using more powerful communication resources than normal nodes [4,21] and establishing better real communication channels (tunnel); • Wormhole nodes operate fully invisible [21];	• Compromising/luring nodes [3] with false and forged routing information; • An attacker locates between two nodes and forwards messages between them; • Using out-of-band or high-bandwidth fast [14] channel; • Wormholes may be used along with Sybil attack; • This attack may combines with selective forwarding or eavesdropping;	• Routing disruption/disorder (false routes, misdirection and forged routing); • False/forged routing information; • Confusion and WSN disruption; • Enable other attacks; • Exploiting the routing race conditions; • Change the network topology; • Prevention of path detection protocol; • Packet destruction/alteration by wormhole nodes; • Changing normal messages stream;
De-synchronization	• Disrupting the established connections between two legitimate nodes by re-synchronizing their transmission[6];	• Sending repeatedly forged or false messages; • Re-synchronizing transmissions;	• Disrupt communication; • Go out the synchronization; • Resource exhaustion;
Denial of Serice (DoS) attacks	• A general attack includes several types other attacks in different layers of WSN, simultaneously [27]; • Reducing WSN's availability [15,27]	• Physical layer, link layer, routing layer, transport layer and application layer attacks techniques;	• Effects of physical layer, link layer, routing layer, transport layer and application layer attacks;

6.1. Link Layer Attacks Classification based on Threat Model of WSNs

In this subsection, we have tried to compare the link layer attacks of WSNs based on attacks' nature and effects, attackers' nature and capabilities, and WSN's threat model; as shown in **Table 1**.

Table 1 shows the most important known attacks on WSNs; this table has three columns, including security class, attack threat and WSNs' threat model. Our purpose of security class is the nature of attacks, includes interruption, interception, modification and fabrication. Attack threat shows which security service attacked or security dimension affected, includes confidentiality, integrity, authenticity and availability. The threat model of WSNs has three sub-columns, that they are presenting attackers' features and capabilities, including based on attacker location (internal/insider or external/outsider), based on attacking devices (mote-class or laptop-class) and based on attacks on WSN's protocols, include active attacks and passive attacks; active attacks are targeting

---

[7] Also called passive information gathering attack; a threat for data confidentiality; the most common attack against privacy; an adversary with powerful resources (powerful receiver and well designed antenna) can gather the data stream from the WSN, if they are not encrypted;

[8] Also called identity spoofing or node replication [26] or multiple identity attacks; identity spoofing and play the role of other one [26]; the attacker assumes the identity of another node in the network, thus receiving messages directed to the node it fakes;

[9] In link layer: using different neighbors to time synchronization; In transport layer: an established connection between two end points can be disrupted by de-synchronization;

availability (packet drop or resource consumption), integrity (information modification) and authenticity (fabrication); passive attacks are aiming confidentiality (interception).

According to **Table 1**, **Figure 5** shows the percentages of security classes' different parameters associated to the nature of WSNs' link layer attacks; it compares these attacks based on their nature by presents the percentage of WSNs' link layer attacks which based on interruption, interception, modification or/and fabrication; so, it represents the importance of the security classes' parameters. As a result, the nature of the most of these attacks is modification (almost 85 percent of them) and interruption-based attacks have lowest effect/importance on this layer (7.6 percent).

The diagram of **Figure 6** shows a comparison of WSNs' link layer attacks based on their security threats factors including confidentiality, integrity, authenticity and availability, in percentage; for example, it presents almost 31 percent of security threat of WSNs' link layer attacks is confidentiality and the nature of 38.4 percent of them is fabrication (fabricating data or identity). As shown in **Figure 6**, the aim of the most WSNs' link layer attacks is attacking integrity and availability.

Figure 7 shows a comparison link layer attacks based on the threat model of WSNs; As shown **Figure 7**, the occurred percentage of WSNs' link layer attacks, in attacker location, are 23 percent internal and 100 percent external; *i.e.* most of WSNs' link layer attacks are occurring from out of WSNs' range and attackers can trigger them by mote-class or laptop-class devices. Also, it presents most of link layer attacks on WSNs are active, except eavesdropping; *i.e.* almost 92 percent of WSNs' link layer attacks are active. Besides, **Figure 7** shows least attacks on link layer of WSNs are internal attacks.

6.2. Link Layer Attacks Comparison based on Their Goals and Results

In link layer, attacker can disrupt the WSN's functionality by tampering with link layer services such as modifying MAC (Media Access Control) protocol, interference in communication channel and replicating/altering data frames. As shown in **Table 4**, it categorizes the link layer attacks of WSNs, based on their goals, effects and results. Also **Table 4** compares WSNs' link layer attacks based on attack or attacker purpose (including passive eavesdrop, disrupt communication, unfairness, authorization and authentication), requirements technical capabilities (such as radio, battery, powerful receiver/antenna and other high-tech and strong attacking devices), vulnerabilities, main target and final result of attacks. Besides, the contributors of all following link layer attacks (shown in

Table 4) are one or many compromised motes, pc or laptop devices on WSNs. The vulnerabilities of these attacks can be physical (hardware), logical or their both; Attacks' main target may be physical (hardware), logical

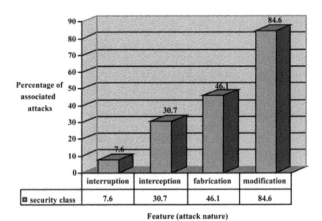

Figure 5. Comparison link layer attacks based on their nature.

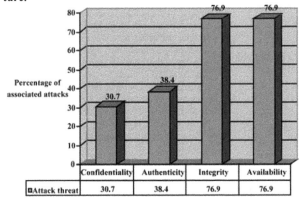

Figure 6. Comparison link layer attacks based on affected/ threaten security dimension.

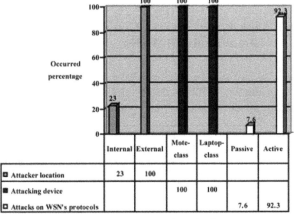

Figure 7. Comparison link layer attacks based on WSN's threat model.

(lis: logical-internal services or lps: logical-provided services) or their both. Final result of these attacks is including passive damage, partial degradation of the WSN functionality and total broken of the WSN's services or functionality.

Figure 8 shows that how much percentage of WSNs' link layer attacks are happened by targeting the fairness, confidentiality, authentication, authorization and disrupt communication on WSNs' functionalities, services and resources; for example, almost 85 percent of these attacks are aiming the fairness of WSNs, and then they lead to unfairness.

Figure 9 is presenting the percentage of every one of kinds of link layer attacks vulnerabilities and their main

target on WSNs, including: 15.4 percent of them are attacking the WSNs' hardware, 61.5 percent of them are aiming the WSNs' logical-internal services (lis) and 92.3 percent are targeting the logical-provided services (lps) by WSNs. Thus, most link layer attacks on WSNs have logical vulnerabilities and only almost 15.4 percent of them have physical harm/effects.

6.3. Detection and Defensive Strategies of WSNs' Link Layer Attacks

In **Table 5** a classification and comparison of detection and defensive techniques on WSNs' link layer attacks is presented.

Table 4. Link layer attacks comparison based on attacks' goals and their results.

Attacks/ features	Purpose[10]	Technical capability	Vulnerability[11]	Main target[12]	Final result[13]
Node outage	Unfairness	-	Logical	lis; lps	PTDB[14]
Link layer jamming [1]	Disrupt communication	Radio	Logical	lps	PTDB
Collision [1]	Unfairness	-	Logical	lis; lps	PTDB
Resource Exhaustion [1]	Unfairness	-	Logical	lis; lps	PTDB
Traffic manipulation	Unfairness	-	Logical	lis; lps	PTDB
Unfairness	Unfairness	-	Logical	lis; lps	PTDB
Acknowledge spoofing	Unfairness	-	Logical	lps	PTDB
Sinkhole [1]	Unfairness	-	Logical	lps	PTDB
Eavesdropping	Passive eavesdrop of data	powerful resources and strong devices[15]	Logical	lps	Passive damage; partial degradation
Impersonation	All purpose	Time and high-tech equipments	Logical; physical	Physical; Logical (lis and lps)	Passive damage; PTDB
Wormholes [1]	Unfairness; to be authenticated; to be authorized	-	Logical	lps	Passive eavesdrop; PTDB
De-synchronization	Disrupt communication; unfairness	-	Logical	lis	PTDB
Denial of Service (DoS) attacks	All purpose	Radio; battery; time and high-tech equipments	Logical; physical	Physical; Logical (lis and lps)	Passive damage; PTDB

[10]Purpose: passive eavesdrop, disrupt communication, unfairness, to be authorized, to be authenticated;

[11]Vulnerabilities: physical (hardware), logical;

[12]Main target: physical (hardware), logical (lis: logical-internal services or lps: logical-provided services);

[13]Final result: passive damage, partial degradation of the WSN duty/functionality, service broken/disruption for the entire WSN (partial or total/entire degradation/broken/disruption of the services/resources/functionality of the WSN);

[14]PTDB: Partial/Total Degradation/Broken;

[15]such as powerful receiver and well designed antenna;

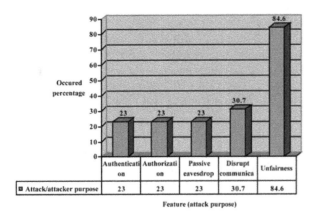

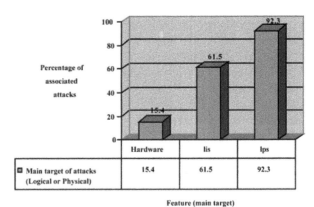

Figure 8. Comparison link layer attacks based on attacks' purpose.

Figure 9. Comparison link layer attacks based on their main target.

Table 5. Link layer attacks on WSNs (classification based on detection and defensive mechanisms).

Attack/criteria	Detection methods	Defensive mechanisms
Node outage	• Node disconnection from the network; • Regular monitoring and nodes' cooperaion; • Existence interference in common operation of node; • Node destruction (physically);	• Providing an alternative path; • Developing appropriate and robust protocols; • Defensive mechanisms against physical and node capture attacks[16];
Link layer jamming	• Misbehavior detection techniques[17]; • False identity detection techniques;	• Limiting the rate of MAC requests; • Use of small frames; • S-MAC defensive method [1][18], L-MAC defensive method [1][19] and B-MAC defensive method [1][20]; • Identity protection[21]; • Link layer encryption;
Collision	• Misbehavior detection techniques;	• All countermeasures of jamming attack; • Error correction codes (such as CRC codes) [1]; • Time diversity;
Resource Exhaustion	• Misbehavior detection techniques;	• Limiting the MAC admission control rate [1]; • Random back-offs; • Using Time-Division multiplexing; • limiting the extraneous responses; • Protection of WSN ID and other information;
Traffic manipulation	• Misbehavior detection techniques;	• Traffic analysis attack defenses; • Collision attack defenses; • Unfairness attack defenses; • Misbehavior detection techniques; • Identity protection; • Link layer encryption; • Limiting the rate of MAC requests; • Use of small frames;
Unfairness	• Misbehavior detection techniques;	• Use of small frames [1,3,5];
Acknowledge spoofing	• Misbehavior detection techniques;	• Using another route; • Authentication, link layer encryption and global shared key techniques;

[16]Using tamper-proofing/tamper-resistant sensor packages; using special alerting hardware/software to the user; camouflaging/hiding sensors;
[17]Include adjustment back-off values, watchdogs/IDS on every node, iterative probing mechanisms, game theory, misbehavior-resilient back-off algorithm, and rating nodes based on replication rate or node's cooperation in communication;
[18]Preventing clustering based analysis by narrowing the distance between the two clusters;
[19]Making the estimation of the clusters more difficult by changing the slot sizes (used for packet transmission) pseudo-randomly as a function of time;
[20]Shortening the preamble in order to make its detection harder;
[21]Using cryptography-based authentication or false identity detection techniques such as Radio resource test (Sybil attack), position verification (detecting immobile attackers), code attestation (differing executing code on malicious or compromised node rather than normal nodes ⇨ detecting attackers by validating executing code on nodes), sequence checking and identity association (associating node identity with used keys on communication by that node);

Sinkhole	• False routing information detection [4,13]; • Cooperating neighboring nodes to each other [13]; • Tree structure and verify by tree [13]; • Verify by Visual Geographical Map;	• Detection on MintRoute [3]; • Geographical routing protocols; • Learning global map (if nodes are static and at known location); • Scalability; • Probabilistic next hop selection; • leveraging global knowledge; • Verifying and to trust information that advertised of neighbor nodes; • Authentication, link layer encryption and global shared key techniques; • Routing access restriction (R) [4]; • Wormhole detection (W) [4]; • Key management (K); • Secure routing (S) [2];
Eavesdropping	• Eavesdropping is a passive behavior, thus it is rarely detectable; • Misbehavior detection techniques;	• Access control; • Reduction in sensed data details; • Distributed processing; • Access restriction; • Strong encryption techniques;
Impersonation	• False identity detection techniques (misbehavior detection techniques); • False routing information detection; • Collision detection techniques;	• Strong and proper authentication techniques; • Using strong data encryption; • Secure routing protocols; • Central certificate authority; • Pair-wise authentication; • Network layer authentication; • Adopt validation techniques; • Identity protection; • Link layer encryption; • Limiting the rate of MAC requests; • Use of small frames for each packet;
Wormholes	• False routing information detection; • Wormhole detection [21]; • Combinational methods [21][22]; • Packet leashes techniques [14, 28];	• Packet leach/leashes techniques [1,14,28][23]; • MAD protocol and OLSR protocol [1,14]; • Directional antennas [1,25]; • Multi-dimensional scaling algorithm (scalability) [1]; • Using local neighborhood information [1]; • DAWWSEN protocol [3][24]; • Designing proper routing protocols (clustering-based and geographical routing protocols); • leveraging global knowledge; • Verifying information that announce of neighbor nodes; • Graphical Position System [25,28]; • Ultrasound [25]; • Global clock synchronization; • Combinational methods (such as radio waves and ultraound); • Authentication, link layer encryption and global shared key techniques; • (R), (W), (K), (S) [2,4];
De-synchroniz-tion	• Strong and un-forgeable authentication mechanisms;	• Strong authentication mechanisms; • Time synchronization, cooperatively; • Maintaining proper timing;
Denial of Service (DoS) attacks	• Detection methods of physical layer, link layer, routing layer, transport layer and application layer attacks;	• Defensive mechanisms of physical layer, link layer, routing layer, transport layer and application layer attacks;

7. Conclusions

In this paper, we analyze different dimensions of WSN's

[22]Such as radio waves and ultrasound, measuring distance between nodes and comparing packet send and receive time with threshold;
[23]Geographical leashes and Temporal leashes ⇨ Physical monitoring of field devices and regular network monitoring by using source routing; monitoring system may use packet leach techniques;
[24]suspicious node detection by signal strength; a proactive routing protocol based on the hierarchical tree construction;

security, present a wide variety of WSNs' link layer attacks and classify them; our approach to classify and compare the WSN's link layer attacks based on different extracted features of WSN's link layer, attacks' and attackers' properties, such as the threat model of WSNs, link layer attacks' nature, goals and results, their strategies and effects and finally their associated detection and defensive techniques against these attacks to handle them, independently and comprehensively. **Table 6** presents how much percentage of WSNs' link layer attacks are occurring based on any one attacks' classifications features. **Figure 10** shows most affected features of WSNs' link layer attacks. Our most important findings are including:

- Discussion typical WSNs' link layer attacks along with their characteristics, in comprehensive;
- Classification and comprehensive comparison of WSNs' link layer attacks to each other;
- Link layer encryption and authentication mechanisms can protect against outsiders, mote-class attackers and link layer attacks such as link layer jamming, traffic manipulation and acknowledgement spoofing;
- Encryption is not enough and inefficient for inside attacks and laptop-class attackers; but clustering protocols can provide most secure solutions against inside attacks and compromised nodes;
- The link layer attacks are often launching combina-

tional;
- The different kinds of link layer attacks may be used same strategies;
- The same type of defensive mechanisms can be used in multiple link layer attacks, such as misbehavior detection;
- The accuracy of solutions against link layer attacks depends on the characteristics of the WSN's application domain;
- As presented in table6, 84.6 percent of link layer attacks' nature is modification; 30.7 percent of link layer attacks threaten confidentiality, *etc*;
- As shown in **Figure 10**, the nature of 84.6 percent of WSNs' link layer attacks is modification; 76.9 percent of them are targeting integrity and availability; most of these attacks are out of the WSNs' range (external: 100 percent) and lead to high-level damages (active attacks: 92.3 percent); 84.6 percent of attacks' purpose is unfairness; 92.3 percent of link layer attacks' main target is WSNs' logical provided services;

This work makes us enable to identify the purpose and capabilities of the attackers; also the goal, final result and effects of the attacks on the WSNs' functionality. The next step of our work is considering other attacks on WSNs. We hope by reading this paper, readers can have a better view of link layer attacks and aware from some defensive techniques against them; as a result, they can take better and more extensive security mechanisms to design secure WSNs.

Table 6. Occurred percentage of each attacks' classification features.

Attack or attacker feature		Criteria	Percent (percentage of occurred)
Security class		Interruption	7.6
		Interception	30.7
		Modification	84.6
		Fabrication	46.1
Attack threat		Confidentiality	30.7
		Integrity	76.9
		Availability	76.9
		Authenticity	38.4
Threat model	**Attacker location**	Internal	23
		External	100
	Attacking device	Mote-class	100
		Laptop-class	100
	Attacks on WSN's protocols	Passive	7.6
		Active	92.3
Attacker purpose		Disrupt communication	30.7
		Authentication	23
		Authorization	23
		Passive eavesdrop	23
		Unfairness	84.6
Attack main target		Physical (hardware)	15.4
		Logical-internal services	61.5
		Logical-provided services	92.3

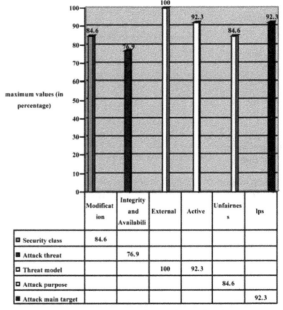

Figure 10. most affected features (have maximum values) on wsns' link layer attacks.

8. Future works

We also can research about following topics:
- Securing wireless communication links against eavesdropping, collision and DoS attacks;
- Resources limitations techniques;
- Using public key cryptography and digital signature in WSNs (of course with attention to WSN's constraints);
- Countermeasures for combinational link layer attacks;
- Designing proper link layer (MAC[25]) protocols for WSNs;
- Optimizing existing WSNs' MAC protocols;

9. References

[1] W. Znaidi, M. Minier and J. P. Babau, "An Ontology for Attacks in Wireless Sensor Networks," Institute National de Recherche en Informatique et en Automatique, October 2008.

[2] M. Saxena, "Security in Wireless Sensor Networks: A Layer-Based Classification," 2011. https://www.cerias.purdue.edu/apps/reports_and_papers/view/3106/

[3] K. Sharma and M. K. Ghose, "Wireless Sensor Networks: An Overview on Its Security Threats," *International Journal of Computers and Their Applications, Special Issue on "Mobile Ad-hoc Networks"*, Vol. 1, 2010, pp. 42-45.

[4] K. Xing, S. S. R. Srinivasan, M. Rivera, J. Li and X. Z. Cheng, "Attacks and Countermeasures in Sensor Networks: A Survey," *Network Security*, Springer, Berlin, 2010, pp. 251-272.

[5] T. A. Zia, "A Security Framework for Wireless Sensor Networks," PhD Thesis, University of Sydney, Sydney, February 2008.

[6] G. Padmavathi and D. Shanmugapriya, "A Survey of Attacks, Security Mechanisms and Challenges in Wireless Sensor Networks," *International Journal of Computer Science and Information Security*, Vol. 4, No. 1-2, 2009, pp. 115-119.

[7] T. Kavitha and D. Sridharan, "Security Vulnerabilities in Wireless Sensor Networks: A Survey," *Journal of Information Assurance and Security*, Vol. 5, 2010, pp. 31-44.

[8] Z. Li and G. Gong, "A Survey on Security in Wireless Sensor Networks," 2011. http://www.cacr.math.uwaterloo.ca/techreports/2008/cacr2008-20.pdf

[9] A. Dimitrievski, V. Pejovska and D. Davcev, "Security Issues and Approaches in WSN," 2011 http://ict-act.org/ICT Innovations.../ictinnovations2009_submission_21.pdf

[10] J. Yick, B. Mukherjee and D. Ghosal, "Wireless Sensor Network Survey," *Computer Networks*, Vol. 52, No. 12, 2008, pp. 2292-2330.

[11] C. Karlof and D. Wagner, "Secure Routing in Wireless Sensor Networks: Attacks and Countermeasures," *Proceedings of the 1st IEEE International Workshop on Sensor Network Protocols and Applications*, Alaska, 11 May 2003, pp. 113-127.

[12] Y. Wang, G. Attebury and B. Ramamurthy, "A Survey of Security Issues in Wireless Sensor Networks," *IEEE Communication Surveys*, 2006.

[13] C. Tumrongwittayapak and R. Varakulsiripunth, "Detecting Sinkhole Attacks in Wireless Sensor Networks," *I CROS-SICE International Joint Conference*, Fukuoka, 18-21 August 2009.

[14] R. H. Khokhar, M. A. Ngadi and S. Mandala, "A Review of Current Routing Attacks in Mobile Ad Hoc Networks," *International Journal of Computer Science and Security*, Vol. 2, No. 3, 2008, pp. 18-29.

[15] Y. Zhou, Y. Fang and Y. Zhang, "Security Wireless Sensor Networks: A Survey," *IEEE Communication Surveys*, 2008.

[16] A. Perrig, R. Szewczyk, V. Wen, D. Culler and D. Tygar, "SPINS: Security Protocols for Sensor Networks," *Proceedings of 7th Annual International Conference on Mobile Computing and Networks*, Rome, July 2001.

[17] I. Krontiris, T. Giannetsos and T. Dimitriou, "Launching a Sinkhole Attack in Wireless Sensor Networks, the Intruder Side," *IEEE International Conference on Wireless & Mobile Computing, Networking & Communication*, Dalian, 12-14 October 2008, pp. 526-531.

[18] A. Perrig, J. Stankovic and D. Wagner, "Security in Wireless Sensor Networks," *Communications of the ACM*, Vol. 47, No. 6, 2004, pp. .

[19] A. Saini and H. Kumar, "Comparison between Various Black Hole Detection Techniques in MANET," *National Conference on Computational Instrumentation*, Chandigarh, 19-20 March 2010, pp. 157-161.

[20] I. Ullah and S. U. Rehman, "Analysis of Black Hole attack On MANETs Using Different MANET Routing Protocols," Master Thesis, Blekinge Institute of Technology, Sweden, 2010.

[21] R. Maheshwari, J. Gao and S. R. Das, "Detecting Wormhole Attacks in Wireless Networks Using Connectivity Information," *IEEE INFOCOM*, Alaska, 2007.

[22] Y-C. Hu, A. Perrig and D. B. Johnson, "Rushing Attacks and Defense in Wireless Ad Hoc Network Routing Protocols," *Proceedings of the 2nd ACM Workshop on Wireless Security ACM*, New York, 2003.

[23] J. R. Douceur, "The Sybil Attack," Proceedings of the 1st International Workshop on Peer-to-Peer Systems (IPTPS), Cambridge, 7-8 March 2002.

[24] J. Newsome, E. Shi, D. Song and A. Perrig, "The Sybil Attack in Sensor Networks: Analysis & Defenses," *3rd International Symposium on Information Processing in Sensor Networks*, Berkeley, 26-27 April 2004.

[25] L. Hu and D. Evans, "Using Directional Antennas to Prevent Wormhole Attacks," *3rd International Symposium on Information Processing in Sensor Networks*,

Berkeley, 26-27 April 2004.

[26] B. Parno, A. Perrig and V. Gligor, "Distributed Detection of Node Replication Attacks in Sensor Networks," *Proceedings of the* 2005 *IEEE Symposium on Security and Privacy*, 8-11 May, 2005, Oakland, pp. 49-63.

[27] A. Wood and J. Stankovic, "Denial of Service in Sensor Networks," IEEE Computer Magazine; Vol. 35, No. 10,

2002, pp. 54-62.

[28] Y. Hu, A. Perrig and D. Johnson, "Packet Leashes: A Defense against Wormhole Attacks in Wireless Networks," *Proceedings of the* 22*nd Annual Joint Conference of the IEEE Computer and Communications Societies*, San Franciso, 30 March-3 April 2003, pp. 1976-1986.

17

Anomalous Network Packet Detection Using Data Stream Mining

Zachary Miller, William Deitrick, Wei Hu[*]
Department of Computer Science, Houghton College, Houghton, USA

Abstract

In recent years, significant research has been devoted to the development of Intrusion Detection Systems (IDS) able to detect anomalous computer network traffic indicative of malicious activity. While signature-based IDS have proven effective in discovering known attacks, anomaly-based IDS hold the even greater promise of being able to automatically detect previously undocumented threats. Traditional IDS are generally trained in batch mode, and therefore cannot adapt to evolving network data streams in real time. To resolve this limitation, data stream mining techniques can be utilized to create a new type of IDS able to dynamically model a stream of network traffic. In this paper, we present two methods for anomalous network packet detection based on the data stream mining paradigm. The first of these is an adapted version of the DenStream algorithm for stream clustering specifically tailored to evaluate network traffic. In this algorithm, individual packets are treated as points and are flagged as normal or abnormal based on their belonging to either normal or outlier clusters. The second algorithm utilizes a histogram to create a model of the evolving network traffic to which incoming traffic can be compared using Pearson correlation. Both of these algorithms were tested using the first week of data from the DARPA'99 dataset with Generic HTTP, Shell-code and Polymorphic attacks inserted. We were able to achieve reasonably high detection rates with moderately low false positive percentages for different types of attacks, though detection rates varied between the two algorithms. Overall, the histogram-based detection algorithm achieved slightly superior results, but required more parameters than the clustering-based algorithm. As a result of its fewer parameter requirements, the clustering approach can be more easily generalized to different types of network traffic streams.

Keywords: Anomaly Detection, Clustering, Data Stream Mining, Intrusion Detection System, Histogram, Payload

1. Introduction

Since the 1990's, internet usage has become an integral part of our daily lives. As a result, computer networks have experienced an increased number of sophisticated malware attacks. Whereas attackers previously attempted to gain access to restricted resources to demonstrate their skill, a new wave of internet-based attacks has shifted the focus primarily towards criminal motives. Due to the availability of software tools designed to exploit vulnerabilities, attackers can create viruses with greater structural complexity and damaging capability using less sophisticated skills. The security challenges resulting from an increasing number of devices connected to the internet has prompted a significant amount of research devoted to network security.

1.1. Intrusion Detection Systems

One notable topic of network security research is the development of Intrusion Detection Systems (IDS), which attempt to detect threats to a network or host through signature-based or anomaly-based methods. To detect intrusions, signature-based IDS generate "signatures" based on characteristics of previous known attacks. This allows the systems to focus on detecting attacks regardless of ordinary network traffic. Signature-based detection is the most common form of intrusion detection because it is simple to implement once a set of signatures has been created. Although this approach is effective in finding known threats to a network, it is unable to identify new threats until a new signature is made. To generate an accurate signature, a human expert is generally needed because this cannot easily be done automatically. Since the detection of new threats in a signature-based system is impossible without the aid of a new signature, an alternative method has been proposed.

In contrast to the signature-based approach, anomaly-based IDS adaptively detect new attacks by first generating a "normal" pattern of network traffic. These systems then find anomalies by comparing incoming packets with the "normal" model. Anything that is considered statistically deviant is classified as anomalous. This allows for the systems to automatically detect new attacks though risking possible misclassification of normal behavior(false positive).In addition to the potential for false positives, anomaly-based systems also fall prey to "mimicry attacks", which attempt to evade the IDS by imitating normal network traffic. One such attack is known as a Polymorphic Blending Attack (PBA), in which the attacker uses byte padding and substitution to avoid detection [1]. Recent research has focused on increasing the efficiency, robustness, and detection rates of these systems while lowering their often high false-positive rates.

One of the first well-developed anomaly-based systems is NIDES [2], which builds a model of normal behavior by monitoring the four-tuple header of packets. The four-tuple contains the source and destination IP addresses and port numbers of packet headers [3]. Another system proposed by Mahoney *et al.* [4] was comprised of two different programs, PHAD and ALAD. Whereas PHAD monitors the data contained in the header fields of individual packets, ALAD looks at distinct TCP connections consisting of multiple packets [3, 4]. To detect anomalies, PHAD and ALAD use port numbers, TCP flags, and keywords found in the payload. Yet another approach, known as NETAD [5], monitors the first 48 bytes of each IP packet header and creates different models based on each individual network protocol. Then, using the information recovered from the packet's header, NETAD creates different models each corresponding to a particular network protocol [6].

Two recently developed network anomaly-based intrusion detection systems are PAYL and McPAD [6,7]. Both used n-grams, sequences of n consecutive bytes in a packet's payload, as features to represent packets

To perform anomaly detection, PAYL utilizes 1-grams. This system first generates a histogram for normal traffic, and then a new histogram for each packet's payload. The two histograms are compared using the simplified Mahalanobis distance. If the distance is above a certain threshold, the new packet is flagged as anomalous [7]. Despite this approach's effectiveness, it suffers from a high false positive rate. To combat this, an extension of PAYL was proposed to use n-grams, creating a more precise detection model [8].

McPAD further develops the effectiveness of the n-gram version of PAYL by using 2-nu-grams, sequences of two bytes separated by a gap of size nu. The 2-gram contains the correlation between two bytes, a feature that 1-gram lacks. By combining the 2-gram with nu, McPAD is able to analyze structural information from higher n-grams while keeping the number of features the same as a 2-gram.By varying the value of nu, McPAD builds multiple one-class support vector machine (SVM) classifiers to detect anomalies as an ensemble. These classifiers are first trained on anomaly free data then tested with mixed normal and abnormal packets [6]. Using this approach, McPAD has successfully detected multiple virus types while maintaining a low false positive rate.

1.2. Stream Data Mining

Although PAYL and McPAD have been able to achieve desirable results, they are not designed to deal with the gradual or abrupt change in the data flows. Also because of the Internet's high speed, systems such as PAYL and McPAD can not efficiently store and evaluate the large amount of traffic generated in real-time. To counter these issues, we propose the application of data stream mining techniques to anomaly detection.

Stream mining differs from the traditional batch setting in a number of ways. First and foremost, because data streams are of extremely large or even infinite size, individual objects within the stream may only beanalyzed once—not repeatedly as is possible in batch mode [9]. The continuous nature of data streams also places significant time constraints on stream mining solutions. For a stream mining approach to be practical and effective, it must be able to process incoming information as quickly as it arrives [10].

One of the salient features of any data stream mining algorithm is the ability to detect fluctuations within a continuous stream of data over an unknown length of time. This dynamic tendency of streaming data is called "concept drift" when a change occurs gradually, or "concept shift" when it occurs more quickly [10]. To deal with this characteristic of streaming data, many stream mining algorithms employ a window of time intervals to temporarily hold the most recent data points in a stream [10,11]. The three types of windows typically implemented are landmark window, sliding window and damped window [11].

2. Materials and Methods

2.1. Data

Two publicly available datasets were used to evaluate the anomaly detection algorithms proposed in this study. These were the DARPA'99 intrusion detection evaluation dataset (http://www.ll.mit.edu/mission/communications/ist/corpora/ideval/data/1999data.html), and the attack dataset provided by [6].

The DARPA'99 dataset was used to provide a sampling of normal network traffic. This dataset simulates network communication from a fictitious United States Air Force base [12], and provides both attack-free and attack-containing network traces. Data samples for this study were obtained from HTTP requests found in outside tcp dump data for each day from week one of the DARPA'99 dataset. This first week of data is provided for training purposes and contains no anomalous network traffic. Using Jpcap, a free Java-based library for network packet manipulation, (http://netresearch.ics.uci.edu/kfujii/Jpcap/doc/), the numeric character values for all HTTP packet payloads with lengths at least 1400 characters were extracted for each day. The resulting dataset provided a total of 5594 packets representing normal network traffic divided by days as is shown in **Table 1**.

The anomalous data used in this study were compiled by [6], and are freely available online (http://roberto.perdisci.com/projects/mcpad). We chose to analyze the algorithms' performance in the detection of three out of the four attack types provided: Generic HTTP Attacks, Shell-code Attacks, and CLET Shell-code attacks. [6] obtained 63 of the attacks included in their Generic HTTP dataset from [13]. These attacks include a variety of HTTP attacks collected in a live environment from test web servers, as well as various archives and databases. The attacks fall into several categories, including buffer overflow, URL decoding error, and input validation error, and were directed against numerous web servers such as Microsoft IIS, Apache, Active Perl ISAPI, CERN 3.0A, etc. [6] further supplements these attacks, bolstering the dataset to include a total of 66 HTTP threats. The Shell-code attack dataset includes 11 shell-code attacks (attacks with packets containing executable code in their payload), which are also included in the Generic HTTP attack dataset. Finally, the CLET attacks were generated by [6] using the CLET polymorphic shell-code engine [14]. This created 96 polymorphic shell-code attacks containing ciphered data meant to evade pattern-matching based detection techniques.

Following the same procedure used to process the DARPA'99 week one data, the numeric character values contained in all HTTP packet payloads from each of the three attack datasets with lengths of at least 1400 characters were extracted using Jpcap. This provided a total of 843 attack packets, with varying numbers of packets from each attack type as is detailed in **Table 2**.

The payload information extracted from the DARPA and attack datasets was used to create training and testing datasets for our anomaly detection systems. For each of the five days in the DARPA dataset, 20% of the day's packets were extracted to be used for training, and the remaining 80% of the day's data were set aside to be used for testing. To simulate the network traffic in real time, anomalous packets were then sporadically inserted into both the training and testing data after an initial interval consisting of only normal traffic (50 packets for training data and 200 packets for testing data). In this way, different datasets were created with each attack type for all five days of DARPA'99 week one (See **Figure 1**). The total number of abnormal packets inserted into both the training and testing data was no more than 10% of all normal data for the given day with payload length 1400 characters or more. In some cases, as shown in **Table 3** and **Table 4**, the number of abnormal packets inserted into data was less than 10% because there was not enough attack data available for that day. For the training data, 20% of the abnormal data was mixed with 20% of the normal data for each day. Likewise, 80% of the abnormal data was mixed with 80% of the normal data selected from each day for testing. For each packet, 256 1-gram and 65,536 2-gram features were extracted to produce separate representations of the training and testing datasets detailed in **Table 3** and **Table 4**. The datasets were stored in the ARFF file format used the by the open source machine learning software WEKA [15].

The payload information extracted from the DARPA and attack datasets was used to create training and testing

Table 1. Packets Extracted from DARPA'99 Week 1.

Day	Number of Packets
Monday	688
Tuesday	968
Wednesday	860
Thursday	2308
Friday	770
Total	5,594

Table 2. Packets extracted from McPAD attack datasets.

Attack Type	Number of Packets
Generic HTTP	122
Shell-code	73
CLET Shell-code	648
Total	843

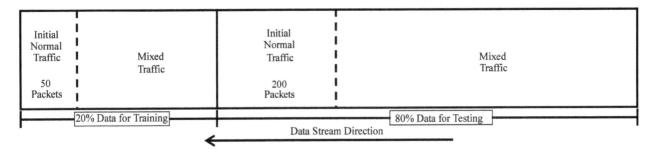

Figure 1. Testing and training data stream diagram.

Table 3. Training dataset.

		CLET	Generic	Shell-code
Mon	Norm.	138	138	138
	Abnorm.	14	14	14
	Total	152	152	152
Tue	Norm.	194	194	194
	Abnorm.	19	19	15
	Total	213	213	209
Wed	Norm.	172	172	172
	Abnorm.	17	17	15
	Total	189	189	187
Thu	Norm.	462	462	462
	Abnorm.	46	24	11
	Total	508	486	473
Fri	Norm.	154	154	154
	Abnorm.	15	15	15
	Total	169	169	169

Table 4. Testing dataset.

		CLET	Generic	Shell-code
Mon	Norm.	550	550	550
	Abnorm.	55	55	55
	Total	605	605	605
Tue	Norm.	774	774	774
	Abnorm.	78	78	58
	Total	852	852	832
Wed	Norm.	688	688	688
	Abnorm.	68	68	54
	Total	756	756	742
Thu	Norm.	1846	1846	1846
	Abnorm.	185	98	58
	Total	2031	1944	1904
Fri	Norm.	616	616	616
	Abnorm.	62	62	50
	Total	678	678	666

datasets for our anomaly detection systems. For each of the five days in the DARPA dataset, 20% of the day's packets were extracted to be used for training, and the remaining 80% of the day's data were set aside to be used for testing. To simulate the network traffic in real time, anomalous packets were then sporadically inserted into both the training and testing data after an initial interval consisting of only normal traffic (50 packets for training data and 200 packets for testing data). In this way, different datasets were created with each attack type for all five days of DARPA'99 week one (See **Figure 1**). The total number of abnormal packets inserted into both the training and testing data was no more than 10% of all normal data for the given day with payload length 1400 characters or more. In some cases, as shown in **Tables 3** and **4**, the number of abnormal packets inserted into data was less than 10% because there was not enough attack data available for that day. For the training data, 20% of the abnormal data was mixed with 20% of

the normal data for each day. Likewise, 80% of the abnormal data was mixed with 80% of the normal data selected from each day for testing. For each packet, 256 1-gram and 65,536 2-gram features were extracted to produce separate representations of the training and testing datasets detailed in **Tables 3** and **4**. The datasets were stored in the ARFF file format used the by the open source machine learning software WEKA [15].

2.2. Clustering-Based Anomaly Detection

Clustering algorithms are commonly used for anomaly detection, and are generally created for the batch environment [16]. However, some batch clustering algorithms, such as DBSCAN, can be modified to process stream data.

2.2.1. DBSCAN
DBSCAN is a density-based clustering algorithm devel-

oped for the batch setting. The algorithm takes two user-defined parameters, epsilon (ε) and minimum points, and relies on the concepts of ε-neighborhood and core-objects. An ε-neighborhood is defined by DBSCAN as being a set of points that have a distance to another point less than the user-defined parameter ε. More specifically, given point p and dataset D, the ε-neighborhood of $p\left(N_\varepsilon\left(p\right)\right)$ is equal to:

$$N_\varepsilon\left(p\right) = \{q \in D|\ dist\left(p,q\right) \le \varepsilon\}, \quad (1)$$

where $dist\left(p,q\right)$ is the Euclidean distance between points p and q [17].

A core-object is defined as a set of points within an ε-neighborhood that contain more points than the minimum points parameter. If p is part of a core-object, DBSCAN will expand the cluster around p.

The basic structure of the algorithm is as follows:

1) DBSCAN takes the ε and minimum points parameters and then chooses a point p that has not been visited.

2) DBSCAN calculates $N_\varepsilon\left(p\right)$. If the size of $N_\varepsilon\left(p\right)$ is greater than minimum points, DBSCAN expands a cluster around p. Otherwise, the point is considered noise.

3) DBSCAN iterates to a new un-visited point and repeats the process [18].

Although DBSCAN was originally developed for a batch environment, it has provided an inspiration for stream clustering algorithms.

2.2.2. DenStream

DenStream is a stream clustering algorithm based on DBSCAN with a damped window model. It expands the concept of an ε-neighborhood in DBSCAN with a fading function to maintain up-to-date information about the data stream. The fading function is defined as:

$$f\left(t\right) = 2^{-\lambda t}, \quad (2)$$

where $\lambda > 0$ represents the decay factor and t represents the time.

DenStream also modifies the core-object concept of DBSCAN, creating a core-micro-cluster with three additional attributes: radius, center and weight. The radius must be less than or equal to ε, and the weight of a cluster must be greater than the user-defined parameter μ [11]. The weight w, center c and radius r of a core-micro-cluster are more formally defined at time t, for a set of close points, $p_1, p_2, \cdots, p_n$ with time-stamps $T_1, T_2, \cdots, T_n$ as:

$$w = \sum_{i=1}^{n} f\left(t - T_i\right), \quad (3)$$

$$c = \frac{\sum_{i=1}^{n} f\left(t - T_i\right)p_i}{w}, \quad (4)$$

$$r = \frac{\sum_{i=1}^{n} f\left(t - T_i\right)dist\left(p_i, c\right)}{w}, \quad (5)$$

where $dist\left(p_i, c\right)$ is the Euclidean distance between the point p_i and the center c.

Because DenStream operates in a stream environment, the core-micro-clusters need to change dynamically as time passes. To facilitate this, a potential core-micro-cluster or p-micro-cluster is introduced. P-micro-clusters are similar to core-micro-clusters, except they differ in that the center and radius values are based on the weighted sum and squared sum of the points ($\overline{CF^1}$ and $\overline{CF^2}$). Also, the weight must be greater than or equal to $\beta\mu$ where β defines the threshold between p-micro-clusters and outliers(described in the next paragraph) such that $0 < \beta \le 1$. $\overline{CF^1}$ and $\overline{CF^2}$ are calculated using the formulas:

$$\overline{CF^1} = \sum_{i=1}^{n} f\left(t - T_i\right)p_i, \quad (6)$$

$$\overline{CF^2} = \sum_{i=1}^{n} f\left(t - T_i\right)p_i^2. \quad (7)$$

This changes the center and radius values to be [11, 19]:

$$c = \frac{\overline{CF^1}}{w}, \quad (8)$$

$$\text{and } r = \sqrt{\frac{\overline{CF^2}}{w} - \left(\frac{\overline{CF^1}}{w}\right)^2}. \quad (9)$$

Although the p-micro-cluster permits the model to be updated dynamically, it generally will not provide a representative view of a data stream as new points appear. To handle this concept drift, DenStream also introduces the outlier-micro-cluster (or o-micro-cluster) and an outlier-buffer that temporarily stores o-micro-clusters and allows them to become p-micro-clusters. The operation of DenStream is as follows:

Initial Step: run DBSCAN on a set of initial points to generate starting p-micro-clusters.

Online Steps, when a new point p arrives in the stream:

1) The algorithm attempts to merge p with the closest p-micro-cluster. If the radius of the potential micro-cluster is less than or equal to the value of ε, the point is merged.

2) If the point is not merged to a p-micro-cluster, it tries to merge p with an existing o-micro-cluster. If the radius is less than ε, it is merged with the o-micro-cluster. Then if the o-micro-cluster now has a weight large enough to become its own p-micro-cluster, it is removed

from the outlier-buffer and added to the model as a p-micro-cluster.

3) If the point cannot be merged to an existing o-micro-cluster, it creates a new o-micro-cluster and gets placed in the outlier-buffer.

After the merging phase of the DenStream algorithm, the lower weight limit is calculated for all o-micro-clusters in the outlier buffer. This is done using the formula:

$$\xi(t_c, t_0) = \frac{2^{-\lambda(t_c - t_0 + T_p)} - 1}{2^{-\lambda T_p} - 1}, \qquad (10)$$

where $\lambda > 0$ represents the decay factor, t_c and t_0 represent the current and starting time for the o-micro-cluster, and T_p is the predetermined time-period.

4) If the weight of a particular cluster is less than the lower weight limit, the o-micro-cluster can be removed from the outlier buffer.

2.2.3. Our DenStream-Based Detection System

To detect anomalous packets, DenStream was modified to create the DenStreamDetection algorithm, which treats incoming packets as points to be clustered. When a packet is merged with a p-micro-cluster, it is classified as normal. Otherwise, it is sent to the outlier-buffer and classified as anomalous. The ability for o-micro-clusters to be promoted to p-micro-clusters was removed because the majority of the packets clustered to the outlier-buffer are abnormal packets. If one of these o-micro-clusters became a p-micro-cluster, the model would be tainted and therefore unable to differentiate between abnormal and normal packets.

The basic structure of DenStreamDetectionis shown in **Algorithm 1**.

2.2.4. Creation of the Detection Model

The anomaly detection model was created in two steps. The first step used the training data to find a range for the parameters in DenStreamDetection such as ε and minimum points. Using 50 initial points, multiple DenStreamDetection models for each day were created to find a range of optimal parameters that could be used in the testing step. We found that ε had a larger impact on the predictions than the minimum points. During the first step, different parameter ranges were identified based on day and abnormal packet type.

The second step used the testing data to make a prediction model, which was evaluated with the sensitivity and false positive rates defined in Section 2.4. A false positive is a normal packet classified as abnormal. The parameters used in this step were 200 initial packets, 10 minimum points and a range of ε values specific to each day and attack type determined from the first step. Using

```
Algorithm: DenStreamDetection (iniP, minP, ε)
Parameters: iniP: number of initial packets
            minP: number of minimum packets in initial p-micro-
                  clusters
            ε: distance threshold
Input: File containing normal and abnormal packets in n-gram
       format.
Output: Predictions of normal and abnormal packets.

1.   Initialize DenStream using iniP and minP to build p-micro-
     clusters.
2.   As each packet p comes in:
3.     Try to merge p into its nearest p-micro-cluster cp
4.     if  radius(cp) ≤ ε  then
5.         Merge p into cp;
6.         Classify as normal packet;
7.     else
8.         Try to merge p into nearest o-micro-cluster c0;
9.         if  radius(c0) ≤ ε  then
10.            Merge p into c0;
11.            Classify as abnormal packet;
12.        else
13.            Create a new o-micro-cluster and insert into outlier-
               buffer;
14.            Classify as abnormal packet;
15.        end if
16.  end if
```

Algorithm 1. DenStream Detection algorithm.

these parameters, models were generated with a range of false positive and sensitivity rates to demonstrate overall performance.

2.3. Histogram-Based Anomaly Detection

Another approach to the detection of anomalous network packets has involved the use of histograms to maintain statistical information about network packet payloads. PAYL is an example of such a system [7], in which a model is created for known normal packet payloads and then compared with incoming packet payloads to determine whether or not the newly arriving packets are anomalous. Due to the evolutionary nature of streaming data, it is important that any abnormal packet detection method is able to update its normal model as concept drift occurs in the incoming data stream. With this in mind, we present a histogram-based classification method capable of modeling dynamic network traffic in real time.

2.3.1. Algorithm Description

The histogram-based detection algorithm provides a simple method for classification of network traffic. The algorithm, summarized in **Algorithm 2**, creates a histogramen compassing a "normal" model of the network packets expected to be encountered. This histogram is generated by counting the frequency of n-gram features

```
Algorithm: HistogramDetection (x, w, q, t, r, h, λ)
Parameters: x: number of initial normal packets
             w: size of Pearson correlation queue
             q: size of rebuild queue
             t: classification threshold
             r: rebuild count
             h: rebuild threshold
             λ: decay factor
Input: File containing normal and abnormal packets in n-gram
       format
Output: Predictions of normal and abnormal packets

1.  Initialize histogram g using x initial packets
2.  Initialize rebuild queue b to queue of size w
3.  Initialize Pearson correlation log l to queue of size w
4.  As each new packet p arrives
5.  decay (g)
6.  Create histogram c from packet p
7.  if pearsonCorrelation(g,c) >t then
8.      Classify p as normal
9.      b.addFirst(p)
10.     if (b.size() >q) then
11.         b.removeLast()
12.     end if
13.     l.addFirst(pearsonCorrelation(g,c))
14.     if (l.size() > w) then
15.         l.removeLast()
16.     end if
17.     Calculate number of packets n in l with values ≤ h
18.     if n ≥ r then
19.         rebuild(g)
20.         l.clear()
21.     else
22.         Classify p as abnormal
23.     end if
24. end if
```

Algorithm 2. Histogram-based detection algorithm.

found within packet payloads. To begin classification of a stream of packets, the algorithm first requires x initial normal packets to construct the normal model histogram. This histogram contains frequency counts from all initial packets for each possible n-gram attribute. Since we are attempting to model normal traffic, it is imperative that no abnormal packets are included when this model is created or else the model will be contaminated and detection rates will decrease. To effectively reflect the evolutionary nature of network traffic, the same fading function with decay factor λ used in DenStream is applied to the histogram after each new packet is processed. This helps to reduce the impact of outdated stream data. After the initial histogram has been built, the algorithm can begin to classify the subsequent packets.

In order to classify an incoming network packet, the algorithm builds a histogram from the newly arrived packet's payload. The histogram generated from the new packet is then compared with the normal model histogram (to which the fading function has been applied as each new packet comes in) by computing the Pearson correlation value between the two histograms. If the

computed Pearson correlation value is above a user-defined threshold t, the packet is classified as normal; otherwise, the packet is classified as abnormal.

To account for the possibility of concept drift and shift occurring in data flows, the normal histogram model may need to be rebuilt using packets that have arrived since the initialization of the normal histogram model. This allows the normal model to stay current, modeling packets most recently classified as normal. In order to facilitate this rebuilding process, the algorithm maintains two queues of user-defined size containing information from previously processed normal packets. One of these queues, of size q, stores the histogram data for the previous packets, while the other, with size w, stores Pearson correlation values computed between the packets and the normal histogram model. Note that only data for packets classified as normal are included in these two queues; any packets classified as abnormal are not taken into account. If the normal histogram is to be rebuilt, a set of user-specified conditions must be met, giving the user control of the rebuilding process. When the model is rebuilt too often, the algorithm's efficiency will decrease significantly; however, if it is not rebuilt enough, accuracy will diminish. To determine when rebuilding the normal model is necessary, the algorithm calculates the number of Pearson correlation values in the stored queue that are below the user-defined threshold h. If this count is found to be of a certain value r, the normal model is rebuilt using packets stored in the histogram data queue and the queue containing previous Pearson correlation values is emptied.

2.3.2. Critical Parameters

Though the histogram-based algorithm requires several parameters, it is important to note that these are not equally important. Rather, two parameters in particular have the greatest effect on the algorithm's ability to detect anomalous packets.

The first of these most critical parameters is q, the size of the queue of previously processed instances used to rebuild the normal histogram model. If this value is too small, the normal histogram model generated when the model is rebuilt will not take into account a sufficient number of previously processed packets. This results in an insufficiently robust model, causing both undesirable sensitivity values and false positive rates.

While q has a noticeable influence on the effectiveness of the histogram detection algorithm, t, which defines the Pearson correlation threshold between instances classified as normal and abnormal, is undoubtedly the most important parameter. This is understandable, as t directly controls the classification of each individual instance as it is processed by the algorithm. Furthermore, t also plays a role in controlling the rebuilding of the normal histogram model. Because parameter h specifies an interval above t, t is directly related the frequency at which the normal model histogram is rebuilt. Thus, the value of t is closely connected to the core functionality of the histogram-based detection algorithm.

2.4. Performance Metrics

To evaluate the performance of the anomaly detection models, the sensitivity and false positive rates were calculated using the following formulas:

$$\text{sensitivity} = \frac{TP}{TP + FN}, \qquad (11)$$

$$\text{false positive rate} = \frac{FP}{TN + FP}, \qquad (12)$$

where TP/FN stand for the number of correctly/incorrectly classified abnormal packets, and TN/FP are the number of correctly/incorrectly classified normal packets. Sensitivity measured how well the model detected abnormal packets, and false positive rate indicated the percentage of false alarms generated.

3. Results and Discussion

3.1. Density-Based Detection Results

After tuning the DenStreamDetection-based system on packets using 2-gram features, we discovered a range of ε values for each day that could be used to evaluate the model. For every day except for Tuesday, the false positive rate was kept between 0% and 10% so that an appropriate detection rate could be found. Tuesday, however, needed the false positive limit to be heavily relaxed in order to achieve a moderate sensitivity. When testing the detection system, the false positive and sensitivity rates for the highest, middle and lowest ε values were generated for both 1-gram and 2-gram feature representations. These are displayed in **Table 5**. The results with highest sensitivity for each virus type were then averaged to find best overall performance.

In general, the DenStreamDetection-based system was able to correctly detect most Shell-code attacks, achieving on average 91% sensitivity with a 14% false positive rate. Similarly, Generic HTTP attacks produced 78% average sensitivity and a 13% false positive rate. CLET attacks, however, had a similar false positive rate of 14%, but a substantially lower average sensitivity of 65%. This disparity was likely due to the polymorphic nature of CLET attacks, which are designed to mimic normal network traffic.

Table 5. DenStreamDetection system results.

DenStreamDetection System Results 2-gram(1-gram)						
Day	ε	CLET		Generic Http		Shell-code	
		FP	Sens	FP	Sens	FP	Sens
Mon	30	7(20)	75(78)	7(20)	78(95)	7(20)	98(100)
	45	7(9)	67(67)	7(10)	76(76)	7(10)	96(95)
	60	6(6)	49(49)	6(7)	73(70)	6(7)	93(93)
Tue	65	35(35)	62(62)	33(35)	74(74)	35(35)	86(86)
	80	34(33)	56(56)	33(34)	72(72)	34(34)	81(81)
	100	33(33)	51(50)	32(33)	69(69)	33(33)	76(79)
Wed	95	11(11)	38(37)	11(11)	63(62)	11(11)	81(81)
	110	9(10)	29(29)	10(10)	60(60)	10(10)	78(78)
	125	8(8)	25(25)	8(8)	54(56)	8(8)	70(72)
Thu	5	6(4)	96(98)	6(3)	99(1)	6(3)	98(1)
	30	3(2)	84(84)	4(1)	90(90)	4(1)	93(93)
	55	0(2)	76(78)	0(1)	81(81)	0(1)	81(82)
Fri	55	9(9)	56(58)	9(9)	76(77)	9(9)	92(94)
	65	8(9)	53(53)	8(9)	74(74)	8(9)	92(92)
	75	8(8)	50(49)	8(8)	71(71)	8(8)	88(88)
Best. Avg		14(16)	65(67)	13(16)	78(82)	14(16)	91(92)

Thursday exhibited the highest detection rates (up to 99%) whilst keeping the false positive rates below 6%. Also, Thursday experienced both the lowest ε value sand the largest ε range to achieve its results.

The models utilizing both 1-gram and 2-gram feature-sproduced similar results. Using the 1-gram representation for the same ε values, the system experienced slightly better detection rates at the expense of higher false positive rates. Also, because the 1-gram representation has a much smaller feature space than 2-gram, the total run-time of 1-gram was significantly less.

3.2. Histogram-Based Detection Results

3.2.1. Optimal Parameters
The histogram-based algorithm was applied to anomalous packet detection in two steps: training and testing. In the training step, favorable parameters for the algorithm were approximated by performing several experiments on the training data. Since the training data included 50 initial normal packets, this value was used for x during the training step. Most critically, appropriate values of t were ascertained for the different attack types on each day, as this parameter has the greatest effect on the performance of the algorithm. Suitable values were also obtained for all other parameters during the training phase. The optimum value of q was found to be 200, as this allowed the algorithm to maintain a fairly accurate model of normal traffic while minimizing the time needed

to for this model to be rebuilt. Also, 30 was generally used for w, with r valued at 10 and h at 0.2. These parameters effectively limited the frequency of rebuilding the normal histogram model while still allowing the algorithm to handle concept drift in the data. A λ value of 0.01 was found to work sufficiently well, as this decay factor helped to better maintain an up-to-date normal model for normal traffic.

Once appropriate parameters were identified, the testing phase began. In this step, the value 200 was assigned to x since the testing data contained 200 initial normal packets. With the rest of the algorithm's parameters remaining static, the algorithm was tested using varying values of t in order to gauge sensitivity values at different false positive rates. This produced the results summarized in **Table 6**, which displays a sampling of t values used for different days and attack types with the resulting sensitivities and false positive rates.

3.2.2. Results Achieved

As can be seen from **Table 6**, we were able to attain fairly consistent results across all days' testing data for each attack type using optimal parameters. The algorithm performed best at detecting shell-code attacks, achieving an average of 97% sensitivity and 1% false positive rate across all shell-code attack testing datasets. Performance was slightly less desirable in detection of Generic HTTP attacks, but was nevertheless acceptable, with an average detection rate of 84% and 3% false positive rate. CLET

Table 6. Histogram-based detection system results.

Histogram Detection System Results 2-gram

Day	CLET			Generic HTTP			Shell-code		
	t	FP	Sens	t	FP	Sens	t	FP	Sens
	0.0025	0	25	0.0025	0	76	0.0005	0	58
Mon	0.0060	7	31	0.0070	5	76	0.0010	0	78
	0.0080	8	60	0.0090	9	76	0.0035	0	96
	0.00005	1	27	0.0002	1	27	0.00001	1	31
Tue	0.0025	7	37	0.0010	2	71	0.0010	2	79
	0.0035	9	40	0.0015	2	83	0.0015	2	97
	0.0020	1	29	0.0004	0	38	0.0005	0	43
Wed	0.0040	2	35	0.0010	0	66	0.0010	0	78
	0.0045	3	44	0.0030	1	81	0.0020	1	96
	0.0050	0	69	0.0005	0	78	0.0005	0	97
Thu	0.1505	3	98	0.0010	0	88	0.0755	2	98
	0.4000	3	100	0.0855	2	100	0.1000	3	100
	0.0005	0	26	0.0005	0	39	0.0010	0	60
Fri	0.0020	2	27	0.0010	0	61	0.0015	1	82
	0.0065	13	63	0.0015	1	79	0.0020	1	96
Best Avg.		7	61		3	84		1	97

attacks proved most difficult for the histogram-based algorithm to detect. In order for reasonable detection rates to be obtained, false positive rates generally had to be pushed much higher than necessary for the other two attack types, to an average of 7% with optimal parameters. Despite this fact, sensitivity remained comparatively low, at an average of 61%. This difficulty detecting CLET attacks was likely due to their polymorphic nature, which also proved troublesome to the DenStream Detection system.

While results were relatively consistent across each days' worth of training data, those achieved using Thursday's testing data were markedly superior. Using optimal parameters, the histogram-based detection algorithm was able to achieve perfect detection on all three types of attacks, each with a false positive rate of 3% or less. There are several possible reasons for this exceptional performance related to the nature of Thursday's testing data as discussed in Section 3.3. Overall, the relatively high t values used indicate greater consistency in Thursday's network traffic. Due to these elevated t values, the algorithm was able to more effectively identify abnormal network packets.

The number of parameters required by the histogram-based detection algorithm necessitated fairly specific tuning for our different datasets in order to perform optimally. This was demonstrated by the algorithm's performance on 1-gram features when the same parameters used for 2-gram were applied. While the clustering-based algorithm was able to achieve comparable results from both 1-gram and 2-gram with the same parameters, the histogram-based algorithm performed poorly on 1-gram when applied with the same parameters as 2-gram. As a result, 1-gram results have not been reported for the histogram-based algorithm.

3.3. Concept Shift

The performance of our anomaly detection systems is heavily influenced by the evolutionary nature of network traffic. To demonstrate this challenge, we calculated the Pearson correlation between segments of ten packets for each day. By measuring the correlation between two consecutive segments, changes in the stream can be visualized (**Figure 2**), which offers a possible explanation to the results observed in **Tables 5** and **6**.

Monday, Wednesday, and Friday exhibit continuous concept shift, particularly during the training phase, as the calculated Pearson correlation values oscillate regularly. Therefore, a robust model for normal traffic was built in each case that responded accurately to the evolving data stream. As a result, greater sensitivity was achieved on each of these three days.

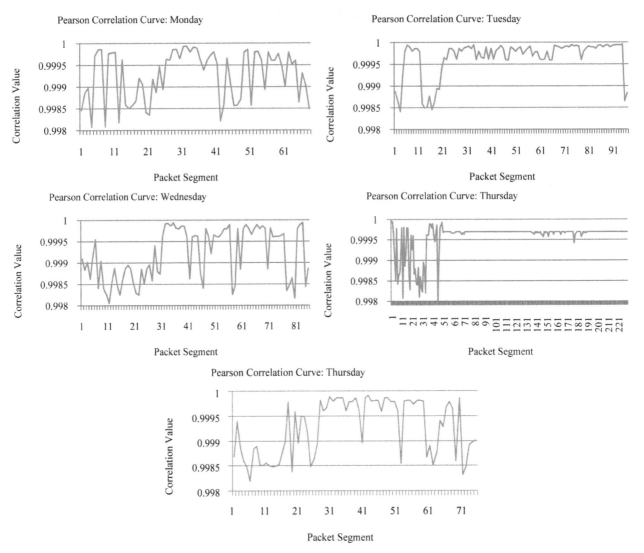

Figure 2. Pearson correlation curves for DARPA'99 week 1.

Tuesday demonstrates a very distinct pattern, as it starts with slight shift, but remains relatively stable throughout the stream. In contrast to Monday, Tuesday experiences only two major shifts, both of which occur during the training phase. Therefore, Tuesday's models may have a less accurate view of the incoming stream, causing decreased performance. Since Tuesday only experienced shift during the training phase, it had a less accurate view of the changing stream environment. This may have led to the performance issues stated previously.

The high sensitivity values for Thursday can also be explained through concept shift. During the training phase, consistent concept shift occurred, allowing Thursday's model to effectively capture the changing pattern of normal network traffic. Following the training step, the remainder of Thursday's data was relatively stable.

Therefore, Thursday likely experienced consistent concept drift, which led to superior detection results.

4. Conclusions

In this paper, two data stream mining techniques were applied to the problem of anomaly detection. First, a stream clustering algorithm was used to detect abnormal packets. Using 1-gram and 2-gram features, this approach achieved moderate success with Generic HTTP and Shell-code attacks but had a higher average false positive rate. Second, a stream adaptation of the relative frequency histogram approach found in [7] was created using Pearson correlation to detect anomalies.

Though the histogram-based approach achieved moderately better results, it required more fine-tuning because of the number of parameters used. In contrast, generalization of the clustering algorithm was easier to achieve since it uses fewer parameters. This was evidenced by the ability of the clustering algorithm to perform effectively on both 1-gram and 2-gram features with the same parameters, while the histogram algorithm required specific parameter tuning for each feature type.

Lastly, to better explain the performance differences between certain days, we analyzed the Pearson correlation between consecutive segments of 10 packets. By plotting these values on a graph, concept drift and shift were visualized, and clear variations were observed between days. The location and frequency of concept shift and drift in the data streams, especially within the training phase, provided an account for the observed changes in performance.

5. Acknowledgements

We would like to thank the Summer Research Institute at Houghton College for providing funding for our research.

6. References

[1] R. Perdisci, G. Gu and W. Lee, "Using an Ensemble of One-Class svm Classifiers to Harden Payload-Based Anomaly Detection Systems," *ICDM'06: Proceedings of the Sixth Integnation Conference on Data Mining*, Hong Kong, 18-22 December 2006, pp. 488-498.

[2] D. Anderson, T. Lunt, H. Javits and A. Tamaru, "Nides: Detecting Unusual Program Behavior Using the Statistical Component of the Next Generation Intrusion Detection Expert System," *Technical Report SRI-CSL-95-06*, Computer Science Laboratory, SRI International, Menlo Park, May 1995.

[3] R. Perdisci, "Statistical Pattern Recognition Techniques for Intrusion Detection in Computer Networks, Challenges and Solutions," University of Cagliari, Italy, 2006.

[4] M. Mahoney and P. Chan, "Learning Non Stationary Models of Normal Network Traffic for Detecting Novel Attacks," *ACM SIGKDD International Conference on Knowledge Discovery and Data Mining*, Edmonton, July 2002, pp. 376-385.

[5] M. Mahoney, "Network Trafic Anomaly Detection Based on Packet Bytes," ACM-SAC, Melbourne, 2003 pp. 346-350.

[6] R. Perdisci, D. Ariu, P. Fogla, G. Giacinto and W. Lee, "McPAD: A Multiple Classifier System for Accurate Payload-based Anomaly Detection," *Computer Networks, Special Issue on Traffic Classification and Its Applications to Modern Networks*, Vol. 5 No. 6, 2009, pp. 864-881.

[7] K. Wang and S. Stolfo, "Anomalous Payload-Based Network Intrusion Detection," *Recent Advances in Intrusion Detection (RAID)*, Vol. 3224, 2004, pp. 203-222.

[8] K. Wang, "Network Payload-Based Anomaly Detection and Content-Based Alert Correlation," Columbia University, New York, 2006.

[9] J. Tang, "An algorithm for Streaming Clustering," MSc. Thesis, Uppsala University, Uppsala, 2011.

[10] A. Bifet, G. Holmes, R. Kirkby and B. Pfahringer, "MOA: Massive Online Analysis," *Journal of Machine Learning Research*, Vol. 11, 2010, pp. 1601-1604.

[11] F. Cao, M. Ester, W. Qian and A. Zhou, "Density-Based Clustering over an Evolving Data Stream with Noise," *SIAM Conference Data Mining*, Bethesda, 2006.

[12] R. Lippmann, J. Haines, D. Fried, J. Korba and K. Das, "The 1999 DARPA Off-Line Intrusion Detection Evaluation," *Computer Networks*, Vol. 34, No. 4, 2000, pp. 579-595.

[13] K. L. Ingham and H. Inoue, "Comparing Anomaly Detection Techniques for HTTP," *Recent Advances in Intrusion Detection (RAID)*, 2007.

[14] T. Detristan, T. Ulenspiegel, Y. Malcom and M. Underduk, "Polymorphic Shellcode Engine Using Spectrum Analysis," *Phrack*, Vol. 11, No. 61, 2003.

[15] I.H. Witten and E. Frank, "Data Mining: Practical Machine Learning Tools and Techniques," 2nd Edition, Morgan Kaufmann Publishers, Waltham, 2005.

[16] L. Portnoy, E. Eskin and S. Stolfo, "Intrusion Detection with Unlabeled Data Using Clustering," *Proceedings of ACM CSS Workshop on Data Mining Applied to Security (DMSA-2001)*, Philadelphia, 2001, pp. 333-342.

[17] M. Ester, H. Kriegel, J. Sander and X. Xu, "A Density-Based Algorithm for Discovering Clusters in Large Spatial Databases with Noise," *International Conference on Knowledge Discovery in Databases and Data Mining (KDD-96)*, Portland, August 1996, pp. 226-231.

[18] K. Mumtaz and K. Duraiswamy, "An Analysis on Density Based Clustering of Multi Dimensional Spatial Data," *Indian Journal of Computer Science and Engineering*, Vol. 1, No. 1, 2010, pp. 8-12.

[19] A. Forestiero, C. Pizzuti and G. Spezzano, "FlockStream: a Bio-Inspired Algorithm for Clustering Evolving Data Streams," *ICTAI'09 Proceedings of the 2009 21st IEEE International Conference on Tools with Artificial Intelligence*, Washington DC, 2009, pp. 1-8.

18

Experimental Evaluation of Juniper Network's Netscreen-5GT Security Device against Layer4 Flood Attacks

Sanjeev Kumar, Raja Sekhar Reddy Gade
Network Security Research Lab, Department of Electrical and Computer Engineering,
The University of Texas–Pan American, Edinburg, USA

Abstract

Cyber attacks are continuing to hamper working of Internet services despite increased use of network security systems such as firewalls and Intrusion protection systems (IPS). Recent Distributed Denial of Service (DDoS) attacks on Dec 8th, 2010 by Wikileak supporters on Visa and Master Card websites made headlines on prime news channels all over the world. Another famous DDoS attacks on Independence Day weekend, on July 4th, 2009 were launched to debilitate the US and South Korean governments' websites. These attacks raised questions about the capabilities of the security systems that were used in the network to counteract such attacks. Firewall and IPS security systems are commonly used today as a front line defense mechanism to defend against DDoS attacks. In many deployments, performances of these security devices are seldom evaluated for their effectiveness. Different security devices perform differently in stopping DDoS attacks. In this paper, we intend to drive the point that it is important to evaluate the capability of Firewall or IPS security devices before they are deployed to protect a network or a server against DDoS attacks. In this paper, we evaluate the effectiveness of a security device called Netscreen 5GT (or NS-5GT) from Juniper Networks under Layer-4 flood attacks at different attack loads. This security device NS-5GT comes with a feature called TCP-SYN proxy protection to protect against TCP-SYN based DDoS attacks, and UDP protection feature to protect against UDP flood attacks. By looking at these security features from the equipments data sheet, one might assume the device to protect the network against such DDoS attacks. In this paper, we conducted real experiments to measure the performance of this security device NS-5GT under the TCP SYN and UDP flood attacks and test the performance of these protection features. It was found that the Juniper's NS-5GT mitigated the effect of DDoS traffic to some extent especially when the attack of lower intensity. However, the device was unable to provide any protection against Layer4 flood attacks when the load exceeded 40Mbps. In order to guarantee a measured level of security, it is important for the network managers to measure the actual capabilities of a security device, using real attack traffic, before they are deployed to protect a critical information infrastructure.

Keywords: Distributed Denial of Service (DDoS), TCP-SYN Flood Attack, TCP-SYN Proxy Protection, Firewall Security, UDP Flood Attack

1. Introduction

Internet is the foremost leading media for multimedia information exchange today. However, the ease of Internet communication comes with the threat of security attacks, which are known to disrupt such communications over Internet. As recently as Dec. 8th, 2010, the servers of Visa, MasterCard, PayPal and several others were brought down by the supporters of WikiLeaks using DDoS attacks [1]. On August 6th 2009, servers like Twitter, Facebook, Live journal, Google's Blogger and Youtube were under DDoS attacks, where Twitter was down for several hours [2]. According to CSI Computer and Security Survey 2008, Firewall type of security technology was used by 94% of the organizations [3]. Many manufacturers are designing firewalls and advanced security devices to provide increased protection for their customers from different types of attacks. Despite widespread use of firewalls to protect corporate and government websites, the damage caused by the denial of service attacks do not seem to have gone away completely. The DDoS attacks, launched during Wikileaks related events starting Dec. 8th, 2010, and the Independence Day DDoS attacks on July 4th, 2009 launched against US and South Korean government websites [4], are now prompting many network managers to question the performance of their firewalls, IPS or other Internet security devices being used in defending against such DDoS attacks [5-13]. In this paper, we evaluate performance of Juniper Network's NetScreen NS-5GT Internet security device [14,15] to measure its effectiveness in defending against two popular layer-4 DDoS attacks, namely the TCP-SYN and UDP flood attacks. The rest of the paper is organized as follows: Section 2 has a discussion on the TCP and UDP flood attacks that are evaluated in this paper, and the protection mechanisms offered by the Juniper Network's NS-5GT security device to protect against these two DDoS attacks. Section 3 provides detail of experimental setup, different scenarios of protection used in the experiments, and discussion on respective results. Section 4 concludes the paper.

2. Juniper's Netscreen NS-5gt Internet Security Device

The Juniper's NetScreen 5GT (NS-5GT) is an Internet Security device that combines functionalities of firewall, Intrusion Prevention System (IPS), VPN and traffic shaping functions [14,15]. NS-5GT device is an enterprise class security solution designed to defend against various security attacks including layer-4 DDoS attacks such as TCP-SYN flood or UDP-flood attacks.

2.1. TCP-SYN Flood Attack

In this type of DDoS attack, the attacker sends a flood of TCP-SYN packets with spoofed addresses. The server responds with corresponding SYN-ACK packets which are never answered with the final ACK packets.

This results in establishment of numerous half open connections at the victim computer (**Figure 1**), which causes excessive consumption of computing resources of the victim computer. This type of DDoS attack is called TCP-SYN flood attack. During this attack, legitimate client connections are dropped as a result of lack of computing resource at the victim computer.

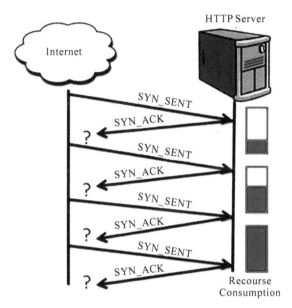

Figure 1. TCP SYN flood attack.

2.2. Protection Provided by NetScreen NS-5GT against TCP-SYN Based DDoS Attacks

The security device NS-5GT from Juniper Networks provides protection against TCP-SYN based DDoS attacks by using a mechanism called SYN Proxy protection method [14,15]. According to this mechanism, the NS-5GT Internet security device is placed between the server (that needs to be protected) and the Internet. In this position, the NS-5GT does the proxy on behalf of the server and participates in the initial TCP 3-Way Handshake process (**Figure 2**) to authenticate genuine client connections to the server.

According to this protection mechanism, first a SYN attack threshold is set in the NS-5GT, which is an upper limit on the number of SYN segments permitted through the device per second. If this threshold is exceeded, then the NS-5GT starts to proxy on behalf of the server and directly participates in 3-way handshake with the clients, to establish a legitimate connection. The NS-5GT replies with SYN_ACK to the initial SYN segments arriving from the clients, and hence opening up a number of half open connections. In the case of genuine client connections, the final ACK segment is sent from the client, and upon receiving it the security device NS-5GT forwards it to the server for establishment of a secure TCP connection. If the final ACK segment doesn't arrive then the half open connection at the intermediate NS-5GT device is terminated or timed out.

2.3. UDP Flood Attack

UDP is another common Layer-4 traffic on internet.

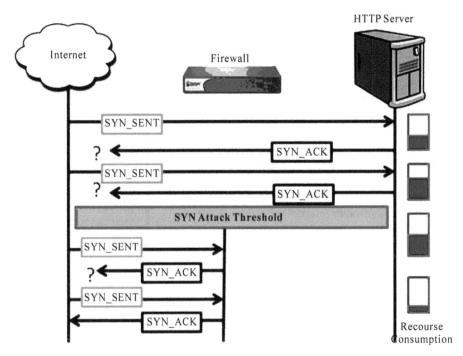

Figure 2. SYN Proxy protection [15].

However unlike TCP traffic, the Web-servers do not receive a lot of UDP traffic. During UDP flood attacks, a flood of UDP packets are sent to the victim computers either on specified ports or on random ports. The victim computer or server processing those UDP packets replies with valid information, if there is an application available on the specified port, otherwise the victim computer sends "ICMP Destination Unreachable" message to the spoofed sender. UDP flood attacks can also consume computing resources on the victim system besides the bandwidth. The Juniper's NetScreen NS-5GT security device also has a protection feature that claims to protect against UDP flood attacks. In this paper, we measure the capability of the NS-5GT to defend against UDP flood attacks.

2.4. Protection Provided by NetScreen NS-5GT against UDP-Flood Based DDoS Attacks

The NetScreen 5GT provides protection against UDP flood attacks by monitoring the rate of incoming UDP datagrams to the NS-5GT. The security device NS-5GT passes the UDP datagrams only if a policy permits them. For example, as shown in **Figure 3**, the UDP packet can be targeted to a DNS server.

In the case of attack, the attacker sends a flood of UDP datagrams to a DNS server, which rides IP packets with spoofed source addresses. The security device protects against this type of UDP flood attack by imposing a limit on the maximum rate i.e. the maximum number of UDP

datagrams that can be allowed to pass through the security device per second. After the threshold is crossed, the security device NS-5GT starts dropping all UDP datagrams from all source addresses and destined to the same subnet for the remaining second and also for the next successive second. During this time period when the threshold is enabled, the UDP packets from the legitimate clients are also dropped. Thus the dropping of all UDP datagrams stays in effect, as long the threshold limit stays violated by the flood of incoming UDP packets.

3. Experimental Setup and Measurements

For experiments, an evaluation network was set up in a controlled lab environment as shown in **Figure 4**, where we launched a TCP-SYN attack and UDP flood attack to measure the performance of Juniper's Netscreen 5GT Security Device. The number of client connections established per second to the server was used as the performance parameter in these experiments. In these experiments, we measured the number of client connections per second against different loads of attack traffic. To compare the effectiveness of the security device, the performance was evaluated with and without respective protections being enabled on the NS-5GT security device to stop the flood attacks from reaching the server. For this experiment, along with the Juniper Networks NS-5GT security device, the Windows Server 2003 with Intel® Xeon™ 3GHz Processor and 4GB RAM were used.

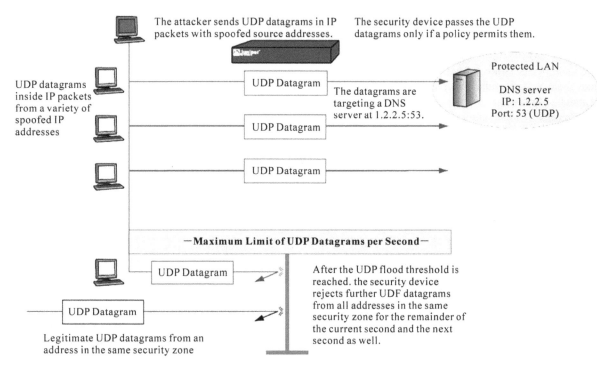

Figure 3. UDP flood protection method used by NS-5GT [15].

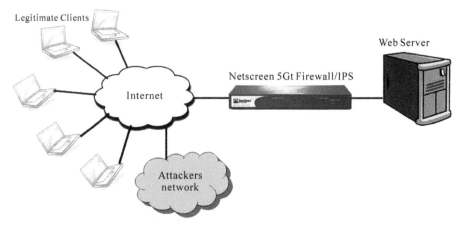

Figure 4. Experimental setup to evaluate the effectiveness of Juniper's NT-5GT security device.

The set up in **Figure 4** shows the legitimate HTTP clients that connect to the server through the security device NS-5GT. Furthermore, the attacker's network is used to simulate the Distributed Denial of Attack (DDoS) attack with the attack traffic being sent with spoofed addresses. Since the Juniper's NS-5GT security device system supported an interface of 100Mbps for internet traffic, the security device was subjected to a range of layer-4 attack traffic load up to 100Mbps.

Prior to starting the experiments, we first measure the baseline performance of the security device NS-5GT in supporting the maximum number of stable client connections per second in the absence of any attack traffic. In the absence of any attack traffic, the maximum number of stable client connection rate established with the server through the NS-5GT security device was measured to be 600 connections per second (baseline performance of the NS-5GT security device).

3.1. TCP SYN Attack on Server without Protection Enabled on Juniper's NS-5GT Security Device

In this case, the security device NS-5GT was setup with no proxy protection enabled against TCP-SYN attacks. A stable connection rate of 600 legitimate client connections per second was established with the server during the experiment. The TCP-SYN attack, with the attack load varying from 10 Mbps to 100Mbps was launched on the server with no SYN proxy protection enabled at the NS-5GT security device. We measured the number of connections per second formed with the end server through the NS-5GT under different loads of TCP-SYN flood attack (**Figure 5**).

Based on the experimental measurements, it was found that the number of legitimate client connection rate was brought down to around 176 connections/sec from the baseline rate of 600 connections/sec under the TCP-SYN attack load of only 15 Mbps. Furthermore, the number of legitimate client connections was brought down to zero when the attack load was increased to 20 Mbps. The number of client connection rate established with the server through the NS-5GT security device (used as a gateway) at different attack loads is shown in **Figure 5**.

3.2. TCP-SYN Attack on Server with SYN-Proxy Protection Enabled on Juniper's NS-5GT Security Device

In this case, the SYN Proxy protection was enabled on the NS-5GT, with default threshold value on the number of TCP SYN permitted through the security device. Despite enabling of the SYN proxy protection, we found that the client connections rate dropped to zero at 45 Mbps of SYN flood attack traffic load as shown in **Figure 6**.

Based on the measurements done for the client connection rate that can be supported with and without TCP proxy protection enabled at the Juniper's NS-5GT security device, such comparison is shown in **Figure 7**. The green bar on the left in **Figure 7** shows the number of successful client connections formed per second without SYN proxy protection enabled at the NS-5GT, whereas the blue bar on the right in **Figure 7** shows the number of successful client connections formed per second with SYN proxy protection enabled at the Juniper's NS-5GT security device.

On one hand, it can be seen that without SYN-proxy protection being enabled at the NS-5GT security device, the legitimate client connection rate fell sharply to zero around 20 Mbps of TCP-SYN attack traffic. On the other hand, it can be seen that when the SYN-proxy protection

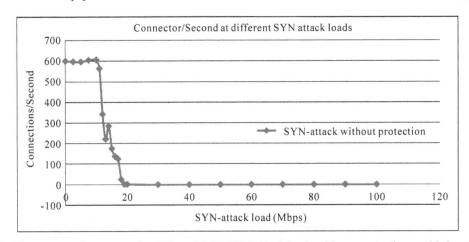

Figure 5. Client connection rate under different TCP-SYN attack loads with no protection enabled on NS-5GT.

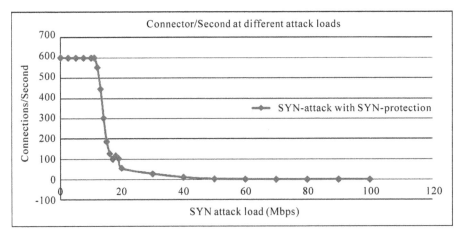

Figure 6. Client connection rate under different TCP-SYN attack loads with SYN-proxy protection enabled on NS-5GT.

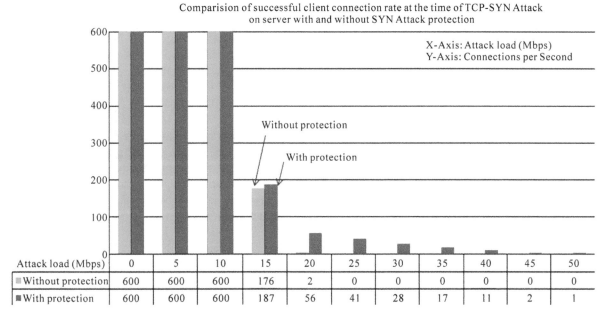

Figure 7. Connections per second compared with and without SYN Proxy protection enabled on the Juniper's NS-5GT security device.

was enabled at the Juniper's NS-5GT security device, it took 45 Mpbs of TCP-SYN attack traffic to completely deny legitimate client connections through the Juniper's Netscreen 5GT security device.

Comparative study and results (**Figure 7**) show that the security effectiveness provided by the Juniper's NS-5GT security device is very marginal in improving the client connection rate, and almost ineffective in protecting against TCP-SYN attacks of higher intensity exceeding 45 Mbps. It is obvious that the security device NS-5GT from Juniper Networks is not capable enough to protect against high intensity TCP-SYN attacks despite offering protection features against such attacks.

3.3. UDP Flood Attack on Server without UDP-Flood Protection Enabled on Juniper's NS-5GT Security Device

In this case, we study the effectiveness of the Juniper's security device NS-5GT in protecting against UDP flood attack. For comparison of its protection mechanism, we consider two scenarios to measure the effect of security provided by the NS-5GT on the connection rate–first scenario, when the UDP flood attack is launched without enabling the UDP flood protection at NS-5GT. Second scenario, when the UDP flood attack is launched after enabling the UDP flood protection at NS-5GT. In this section, we cover the first scenario when the security device NS-5GT was setup with no UDP-flood protection, and the server maintained an initial (baseline) client connection rate of 600 connections per second during the

experiments. The UDP flood attack traffic varying from 10 Mbps to 100 Mbps in steps of 10 Mbps was sent towards the server through the security device NS-5GT. The effect of attack traffic loads on the client connection rate was measured and plotted in **Figure 8**.

When the server is flooded with the spoofed UDP traffic, the UDP packet received by the server processes the packets and checks for the application on the requested port number. If there was no application found on that requested port then the server sends the destination unreachable packet as reply for the received packets.

Results in **Figure 8** show that the number of client connections dropped to half of its maximum baseline capacity under UDP flood attack load of 35 Mbps. Furthermore, without UDP flood protection on the NS-5GT security device, no client connection could be established under UDP attack load of 40 Mbps or higher.

3.4. UDP Flood Attack on Server with UDP Flood Protection Enabled on Juniper's Security Device NS-5GT

In this case, the UDP flood attack protection (**Figure 3**) was enabled on the Juniper's NS-5GT security device to evaluate its effectiveness in mitigating the attack, and in improving the number of client connections under UDP flood attack conditions. Initially, in the absence of attack conditions, the baseline client connection rate of 600 connections per second was maintained during the experiment. The UDP flood attack load varying from 10 Mbps to 100 Mbps in steps of 10 Mbps was sent towards the server, through the Juniper's security device NS-5GT gateway, in order to measure its effectiveness in preventing the attack. The number of connections per second was measured against different loads of attack.

When the UDP flood protection was enabled on the Juniper Networks security device NS-5GT, it was found that under an UDP attack traffic load of 30 Mbps, the connection rate dropped from baseline connection rate of 600 connections/sec to around 373 connections/sec, *i.e.* a decrease of around 38% in the baseline performance.

Whereas, without such UDP flood protection being enabled on the security device NS-5GT (**Figure 8**), only 97 connections/sec could be supported under the UDP attack load of 30 Mbps *i.e.* around 84% decrease in the baseline performance. The relative improvement in the connection rate provided by the UDP protection mechanism of the security device can be calculated as 46% for the attack load of 30 Mbps. It can be seen that at lower attack loads, there was some improvement in the connection rate provided by the security device NS-5GT, however when the UDP attack load was increased to 45Mbps or higher, no client connections could be established *i.e.*

0% improvement in the connection rate despite claims of providing protection against UDP attacks by the NS-5GT security device.

The results show that the NS-5GT provides some protection against the UDP flood attack of lower intensity (below 40 Mbps), however it is not effective in preventing against UDP flood attacks of higher intensity (*i.e.* exceeding 40 Mbps).

Based on the measurements done for the number of client connection rate that can be supported with and without UDP flood protection enabled at the Juniper's NS-5GT security device, we show such comparison in **Figure 10**. The green bars on the left in **Figure 10** show the number of successful client connections formed per second when no UDP flood protection was enabled at the NS-5GT. Whereas the blue bars on the right in **Figure 10** show the number of successful client connections formed per second with UDP flood protection enabled at the Juniper's NS-5GT security device.

From **Figure 10**, it can be observed that without UDP flood-protection enabled at the NS-5GT security device, the client connection rate goes to almost zero at 35 Mbps

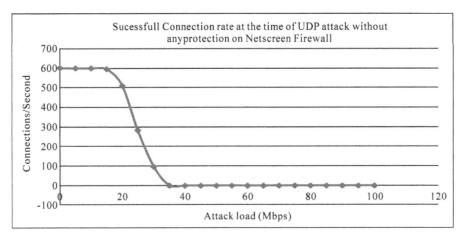

Figure 8. Client connections established under different UDP flood attack loads with no protection enabled on NS-5GT.

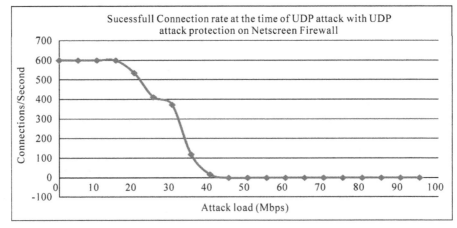

Figure 9. Client connections established under different UDP flood attack loads with UDP-protection enabled on NS-5GT.

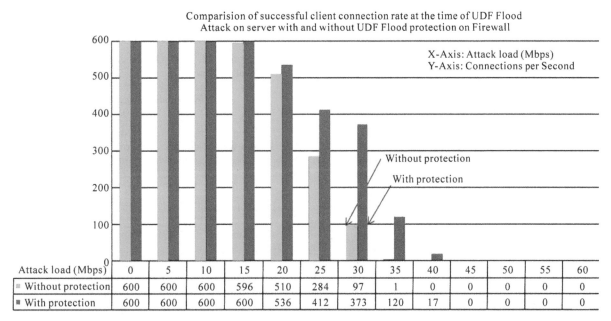

Figure 10. Comparison of successful client connection rate at the time of UDF Flood Attack on server with and without UDF Flood protection on Firewall

X-Axis: Attack load (Mbps)
Y-Axis: Connections per Second

Attack load (Mbps)	0	5	10	15	20	25	30	35	40	45	50	55	60
Without protection	600	600	600	596	510	284	97	1	0	0	0	0	0
With protection	600	600	600	600	536	412	373	120	17	0	0	0	0

Figure 10. Comparison of Connection rate with and without UDP-flood protection enabled on the NS-5GT security device.

of UDP-flood attack traffic. Whereas when the UDP-flood attack protection is enabled on the NS-5GT, the connection rate goes to zero at a little higher traffic load of 45 Mbps. The connection drop rate is found to be somewhat slower when the protection is enabled at the NS-5GT security device for lower attack loads (**Figure 10**). Overall the protection provided by the security device NS-5GT is marginal against prevention of the UDP flood attacks considered in this paper.

4. Conclusion

In this paper, we evaluated the performance of a Juniper Network security device NS-5GT to measure its effectiveness in providing protection against Layer-4 TCP-SYN and UDP based DDoS attacks. It was found that the protection provided by NS-5GT was capable in defending to some extent against lower loads of TCP-SYN and UDP based DDoS attacks, however at higher attack loads exceeding 40 Mbps, the NS-5GT security device was not capable of establishing client connections in the face of such flood attacks. Despite the security protection offered by the security device NS-5GT, the evaluation results showed the Juniper's security device NS-5GT to be of limited capability in preventing layer4 DDoS attacks. The Juniper Network security device NS-5GT, claimed to provide protection against TCP SYN attacks and UDP flood attacks, however the protection was measured to be not effective in defending against higher intensity of such attacks exceeding 40 Mbps. Before deploying a network security device to protect a critical information infrastructure, it is important for the network administra-

tors to seek actual performance evaluation results from the manufacturers to determine the actual capabilities of the Internet security devices in preventing against DDoS attacks.

5. Acknowledgements

This research work is based upon work supported in part by US National Science Foundation under Grant No. 0421585. Authors would like to thank Hari Vallelacheruvu and Sirisha Surisetty of the networking research lab for their helpful discussion and assistance with the experiments.

6. References

[1] "WikiLeaks Supporters Tear down VISA in DDoS Attack," December 9, 2010. http://www.digitaltrends.com/computing/wikileaks-supporters-tear-down-visa-in-ddos-attack/.

[2] Cnet news, "Twitter Crippled by Denial-of-Service Attack", 15 October 2010. http://news.cnet.com/8301-1357 7_3-10304633-36. html

[3] R. Richardson, "2008 CSI Computer Crime & Security Survey," CSI, 2008.

[4] "US Suspects N Korea Launched Internet Attack on July 4," 15 October 2010. http://ibnlive.in.com/news/us-sus-pects-n-korea-laun-ched-internettack-on-%20%20%20%20%20july-4/96715 -2.html

[5] "Computer Emergency Response Team (CERT)® Advisory CA-2001-20," 15 October 2010. http://www.cert.org/tech_tips/home_ networks.html

[6] "Computer Emergency Response Team (CERT)®,"

Trends in Denial of Service Attacks Technology. 15 October 2010. http:// www.cert.org/archive/pdf/DoS_trends.pdf

[7] C. Douligeris and A. Mitrokotsa, "DDOS Attacks and Defense Mechanisms: A Classification," *Proceedings of the 3rd IEEE International Symposium on Signal Processing and Information Technology*, 14-17 December 2003, pp. 190-193. doi:10.1109/ISSPIT.2003.1341092

[8] J. Mirkovic and P. Reiher. "A Taxonomy of DDoS Attacks and DDoS Defense Mechanisms," *ACM SIGCOMM Computer Communications Review*, Vol. 349, No. 2, April 2004, pp. 39-54. doi:10.1145/997150.997156

[9] S. Kumar, "Smurf Based Denial of Service Attack Amplification in Internet," *IEEE Computer Society*, ICIMP, 2007.

[10] M. R. Lyu and L. K. Y. Lau, "Firewall Security: Policies, Testing and Performance Evaluation," *The 24th Annual International Computer Software and Applications Conference*, Taipe, 25-27 October 2000, pp. 116-121.

[11] R. K. C. Chang "Defending Against Flooding-Based

Distributed Denial-of-Service Attacks: A Tutorial," *IEEE Communications*, Vol. 40, No. 10, April 2002, pp. 42-51. doi:10.1109/MCOM.2002.1039856

[12] S. Kumar, M. Azad, O. Gomez and R. Valdez, "Can Microsoft's Service Pack-2 (SP2) Security Software Prevents Smurf Attacks?" *Advanced International Conference on Telecommunications*, Guadeloupe, September 2006, pp. 89-93.

[13] S. Kumar and E. Petana, "Mitigation of TCP-SYN Attacks with Microsoft's Windows XP Service Pack2 (SP2) Software," *Seventh International Conference on Networking*, Cancun, 13-18 April 2008, pp. 238-242. doi: 10.1109/ICN.2008.77

[14] "Juniper Networks NetScreen NS 5GT Security Policy," 15 October 2010. http://csrc.nist.gov/groups/STM/cmvp/documents/140-1/140sp/140sp629.pdf

[15] Juniper Networks, Inc., "Attack Detection and Defense Mechanisms," 2008. http://www.juniper.net/techpubs/software/screenos/screenos5x/ce_v4_5_0.pdf

19

On Secure Digital Image Watermarking Techniques

Manjit Thapa[1], Sandeep Kumar Sood[2*]

[1]*Department of Computer Science, Sri Sai College of Engineering & Technonogy, Badhani, Pathankot, India*
[2]*Department of Computer Science and Engineering, G.N.D.U.R.C., Gurdaspur, Punjab, India*

Abstract

Digital watermarking is used to hide the information inside a signal, which can not be easily extracted by the third party. Its widely used application is copyright protection of digital information. It is different from the encryption in the sense that it allows the user to access, view and interpret the signal but protect the ownership of the content. One of the current research areas is to protect digital watermark inside the information so that ownership of the information cannot be claimed by third party. With a lot of information available on various search engines, to protect the ownership of information is a crucial area of research. In latest years, several digital watermarking techniques are presented based on discrete cosine transform (DCT), discrete wavelets transform (DWT) and discrete fourier transforms (DFT). In this paper, we propose an algorithm for digital image watermarking technique based on singular value decomposition; both of the L and U components are explored for watermarking algorithm. This technique refers to the watermark embedding algorithm and watermark extracting algorithm. The experimental results prove that the quality of the watermarked image is excellent and there is strong resistant against many geometrical attacks.

Keywords: Digital Image Watermarking, Singular Value Decomposition, Watermark Embedding Algorithm, Watermark Extracting Algorithm, Ratio Analysis, Security Analysis

1. Introduction

Digital watermarking is a technique that embeds data called watermark into a multimedia object so that watermark can be detected to make an assertion about the objects. It can be categorized as visible or invisible. Example of visible watermarking is the logo visible superimposed on the corner of television channel in a television picture. On the other hand, invisible watermark is hidden in the object, which can be detected by an authorized person. Such watermarks are used for suit the author authentication and detecting unauthorized copying. The novel technology of digital watermarking has been sponsored by many consultants as the best method for such multimedia copyright protection problem [1,2]. Digital watermarking is having a variety of useful applications such as digital cameras, medical imaging, image databases, video on demand systems, and many others. In recent years, many digital image watermarking techniques have been proposed in the literature which is based on spatial domain technique and frequency domain technique. These techniques are used in watermark em-

bedding algorithm and watermark extracting algorithm. In 2002, Ali [3] proposed an approach based on DWT and DCT to improve the performance of the DWT-based watermarking algorithms. In this method, watermarking is done by embedding the watermark in first and second level of DWT sub-bands of the host image, followed by the application of DCT on the selected DWT sub-bands. The combination of these two transforms improved the watermarking performance considerably in comparison with only watermarking approaches. They showed that the quality of watermark image is very good. In 2005, Chen [4] proposed a singular value decomposition scheme based on components of D and U without using DWT, DCT and DFT transforms. They showed that quality of watermarked image is good on their schemes. In 2007, Seed [5] introduced a novel digital watermarking method based on single key image for extracting different watermarks. In this method, they used Arnold transform technique in watermark embedding and extraction, which is based on DWT and DCT algorithm. With the popularity of internet and availability of large storage devices, storing and transferring an image is simple and feasible. They showed that robustness of the algorithm against many signal processing operations. In 2010, Lamma and Ali [6] suggested two blind, imperceptible and robust video watermarking algorithms that are based on singular value decomposition. Each algorithm integrates the watermark in the transform domain. They used the components of matrices such as U and V. Their schemes are shown to provide very good performance in watermarked video as compared to Chan [4].

Most of the domain transformation watermarking techniques works with DCT and DWT. However singular value decomposition (SVD) is one of the most powerful numeric analysis techniques and used in various requirements. These requirements can be organized and described as follows [7-10].

Undeletable: An embedded watermark is difficult to detect and cannot be removed by an illegal person. Also the algorithm must resist different attacks.

Perceptually visible: The original images and watermarked images cannot be distinguished by the human eye. This means that there is not enough alteration of a watermarked image to prevent motivation to an illegal person.

Unambiguous: An embedded watermark selected from a watermarked image that must be clear enough for ownership to be determined. In this way, the extracted watermark cannot be distorted to such an extent that the original watermark cannot be recognized.

In this paper, we will describe a digital image watermarking algorithm based on singular value decomposition technique. This paper is organized as follows. In Section 2, we introduce the SVD transformation and SVD based watermarking techniques briefly. In Section 3, we propose the embedding and extracting algorithm. In Section 4, we evaluate the performance of watermark image. In section 5, we show the experimental results and Section 6 conclude the paper.

2. A Review of Related Work

Singular value decomposition (SVD) is a mathematical technique based on linear algebra and used by factorization of a real matrix or complex matrix, with many useful applications in signal processing and statistics.

2.1. Singular Value Decomposition (SVD)

Singular value decomposition is one of a number of valuable numerical analysis tools which is used to analyze matrices. It can be appeared from three jointly compatible points of view. On the other hand, we can see it as a method for transforming correlated variables into a set of uncorrelated ones that better expose the various

relationships among the original data items. At the same time, SVD is a method for identifying and ordering the dimensions along which data points demonstrate the most variation. This attach the third way of viewing singular value decomposition, which accepted the most variation, it's possible to find the best approximation of the original data points using less dimensions. Hence, SVD can be seen as a method for data reduction. In SVD transformation, a matrix can be decayed into three matrices that are having the same size as the original matrix. It is useful to establish a contrast with Gaussian elimination and its equation. Given A is a $n \times n$ square matrix, this matrix can be decomposed into three components, L, D and U, respectively such that

$$[L\ D\ U] = SVD\ (A),\ A' = LDU^T,\quad L^{-1}\ \text{where } A = LDU.$$

$$\begin{pmatrix} l_{1,1} & l_{1,2} & l_{1,n} \\ l_{2,1} & l_{2,2} & l_{2,n} \\ l_{3,1} & l_{3,2} & l_{3,n} \end{pmatrix} \begin{pmatrix} \sigma_{1,1} & \sigma_{1,2} & \sigma_{1,n} \\ \sigma_{2,1} & \sigma_{2,2} & \sigma_{2,n} \\ \sigma_{3,1} & \sigma_{3,2} & \sigma_{3,n} \end{pmatrix}$$

$$\begin{pmatrix} u_{1,1} & u_{1,2} & u_{1,n} \\ u_{2,1} & u_{2,2} & u_{2,n} \\ u_{3,1} & u_{3,2} & u_{3,n} \end{pmatrix} = \sum_{i=1}^{n} \sigma_i l_i u_i^T \quad (1)$$

where the L and U components are real unitary matrices or complex matrices with small singular values, and the D component is an $n \times n$ diagonal matrix with larger singular value or eigen vector values entries which specify $\sigma_{1,1} >> \sigma_{2,2} >> \cdots \sigma_{k,k+1} = \cdots \sigma_{n,n} = 0$. $\sum$ are non zero matrix by diagonals of A. SVD is nonlinear because the orthogonal matrices L and U depend on A and shown in Equation (1). A' is the reconstructed matrix after the inverse SVD transformation. Reduced singular value decomposition is the mathematical technique underlying a type of document retrieval and word semblance method. These are also known as Latent Semantic Indexing or Latent Semantic Analysis. In this way, the three components of matrices L, D, and U specify $Au_i = \sigma_i l_i$ and $\mu_i^T A = \sigma_i u_i^T$.

SVD Example

A matrix is said to be square if it has the same number of rows as columns. To designate the size of a square matrix with n rows and columns, it is called n-square matrix. For example, the matrix below is 3-square. As an example to simplify SVD transformation, suppose

$$A = \begin{pmatrix} 10 & 21 & 15 \\ 30 & 9 & 23 \\ 18 & 53 & 29 \end{pmatrix}$$

If SVD operation is useful on this matrix, then the matrix A will be decomposed into equivalent three matrices as follows:

$$L = \begin{pmatrix} -0.4019 & 0.1202 & -0.9079 \\ -0.4749 & -0.8749 & 0.9417 \\ -0.7830 & 0.4690 & 0.4083 \end{pmatrix},$$

$$D = \begin{pmatrix} 68.5399 & 0 & 0 \\ 0 & 24.2485 & 0 \\ 0 & 0 & 0.5342 \end{pmatrix},$$

$$U = \begin{pmatrix} -0.4492 & -0.7233 & 0.5242 \\ -0.6995 & 0.6498 & 0.2972 \\ -0.5557 & -0.2332 & -0.7979 \end{pmatrix}$$

Here diagonal elements of matrix D are singular values and we observe that these values satisfy the non increasing order: $68.5399 \geq 24.2485 \geq 0.5342$.

Digital image watermarking techniques has several advantages that used singular value decomposition. Firstly, SVD transformation from the size of memory is not fixed and can be represented by a rectangle or square matrices. Secondly, SVD increase accuracy and decrease the memory requirement. Thirdly, digital images in singular values are less affected if general image watermark is executed. Fourth, singular value decomposition include by algebraic properties.

2.2. SVD-Transformation

We will describe a digital image watermarking technique which is based on singular value decomposition transform, such as DWT and DCT. Watermarking is established by the wavelet coefficient of selected sub bands and followed by the requirements of DCT transform on the selected sub-bands [11-14]. In this section, we will introduce the transformation of digital watermarking technique.

The DCT Transform: The discrete cosine transform is a transformation technique based on digital watermarking algorithm and spatial domain technique. The discrete cosine transform is derived from discrete Fourier transforms and represents data in terms of frequency space rather than an amplitude space. The spatial domain technique can be transformed into the frequency domain, and the frequency domain technique can be transformed back to the spatial domain by using inverse discrete cosine transform. The discrete cosine transform (DCT) is a technique for converting a signal into effortless frequency components. It represents an image as a sum of sinusoids of varying magnitudes and frequencies. With an input image, k and the DCT coefficients for the transformed output image, L is computed according to Equation (2) as shown below. In the equation, k, is the input image having $N \times M$ pixels, $k(m, n)$ is the intensity of the pixel in row m and column n of the image and $L(u, v)$ is

the DCT coefficient in row u and column v of the DCT matrix. The DCT formulas are as follows.

The general equation for a one dimension (N data items) DCT is defined by the following equation:

$$L(u) = \sqrt{\frac{2}{M}} \beta m \sum_{x=0}^{M-1} \frac{\cos(2m+1)\pi u}{2M} k(m) \qquad (2)$$

and the corresponding inverse 1D DCT transform is simple $L^{-1}(u)$
where

$$\beta m = \begin{cases} \dfrac{1}{\sqrt{2}} & u = 0 \\ 1 & u = 1, 2, \text{ otherwise} \end{cases}$$

The βm function computes the two-dimensional discrete cosine transform (DCT) of an image. The DCT has the property that, for a typical image, most of the visually significant information about the image is concentrated in just a few coefficients of the DCT. For this reason, the DCT is often used in image compression applications. The general equation for a 2D (N by M image) DCT is defined by the following Equation (3):

$$L(u,v) = \sqrt{\frac{2}{M}} \sqrt{\frac{2}{N}} \beta m \beta n$$
$$\sum_{x=0}^{M-1} \sum_{y=0}^{N-1} \frac{\cos(2m+1)\pi u}{2M} \frac{\cos(2n+1)\pi u}{2N} k(m,n) \qquad (3)$$

and the corresponding inverse 2D DCT transform is simple $L^{-1}(u, v)$, i.e.:
where

$$\beta m = \begin{cases} \dfrac{1}{\sqrt{2}} & u = 0 \\ 1 & u = 1, 2, \cdots, M-1 \end{cases}$$

$$\beta n = \begin{cases} \dfrac{1}{\sqrt{2}} & v = 0 \\ 1 & v = 1, 2, \cdots, N-1 \end{cases}$$

The image is reconstructed by applying inverse DCT operation according to Equation (4):

$$K(m,n) = \sqrt{\frac{2}{M}} \sqrt{\frac{2}{N}} \beta m \beta n$$
$$\sum_{u=0}^{M-1} \sum_{v=0}^{N-1} \frac{\cos(2m+1)\pi u}{2M} \frac{\cos(2n+1)\pi u}{2N} l(u,v) \qquad (4)$$

Examples for Transformation: The grayscale Lena image of 256×256 pixels, with 4-bit representation for each pixel is used as the test input. The input image is divided into 4-by-4 or 8-by-8 blocks, and the two-dimensional DCT is computed for each block. The DCT coefficients are then quantized, coded, and transmitted.

The JPEG receiver (or JPEG file reader) decodes the quantized DCT coefficients, computes the inverse two-dimensional DCT of each block, and then puts the blocks back together into a single image. For typical images, many of the DCT coefficients have values close to zero; these coefficients can be discarded without seriously affecting the quality of the reconstructed image as shown in **Figure 1**. The transform matrix computation method is used. The test image was compressed to different scales, from one to three and the compression ratio as well as the mean square root error of the reconstructed image were calculated for minimal error case and quantised case.

The popular block-based DCT transform segments is an image non-overlapping blocks and applies DCT to each block. This result in giving three frequency coefficient sets: low frequency sub-band, mid frequency sub-band, and high frequency sub band. The digital watermarking based on two facts. The first fact is that much of the signal energy lies at low- frequency sub-band which includes the most important visual parts of the image. The second fact is that high frequency components of the image are generally detached through compression and noise attacks. The watermark is surrounded by modifying the coefficients of the middle frequency sub-band so that the visibility of the image will not be overstated and the watermark will not be removed by compression.

Discrete Wavelet Transform: The transformation product is a set of coefficients organized in the way that enables not only spectrum analyses of the signal, but also spectral behavior of the signal in time. This is achieved by decomposing signal, breaking it into two components, each concerned information about source signal. Filters from the filter bank used for decomposition come in pairs: low pass and high pass. Low pass filtered signal contains information about slow changing component of the signal, looking very similar to the original signal, only two times shorter in term of number of samples. High pass filtered signal be full of information about fast

changing component of the signal. In most cases, high pass component is not so rich with data offering good property for compression. In some cases, such as audio or video signal, it is possible to contend with some of the samples of the high pass component without noticing any significant changes in signal. Filters from the filter bank are called wavelets and as shown in **Figure 2**.

For 2-D images, applying DWT corresponds to processing the image by 2-D filters in each dimension. The filters divide the input image into four non-overlapping multi-resolution sub-bands LL_1, LH_1, HL_1 and HH_1. The sub-band LL_1 represents the coarse-scale DWT coefficients while the sub-bands LH_1, HL_1 and HH_1 represent the fine-scale of DWT coefficients. To obtain the next coarser scale of wavelet coefficients, the sub-band LL_1 is further processed until some final scale N is reached. When N is reached we will have $3N + 1$ sub-bands consisting of the multi-resolution sub-bands LL_y and LH_y, HL_y and HH_y where y ranges from 1 until N. It has the following steps in digital image watermarking transformation such as

Step 1: Present DWT on the original image to decompose it into four non-overlapping multi-resolution coefficient sets, such as LL_1, HL_1, LH_1 and HH_1.

Step 2: Present DWT again on two HL_1 and LH_1 sub-bands to get eight smaller sub-bands and prefer four coefficient sets: HL_{12}, LH_{12}, HL_{22} and LH_{22} as shown in **Figure 1**.

Figure 1. Reconstructed image, compression image and quantization image by using DCT.

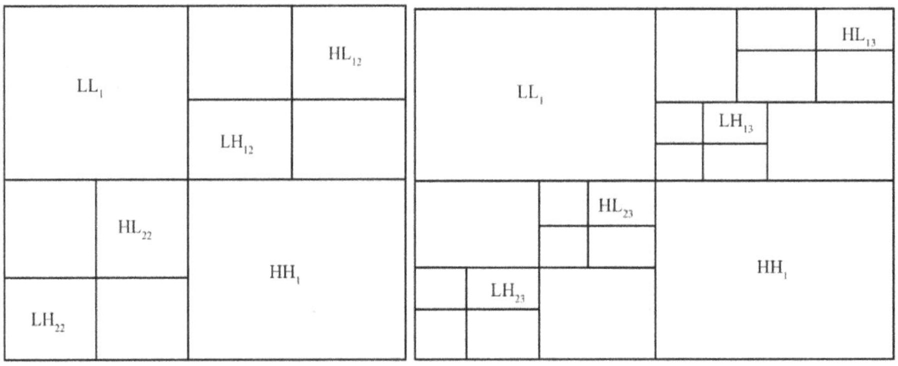

Figure 2. Sketch map of DWT and DCT decomposed sub-bands.

Step 3: Present DWT again on four sub-bands, such as HL$_{12}$, LH$_{12}$, HL$_{22}$ and LH$_{22}$ to get sixteen smaller coefficient sets and prefer four coefficient sets, such as HL$_{13}$, LH$_{13}$, HL$_{13}$ and LH$_{13}$ as shown in **Figure 1**.

Step 4: Divide four coefficient sets such as HL$_{13}$, LH$_{13}$, HL$_{23}$ and LH$_{23}$ into 4 × 4 blocks.

Step 5: Present DCT to each block in the chosen sub-bands (HL$_{13}$, LH$_{13}$, HL$_{23}$ and LH$_{23}$). These coefficient sets are chosen to inquire both of imperceptibility and strength of algorithm equally.

The DWT is very suitable to identify the areas in the original image where a watermark can be embedded effectively. This property allows the utilization of the masking effect of the human visual system such that if a DWT coefficient is modified, only the region corresponding to that coefficient will be modified. In general most of the image energy is concentrated at the lower frequency sub-bands LLx and therefore embedding watermarks in these sub-bands may humiliate the image appreciably. Embedding in the low frequency sub-bands, however, could increase robustness appreciably. On the other hand, the high frequency sub-bands HHx include the edges and textures of the image and the human eye is not generally sensitive to changes in such sub-bands. This allows the watermark to be embedded without being superficial by the human eye. The compromise accepted by many DWT-based watermarking algorithm, is to embed the watermark in the middle frequency sub-bands LHy and HLy where good enough performance of imperceptibility and robustness could be achieved.

3. Proposed Watermarking Techniques

We proposed a singular value decomposition technique and quantization based watermarking technique. The watermarking techniques can be represented by three components, L, D and U. It relies on row and column operations. Row operations involve pre-multiplying matrix and column operations involve post-multiplying matrix. The D component can be explored with a diagonal matrix. These techniques depend upon the watermark embedding algorithm and watermark extracting algorithm.

3.1. Watermark Embedding Algorithm

The digital image watermarking algorithm can be followed by singular value decomposition techniques, which involve the characteristics of the D and U components. In the embedding algorithm, the largest coefficients in D component were customized and used to embed a watermark. The adaptation was determined by the quantization method. We will start the algorithm by applying

SVD transformation on original image and to reconstruct the watermarked image. Because the largest coefficients in the D component can oppose with general image processing, the embedded watermark was not really affected. In this way, the quality of the watermarked image can be decomposed by quantization method. In our inspection, two important features of the D and U components are found. In the first feature, the number of non zero coefficients in the D component could be used to determine the complexity of a matrix. Commonly, the greater number of the non-zero coefficient can be specified by greater complexity. In the second feature, the relationship between the coefficients in the first column of the L component could be sealed, when usually image processing was presented as shown in **Figure 3**. The watermarks embedding algorithm can be described as follows.

Step 1: Read the original host image.

Step 2: Partition the image into blocks of n × n pixels.

Examples: Perform combination of two filters as prefiltering operation. The first filter is 3 × 3 sharpening filter which is defined as Equation (5).

$$\begin{pmatrix} 0 & -1 & 0 \\ -1 & 3 & -1 \\ 0 & -1 & 0 \end{pmatrix} \tag{5}$$

This filter enhances contrast of watermarked image. The second filter is designed by Laplacian of Gaussian filter and defined by general equation as 6.

$$G(x) = \frac{1}{\sqrt{2\pi\sigma^2}} e^{-\frac{x^2}{2\sigma^2}} \tag{6}$$

The Gaussian blur is types of image-blurring filter that uses a Gaussian function (which also expresses the normal distribution in statistics) for calculating the transformation to apply to each pixel in the image as shown by Equation (7).

$$G(x,y) = \frac{1}{2\pi\sigma^2} e^{-\frac{x^2+y^2}{2\sigma^2}} \tag{7}$$

where x is the distance from the origin in the horizontal axis, y is the distance from the origin in the vertical axis, and σ is the standard deviation of the Gaussian distribution. The default value for them in $g = 4$ and $\sigma = 0.5$.

Performing these two filters on watermarked image could caused details of image become more visible, its means that watermark information which is different from image background become recognizable uncomplicatedly.

Step 3: Perform singular value decomposition (SVD) transformation.

Step 4: Extract the greater coefficient D(1, 1) from each D component and quantize by using a predefined quantization coefficients A. Suppose that S = D(1, 1) mod A.

Step 5: Perform embed the two pseudo-random sequences PN0, PN1, that is applied to the mid-band coefficients. If A is the matrix of the mid band coefficients of SVD transformed block, then embedding is done as follows:

If the watermark bit is 0 then,
D′(1, 1) = D(1, 1) + K/4 − A, so that [A < 3K/4]

Otherwise, if the watermark bit is 1 then,
D′(1, 1) = D(1, 1) −K/4 + A, so that [A < K/4]

Step 6: Perform the inverse of singular value decomposition transformation to reform the watermarked image.

3.2. Watermark Extracting Algorithm

The watermark extracting algorithm is similar to the watermark embedding algorithm. Extraction algorithm is the same as embedding and pre-filtering is used before applying SVD transform to superior split watermark information from original image. The watermark extraction algorithm is performed as described by the following steps. The first three steps of the watermark extracting algorithms are same as the watermark embedding algorithm except that the original image is replaced with the watermarked image. Previously, an embedded block is detected according to the feature of the D component and PRNG, the relationship of the U component coefficients is observed. If a positive relationship is detected, the extracted watermark has assigned a bit value of 1. Otherwise, the extracted watermark has assigned a bit value of 0. These extracted bit values convert the original image SVD from the extracted watermark. The extracted watermark can be specified by original watermarked image and as shown in **Figure 4**.

Step 1: Read the watermarked image.

Step 2: watermarked it into blocks of n × n pixels.

Step 3: Perform the SVD transformation.

Step 4: Extract the greater coefficients D″(1, 1) from each D component and quantize by using a predefined quantization coefficients A. Suppose that S = D′(1, 1) mod A.

Step 5: Regenerate the two pseudo random sequences number using the same key, which is used in the watermark embedding algorithm.

Step 6: For an extraction watermark bit valued of zero, if A < K/2. On the other hand, the extraction watermark bit value of one, if A > K/2.

Step 7: The watermark is restructured using the ex-

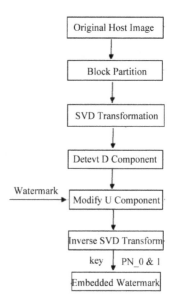

Figure 3. Flow chart for watermark embedding algorithm.

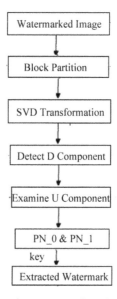

Figure 4. Flow chart for watermark embedding algorithm.

tracted watermark bits, and compute the similarity between the original watermark and extracted watermarks.

4. Performance Evaluation

We evaluated the performance of the SVD image watermarking algorithms. The performance of the watermarking methods can be measured by imperceptibility and robust capabilities. Imperceptibility means that the superficial quality of the original image should not be distorted by the presence of watermark image and as shown by Equation (8). On the other hand, the robustness is a measure of the intentionally attacks and unintentionally attacks. It was found that the image quality measured by peak signal to noise ratio among the watermarked images was larger than 42 db [15]. This peak signal to noise ratio is defined as

$$PSNR(o,o^1) = 10\log_{10}\left(\frac{255\times255}{\sum_{i=1}^{m}\sum_{j=1}^{n}\frac{1}{xy}\left(o-o^1\right)^2}\right) \quad (8)$$

The PSNR is employed to evaluate the difference between an original image o and watermarked image o^1. For the robust capability, mean absolute error (MSE) measures the difference between an original watermark W and corresponding extracted watermark W^1 as shown by Equation (9).

$$MSE(w^0,w^1) = \sum_{i=0}^{d}\left(\frac{w^0-w^1}{w}\right) \quad (9)$$

Generally, if PSNR value is larger than 40 db the watermarked image is within acceptable degradation levels, *i.e.* the watermarked is almost invisible to human visual system. A lower mean absolute error reveals that the extracted watermark w^0 resembles the w^1 more closely. The strength of digital watermarking method is accessed from the watermarked image o^1, which is further degraded by attacks and the digital watermarking performance of proposed method is compared with that of Chen [4]. If a method has a lower $MSE(w^0, w^1)$, it is more robust.

5. Experimental Results

The experimental results are simulated with the software MATLAB 7.10 version. It provides a single platform for computation, visualization, programming and software development. All problems and solutions in Matlab are expressed in notation used in linear algebra and essentially involve operations using matrices and vectors. We are using a 256 × 256 "Lena", "facial", and "Moon" as the gray scale original host image, and a 256 × 256 greyscale image of the watermark image. The three images are shown in **Figures 5** and **6** respectively. In the proposed method, we select the largest complexity of blocks; the original images can be separated into blocks

of 4 × 4 pixels. Each block can be transformed into L, D, and U components by singular value decomposition. And then, a set of blocks with the same size as the watermark was selected, according to the feature of the D component. For an embedding watermark block, the relationship between the L component coefficients can be examined and the coefficients were modified, according to the watermark to be embedded. In our experiment, the original image and watermarked image quality is shown in **Figure 5**.

We claimed the embedding algorithm and extracting algorithm to identify the ownership of the original watermarked image as shown in **Tables 1** and **2**. We can see that the performance of our algorithm against the different attacks. Further, the proposed watermarking algorithm can be used for protecting the copyright of digital images. It can be observed from **Tables 1** and **2** that the future method provides excellent results in the geometrical attacks.

Simulation results suggest that this digital watermarking algorithm is robust against many common different types of attacks such as cropping attacks, pyramid at-

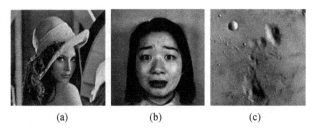

(a)   (b)   (c)

Figure 5. Three original images of 256 × 256 pixels (a) The original lena image (b) The original facial image (c) The original moon image.

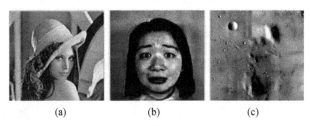

(a)   (b)   (c)

Figure 6. Three watermarked images of 256 × 256 pixels (a) The watermarked lena image; (b) The watermarked facial image; (c) The watermarked moon image.

Table 1. The experimental results of the error ratio of the embedded watermark after different attacks by proposed method.

Images Type	Without Attacks	Cropping Attacks	Pyramid Attacks	Rotation Attacks	Noise Attacks	Blurring Attacks	PSNR (DB)
Lena Image	29.2752	38.7569	45.3102	30.0444	26.8879	29.2752	$\alpha = 0.2$
Facial Image	29.9337	35.2695	46.3784	31.3159	26.5601	29.9337	$\alpha = 0.2$
Moon Image	24.0375	36.3759	42.8253	26.2853	24.0375	24.0375	$\alpha = 0.2$

Table 2. The experimental results of the error ratio of the extracted watermark after different attacks by the proposed method.

Images Type	Without Attacks	Cropping Attacks	Pyramid Attacks	Rotation Attacks	Noise Attacks	Blurring Attacks	PSNR (DB)
Lena Image	272.2211	279.3277	282.3816	273.8656	283.2165	272.2217	$\alpha = 0.2$
Facial Image	284.1641	283.9997	280.3740	285.8853	279.7679	284.1641	$\alpha = 0.2$
Moon Image	275.1305	271.2818	287.8321	278.3293	275.1305	275.1305	$\alpha = 0.2$

tacks, rotation attacks, and noise attacks and blurring attacks **Figures 7-12**. However, cropping is a geometrical manipulation and rotation is a geometrical distortion in practical application. If alpha's value is more than 0.2 then quality of original image and watermarked image is not good. So we are using the dumpy value in these techniques.

We are using the different coefficent of parameters by proposed method based on digital image watermarking embedding algorithm and extracting algorithm as a shown by **Tables 3** and **4**. Its depends upon the security analysis and as shown in **Figures 13-30**. The parameters are to be satisfying by E1, E2 and E3.

E1 is the parameter of "Lena Image",
E2 is the parameter of "Facial Image" and
E3 is the parameter of "Moon Image".

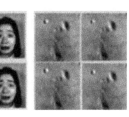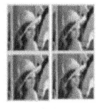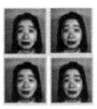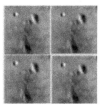

Figure 7. Grey level of original image and watermarked image under without attacks and the corresponding qualities: (a) Lena (29.2752 db), (272.2211 db), (b) Facial (29.9337 db), (284.1641 db), (c) Moon (24.0375 db), (275.1305 db).

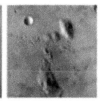

Figure 8. Grey level of original image and watermarked image under cropping attacks and the corresponding qualities: (a) Lena (38.7569 db), (279.3277 db), (b) Facial (35.2695 db), (283.9997 db), (c) Moon (36.3759 db), (271.2718 db).

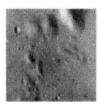

Figure 9. Grey level of original image and watermarked image under pyramid attacks and the corresponding qualities: (a) Lena (45.3102 db), (288.3216 db), (b) Facial (46.3784 db), (280.3740 db) (c) Moon (42.8253 db), (287.8721 db).

Figure 10. Grey level of original image and wtaremarked image under rotation attacks and the corresponding qualities: (a) Lena (30.0444 db), 273.8656 (db), (b) Facial (31.3159 db), 285.8853 (db) (c) Moon (26.2853 db), 278.3293(db).

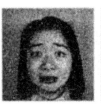

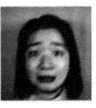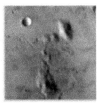

Figure 11. Grey level of original image and watermarked image under noise attacks and the corresponding qualities: (a) Lena (26.8879 db), 283.2165 (db) (b) Facial (26.5601 db), 279.7678 (db) (c) Moon (24.0375 db), 275.1305 (db).

Figure 12. Grey level of original image and watermarked image under blurred attacks and the corresponding qualities: (a) Lena (26.8879 db), 272.2217 (db), (b) Facial (26.5601 db), 284.1641 (db), (c) Moon (24.0375 db), 275.1305 (db).

Table 3. A similarity between coefficients of original image and watermarked image using different parameters by proposed method under embedded algorithm.

Coefficent of Parameters	Without Attacks	Cropping Attacks	Pyramid Attacks	Rotation Attacks	Noise Attacks	Blurring Attacks	PSNR (DB)
E1	29.2753	38.7691	29.2752	30.4487	27.4361	23.5507	$\alpha = 0.2$
E2	29.9334	35.3072	38.4104	10.0200	27.5376	29.9347	$\alpha = 0.2$
E3	24.0375	36.3290	24.0375	11.1151	12.4233	23.5507	$\alpha = 0.2$

Table 4. A similarity between coefficients of original image and watermarked image using different parameters by proposed method under extracted algorithm.

Coefficent of Parameters	Without Attacks	Cropping Attacks	Pyramid Attacks	Rotation Attacks	Noise Attacks	Blurring Attacks	PSNR (DB)
E1	272.2212	279.3657	272.2212	273.8651	271.7452	272.4247	$\alpha = 0.2$
E2	241.1641	285.0083	278.8258	284.1675	284.8783	284.1667	$\alpha = 0.2$
E3	275.1305	291.1681	275.5309	275.1345	273.5305	276.7801	$\alpha = 0.2$

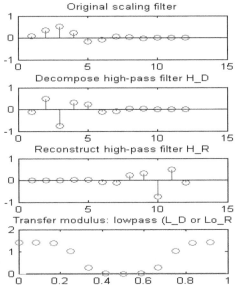

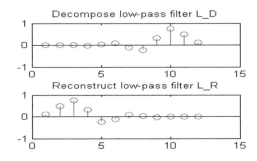

Figure 13. A similarity between coefficents of original watermarked image under without attacks: (a) Lena without attacks (29.2753 db), (272.2212 db).

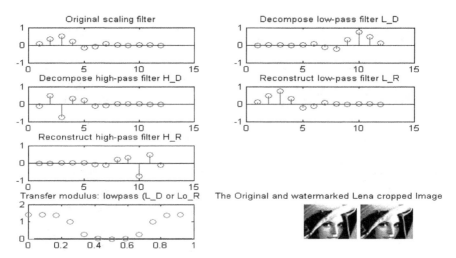

Figure 14. A similarity between coefficents of original watermarked image under cropping attacks: (a) Lena cropped attacks (38.7691 db, 279.3657db).

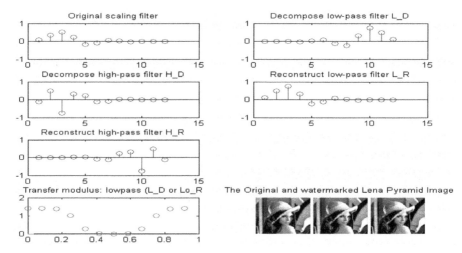

Figure 15. A similarity between coefficents of original watermarked image under pyramid attacks: (a) Lena pyramid attacks (29.2752), (272.2212 db).

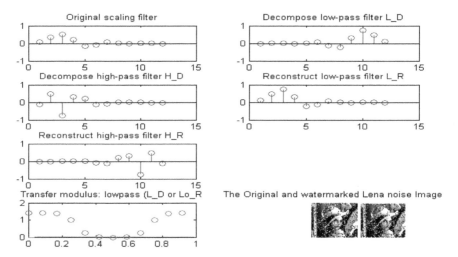

Figure 16. A similarity between coefficents of original watermarked image under noise attacks: (a) Noise attacks (27.4361 db), (271.7452 db).

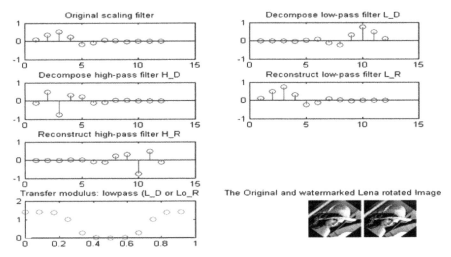

Fgure 17. A similarity between coefficents of original watermarked image under rotated attacks: (a) Lena rotated attacks (30.4487 db), (273.865 db).

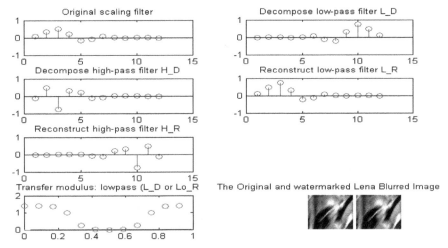

Figure 18. A similarity between coefficents of original watermarked image under blurring attacks: (a) Lena blurring attacks (23.5507 db), (272.4247 db).

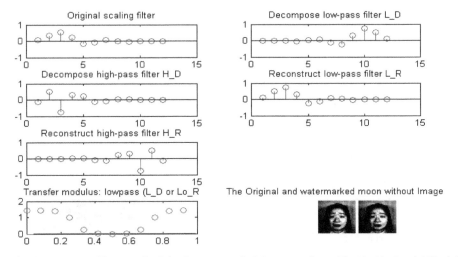

Figure 19. A similarity between coefficents of original watermarked image under without attacks: (a) Facial without attacks (29.9337 db), (284.1641 db).

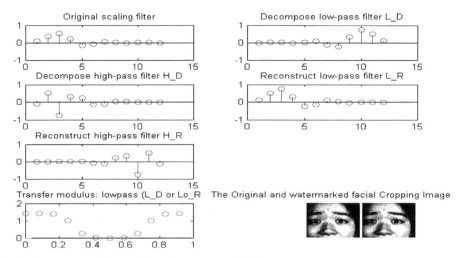

Figure 20. A similarity between coefficents of original watermarked image under cropped attacks: (a) Facial cropped attacks (35.3072 db), (285.0083 db).

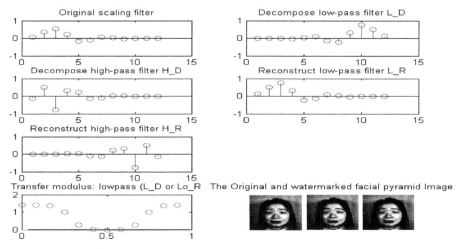

Figure 21. A similarity between coefficents of original watermarked image under pyramid attacks: (a) Facial pyramid attacks (38.4104 db), (278.8258 db).

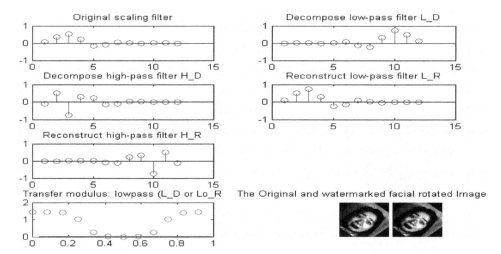

Figure 22. A similarity between coefficents of original watermarked image under rotated attacks: (a) Facial rotated attacks (10.0200 db), (284.1675 db).

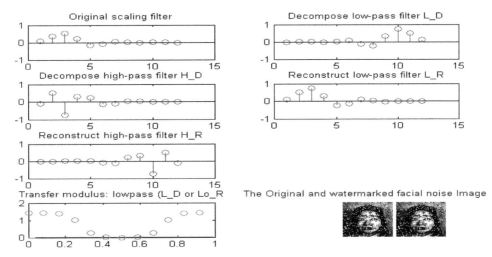

Figure 23. A similarity between coefficents of original watermarked image under noise attacks: (a) Facial noise attacks (27.5376 db), (284.8483 db).

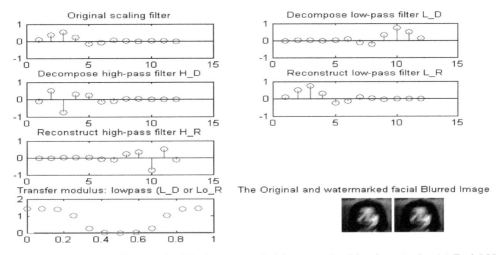

Figure 24. A similarity between coefficents of original watermarked image under blurring attacks: (a) Facial blurred attacks (29.9347 db), (284.1667 db).

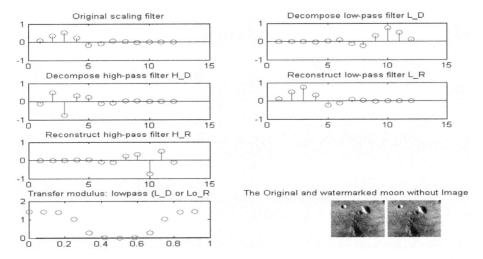

Figure 25. A similarity between coefficents of original watermarked image under without attacks (a) Moon without attacks (24.0375 db), (275.1305 db).

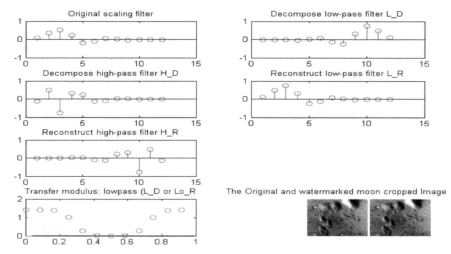

Figure 26. A similarity between coefficents of original watermarked image under cropped attacks: (a) Moon cropped attacks (36.329 db), (291.1681 db).

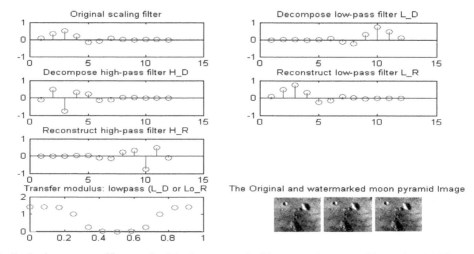

Figure 27. A similarity between coefficents of original watermarked image under pyramid attacks: (a) Moon pyramid attacks (24.0375 db), (275.5309 db).

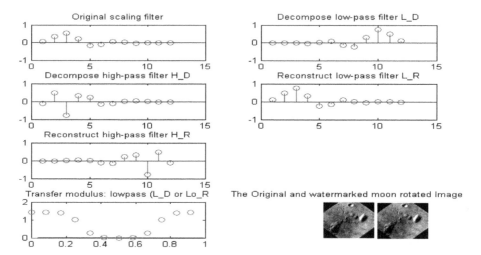

Figure 28. A similarity between coefficents of original watermarked image under rotated attacks: (a) Moon rotated attacks (12.4233 db), (273.5305 db).

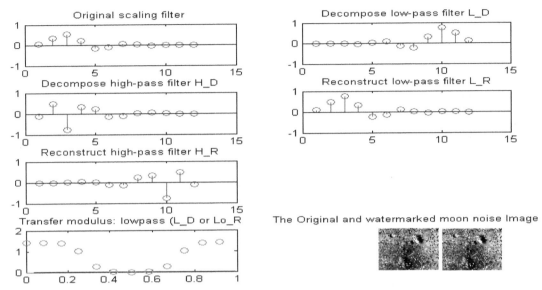

Figure 29. A similarity between coefficents of original watermarked image under noise attacks: (a) Moon noise attacks (11.1151 db), (274.1345 db).

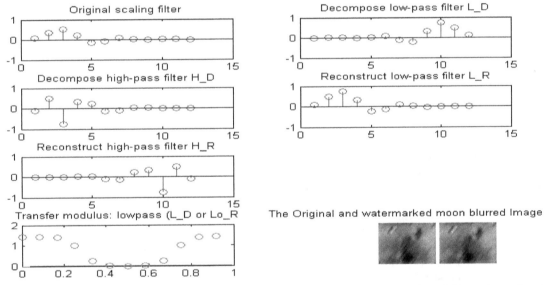

Figure 30. A similarity between coefficents of original watermarked image under without and blurred attacks: (a) Moon blurred attacks (23.5507 db), (276.7801 db).

In this way, we designed a singular value decomposition algorithm based on digital image watermarking technique and are to be following by this **Figure 31**.

6. Conclusions

Digital watermarking is one of emerging area of research. In this paper, we proposed a digital image watermarking algorithm based on singular value decomposition. The algorithm is used for watermarking embedding and watermark extraction. The feautre of the D component and the realation ship between the U Component coefficents

were explored in the proposed technique that provide stronger robustness against different attacks and better image quality. So, Digital image watermarking techniques are secure on this algorithm. If alpha has a less than 0.2 value then quality of the original image and watermarked image is good. The experimental results also recognized the effectiveness of the proposed technique. Because of these properties, SVD is used for DCT, DFT, and DWT transformations, and one-way non-symmetrical decomposition. These provide the advantages of various sizes of transformation and more security. That is a good performance of the proposed scheme both in

```
%Embedding Watermarked Image
clear;
clc
% Read Original Image
img= imread('filename');
img=imresize(img,[size]);
[X,Y]=size(img);
img=double(img);
[Limg,Dimg,Uimg]=svd(img);
Dimg_temp=Dimg;
% Read Watermark Image
Img = imread('filename');
img =imresize(img ,[size]);
% Cropping Image
img = imcrop(rect);
% Pyramid Image
img = impyramid(img,'direction');
imshow(img)
% Rotation Image
img = mat2gray(img);
img = imrotate(img, angle, method, 'box');
% Noise Image
I= double(imread('circles.png'));
Img = imnoise(img,'salt & pepper',.2);
% Blurring Image
LEN = [ ];
THETA =[ ];
PSF = fspecial('motion',LEN,THETA);
Blurred=imfilter(img,PSF,'circular',');
img_wat= imnoise(img,'salt & pepper',.[ ]);
figure; imshow(Blurred);
% Input Alpha
alfa= input('The alfa Value = ');
[x y]=size(img_wat);
img_wat=double(img_wat);
```

```
% SVD for Simg
[L_SHL_w,D_SHL_w,U_SHL_w]=svd
(Dimg);
Wimg =Limg* D_SHL_w * Uimg';
% Show Image
figure(1)
imshow(uint8(img_wat));
title('The watermarked Image')
figure(2)
imshow(uint8(img_wat));
title('The Watermark ')
figure(3)
imshow(uint8(Blurred));
title('The Watermark ')
figure(4)
% Extraction Watermarked Image
% Read Watermark Image
Img = imgread(''filename');
% SVD for Wimg (WM)
[LWimg,DWimg,UWimg]=svd(Wimg);
D_1=L_SHL_w * DWimg * U_SHL_w';
for i=1:x
for j=1:y
Watermark(i,j)=          (D_1(i,j)    -
Dimg_temp(i,j) )/alfa ;
end
end
Calculate Image Quality humiliation after
inserting watermark
mse=mean(squeeze(sum(sum((double(im
g)-double(Wimg)).^2))/(X*Y)));
PSNR=10*log10(A^2./mse);
msg=sprintf('n n--------------------
nWatermark by
disp(msg);
```

Figure 31. SVD algorithm

terms of robustness and security.

7. References

[1] D. Kundur and D. Hatzinakos, "Digital Watermarking Using Multiresolution Wavelet Decomposition," *Speech and Signal Processing Proceedings*, Acoustics, 1997, pp. 2969-2972.

[2] P. Zeng and C. Jin, "Image Adaptive Watermarking Using Visual Models," *IEEE Journal on Selected Areas in Communications*, Vol. 16, No. 4, 1998, pp. 525-539.

[3] L. Rajab, T. Khatib and A. Haj, "Combined DWT-DCT Digital Image Watermarking," *Journal of Computer Science*, Vol. 3, 2002, pp. 740-749.

[4] C. C. Chang and P. Tsai, "SVD-based Digital Image Watermarking Scheme," *Pattern Recognition Letters*, Vol. 26, No. 10, 2005, pp. 1577-1586.

[5] T. V. Nguyen and J. C. Patra, "A Simple ICA Based Digital Image Watermarking Scheme," *Digital Signal Processing*, Vol. 18, No. 5, 2007, pp. 762-776.

[6] A. H. Ali and M. Ahmad, "Digital Audio Watermarking Based on the Discrete Wavelets Transform and Singular Value Decomposition," *Europe Journal of Science Research*, Vol. 39, No. 1, 2010, pp. 6-21.

[7] C. I. Podilchuk and E. J. Delp, "Digital Watermarking: Algorithms and Applications," *IEEE Signal Processing Magazine*, Vol. 18, No. 4, 2001, pp. 33-46.

[8] B. Kim, J. G. Choi and D. Min, "Robust Digital Watermarking Method Against Geometric Attacks," *Real Time Imaging Processing*, Vol. 9, No. 2, 2003, pp. 139-149.

[9] H. Tina, W. Lu, R. prawn and Y. Ming, "A Fragile Watermarking Scheme for 3D Meshes," MM-SEC'05, ACM, pp. 117-123, 2008.

[10] W. Loo and X. Kingsbury, "Digital Watermarking using Complex Wavelets," *International Conference on Image Processing*, Vol. 3, 1999, pp. 29-32.

[11] M. Jiansheng and L. Sukang, "A Digital Watermarking Algorithm Based on DCT and DWT," *International Symposium on Web Information System and Application (WISA)*, 2009, pp. 104-107.

[12] A. H. Ali and M. Ahmad, "Digital Audio Watermarking Based on the Discrete Wavelets Transform and Singular Value Decomposition," *Europe Journal of Science Research*, Vol. 39, No. 1, 2010, pp. 6-21.

[13] W. Lu, H. Lu and F. L. Chung, "Feature Based Watermarking Using Watermark Template Match," *Applied Mathematics and Computation*, Vol. 177, No. 1, 2011, pp. 886-893.

[14] Y. Lu, K. Uehira and K. Yanaka, "Practical Evaluation of Illumination Watermarking Technique Using Orthogonal Transforms," *Journal of Display Technology*, Vol. 6, No. 9, 2010, pp. 351-358.

Permissions

The contributors of this book come from diverse backgrounds, making this book a truly international effort. This book will bring forth new frontiers with its revolutionizing research information and detailed analysis of the nascent developments around the world.

We would like to thank all the contributing authors for lending their expertise to make the book truly unique. They have played a crucial role in the development of this book. Without their invaluable contributions this book wouldn't have been possible. They have made vital efforts to compile up to date information on the varied aspects of this subject to make this book a valuable addition to the collection of many professionals and students.

This book was conceptualized with the vision of imparting up-to-date information and advanced data in this field. To ensure the same, a matchless editorial board was set up. Every individual on the board went through rigorous rounds of assessment to prove their worth. After which they invested a large part of their time researching and compiling the most relevant data for our readers. Conferences and sessions were held from time to time between the editorial board and the contributing authors to present the data in the most comprehensible form. The editorial team has worked tirelessly to provide valuable and valid information to help people across the globe.

Every chapter published in this book has been scrutinized by our experts. Their significance has been extensively debated. The topics covered herein carry significant findings which will fuel the growth of the discipline. They may even be implemented as practical applications or may be referred to as a beginning point for another development. Chapters in this book were first published by Scientific Research Publishing Inc.; hereby published with permission under the Creative Commons Attribution License or equivalent.

The editorial board has been involved in producing this book since its inception. They have spent rigorous hours researching and exploring the diverse topics which have resulted in the successful publishing of this book. They have passed on their knowledge of decades through this book. To expedite this challenging task, the publisher supported the team at every step. A small team of assistant editors was also appointed to further simplify the editing procedure and attain best results for the readers.

Our editorial team has been hand-picked from every corner of the world. Their multi-ethnicity adds dynamic inputs to the discussions which result in innovative outcomes. These outcomes are then further discussed with the researchers and contributors who give their valuable feedback and opinion regarding the same. The feedback is then collaborated with the researches and they are edited in a comprehensive manner to aid the understanding of the subject.

Apart from the editorial board, the designing team has also invested a significant amount of their time in understanding the subject and creating the most relevant covers. They scrutinized every image to scout for the most suitable representation of the subject and create an appropriate cover for the book.

The publishing team has been involved in this book since its early stages. They were actively engaged in every process, be it collecting the data, connecting with the contributors or procuring relevant information. The team has been an ardent support to the editorial, designing and production team. Their endless efforts to recruit the best for this project, has resulted in the accomplishment of this book. They are a veteran in the field of academics and their pool of knowledge is as vast as their experience in printing. Their expertise and guidance has proved useful at every step. Their uncompromising quality standards have made this book an exceptional effort. Their encouragement from time to time has been an inspiration for everyone.

The publisher and the editorial board hope that this book will prove to be a valuable piece of knowledge for researchers, students, practitioners and scholars across the globe.

List of Contributors

Hari Krishna Vellalacheruvu and Sanjeev Kumar
Networking Security Research Lab, Department of Electrical and Computer Engineering, The University of Texas-Pan American, Edinburg, USA

Alok Sharma and Sunil Pranit Lal
Faculty of Science, Technology and Environment, University of the South Pacific, Suva, Fiji

Charlie Obimbo and Benjamin Ferriman
School of Computer Science, University of Guelph, Guelph, Canada

Basant Kumar
Motilal Nehru National Institute of Technology, Allahabad, India

Harsh Vikram Singh
Kamla Nehru Institute of Technology, Sultanpur, India

Surya Pal Singh and Anand Mohan
Institute of Technology, Banaras Hindu University, Varanasi, India

Shaojun Zhang
School of Information Security Engineering, Shanghai Jiao Tong University, Shanghai, China

Shanshan Song
Information Technology Department, Guotai Junan Futures Co., Ltd, Shanghai, China

Tao Xu and Chunxiao Yi
College of Computer Science and Technology, Civil Aviation University of China, Tianjin, China

Zakaria I. Saleh, Heba Refai and Ahmad Mashhour
Faculty of Computer Science and Information Systems, Yarmouk University, Jordan

Aqeel ur Rehman and Qinglu Ma
Department of Computer Science, Chongqing University, Chongqing, China

Xiaofeng Liao
Faculty of Computer Science, Senior Member IEEE, Chongqing University, Chongqing, China

Saleem-Ullah Lar
Department of Computer Science, Chongqing University, Chongqing, China
Department of Computer Science and IT, The Islamia University Bahawalpur, Pakistan

Alok Sharma and Sunil Pranit Lal
Faculty of Science, Technology and Environment, University of the South Pacific, Suva, Fiji

Yasunari Yoshitomi, Taro Asada, Yohei Kinugawa and Masayoshi Tabuse
Graduate School of Life and Environmental Sciences, Kyoto Prefectural University, Kyoto, Japan

Tarek S. Sobh and Yasser Aly
Information Systems Department, Egyptian Armed Forces, Cairo, Egypt

Kamlesh Gupta
Department of Computer Science, Jaypee University of Engineering and Technology, Guna, India

Sanjay Silakari
Department of Computer Science, Rajiv Gandhi Technical University, Bhopal, India

Sirisha Surisetty and Sanjeev Kumar
Network Security Research Lab, Department of Electrical/Computer Engineering, The University of Texas-Pan American, Edinburg, USA

Shinichi Murata
Panasonic Corporation, Kadoma, Osaka, Japan

Yasunari Yoshitomi
Graduate School of Life and Environmental Sciences, Kyoto Prefectural University, Kyoto, Japan

Hiroaki Ishii
School of Science and Technology, Kwansei Gakuin University, Sanda, Hyogo, Japan

Indraneel Mukhopadhyay and Mohuya Chakraborty
Department of Information Technology, Institute of Engineering & Management, Kolkata, India

Satyajit Chakrabarti
Institute of Engineering & Management, Kolkata, India

Shahriar Mohammadi
Department of Industrial Engineering, K. N. Tossi University of Technology, Tehran, Iran

Reza Ebrahimi Atani
Department of Computer Engineering, University of Guilan, Rasht, Iran

Hossein Jadidoleslamy
Department of Information Technology, Anzali International Branch, The University of Guilan, Rasht, Iran

Zachary Miller, William Deitrick and Wei Hu
Department of Computer Science, Houghton College, Houghton, USA

Sanjeev Kumar and Raja Sekhar Reddy Gade
Network Security Research Lab, Department of Electrical and Computer Engineering, The University of Texas–Pan American, Edinburg, USA

Manjit Thapa
Department of Computer Science, Sri Sai College of Engineering & Technology, Badhani, Pathankot, India

Sandeep Kumar Sood
Department of Computer Science and Engineering, G.N.D.U.R.C., Gurdaspur, Punjab, India

Printed in the USA
CPSIA information can be obtained
at www.ICGtesting.com
JSHW051442221024
72173JS00006B/1549